Secure Key Establishment

Advances in Information Security

Sushil Jajodia

Consulting Editor
Center for Secure Information Systems
George Mason University
Fairfax, VA 22030-4444
email: jajodia@gmu.edu

The goals of the Springer International Series on ADVANCES IN INFORMATION SECURITY are, one, to establish the state of the art of, and set the course for future research in information security and, two, to serve as a central reference source for advanced and timely topics in information security research and development. The scope of this series includes all aspects of computer and network security and related areas such as fault tolerance and software assurance.

ADVANCES IN INFORMATION SECURITY aims to publish thorough and cohesive overviews of specific topics in information security, as well as works that are larger in scope or that contain more detailed background information than can be accommodated in shorter survey articles. The series also serves as a forum for topics that may not have reached a level of maturity to warrant a comprehensive textbook treatment.

Researchers, as well as developers, are encouraged to contact Professor Sushil Jajodia with ideas for books under this series.

Additional titles in the series:

SECURITY FOR TELECOMMUNICATIONS NETWORKS by Patrick Traynor, Patrick McDaniel and Thomas La Porta; ISBN: 978-0-387-72441-6

INSIDER ATTACK AND CYBER SECURITY: Beyond the Hacker edited by Salvatore Stolfo, Steven M. Bellovin, Angelos D. Keromytis, Sara Sinclaire, Sean W. Smith; ISBN: 978-0-387-77321-6

INTRUSION DETECTION SYSTEMS edited by Robert Di Pietro and Luigi V. Mancini; ISBN: 978-0-387-77265-3

VULNERABILITY ANALYSIS AND DEFENSE FOR THE INTERNET edited by Abhishek Singh; ISBN: 978-0-387-74389-9

BOTNET DETECTION: Countering the Largest Security Threat edited by Wenke Lee, Cliff Wang and David Dagon; ISBN: 978-0-387-68766-7

PRIVACY-RESPECTING INTRUSION DETECTION by Ulrich Flegel; ISBN: 978-0-387-68254-9

SYNCHRONIZING INTERNET PROTOCOL SECURITY (SIPSec) by Charles A. Shoniregun; ISBN: 978-0-387-32724-2

SECURE DATA MANAGEMENT IN DECENTRALIZED SYSTEMS edited by Ting Yu and Sushil Jajodia; ISBN: 978-0-387-27694-6

NETWORK SECURITY POLICIES AND PROCEDURES by Douglas W. Frye; ISBN: 0-387-30937-3

DATA WAREHOUSING AND DATA MINING TECHNIQUES FOR CYBER SECURITY by Anoop Singhal; ISBN: 978-0-387-26409-7

Additional information about this series can be obtained from http://www.springer.com

Secure Key Establishment

by

Kim-Kwang Raymond Choo
Australian Institute of Criminology
Australia

 Springer

Author:
Kim-Kwang Raymond Choo
Australian Institute of Criminology
GPO Box 2944
Canberra 2601, Australia
raymond.choo.au@gmail.com

ISBN 978-1-4419-4689-8   e-ISBN-13: 978-0-387-87969-7

Printed on acid-free paper

springer.com

Foreword

Around the year 1990 I received a letter from the late Roger Needham in which he informed me that he had thought he had the subject of key establishment "weighed off years ago". He likely had in mind his landmark paper with Schroeder from 1978 in which he had designed the fundamental architecture of server-based key establishment still in wide use today. Needham's letter came in response to a request for a copy of his paper with Burrows and Abadi which introduced what quickly became known as the BAN logic. BAN logic was one of the early examples of mathematical approaches to analysis of key establishment protocols. It represents another of Needham's major contributions to the understanding of key establishment and his remark referred to the surprising new insights that he and his co-authors gained from developing and applying the logic.

Today we find ourselves almost 20 years on from the introduction of BAN logic and yet key establishment continues to be a subject of active research. There are several reasons for this situation. One is that key establishment today includes many more demands than before; new properties such as forward secrecy, resistance to key compromise impersonation, key integrity, anonymity, and deniability are often added to the list of basic requirements involving authentication and key confidentiality. Another reason is that different architectures and infrastructures need to be considered such as multi-party scenarios, or identity-based cryptography. However, amidst all this extra compexity one question is paramount for any key establishment protocol: how can we be sure that it is secure? This is the question that is addressed in the current volume.

It is fair to say that while the BAN logic is no longer widely used, it played an important role in pioneering new mathematical ways to analyse and prove the security of key establishment protocols. In the cryptographic community it is now commonplace to use reductionist proofs of security to show that a protocol cannot be broken unless some computational assumption is false. Such proofs are normally constructed 'by hand' and intended to be read by humans. I can tell you from personal experience that writing such proofs accurately is not an easy task - the evidence is in this book. As supervisor (advisor) of the PhD thesis on which this book is based, I had to get used to my student mercilessly examining my own work for faults as well as that of many others! Raymond developed an uncanny, and to some of us intimidating, knack of identifying flaws or omissions in the proof logic.

The difficulty of ensuring that hand written proofs are correct has been widely recognised by the research community in recent years. The contributions of this book have played an important part in demonstrating the validity of this assertion. Although finding attacks on protocols with supposed proofs of security is always a surprising and noteworthy contribution, more long-lasting are methods for avoiding such attacks from the beginning; this book contains several advances in this direction. The first thing to sort out is what is the correct model to use – a comprehensive comparison of the models can be found in Chapter 5. Having established the model, methods for designing protocols amenable to proof form a very helpful practical tool. The chapter on session key construction is just such a tool. Finally, automatic tools can be used to check that proofs do not contain errors - Chapters 10 and 11 give a method and examples for how this can be achieved.

This book is an essential companion for researchers and practitioners who want to understand how proofs for security of key establishment can and should work. The lessons from previous errors and the techniques for protocol modelling and design contained in the book also make it invaluable for those who wish to provide new security proofs which are sound. I believe that Roger Needham would have been delighted to see this book, demonstrating as it does that the struggle to understand and master the security of key establishment protocols continues still.

Brisbane, September 2008   *Colin Boyd*

Preface

We study the problem of secure key establishment. We critically examine the security models of Bellare and Rogaway (1993) and Canetti and Krawczyk (2001) in the computational complexity approach, as these models are central in the understanding of the provable security paradigm. We show that the partnership definition used in the three-party key distribution (3PKD) protocol of Bellare and Rogaway (1995) is flawed, which invalidates the proof for the 3PKD protocol. We present an improved protocol with a new proof of security.

We identify several variants of the key sharing requirement (i.e., two entities who have completed matching sessions, partners, are required to accept the same session key). We then present a brief discussion about the key sharing requirement. We identify several variants of the Bellare and Rogaway (1993) model. We present a comparative study of the relative strengths of security notions between the several variants of the Bellare–Rogaway model and the Canetti–Krawczyk model. In our comparative study, we reveal a drawback in the Bellare, Pointcheval, and Rogaway (2000) model with the protocol of Abdalla and Pointcheval (2005) as a case study.

We prove a revised protocol of Boyd (1996) secure in the Bellare–Rogaway model. We then extend the model in order to allow more realistic adversary capabilities by incorporating the notion of resetting the long-term compromised key of some entity. This allows us to detect a known weakness of the protocol that cannot be captured in the original model. We also present an alternative protocol that is efficient in both messages and rounds. We prove the protocol secure in the extended model.

Although the Yahalom protocol, proposed by Burrows, Abadi, and Needham in 1990, is one of the most prominent key establishment protocols analyzed by researchers from the computer security community (using automated proof tools), a simplified version of the protocol is only recently proven secure by Backes and Pfitzmann (2006) in their cryptographic library framework. We present a protocol for key establishment that is closely based on the Yahalom protocol. We then present a security proof in the Bellare and Rogaway (1993) model and the random oracle model. We also observe that no partnering mechanism is specified within the Yahalom protocol. We then present a brief discussion on the role and the possible construct of session identifiers as a form of partnering mechanism, which allows the right session key to be identified in concurrent protocol executions.

We point out previously unknown flaws in several published protocols and a message authenticator of Bellare, Canetti, and Krawczyk (1998) by refuting claimed proofs of security. We also point out corresponding flaws in their existing proofs. We propose fixes to these protocols and their proofs. In some cases, we present new protocols with full proofs of security.

We examine the role of session key construction in key establishment protocols, and demonstrate that a small change to the way that session keys are constructed can have significant benefits. Protocols that were proven secure in a restricted Bellare–Rogaway model can then be proven secure in the full model. We present a brief discussion on ways to construct session keys in key establishment protocols and also prove the protocol of Chen and Kudla (2003) secure in a less restrictive Bellare–Rogaway model.

To complement the computational complexity approach, we provide a formal specification and machine analysis of the Bellare–Pointcheval–Rogaway model using an automated model checker, Simple Homomorphism Verification Tool (SHVT). We demonstrate that structural flaws in protocols can be revealed using our framework. We reveal previously unknown flaws in the unpublished pre-proceedings version of the protocol due to Jakobsson and Pointcheval (2001) and several published protocols with only heuristic security arguments.

We extend the work to automatically repair protocols that are found to be insecure. The three-party identity-based secret public key protocol (3P-ID-SPK) protocol of Lim and Paterson (2006) is used as a case study.

We conclude this book with a listing of some open problems that were encountered in the study.

Comments and Errata

Although we hope that there are no errors or typos in this book, we would greatly appreciate if you let us know if you do find any. Comments and errate can be emailed to raymond.choo.au@gmail.com with the book title as the subject heading.

Kim-Kwang Raymond Choo

Acknowledgements

I am privileged to have numerous researchers contributing towards in the shaping of this book (based on my Ph.D. thesis entitled "Key Establishment: Proofs and Refutations"[1]), especially my principal supervisor, Professor Colin Boyd, and my associate supervisor, Dr. Yvonne Hitchcock. Both Colin and Yvonne offered me hours of their precious time each week during my doctoral research endeavour for the entire three years of my doctoral research. Their approachability, inspirational advice, and constructive criticism, taught me a lot about doing research and presenting the research results and for which I will remain forever grateful. Also I am privileged to have Dr. Greg Maitland for his invaluable guidance and for continued supervision of my doctoral research. Colin, Yvonne, and Greg gave me the freedom to explore and make mistakes while always ensuring that I was progressing and learned from my mistakes. Much of what I understand about protocols, provable security, cryptography, research, and paper writing, I learned from Colin, Yvonne, and Greg. If there is anything right and of value in this book, it probably stems from them.

Along the way I have also been privileged to be assisted by many people and I have formed many valuable friendships. I wish to thank them all for helping to provide the environment which made this work possible. I am also fortunate to have a team of enthusiastic, dedicated, knowledgeable, and meticulous panel for my doctoral defense seminar, namely: Professor Colin Boyd, Professor Colin Fidge, and Dr. Greg Maitland. This thesis benefited immeasurably from their scrutiny, their relentless precision, and their impeccable taste.

My wife, Jin Nie Goh, has been a constant source of loving encouragement and unwavering support over the entire doctoral candidature, in particular through the inevitable ups and downs, fustrations and elations, certainties and uncertainties. For this, and for all that she has given over the years, she is as much the author as I. Special thanks must also go to my family (back in Singapore), for their loving support,

---

[1] http://adt.library.qut.edu.au/adt-qut/public/adt-QUT20060928.114022/

not only during the time spent on this thesis, but also throughout the many years of education which preceded it. This manuscript is a witness to their love, their unwavering faith, and their unfailing hope.

I am also extremely grateful to Susan Lagerstrom-Fife, Senior Publishing Editor/CS for Springer, and Sharon Palleschi, Editorial Assistant at Springer, for their support in this project. It is not easy to keep on schedule but they were relentless ... in a good way.

The permission of Elsevier (Chapter 10), IEEE (Chapter 10), IOS Press (Chapter 11), Oxford University Press (Chapter 7) Springer (Chapters 3 to 6, and 8 to 10) for permission to reprint the respective copyrighted material is acknowledged.

Last, but by no means least, I thank God for his never ending help and it goes without saying that all opinions expressed here are my own.

Contents

1 Introduction 1
  1.1 The Key Distribution Problem 1
  1.2 Solution: Key Establishment Protocols 3
      1.2.1 Computer Security Approach 4
      1.2.2 Computational Complexity Approach 5
      1.2.3 Research Objectives and Deliverables 6
  1.3 Structure of Book and Contributions to Knowledge 6
  References 10

2 Background Materials 19
  2.1 Mathematical Background 19
      2.1.1 Abstract Algebra and the Main Groups 19
      2.1.2 Bilinear Maps from Elliptic Curve Pairings 20
      2.1.3 Computational Problems and Assumptions 21
      2.1.4 Cryptographic Tools 23
          2.1.4.1 Encryption Schemes: Asymmetric Setting 23
          2.1.4.2 Encryption Schemes: Symmetric Setting 25
          2.1.4.3 Digital Signature Schemes 26
          2.1.4.4 Message Authentication Codes 26
          2.1.4.5 Cryptographic Hash Functions 27
          2.1.4.6 Random Oracles 28
  2.2 Key Establishment Protocols and their Basis 29
      2.2.1 Protocol Architectures 30
          2.2.1.1 Existing Cryptographic Keys 31
          2.2.1.2 Method of Session Key Generation 31
          2.2.1.3 Number of Entities 33
      2.2.2 Protocol Goals and Attacks 33
          2.2.2.1 Protocol Goals 33
          2.2.2.2 Additional Security Attributes 34
          2.2.2.3 Types of Attacks 36
          2.2.2.4 A Need for Rigorous Treatment 38

2.3   The Computational Complexity Approach   38
      2.3.1   Adversarial Powers   39
      2.3.2   Definition of Freshness   41
      2.3.3   Definition of Security   41
      2.3.4   The Bellare–Rogaway Models   42
              2.3.4.1   The BR93 Model   43
              2.3.4.2   The BR95 Model   44
              2.3.4.3   The BPR2000 Model   45
      2.3.5   The Canetti–Krawczyk Model   46
      2.3.6   Protocol Security   48
2.4   Summary   49
References   49

3   **A Flawed BR95 Partnership Function**   57
    3.1   A Flaw in the Security Proof for 3PKD Protocol   58
          3.1.1   The 3PKD Protocol   58
          3.1.2   Key Replicating Attack on 3PKD Protocol   59
          3.1.3   The Partner Function used in the BR95 Proof   60
    3.2   A Revised 3PKD Protocol in Bellare–Rogaway Model   62
          3.2.1   Defining SIDs in the 3PKD Protocol   62
          3.2.2   An Improved Provably Secure 3PKD Protocol   62
          3.2.3   Security Proof for the Improved 3PKD Protocol   63
                  3.2.3.1   Adaptive MAC Forger $\mathcal{F}$ 64
                  3.2.3.2   Multiple Eavesdropper Attacker $\mathcal{ME}$ 65
                  3.2.3.3   Conclusion of Proof   69
    3.3   Summary   70
    References   70

4   **On The Key Sharing Requirement**   71
    4.1   Bellare–Rogaway 3PKD Protocol in CK2001 Model   72
          4.1.1   The 3PKD Protocol   72
          4.1.2   New Attack on 3PKD Protocol   73
          4.1.3   A New Provably-Secure 3PKD Protocol in CK2001 Model .   74
    4.2   Jeong–Katz–Lee Protocol $\mathcal{TS}2$ 76
          4.2.1   Protocol $\mathcal{TS}2$ 76
          4.2.2   New Attack on Protocol $\mathcal{TS}2$ 77
          4.2.3   An Improved Protocol $\mathcal{TS}2$ 77
    4.3   The Key Sharing Requirement   78
    4.4   Summary   80
    References   80

5   **Comparison of Bellare–Rogaway and Canetti–Krawczyk Models**   83
    5.1   Relating The Notions of Security   86
          5.1.1   Proving BR93 (EA+KE) $\rightarrow$ BPR2000 (EA+KE)   88
                  5.1.1.1   Proof for the key establishment goal   88

　　　　5.1.1.2　Proof for the entity authentication goal 89
　　5.1.2　Proving CK2001 → BPR2000 (KE) 90
　　5.1.3　Proving CK2001 → BR93 (KE) 91
　　5.1.4　BR93 (KE) → BR95 and BR93 (KE), CK2001 ↚ BR95 . . . 92
　　5.1.5　BR93 (KE) / CK2001 ↚ BPR2000 (KE) 93
　　5.1.6　CK2001 ↚ BR93 (EA+KE) 93
　　5.1.7　BR93 (KE) ↚ CK2001 94
　　5.1.8　BPR2000 (KE) ↚ BR95 96
　5.2　A Drawback in the BPR2000 Model 96
　　5.2.1　Case Study: Abdalla–Pointcheval 3PAKE 96
　　5.2.2　Unknown Key Share Attack on 3PAKE 97
　5.3　Summary 99
　References 99

6　An Extension to the Bellare–Rogaway Model 101
　6.1　A Provably-Secure Revised Protocol of Boyd 102
　　6.1.1　Secure Authenticated Encryption Schemes 102
　　6.1.2　Revised Protocol of Boyd 103
　　6.1.3　Security Proof 104
　　　　6.1.3.1　Integrity attacker 105
　　　　6.1.3.2　Confidentiality attacker 106
　　　　6.1.3.3　Conclusion of Security Proof 108
　6.2　An Extension to the BR93 Model 108
　6.3　An Efficient Protocol in Extended Model 110
　　6.3.1　An Efficient Protocol 110
　　6.3.2　Security Proof 111
　　　　6.3.2.1　Integrity Breaker 112
　　　　6.3.2.2　Confidentiality Breaker 112
　　　　6.3.2.3　Conclusion of Security Proof 114
　6.4　Comparative Security and Efficiency 114
　6.5　Summary 115
　References 116

7　A Proof of Revised Yahalom Protocol 117
　7.1　The Yahalom Protocol and its Simplified Version 118
　7.2　A New Provably-Secure Protocol 119
　　7.2.1　Proof for Protocol 7.2 120
　　　　7.2.1.1　Integrity attacker 121
　　　　7.2.1.2　Confidentiality attacker 122
　　　　7.2.1.3　Conclusion of Proof for Theorem 7.2.1 123
　　7.2.2　An Extension to Protocol 7.2 123
　7.3　Partnering Mechanism: A Brief Discussion 124
　7.4　Summary 126
　References 127

8   Errors in Computational Complexity Proofs for Protocols 129
  8.1   Boyd–González Nieto Protocol 130
     8.1.1   Unknown Key Share Attack on Protocol 131
     8.1.2   An Improved Conference Key Agreement Protocol 132
     8.1.3   Limitations of Existing Proof 133
  8.2   Jakobsson–Pointcheval MAKEP 134
     8.2.1   Unknown Key Share Attack on JP-MAKEP 135
     8.2.2   Flaws in Existing Security Proof for JP-MAKEP 135
  8.3   Wong–Chan MAKEP 136
     8.3.1   A New Attack on WC-MAKEP 136
     8.3.2   Preventing the Attack 137
     8.3.3   Flaws in Existing Security Proof for WC-MAKEP 137
  8.4   An MT-Authenticator 138
     8.4.1   Encryption-Based MT-Authenticator 138
     8.4.2   Flaw in Existing Security Proof Revealed 139
     8.4.3   Addressing the Flaw 140
     8.4.4   An Example Protocol as a Case Study 140
  8.5   Summary 142
  References 143

9   On Session Key Construction 147
  9.1   Chen–Kudla ID-Based Protocol 148
     9.1.1   The ID-Based Protocol 149
     9.1.2   Existing Arguments on Restriction of Reveal Query 149
     9.1.3   Improved Chen–Kudla Protocol 150
     9.1.4   Security Proof for Improved Chen–Kudla Protocol 151
  9.2   McCullagh–Barreto 2P-IDAKA Protocol 153
     9.2.1   The 2P-IDAKA Protocol 153
     9.2.2   Why Reveal Query is Restricted 153
     9.2.3   Errors in Existing Proof for 2P-IDAKA Protocol 154
        9.2.3.1   Error 1 154
        9.2.3.2   Error 2 155
     9.2.4   Improved 2P-IDAKA Protocol 156
  9.3   A Proposal for Session Key Construction 157
  9.4   Another Case Study 158
     9.4.1   Reflection Attack on Lee–Kim–Yoo Protocol 159
     9.4.2   Preventing the Attack 160
  9.5   Summary 160
  References 161

10   Complementing Computational Protocol Analysis 163
  10.1 The Formal Framework 164
  10.2 Analysing a Provably-Secure Protocol 165
     10.2.1 Protocol Specification 166
        10.2.1.1 Initial State of Protocol 10.1 166

10.2.1.2 Step 1 of Protocol 10.1 167

10.2.1.3 A Malicious State Transition................... 167

10.2.2 Protocol Analysis 168

10.2.2.1 Hijacking Attack 169

10.2.2.2 New Attack 1 169

10.2.2.3 New Attack 2 171

10.3 Analysing Another Two Protocols With Claimed Proofs of Security 172

10.3.1 Protocol Analysis 173

10.3.1.1 Analysis of Protocol 10.2 174

10.3.1.2 Analysis of Protocol 10.3 174

10.3.2 Flaws in Refuted Proofs.............................. 177

10.3.3 A Possible Fix....................................... 177

10.4 Analysing Protocols with Heuristic Security Arguments 178

10.4.1 Case Studies 178

10.4.1.1 Jan–Chen Mutual Protocol 178

10.4.1.2 Yang–Shen–Shieh Protocols 178

10.4.1.3 Kim–Huh–Hwang–Lee Protocol 180

10.4.1.4 Lin–Sun–Hwang Key Protocols MDHEKE I and II 181

10.4.1.5 Yeh–Sun Key Protocol........................ 181

10.4.2 Protocol Analyses.................................... 181

10.4.2.1 Protocol Analysis 1 182

10.4.2.2 Protocol Analysis 2 183

10.4.2.3 Protocol Analysis 3 184

10.4.2.4 Protocol Analysis 4 184

10.4.2.5 Protocol Analysis 5 186

10.4.2.6 Protocol Analysis 6 186

10.4.2.7 Protocol Analysis 7 187

10.5 Summary 188

References 188

11 An Integrative Framework to Protocol Analysis and Repair........ 191

11.1 Case Study Protocol 193

11.2 Proposed Integrative Framework 194

11.2.1 Protocols Specification 194

11.2.1.1 Defining SIDs in Protocol 11.1 195

11.2.1.2 Description of Goal State 196

11.2.1.3 Description of Possible Actions 196

11.2.2 Protocols Analysis 197

11.2.3 Protocol Repair...................................... 199

11.3 Summary 201

References 202

12 Conclusion and Future Work 205
 12.1 Research Summary 205
 12.2 Open Problems and Future Directions 206
 References 208

Index 211

List of Protocols

2.1   ISO/IEC key transport mechanism 1 32

2.2   Gong's hybrid protocol 32

3.1   3PKD protocol 59

3.2   An Improved Provably Secure 3PKD Protocol 63

4.1   3PKD protocol proven secure by Tin, Boyd, and González Nieto 72

4.2   Tin–Boyd–González Nieto protocol AM-3PKD 74

4.3   A new provably-secure 3PKD protocol in the CK2001 (UM) 75

4.4   Jeong–Katz–Lee protocol $\mathcal{TS}2$ 77

4.5   An improved Protocol 4.4 78

4.6   Yahalom protocol 80

5.1   Wong–Chan MAKEP 94

5.2   A modified (Canetti–Krawczyk) Diffie–Hellman protocol 95

5.3   Abdalla–Pointcheval 3PAKE 97

6.1   A revised key agreement protocol of Boyd 104

6.2   A new key agreement protocol 110

6.3   An extension to Protocol 6.2 115

7.1   The Yahalom protocol 118

7.2   A revised Yahalom protocol 120

7.3   An extension to Protocol 7.2 (i.e., re-authentication) 124

8.1   Boyd–González Nieto conference key agreement protocol 130

8.2   An improved Protocol 8.1 133

8.3   Jakobsson–Pointcheval MAKEP 134

8.4   Wong–Chan MAKEP 136

8.5   Hitchcock–Tin–Boyd–González Nieto–Montague protocol 2DHPE . . 141

9.1   Chen–Kudla Protocol 2 149

9.2   McCullagh–Barreto 2P-IDAKA protocol 153

9.3   Lee, Kim, and Yoo (2005) authenticated key agreement protocol 159

10.1 Original unpublished version of Protocol 8.3 166

10.2 Hitchcock–Boyd–González Nieto tripartite key exchange protocol 8 . 173

10.3 Hitchcock–Boyd–González Nieto tripartite key exchange protocol 9 . 173

10.4 Jan–Chen MAKEP 179

10.5   Yang–Shen–Shieh protocol 1 179
10.6   Yang–Shen–Shieh protocol 2 179
10.7   Kim–Huh–Hwang–Lee key agreement protocol 180
10.8   Lin–Sun–Hwang Key improved protocol MDHEKE I 181
10.9   Lin–Sun–Hwang Key improved protocol MDHEKE II 181
10.10 Yeh–Sun authenticated key agreement protocol 182
11.1   Lim–Paterson three-party identity-based secret public key protocol . . 193
11.2   A repaired Protocol 11.1 200

List of Attacks

3.1 Key replicating attack on Protocol 3.1 59
4.1 Execution of Protocol 4.1 in the presence of a malicious adversary .. 73
4.2 Execution of Protocol 4.4 in the presence of a malicious adversary .. 77
5.1 Execution of Protocol 3.1 in the presence of a malicious adversary .. 92
5.2 Execution of Protocol 3.2 in the presence of a malicious adversary .. 93
5.3 Execution of Protocol 5.1 in the presence of a malicious adversary .. 95
5.4 Execution of Protocol 5.2 in the presence of a malicious adversary .. 95
5.5 Unknown key share attack on Protocol 5.3 98
8.1 Unknown key share attack on Protocol 8.1 131
8.2 Unknown key attack on Protocol 8.3 135
8.3 Key replicating attack on Protocol 8.4 137
8.4 An example execution of encryption-based MT-authenticator 139
8.5 Execution of Protocol 8.5 in the presence of a malicious adversary .. 141
9.1 Key replicating attack on Protocol 9.1 150
9.2 Key replicating attack on Protocol 9.2 154
9.3 Execution of Protocol 9.3 in the presence of a malicious adversary .. 159
10.1 A hijacking attack on Protocol 10.1 170
10.2 New attack 1 on Protocol 10.1 171
10.3 New attack 2 on Protocol 10.1 172
10.4 Attack Sequence on Protocol 10.2 175
10.5 Attack Sequence on Protocol 10.3 176
10.6 Offline dictionary attack on Protocol 10.7 180
10.7 Attack sequence on mutual authentication goal of Protocol 10.4 183
10.8 Attack sequence on key establishment goal of Protocol 10.4 183
10.9 Attack sequence on Protocol 10.5 184
10.10 Attack sequence on Protocol 10.6 185
10.11 Attack sequence on Protocol 10.7 185
10.12 Attack sequence on Protocol 10.8 186
10.13 Attack sequence on Protocol 10.9 187
10.14 Attack sequence on Protocol 10.10 187
11.1 Attack Sequence on Protocol 11.1 198

List of Figures

2.1 Game simulation $\mathcal{G}$ 42
2.2 Matching conversation 43
2.3 Translating protocol in AM to UM 47

3.1 Game $\mathcal{G}_{\mathcal{ME}}$ 66

4.1 Canetti–Krawczyk MAC-based MT-authenticator............... 74

5.1 The proof models and their variants 85
5.2 Notions of security 85
5.3 Additional comparisons 86
5.4 An example protocol execution 89

8.1 Insiders vs outsider 133
8.2 Bellare–Canetti–Krawczyk encryption-based MT-authenticator 138
8.3 A revised encryption-based MT-authenticator 140

9.1 An example simulation of Protocol 9.1........................ 152
9.2 Illustration of error 1....................................... 154
9.3 Illustration of error 2....................................... 155
9.4 An example simulation of Protocol 9.2........................ 157

10.1 Examples of basic types and functions 167
10.2 Initial state of Protocol 10.1 167
10.3 State transition - step 1 of Protocol 10.1 168
10.4 A malicious state transition 169
10.5 Analysis statistics 169
10.6 Analysis statistics 174

11.1 A reachability graph: protocol analysis in SHVT 197
11.2 Analysis statistics of Protocol 11.1 198

List of Tables

2.1 Summary of notations 20
2.2 Summary of generic formal goals 34
2.3 Summary of adversarial powers................................ 40

3.1 Oracle queries associated with Attack 3.1 60

4.1 Comparison of the computational loads 76
4.2 Variants of key sharing requirement 79

6.1 A comparative summary...................................... 114

7.1 A comparative summary...................................... 126

8.1 Internal states of players U_1, U_2, and U_3 132

9.1 $\mathscr{A}_{\mathscr{BDH}}$ simulating the view of $\mathscr{A}$ 152
9.2 Construction of session key in key establishment protocols 158

10.1 Violations of Definition 10.1.1 in protocol analyses 182

Chapter 1
Introduction

The aim of this chapter is to provide an introduction and to present the overall structure of the book, which is based on the author's Ph.D. thesis entitled "Key Establishment: Proofs and Refutations" [40]. This chapter also describes the main contributions of the book to the study of key establishment protocols.

1.1 The Key Distribution Problem

As the Internet evolves from an academic and research network into a commercial network, more organizations and individuals are connecting their internal networks and computers to the (insecure) Internet. Investment in network expansion by telecommunications companies will see a further expansion in capacity that will result in an increase in bandwidth availability and greater adoption of wireless and mobile technologies. As businesses continue to engage in electronic commerce, they will become increasingly globalised and interconnected [51]. This is perhaps due to the cost of an internet-based transaction being a small fraction of a bricks-and-mortar based transaction. The propensity for consumers to buy online is indicated in a recent article that online spending on retail websites in United States has exceeded US$100 billion [7].

These, and other developments, create not only benefits for the community but also risks of technology-enabled crime [50, 51]. Cybercriminals, for example, aim to disrupt one or more combinations of the following security notions: data confidentiality, data integrity and data availability. The ability to provide security guarantees is of paramount importance and several initiatives have been proposed to address this concern (including the use of cryptographic data encryption and authentication). Typically security guarantees are provided by means of protocols that make use of security primitives such as encryption, digital signatures, and hashing.

Menezes, van Oorschot, and Vanstone [94, Chapter 1] and Boyd and Mathuria [28,

Chapter 1] identify the following possible different services that may be provided by the employment of cryptographic algorithms.

Confidentiality   ensures the data is available only to the authorised parties involved. To achieve this notion, encryption using mathematical algorithms is typically used to encrypt the data and render the encrypted data unintelligible to anyone else, other than the authorised parties even if the unauthorised party (commonly referred to as the adversary in the literature) has access to the encrypted data. In cryptographic protocols, confidentiality ensures that keys and other data are only available to the authorised principals (entities) as intended and trusted third party server if applicable.

Data integrity   ensures the data has not been tampered with or modified. To achieve this notion, several approaches such as the use of a secure hash function together with encryption or use of a message authentication code (MAC), have been adopted to detect data manipulation such as insertion, deletion, and substitution.

Authentication   ensures the identification of either the data (*Data Origin Authentication*) or the entity (*Entity Authentication*). *Data origin authentication* implicitly provides data integrity since the unauthorised alteration of the data implies that the origin of the data is changed, as the origin of data can only be guaranteed if the data integrity has not been compromised in any way. The use of a one-way hash function together with encryption or use of a message authentication code (MAC) can help to achieve data origin authentication. *Entity authentication* is a communication process by which a principal establishes a live correspondence with a second principal whose identity should be that which is sought by the first principal. In cryptographic protocols, both entity authentication and data origin authentication are essential to establish the key.

Cryptographic protocols are designed to provide one or more of these security services between communicating agents in a hostile environment. To achieve confidentiality of data in a session established by some entity A, with another intended entity B, one may use a cryptographic primitive, called *symmetric key encryption*. This cryptographic algorithm produces a ciphertext message, c, when given some plaintext message, m. A then sends B the ciphertext c over the insecure communication channel. Only B who has a pre-established secret information (with A), known as a *shared key*, can decrypt c to obtain m, achieving the notion of data confidentiality.

The shared key can be a long-term key associated with some identities, a symmetric encryption key shared between two entities, or a session key. In a real world setting, it is normal to assume that a host can establish several concurrent sessions with many different parties. Therefore, the session key has to be fresh and unique for each session as sessions are specific to both the communicating parties.

The above security services are usually meaningful when guaranteed during a complete session of closely related interactions over a communication channel and in many cases, open and insecure communication channels. In most of these cases, there is a need for some temporary keys. For example, an encryption key for a shared-key encryption scheme in the above-mentioned scenario.

The advantages of using temporary (session) keys relative to using long-term keys directly are four-fold:

1. to limit the amount of cryptographic material available to cryptanalytic attacks;
2. to limit the exposure of messages when keys are lost,
3. to create independence between different and unrelated sessions, and
4. to achieve efficiency, e.g., if long-term keys are based on asymmetric cryptography, using session keys based on (faster) symmetric cryptography can bring a considerable gain in efficiency.

The establishment of session keys often involves interactive cryptographic protocols or also known as authentication and/or key establishment protocols. Such protocols are increasingly being considered as the *sine qua non* of many diverse secure electronic communications and electronic commerce applications. They are the focus of this book.

1.2 Solution: Key Establishment Protocols

Although technological advances have brought us many conveniences and benefits, they have also resulted in the erosion of many assumptions which influence the design of key establishment protocols[1]. For example, in the past computers tended to be shared with limited disk space and memory, resulting in a user-to-user confidentiality requirement. With the current technology, computers tend to be personal, with much more generous disk space and memory, resulting in a firewall-to-firewall confidentiality requirement. As a result, the environment for security protocols has changed drastically over the years. One thing that has not changed with time is that the design of cryptographic protocols is still notoriously hard. Frequently errors were found in many such protocols years after they were published [1, 3, 12, 13, 16, 17, 29, 33, 37, 39, 41, 42, 43, 45, 46, 44, 48, 49, 60, 69, 70, 73, 76, 77, 80, 82, 86, 95, 97, 98, 99, 100, 109, 110, 111, 104, 105, 106, 114, 119, 120, 121, 124, 125, 126, 128, 129, 130, 133, 131, 132, 134]. Long gone are the days where protocols are considered secure in an iterative process of fixing discovered attacks, as it is normally accepted that protocols designed in this manner do not achieve any security guarantee. Such an ad-hoc approach usually only buries the problem, rather than eliminates it. Moreover, many important protocols such as electronic auction protocols, electronic payment protocols, fair contract signing protocols, and internet

---

[1] The first key establishment protocol with public key properties is published by Diffie and Hellman [58]. Although a later protocol of Merkle [93] – Merkle's puzzles – also achieves the key distribution goal, the protocol of Diffie and Hellman enjoys a better ratio between security and efficiency [127].

key exchange protocols have become far too complex for such an approach.

The study of protocols for key establishment and authentication has led to a dichotomy in cryptographic protocol analysis techniques between the computational complexity approach [2, 20, 18, 27, 24, 35, 36, 115] and the computer security approach [62, 31, 85, 90, 91, 92].

1.2.1 Computer Security Approach

In the 1990s academic cryptography started its move toward a mature discipline by demanding new standards of proof, with many researchers shifting their attention to using formal methods, especially in the last decade. Emphasis in the computer security approach is placed on automated machine specification and analysis. Researchers have attempted to verify, prove, and/or design cryptographic protocols with automated theorem provers [15, 88, 102, 103, 122], model checkers [8, 9, 53, 52, 96], logic-based approaches (including belief logic) [5, 23, 55, 65, 71], and other tools (including specific cryptographic protocol programming languages) [6, 26, 25, 30, 54, 56, 61, 63, 66, 79, 83, 84, 85, 87, 89, 107, 108, 112]. The main goal is to relieve humans of the tedious and error prone parts of the mathematical proofs.

The Dolev and Yao [59] adversarial model is the de-facto standard used in formal specifications, where cryptographic operations are often used in a "black box" fashion ignoring some of the cryptographic properties. This resulted in possible loss of partial information. For the foreseeable future, this approach requires abstractions of cryptographic primitives because the tools cannot handle the cryptographic details. However, all the classical abstractions were made ad-hoc.

Cervesato, Durgin, Lincoln, Mitchell, and Scedrov [38] also pointed out that the main obstacles in this automated approach are undecidability and intractability. Messages from an adversary are unbounded in structural depth and the number of possible values for some data fields is infinite. The adversary can have a large set of possible actions, which results in a state explosion. It is generally acknowledged that protocols proven secure in such a manner could possibly be flawed – giving a false positive result [10]. However, this approach has the benefit of providing unambiguous specification of system requirements and mathematically precise proofs of system properties [11, 101]. This approach should also be credited for finding both known and previously unknown flaws in protocols [6, 16, 17, 26, 43, 47, 53, 68, 85, 118, 119].

1.2.2 Computational Complexity Approach

The computational complexity approach adopts a deductive reasoning process. Emphasis is placed on showing a reduction from the problem of breaking the protocol to another problem believed to be hard. The first treatment of computational complexity analysis for cryptography began in the 1980s [64]. It was made popular for key establishment protocols by Bellare and Rogaway. In fact, Bellare and Rogaway [20] provided the first formal definition for a model of adversarial capabilities with an associated definition of security (hereafter referred to as the BR93 model).

A complete (human-generated) mathematical proof with respect to cryptographic definitions provides a strong assurance that a protocol is behaving as desired. The history of mathematics is, however, full of erroneous proofs [32]. The difficulty of obtaining correct mathematical proofs has been illustrated in the *virtuoso* work of Lakatos [78] whereby the many proofs and refutations for Euler's characteristic in algebraic topology are presented as a comedy of errors. Many formulations for Euler's characteristic in algebraic topology, a theorem about the properties of polyhedra, have been proposed, only to be refuted and replaced by another formulation.

The difficulty of obtaining correct computational proofs of security is also dramatically illustrated by the well-known problem with the OAEP mode for public key encryption [116, 117]. Although OAEP [21] was one of the most widely used and implemented algorithms, it was several years after the publication of the original proof that a problem was found (and subsequently fixed in the case of RSA). Problems with proofs of protocol security have occurred too. Furthermore, such security proofs usually entail lengthy and complicated mathematical proofs, which are daunting to most readers [74, 75]. The breaking of provably-secure protocols [43, 45, 48, 49, 124, 128] after publication is evidence of the difficulty of obtaining correct computational proofs of protocol security. Despite these setbacks, we advocate that proofs are invaluable for arguing about security and certainly are one very important tool in getting protocols right.

The BR93 model has been further revised several times. In 1995, Bellare and Rogaway analysed a three-party server-based key distribution (3PKD) protocol [22] using an extension to the BR93 model, which will be referred to as the BR95 model. A more recent revision to the model was proposed in 2000 by Bellare, Pointcheval and Rogaway [19], hereafter referred to as the BPR2000 model. Collectively, the BR93, BR95, and BPR2000 models will be referred to as the Bellare–Rogaway model.

In independent yet related work, Bellare, Canetti, and Krawczyk [18] built on the BR93 model and introduced a modular proof model. However, some drawbacks with this formulation were discovered and this modular proof model was subsequently modified by Canetti and Krawczyk [35], and will be referred to as the CK2001 model in this book. Although the trend towards such formal approaches has been gaining momentum in recent years, the number of protocols that possess a rigorous proof of security remains relatively small.

1.2.3 Research Objectives and Deliverables

The main objective of this book is to study cryptographic protocol analysis techniques. The emphasis is on the current computational complexity (cryptography-oriented) approach to proofs for protocols, but the computer security proof (formal methods) approach to protocol analysis is also considered as a complimentary tool for finding human error in cryptography oriented analysis. The design of such protocols remains a hard problem despite years of research, evidenced by the number of protocols (including some well-studied and widely-cited ones) being broken after publication.

To achieve the main objective of this book, the following four related research goals are defined.

1. To examine the security models in the computational complexity approach critically, as the security models are the central component in the design and analysis of key establishment protocols in the provable security paradigm.
2. To analyse published protocols in the literature, including protocols that carry heuristic security arguments and protocols that carry proofs of security.
3. To contribute towards the design principles for provably-secure key establishment protocols.
4. To design new provably secure key establishment protocols, which need to be as efficient in performance as the existing protocols.

1.3 Structure of Book and Contributions to Knowledge

We present a brief outline of the structure of this book and the main contributions.

Chapter 2.   In this chapter, we cover the nomenclature and definitions necessary for understanding the remainder of the book and the notation used throughout the book. We present the necessary background material on the topic of cryptographic protocols, and in particular key establishment protocols. We also present overviews of the Bellare–Rogaway [19, 20, 22] and Canetti–Krawczyk [18, 35] computational complexity models which will serve as building blocks in this book. We mainly work in these models and several protocols proposed in this book are proven secure in one of these models.

Chapter 3.   In this chapter, we show that the BR95 partnership function used in the three-party key distribution (3PKD) protocol [22] is flawed, which invalidates the proof. We then show that there is no way to define a session identifier (SID) for the 3PKD protocol that will preserve the proof of security. We conclude with an improved provably-secure 3PKD protocol.

Material presented in this chapter has appeared in the following publication:

- Kim-Kwang Raymond Choo, Colin Boyd, Yvonne Hitchcock, and Greg Maitland. On Session Identifiers in Provably Secure Protocols: The Bellare–Rogaway Three-Party Key Distribution Protocol Revisited. In Blundo Carlo and Stelvio Cimato, editors, 4th Conference on Security in Communication Networks - SCN 2004, volume 3352/2005 of Lecture Notes in Computer Science, pages 352–367. Springer-Verlag, 2004.

Chapter 4. In this chapter, we present our observation that the definitions of security in the Bellare–Rogaway and Canetti–Krawczyk models require two partners in the presence of a malicious adversary to accept the same session key, which we term a key sharing requirement. We identify several variants of the key sharing requirement and present a brief discussion. We also reveal previously unknown flaws in two protocols, which carry claimed proofs of security. We then present an improved provably-secure protocol and a revised protocol. The new provably-secure protocol is included in a submission to the IEEE 802.11, the working group setting the standards for wireless LANs, by researchers from Fujitsu Labs in America [4] and in another independent submission to The Internet Engineering Task Force (IETF) / Network Working Group [67].

Material presented in this chapter has appeared in the following publication:

- Kim-Kwang Raymond Choo and Yvonne Hitchcock. Security Requirements for Key Establishment Proof Models: Revisiting Bellare–Rogaway and Jeong–Katz–Lee Protocols. In Colin Boyd and Juan Manuel González Nieto, editors, 10th Australasian Conference on Information Security and Privacy - ACISP 2005, volume 3574/2005 of Lecture Notes in Computer Science, pages 429–442. Springer-Verlag, 2005. [Received the Best Student Paper award]

Chapter 5. In this chapter, we identify several variants of the Bellare–Rogaway model, identify several subtle differences between these Bellare–Rogaway variants and CK2001 model. We compare the relative strengths of the notions of security between these models. We also reveal a drawback with the original formulation of the BPR2000 model, whereby the Corrupt query is not allowed.

Material presented in this chapter has appeared in the following publication:

- Kim-Kwang Raymond Choo, Colin Boyd, and Yvonne Hitchcock. Examining Indistinguishability-Based Proof Models for Key Establishment Protocols. In Bimal Roy, editor, Advances in Cryptology - Asiacrypt 2005, volume 3788/2005 of Lecture Notes in Computer Science, pages 585–604, Springer-Verlag, 2005.

Chapter 6. In this chapter, we extend the Bellare–Rogaway model. We include the compromise of long-term keys which is not currently captured in the existing model. We also present two new protocols with proofs of security, one of which is in the extended model.

Material presented in this chapter has appeared in the following publication:

- Colin Boyd and Kim-Kwang Raymond Choo and Anish Mathuria. An Extension to Bellare and Rogaway (1993) Model: Resetting Compromised Long-Term Keys. In Lynn Margaret Batten and Reihaneh Safavi-Naini, editors, 11th Australasian Conference on Information Security and Privacy - ACISP 2006, volume 4058/2006 of Lecture Notes in Computer Science, pages 371–382, Springer-Verlag, 2006.

Chapter 7. In this chapter, we present a protocol for key establishment that is closely based on the Yahalom protocol [34], one of the most prominent key establishment protocols analyzed by researchers from the computer security community. We then present a security proof in the Bellare–Rogaway model and the random oracle model. We also observe that no partnering mechanism is specified within the Yahalom protocol. We then present a brief discussion on the role and the possible construct of session identifiers as a form of partnering mechanism, which allows the right session key to be identified in concurrent protocol executions. We then recommend that session identifiers should be included within protocol specification rather than consider session identifiers as artefacts in protocol proof.

Material presented in this chapter has appeared in the following publication:

- Kim-Kwang Raymond Choo. A Proof of Revised Yahalom Protocol in the Bellare and Rogaway (1993) Model. *The Computer Journal*, 50(5):591–601, 2007. [Received the Wilkes Award for the best paper published in the 2007 volume of *The Computer Journal*]

Chapter 8. In this chapter, we examine several protocols with claimed proofs of security by Boyd and González Nieto [29], Jakobsson and Pointcheval [72], and Wong and Chan [128], and an authenticator by Bellare, Canetti, and Krawczyk [18]. Using these protocols and the MT-authenticator as case studies, we reveal previously unknown flaws in these protocols and the MT-authenticator by refuting claimed proofs. We also identify three areas where computational proofs are likely to fail; namely an inappropriate proof model environment, Send, Session-Key Reveal, Session-State Reveal, and Corrupt queries not adequately considered in the proof simulations, and the omission of proof simulations.

Material presented in this chapter has appeared in the following publication:

- Kim-Kwang Raymond Choo, Colin Boyd, and Yvonne Hitchcock. Errors in Computational Complexity Proofs for Protocols. In Bimal Roy, editor, Advances in Cryptology - Asiacrypt 2005, volume 3788/2005 of Lecture Notes in Computer Science, pages 624–643. Springer-Verlag, 2005.

Chapter 9.   In this chapter, we examine the role of session key construction in provably-secure key establishment protocols. We demonstrate that a small change in the way that session keys are constructed in the protocols can have significant benefits. Protocols that were proven secure in a restricted model can then be proven secure in a less restrictive model or the full model under certain assumption. We present a brief discussion on ways to construct session keys in key establishment protocols. We also show that such key construction can help to avoid certain attacks.

Our observation on the session key construction is cited in a special publication (SP 800-56A) – Recommendation for Pair-Wise Key Establishment Schemes Using Discrete Logarithm Cryptography by National Institute of Standards and Technology (NIST) [14].

Material presented in this chapter has appeared in the following publications:

- Kim-Kwang Raymond Choo, Colin Boyd, and Yvonne Hitchcock. On Session Key Construction in Provably Secure Protocols. In Ed Dawson and Serge Vaudenay, editors, 1st International Conference on Cryptology in Malaysia - Mycrypt 2005, volume 3715/2005 of Lecture Notes in Computer Science, pages 116–131. Springer-Verlag, 2005.
- Kim-Kwang Raymond Choo. Revisit Of McCullagh–Barreto Two-Party ID-Based Authenticated Key Agreement Protocols (Preliminary version available from http://eprint.iacr.org/2004/343/). *International Journal of Network Security*, 1(3):154–160, 2005.
- Kim-Kwang Raymond Choo. Revisiting Lee, Kim, and Yoo Authenticated Key Agreement Protocol. *International Journal of Network Security*, 2(1):64–68, 2006.

Chapter 10.   In this chapter, we adopt the computer security approach. We provide a formal specification and machine analysis of the BPR2000 adversarial model using a model checker tool. Previously unknown flaws in several protocols will be revealed using this approach.

Material presented in this chapter has appeared in the following publications:

- Kim-Kwang Raymond Choo, Colin Boyd, Yvonne Hitchcock, and Greg Maitland. Complementing Computational Protocol Analysis with Formal Specifications. In Theo Dimitrakos and Fabio Martinelli, editors, IFIP TC1 WG1.7 2nd International Workshop on Formal Aspects in Security and Trust - FAST 2004, volume 173/2005 of IFIP International Federation for Information Processing Series, pages 129–144. Springer-Verlag, 2004.
- Kim-Kwang Raymond Choo, Colin Boyd, and Yvonne Hitchcock. The Importance of Proofs of Security for Key Establishment Protocols: Formal

Analysis of Jan–Chen, Yang–Shen–Shieh, Kim–Huh–Hwang–Lee, Lin–Sun–Hwang, & Yeh–Sun Protocols. *Computer Communications*, 29(15):2788–2797, 2006.

- Kim-Kwang Raymond Choo. Refuting Security Proofs for Tripartite Key Exchange with Model Checker in Planning Problem Setting. In 19th IEEE Computer Security Foundations Workshop - CSFW-19, pages 297–308. IEEE Computer Society, 2006.

Chapter 11. In this chapter, we extend the work in Chapter 10 and reveal a previously unknown flaw in the three-party identity-based secret public key protocol (3P-ID-SPK) protocol of Lim and Paterson [81]. We then show how our approach can automatically repair the protocol. This is, to the best of our knowledge, the first work that integrates an adversarial model from the computational complexity paradigm with an automated tool from the computer security paradigm to analyse protocols in an artificial intelligence problem setting – planning problem – and, most importantly, to repair protocols..

Material presented in this chapter has appeared in the following publication:

- Kim-Kwang Raymond Choo. An Integrative Framework to Protocol Analysis and Repair: Bellare-Rogaway Model + Planning + Model Checker . *Informatica*, 18(4):547–568, 2007.

Chapter 12. In this chapter, a summary of the book and a discussion of open problems and possible research directions is presented.

References

1. Michel Abdalla, Emmanuel Bresson, Olivier Chevassut & David Pointcheval 2006. Password-based Group Key Exchange in a Constant Number of Rounds, in Yung M, Dodis Y, Kiayias A & Malkin T (eds), Proceedings of Public Key Cryptography - PKC 2006. Lecture Notes in Computer Science 3958/2006: 427–442
2. Michel Abdalla, Pierre-Alain Fouqu & David Pointcheval 2005. Password-Based Authenticated Key Exchange in the Three-Party Setting, in Serge Vaudenay (ed), Proceedings of Public Key Cryptography - PKC 2005. Lecture Notes in Computer Science 3386/2005: 65–84
3. Martín Abadi 1997. Explicit Communication Revisited: Two New Attacks on Authentication Protocols. *IEEE Transactions on Software Engineering* 23(3): 185–186.
4. Jonathan Agre, Wei-Peng Chen, Mohammed Refaei, Anuja Sonalker, Chenxi Zhu & Xun Yuan 2005. Secure NOmadic Wireless Mesh (SnowMesh). Submission to the IEEE 802.11, The Working Group Setting the Standards for Wireless LANs. http://www.flacp.fujitsulabs.com/publications.html
5. Luigia Carlucci Aiello & Fabio Massacci 2001. Verifying Security Protocols as Planning in Logic Programming. *ACM Transactions on Computational Logic* 2(4): 542–580
6. Xavier Allamigeon & Bruno Blanchet 2005. Reconstruction of Attacks against Cryptographic Protocols, in Proceedings of 18th IEEE Computer Security Foundations Workshop - CSFW 2005. IEEE Computer Society Press: 140–154

7. Ben Ames (2007) Online spending tops US$100 billion. *Computerworld.com.au* 5 May. http://www.computerworld.com.au/index.php/id;732481904
8. Michael Backes 2004. A Cryptographically Sound Dolev-Yao Style Security Proof of the Needham–Schroeder–Lowe Public–Key Protocol. *IEEE Journal on Selected Areas in Communications* 22(10): 2075–2086
9. Michael Backes 2004. A Cryptographically Sound Dolev-Yao Style Security Proof of the Otway-Rees Protocol, in Samarati P & Gollmann D (eds), Proceedings of 9th European Symposium on Research in Computer Security - ESORICS 2004. Lecture Notes in Computer Science 3193/2004: 89–108
10. Michael Backes & Christian Jacobi 2003. Cryptographically Sound and Machine-Assisted Verification of Security Protocols, in Alt H & Habib M (eds), Proceedings of 20th International Symposium on Theoretical Aspects of Computer Science - STACS 2003. Lecture Notes in Computer Science 2607/2003: 310–329
11. Michael Backes, Christian Jacobi & Birgit Pfitzmann 2002. Deriving Cryptographically Sound Implementations Using Composition and Formally Verified Bisimulation, in Lars-Henrik Eriksson & Peter A Lindsay (eds), Proceedings of International Symposium of Formal Methods Europe – FME 2002. Lecture Notes in Computer Science 2391/2002: 310–329
12. Feng Bao 2003. Security Analysis of a Password Authenticated Key Exchange Protocol, in Colin Boyd & Wenbo Mao (eds), Proceedings of 6th Information Security Conference - ISC 2003. Lecture Notes in Computer Science 2851/2003: 208–217
13. Feng Bao 2004. Colluding Attacks to a Payment Protocol and Two Signature Exchange Schemes, in Pil Joong Lee (ed), Proceedings of Advances in Cryptology - ASIACRYPT 2004. Lecture Notes in Computer Science 3329/2004: 417–429
14. Elaine Barker, Don Johnson, & Miles Smid 2006. Recommendation for Pair-Wise Key Establishment Schemes Using Discrete Logarithm Cryptography. *Special Publication (SP 800-56A)*. National Institute of Standards and Technology
15. Gilles Barthe, Jan Cederquist & Sabrina Tarento 2004. A Machine-Checked Formalization of the Generic Model and the Random Oracle Model, in David A. Basin and Michaël Rusinowitch (eds), Proceedings of 2nd International Joint Conference on Automated Reasoning - IJCAR 2004. Lecture Notes in Computer Science 3097/2005: 385–399
16. David A. Basin and Sebastian Mödersheim and Luca Viganó 2003. An On-the-Fly Model-Checker for Security Protocol Analysis. *Technical report* no 404. Information Security Group, ETH Zentrum
17. David A. Basin and Sebastian Mödersheim and Luca Viganó 2003. An On-the-Fly Model-Checker for Security Protocol Analysis, in Einar Snekkenes & Dieter Gollmann (eds), Proceedings of 8th European Symposium on Research in Computer Security - ESORICS 2003. Lecture Notes in Computer Science 2808/2003: 253–270
18. Mihir Bellare, Ran Canetti & Hugo Krawczyk 1998. A Modular Approach to The Design and Analysis of Authentication and Key Exchange Protocols, in Jeffrey Vitter (ed), Proceedings of 30th ACM Symposium on the Theory of Computing - ACM STOC 1998. ACM Press: 419–428
19. Mihir Bellare, David Pointcheval & Phillip Rogaway 2000. Authenticated Key Exchange Secure Against Dictionary Attacks, in Bart Preneel (ed), Proceedings of Advances in Cryptology - EUROCRYPT 2000. Lecture Notes in Computer Science 1807/2000: 139 – 155
20. Mihir Bellare & Phillip Rogaway 1993. Entity Authentication and Key Distribution, in Douglas R. Stinson (ed), Proceedings of Advances in Cryptology - CRYPTO 1993. Lecture Notes in Computer Science 773/1993: 110–125
21. Mihir Bellare & Phillip Rogaway 1994. Optimal Asymmetric Encryption, in Alfredo De Santis (ed), Proceedings of Advances in Cryptology - EUROCRYPT 1994. Lecture Notes in Computer Science 950/199: 92–111.
22. Mihir Bellare & Phillip Rogaway 1995. Provably Secure Session Key Distribution: The Three Party Case, in F. Tom Leighton & Allan Borodin (eds), Proceedings of 27th ACM Symposium on the Theory of Computing - ACM STOC 1995. ACM Press: 57–66
23. Massimo Benerecetti & Fausto Giunchiglia 2000. Model Checking Security Protocols Using a Logic of Belief, in Susanne Graf & Michael I Schwartzbach (eds), Proceedings of 6th

International Workshop on Tools and Algorithms for Construction and Analysis of Systems - TACAS 2000. Lecture Notes in Computer Science 1785/2000: 519–534

24. Simon Blake-Wilson, Don Johnson & Alfred Menezes 1997. Key Agreement Protocols and their Security Analysis, in Michael Darnell (ed), Proceedings of 6th IMA International Conference on Cryptography and Coding. Lecture Notes in Computer Science 1335/1997: 30–45

25. Bruno Blanchet 2004. Automatic Proof of Strong Secrecy for Security Protocols, in David A Wagner and Michael Waidner (eds), Proceedings of IEEE Symposium on Research in Security and Privacy 2004. IEEE Computer Society Press: 86–100

26. Chiara Bodei, Mikael Buchholtz, Pierpaolo Degano, Flemming Nielson & Hanne Riis Nielson 2003. Automatic Validation of Protocol Narration, in Riccardo Focardi (ed), Proceedings of 16th IEEE Computer Security Foundations Workshop - CSFW 2003. IEEE Computer Society Press: 126–140

27. Colin Boyd, Kim-Kwang Raymond Choo & Anish Mathuria. An Extension to Bellare and Rogaway (1993) Model: Resetting Compromised Long-Term Keys, in Lynn Margaret Batten & Reihaneh Safavi-Naini (eds), Proceedings of 11th Australasian Conference on Information Security and Privacy - ACISP 2006. Lecture Notes in Computer Science 4058/2006: 371–382

28. Colin Boyd & Anish Mathuria 2003. *Protocols for Authentication and Key Establishment.* Springer-Verlag

29. Colin Boyd & Juan Manuel González Nieto 2003. Round-optimal Contributory Conference Key Agreement, in Yvo Desmedt (ed), Proceedings of Public Key Cryptography - PKC 2003. Lecture Notes in Computer Science 2567/2003: 161–174

30. Francesco Buccafurri, Thomas Eiter, Georg Gottlob & Nicola Leone 1999. Enhancing Model Checking in Verification by AI Techniques. *Artificial Intelligence* 112(1-2): 57–104

31. Michele Bugliesi, Riccardo Focardi & Matteo Maffei 2005. Analysis of Typed Analyses of Authentication Protocols, in Joshua Guttman (ed), Proceedings of 18th IEEE Computer Security Foundations Workshop - CSFW 2005. IEEE Computer Society Press: 112–125

32. Alan Bundy, Mateja Jamnik & Andrew Fugard 2005. What is a Proof?. *Philosophical Transactions of the Royal Society A: Mathematical, Physical and Engineering Sciences* 363(1835): 2377–2391

33. Mike Burmester. Cryptanalysis of the Chang-Wu-Chen Key Distribution System, in Tor Helleseth (ed), Proceedings of Advances in Cryptology - EUROCRYPT 1993. Lecture Notes in Computer Science 2656/1993: 440–442

34. Michael Burrows, Martín Abadi & Roger Needham 1990. A Logic of Authentication. *ACM Transactions on Computer Systems* 8(1): 18–36

35. Ran Canetti & Hugo Krawczyk 2001. Analysis of Key-Exchange Protocols and Their Use for Building Secure Channels, in Birgit Pfitzmann (ed), Proceedings of Advances in Cryptology - EUROCRYPT 2001. Lecture Notes in Computer Science 2045/2001: 453–474. Extended version available from http://eprint.iacr.org/2001/040/

36. Ran Canetti & Hugo Krawczyk 2002. Universally Composable Notions of Key Exchange and Secure Channels, in Lars R Knudsen (ed), Proceedings of Advances in Cryptology - EUROCRYPT 2002. Lecture Notes in Computer Science 2332/2002: 337–351. Extended version available from http://eprint.iacr.org/2002/059/

37. Tianjie Cao, Xianping Mao & Dongdai Lin 2006. Security Analysis of a Server-Aided RSA Key Generation Protocol, in Kefei Chen, Robert H Deng, Xuejia Lai & Jianying Zhou (eds), Proceedings of 2nd Information Security Practice and Experience Conference - ISPEC 2006. Lecture Notes in Computer Science 3903/2006: 314–320

38. Iliano Cervesato, Nancy Durgin, Patrick D Lincoln, John C Mitchell & Andre Scedrov 1999. A Meta-Notation for Protocol Analysis, in Paul Syverson (ed), Proceedings of 12th Computer Security Foundations Workshop - CSFW 1999. IEEE Computer Society Press: 55–71

39. Zhaohui Cheng & Richard Comley 2006. Attacks on An ISO/IEC 11770-2 Key Establishment Protocol. *International Journal of Network Security* 3(2): 238–243. Preliminary version available from http://eprint.iacr.org/2004/249/

40. Kim-Kwang Raymond Choo. Key Establishment : Proofs and Refutations. Ph.D. Thesis. Brisbane: Queensland University of Technology.

41. Kim-Kwang Raymond Choo 2006. On the Security Analysis of Lee, Hwang & Lee (2004) and Song & Kim (2000) Key Exchange / Agreement Protocols. *Informatica* 17(4): 467–480
42. Kim-Kwang Raymond Choo 2006. On the Security of Lee, Kim, Kim, & Oh Key Agreement Protocol. *International Journal of Network Security* 3(1): 85–94
43. Kim-Kwang Raymond Choo 2006. Refuting Security Proofs for Tripartite Key Exchange with Model Checker in Planning Problem Setting, in Joshua Guttman (ed), Proceedings of 19th Computer Security Foundations Workshop - CSFW 2006. IEEE Computer Society Press: 297–308
44. Kim-Kwang Raymond Choo, Colin Boyd & Yvonne Hitchcock 2005. The Importance of Proofs of Security for Key Establishment Protocols: Formal Analysis of Jan–Chen, Yang–Shen–Shieh, Kim–Huh–Hwang–Lee, Lin–Sun–Hwang, & Yeh–Sun Protocols. *Computer Communications* 29(15): 2788–2797
45. Kim-Kwang Raymond Choo, Colin Boyd & Yvonne Hitchcock 2005. Errors in Computational Complexity Proofs for Protocols, in Bimal Roy (ed), Proceedings of Advances in Cryptology - ASIACRYPT 2005. Lecture Notes in Computer Science 3788/2005: 624–643. Extended version available from http://eprint.iacr.org/2005/351
46. Kim-Kwang Raymond Choo, Colin Boyd & Yvonne Hitchcock 2005. Examining Indistinguishability-Based Proof Models for Key Establishment Protocols, in Bimal Roy (ed), Proceedings of Advances in Cryptology - ASIACRYPT 2005. Lecture Notes in Computer Science 3788/2005: 585–604. Extended version available from http://eprint.iacr.org/2005/270
47. Kim-Kwang Raymond Choo, Colin Boyd, Yvonne Hitchcock & Greg Maitland 2004. Complementing Computational Protocol Analysis with Formal Specifications, in Theo Dimitrakos & Fabio Martinelli (eds), Proceedings of IFIP TC1 WG1.7 2nd International Workshop on Formal Aspects in Security and Trust - FAST 2004. IFIP International Federation for Information Processing Series 173/2005: 129–144
48. Kim-Kwang Raymond Choo, Colin Boyd, Yvonne Hitchcock & Greg Maitland 2004. On Session Identifiers in Provably Secure Protocols: The Bellare-Rogaway Three-Party Key Distribution Protocol Revisited, in Blundo Carlo & Stelvio Cimato (eds), Proceedings of 4th Conference on Security in Communication Networks - SCN 2004. Lecture Notes in Computer Science 3352/2005: 352–367. Extended version available from http://eprint.iacr.org/2004/345
49. Kim-Kwang Raymond Choo & Yvonne Hitchcock 2005. Security Requirements for Key Establishment Proof Models: Revisiting Bellare–Rogaway and Jeong–Katz–Lee Protocols, in Colin Boyd & Juan Manuel González Nieto (eds), Proceedings of 10th Australasian Conference on Information Security and Privacy - ACISP 2005. Lecture Notes in Computer Science 3574/2005: 429–442. Received the Best Student Paper award
50. Kim-Kwang Raymond Choo & Russell G Smith 2008. Criminal Exploitation of Online Systems by Organised Crime Groups. *Asian Journal of Criminology* 3(1): 37–59
51. Kim-Kwang Raymond Choo, Russell G Smith & Rob McCusker 2007. Future directions in technology-enabled crime : 2007-09. *Research and public policy series* no 78. Canberra: Australian Institute of Criminology. http://www.aic.gov.au/publications/rpp/78/index.html
52. . Edmund M. Clarke, Orna Grumberg & Doron A Peled 2000. *Model Checking*. MIT Press
53. Edmund M Clarke, S Jha & W Marrero 2000. Verifying Security Protocols with Brutus. *ACM Transactions on Software Engineering and Methodology* 9(4): 443–487
54. Ricardo Corin & Sandro Etalle 2002. An Improved Constraint-Based System for the Verification of Security Protocols, in Manuel V Hermenegildo & Germn Puebla (eds), Proceedings of 9th International Symposium on Static Analysis - SAS 2002. Lecture Notes in Computer Science 2477/2002: 326–341
55. Ricardo Corin, Ari Saptawijaya & Sandro Etalle 2006. A Logic for Constraint-based Security Protocol Analysis, in Vern Paxson & Birgit Pfitzmann (eds), Proceedings of IEEE Symposium on Research in Security and Privacy 2006. IEEE Computer Society Press: 155–168

56. Vronique Cortier & Bogdan Warinschi 2005. Computationally Sound, Automated Proofs for Security Protocols, in Mooly Sagiv (ed), Proceedings of 14th European Symposium on Programming: Programming Languages and Systems - ESOP 2005. Lecture Notes in Computer Scienc 3444/2005: 157–171

57. Dorothy E Denning & Giovanni Maria Sacco 1981. Timestamps in Key Distribution Protocols. *ACM Journal of Communications* 24(8): 533–536

58. Whitfield Diffie & Martin Hellman 1976. New Directions in Cryptography. *IEEE Transaction on Information Theory* 22(6): 644–654

59. Danny Dolev & Andrew C Yao 1983. On the Security of Public Key Protocols. *IEEE Transaction of Information Technology* 29(2): 198–208

60. Ben Donovan, Paul Norris & Gavin Lowe 1999. Analyzing a Library of Security Protocols using Casper and FDR, in *Proceedings of Workshop on Formal Methods and Security Protocols*. http://web.comlab.ox.ac.uk/oucl/work/gavin.lowe/Security/Papers/prots.ps

61. Santiago Escobar, Catherine Meadows & José Meseguer 2005. A Rewriting-based Inference System for the NRL Protocol Analyzer: Grammar Generation, in Vijay Atluri, Pierangela Samarati, Ralf Ksters & John Mitchell (eds), Proceedings of ACM workshop on Formal methods in security engineering - FMSE 2005. ACM Press: 1–12

62. Colin J Fidge 2001. *A Survey of Verification Techniques for Security Protocols*. http://espace.uq.edu.au/view/UQ:10577

63. Marcelo P Fiore & Martín Abadi 2001. Computing Symbolic Models for Verifying Cryptographic Protocols, in Steve Schneider (ed), Proceedings of IEEE Computer Security Foundation Workshop - CSFW 2001. IEEE Computer Society Press: 160–173

64. Shafi Goldwasser & S Micali 1984. Probabilisitic Encryption. *Journal of Computer and System Sciences* 28(3): 270–299. http://people.csail.mit.edu/joanne/shafi-pubs.html

65. Prateek Gupta & Vitaly Shmatikov 2005. Towards Computationally Sound Symbolic Analysis of Key Exchange Protocols, in Vijay Atluri, Pierangela Samarati, Ralf Ksters & John Mitchell (eds), Proceedings of ACM workshop on Formal methods in security engineering - FMSE 2005. ACM Press: 23–32. Extended version available from http://eprint.iacr.org/2005/171

66. Joshua D Guttman, Jonathan C Herzog, John D Ramsdell & Brian T Sniffen 2005. Programming Cryptographic Protocols, in Rocco De Nicola & Davide Sangiorgi (eds), Proceedings of Trustworthy Global Computing, International Symposium - TGC 2005. Lecture Notes in Computer Science 3705/2005: 116–145

67. Dan Harkins, Yoshihiro Ohba, Madjid Nakhjiri & Rafael Marin Lopez 2007. Problem Statement and Requirements on a 3-Party Key Distribution Protocol for Handover Keying. Submission to The Internet Engineering Task Force (IETF) / Network Working Group. http://tools.ietf.org/html/draft-ohba-hokey-3party-keydist-ps-01

68. Jonathon Herzog 2002. Computational Soundness of Formal Adversaries. Master of Science Thesis: Department of Electrical Engineering and Computer Science, Massachusetts Institute of Technology

69. Bin-Tsan Hsieh, Hung-Min Sun & Tzonelih Hwang 2002. Cryptanalysis of Enhancement for Simple Authentication Key Agreement Algorithm. *IEE Electronics Letters* 38(1): 20–21

70. Min-Shiang Hwang, Ting-Yi Chang, Shu-Chen Lin & Chwei-Shyong Tsai 2004. On the Security of an Enhanced Authentication Key Exchange Protocol, in *Proceedings of 18th International Conference on Advanced Information Networking and Applications - AINA 2004*. IEEE Computer Society: 160–163

71. Kenji Imamoto & Kouichi Sakurai 2005. Design and Analysis of Diffie–Hellman-Based Key Exchange Using One-time ID by SVO Logic. *Electronic Notes in Theoretical Computer Science* 135(1): 79–94

72. Markus Jakobsson & David Pointcheval 2001. Mutual Authentication and Key Exchange Protocol for Low Power Devices, in Paul F Syverson (ed), Proceedings of 5th International Conference on Financial Cryptography - FC 2001. Lecture Notes in Computer Science 2339/2002: 169–186

73. Burton S Kaliski 2001. An Unknown Key-Share Attack on the MQV Key Agreement Protocol. *ACM Transactions on Information and System Security (TISSEC)* 4(3): 275–288

74. Neal Koblitz & Alfred Menezes 2004. Another Look at "Provable Security". *Technical report* no CORR 2004-20. Centre for Applied Cryptographic Research, University of Waterloo, Canada. http://eprint.iacr.org/2004/152/

75. Neal Koblitz & Alfred Menezes 2006. Another Look at "Provable Security". *Journal of Cryptology* 20(1): 3–37

76. Wei-Chi Ku & Sheng-De Wang 2000. Cryptanalysis of Modified Authenticated Key Agreement Protocol. *IEE Electronics Letters* 36(21): 1770–1771

77. Taekyoung Kwon, Young-Ho Park & Hee Jung Lee 2005. Security Analysis and Improvement of the Efficient Password-based Authentication Protocol. *IEEE Communications Letters* 9(1): 93–95

78. Imre Lakatos 1976. *Proofs and Refutations : The Logic of Mathematical Discovery.* Cambridge University Press

79. Peter Laud 2005. Secrecy Types for a Simulatable Cryptographic Library, in *Proceedings of 12th ACM Conference on Computer and Communications Security - ACM CCS 2005.* ACM Press: 26–35

80. Kristin Lauter & Anton Mityagin 2006. Security Analysis of KEA Authenticated Key Exchange, in Moti Yung, Yevgeniy Dodis, Aggelos Kiayias & Tal Malkin (eds), Proceedings of Public Key Cryptography - PKC 2006. Lecture Notes in Computer Science 3958/2006: 378–394

81. Hoon Wei Lim & Kenneth G Paterson 2006. Secret Public Key Protocols Revisited in *Proceedings of Security Protocols Workshop 2006.* http://www.isg.rhul.ac.uk/~kp/

82. Chun-Li Lin, Hung-Min Sun & Tzonelih Hwang 2000. Three-Party Encrypted Key Exchange: Attacks and A Solution. *ACM SIGOPS Operating Systems Review* 34(4): 12–20

83. Javier Lopez, Juan J Ortega & José M Troya 2002. Verification of Authentication Protocols using SDL-method, in Roberto Moya & Eduardo Fernández-Medina (eds), Proceedings of 1st International Workshop on Security in Information Systems - SIS 2002. ICEIS Press: 61–71

84. Javier Lopez, Juan J Ortega & José M Troya 2005. Security Protocols Analysis: A SDL-based Approach. *Computer Standards & Interfaces* 27(5): 489–499

85. Gavin Lowe 1996. Breaking and Fixing the Needham-Schroeder Public Key Protocol using FDR, in Tiziana Margaria & Bernhard Steffen (eds), Proceedings of 2nd International Workshop on Tools and Algorithms for Construction and Analysis of Systems - TACAS 1996. Lecture Notes in Computer Science 1055/1996: 147–166

86. Gavin Lowe 1996. Some New Attacks upon Security Protocols, in *Proceedings of IEEE Computer Security Foundations Workshop - CSFW 1996.* IEEE Computer Society Press: 162–169

87. Gavin Lowe 1997. Casper: A Compiler for the Analysis of Security Protocols, in *Proceedings of IEEE Computer Security Foundations Workshop - CSFW 1997.* IEEE Computer Society Press: 18–30

88. Nancy A Lynch 1999. I/O Automaton Models and Proofs for Shared-Key Communication Systems, in *Proceedings of IEEE Computer Security Foundations Workshop - CSFW 1999.* IEEE Computer Society Press: 14–29

89. Wenbo Mao 2005. A Structured Operational Semantic Modelling of the Dolev-Yao Threat Environment and its Composition with Cryptographic Protocols. *Computer Standards & Interfaces* 27(5): 479–489

90. Catherine Meadows 1997. Languages for Formal Specification of Security Protocols, in *Proceedings of 9th IEEE Computer Security Foundations Workshop - CSFW 1997.* IEEE Computer Society Press: 96–97

91. Catherine Meadows 2001. Open Issues in Formal Methods for Cryptographic Protocol Analysis, in *Proceedings of DARPA Information Survivability Conference and Exposition.* IEEE Computer Society Press: 237–250

92. Catherine Meadows 2003. Formal Methods for Cryptographic Protocol Analysis: Emerging Issues and Trends. *IEEE Journal on Selected Area in Communications* 21(1): 44–54

93. Ralph C Merkle 1978. Secure Communications over Insecure Channels. *Communications of the ACM* 21(4): 294–299

94. Alfred J Menezes, Paul C van Oorschot & Scott A Vanstone 1997. *Handbook of Applied Cryptography*. CRC Press

95. Chris J Mitchell 2001. Breaking the Simple Authenticated Key Agreement (SAKA) Protocol. *Technical report* no RHUL-MA-2001-2. Royal Holloway, University of London

96. John C Mitchell, Mark Mitchell & Ulrich Stern 1997. Automated Analysis of Cryptographic Protocols using Murphi, *Proceedings of IEEE Symposium on Research in Security and Privacy 1997*. IEEE Computer Society Press: 141–153

97. Chris J Mitchell & Chan Yeob Yeun 1998. Fixing a Problem in the Helsinki Protocol. *ACM Operating Systems Review* 32(4): 21–24

98. Alexei G Myasnikov, Vladimir Shpilrain & Alexander Ushakov 2005. A Practical Attack on a Braid Group Based Cryptographic Protocol, in Victor Shoup (ed), Proceedings of Advances in Cryptology - CRYPTO 2005. Lecture Notes in Computer Science 3621/200: 86–96

99. Junghyun Nam, Seungjoo Kim & Dongho Won 2004. Attacks on Bresson-Chevassut-Essiari-Pointcheval's Group Key Agreement Scheme. Cryptology ePrint Archive, Report 2004/251. http://eprint.iacr.org/2004/251/

100. Junghyun Nam, Seungjoo Kim & Dongho Won 2005. Security Weakness in Ren et al.s Group Key Agreement Scheme Built on Secure Two-Party Protocols, in JooSeok Song, Taekyoung Kwon & Moti Yung (eds), Proceedings of 6th International Workshop on Information Security Applications - WISA 2005. Lecture Notes in Computer Science 3325/2005: 1–9

101. Claus Pahl 2002. Interference Analysis for Dependance Systems Using Refinement and Abstraction, in Lars-Henrik Eriksson & Peter A Lindsay (eds), Proceedings of Formal Methods - Getting IT Right. Lecture Notes in Computer Science 2391/2002: 330–349

102. Lawrence C Paulson 1997. Proving Properties of Security Protocols by Induction, in *Proceedings of IEEE Computer Security Foundation Workshop - CSFW 1997*. IEEE Computer Society Press: 70–83

103. Lawrence C Paulson 1998. The Inductive Approach to Verifying Cryptographic Protocols. *Journal of Computer Security* 6(1/2): 85–128

104. Olivier Pereira & Jean-Jacques Quisquater 2001. A Security Analysis of the Cliques Protocol Suites, in *Proceedings of IEEE Computer Security Foundation Workshop - CSFW 2001*. IEEE Computer Society Press: 73–81

105. Olivier Pereira & Jean-Jacques Quisquater 2001. Security Analysis of the Cliques Protocols Suites: First Results, in Michel Dupuy & Pierre Paradinas (eds), Proceedings of IFIP TC11 Sixteenth Annual Working Conference on Information Security - SEC 2001. IFIP Conference Proceedings 193/2001: 151–166

106. Olivier Pereira & Jean-Jacques Quisquater 2003. Some Attacks Upon Authenticated Group Key Agreement Protocols. *Journal of Computer Security* 11(4): 555–580

107. Adrian Perrig & Dawn Song 2000. A First Step towards the Automatic Generation of Security Protocols, in *Proceedings of ISOC Networks and Distributed Security Systems - NDSS 2000*. Internet Society Press: 73–83

108. Adrian Perrig & Dawn Song 2000. Looking for Diamonds in the Desert: Extending Automatic Protocol Generation to Three-Party Authentication and Key Agreement Protocols, in *Proceedings of IEEE Computer Security Foundation Workshop - CSFW 2000*. IEEE Computer Society Press: 64–76

109. Raphael C-W Phan & Bok-Min Goi 2005. Cryptanalysis of an Improved Client-to-Client Password-Authenticated Key Exchange (C2C-PAKE) Scheme, in Angelos Keromytis & Moti Yung (eds), Proceedings of Applied Cryptography and Network Security - ACNS 2005. Lecture Notes in Computer Science 3531/2005: 33–39

110. Raphael C-W Phan & Bok-Min Goi 2005. On the Rila-Mitchell Security Protocols for Biometrics-Based Cardholder Authentication in Smartcards, in Osvaldo Gervasi, Marina L Gavrilova, Vipin Kumar, Antonio Lagan, Heow Pueh Lee, Youngsong Mun, David Taniar & Chih Jeng Kenneth Tan (eds), Proceedings of International Conference On Computational Science And Its Applications - ICCSA 2005. Lecture Notes in Computer Science 3480/2005: 488-497

111. Raphael C-W Phan & Bok-Min Goi 2006. Cryptanalysis of the N-Party Encrypted Diffie–Hellman Key Exchange Using Different Passwords, in Jianying Zhou, Moti Yung & Feng Bao

(eds), Proceedings of Applied Cryptography and Network Security - ACNS 2006. Lecture Notes in Computer Science 3989/2006: 226-238

112. Steve Schneider 1997. Verifying Authentication Protocols with CSP, in *Proceedings of IEEE Computer Security Foundation Workshop - CSFW 1997*. IEEE Computer Society Press: 3–17

113. Shiuh-Pyng Shieh, Wen-Her Yang & H M Sun 1997. An Authentication Protocol without Trusted Third Party. *IEEE Communications Letters* 1(3): 87–89

114. Kyungah Shim 2003. Cryptanalysis of Mutual Authentication and Key Exchange for Low Power Wireless Communications. *IEEE Communications Letters* 7(5): 248–250

115. Victor Shoup 1999. On Formal Models for Secure Key Exchange (Version 4). *Technical report* no RZ 3120 (#93166). IBM Research, Zurich

116. Victor Shoup. OAEP Reconsidered, in Joe Kilian (ed), Proceedings of Advances in Cryptology - CRYPTO 2001. Lecture Notes in Computer Science 2139/2001: 239–259

117. Victor Shoup 2002. OAEP Reconsidered. *Journal of Cryptology* 15(4): 223–249

118. Jason Smith, Suratose Tritilanunt, Colin Boyd, Juan Manuel González Nieto & Ernest Foo 2006. Denial-of-Service Resistance in Key Establishment. *International Journal of Wireless and Mobile Computing* 2(1): 59–91

119. Graham Steel & Alan Bundy 2005. Attacking Group Multicast Key Management Protocols Using Coral, in Alessandro Armando & Luca Viganó (eds), Proceedings of 2nd International Joint Conference on Automated Reasoning - ARSPA 2004. Electronic Notes in Theoretical Computer Science 125(1)/2005: 125–144

120. Graham Steel, Alan Bundy & Monika Maidl 2004. Attacking a Protocol for Group Key Agreement by Refuting Incorrect Inductive Conjectures, in David A Basin & Michaël Rusinowitch (eds), Proceedings of 2nd International Joint Conference on Automated Reasoning - IJCAR 2004. Lecture Notes in Computer Science 3097/2005: 137–151

121. Adam Stubblefield, John Ioannidis & Aviel D Rubin 2004. A Key Recovery Attack on the 802.11b Wired Equivalent Privacy Protocol (WEP). *ACM Transactions on Information and System Security (TISSEC)* 7(2): 319–332

122. Sabrina Tarento 2005. Machine-Checked Security Proofs of Cryptographic Signature Schemes, in Sabrina de Capitani di Vimercati, Paul Syverson & Dieter Gollmann (eds), Proceedings of 10th European Symposium on Research in Computer Security - ESORICS 2005. Lecture Notes in Computer Science 3679/2005: 140–158

123. Xiaojian Tian & Duncan S Wong 2006. Session Corruption Attack and Improvements on Encryption Based MT-Authenticators, in David Pointcheval (ed), Proceedings of Cryptographers' Track at RSA Conference - CT-RSA 2006. Lecture Notes in Computer Science 3860/2006: 34–51

124. Zhiguo Wan & Shuhong Wang 2004. Cryptanalysis of Two Password-Authenticated Key Exchange Protocols, in Huaxiong Wang, Josef Pieprzyk & Vijay Varadharajan (eds), Proceedings of 9th Australasian Conference on Information Security and Privacy - ACISP 2004. Lecture Notes in Computer Science 3108/2004: 164–175

125. Shuhong Wang, Jie Wang & Maozhi Xu 2004. Weaknesses of a Password-Authenticated Key Exchange Protocol between Clients with Different Passwords, in Markus Jakobsson, Moti Yung & Jianying Zhou (eds), Proceedings of Applied Cryptography and Network Security - ACNS 2004. Lecture Notes in Computer Science 3089/2004: 414-425

126. Jeannette M Wing 1998. A Symbiotic Relationship Between Formal Methods and Security, in *Proceedings of Workshops on Computer Security, Fault Tolerance, and Software Assurance: From Needs to Solution*. IEEE Computer Press

127. Stefan Wolf 1999. Information-Theoretically and Computationally Secure Key Agreement in Cryptography. Ph.D. Thesis. ETH Zurich, Swiss Federal Institute of Technology Zurich. http://www.iro.umontreal.ca/~wolf/papers.html

128. Duncan S Wong & Agnes H Chan 2001. Efficient and Mutually Authenticated Key Exchange for Low Power Computing Devices, in Colin Boyd (ed), Proceedings of Advances in Cryptology - ASIACRYPT 2001. Lecture Notes in Computer Science 2248/2001: 172–289

129. Yacov Yacobi 1987. Attack on the Koyama-Ohta Identity Based Key Distribution Scheme, in Carl Pomerance (ed), Proceedings of Advances in Cryptology - CRYPTO 1987. Lecture Notes in Computer Science 293/1988: 429–433

130. Xun Yi, Chee Kheong Siew, Hung-Min Sun, Her-Tyan Yeh, Chun-Li Lin & Tzonelih Hwang 2003. Security of Park-Lim Key Agreement Scheme for VSAT Satellite Communications. *IEEE Transactions on Vehicular Technology* 52(2): 465–468

131. Muxiang Zhang 2004. Further Analysis of Password Authenticated Key Exchange Protocol Based on RSA for Imbalanced Wireless Networks, in Kan Zhang & Yuliang Zheng (eds), Proceedings of 7th Information Security Conference - ISC 2004. Lecture Notes in Computer Science 3225/2004: 13-24

132. Muxiang Zhang 2005. Breaking an Improved Password Authenticated Key Exchange Protocol for Imbalanced Wireless Networks. *IEEE Communications Letters* 9(3): 276–278

133. Zhu Zhao, Zhongqi Dong & Yongge Wang 2006. Security Analysis of a Password-based Authentication Protocol Proposed to IEEE 1363. *Theoretical Computer Science* 352(1-3): 280–287

134. Jianying Zhou 2000. Further Analysis of the Internet Key Exchange Protocol. *Journal of Computer Communications* 23(17): 1606–1612

Chapter 2
Background Materials

In this chapter, we cover the nomenclature and definitions necessary for understanding the remainder of the book. Necessary background material on the topic of cryptographic protocols, and in particular key establishment protocols, is presented. We also present overviews of the Bellare–Rogaway [13, 14, 16] and Canetti–Krawczyk [10, 30] computational complexity models which will serve as building blocks in this book. We mainly work in these models and several protocols proposed in this book are proven secure in one of these models.

2.1 Mathematical Background

This section introduces the basic ideas of complexity theory, introduces several different cryptographic definitions, and provides the necessary mathematical background required for the book. The notation used throughout the book is presented in Table 2.1.

2.1.1 Abstract Algebra and the Main Groups

$\mathbb{G}$ denotes a group which is a set with some binary operation. We denote $\mathbb{G}^*$ as the set of non-identity elements of the group.

Definition 2.1.1 *A group is an algebraic structure consisting of a set $\mathbb{G}$ of group elements and a binary group operation $\cdot : \mathbb{G} \times \mathbb{G} \to \mathbb{G}$ such that the following conditions hold:*

1. *if $a, b \in \mathbb{G}$, then $a \cdot b \in \mathbb{G}$,*
2. *the group operation is associative (i.e., $a \cdot (b \cdot c) = (a \cdot b) \cdot c$ for all $a, b, c \in \mathbb{G}$),*
3. *there is an identity element $1 \in \mathbb{G}$ such that $a \cdot 1 = a = 1 \cdot a$ for all $a \in \mathbb{G}$, and*
4. *for each $a \in \mathbb{G}$ there is an inverse $a^{-1} \in \mathbb{G}$ such that $a \cdot a^{-1} = 1 = a^{-1} \cdot a$.*

Principals	Denotes protocol participants or entities.
A and B	Denote honest parties where A is usually the initiator entity and B the responder entity (unless otherwise stated).
$x \in_R \{0,1\}^k$	Denotes that x is randomly chosen from $\{0,1\}^k$ where the superscript k symbolises the security parameter.
$x\|y$	If x and y are strings, then $x\|y$ denotes their concatenation.
$x \stackrel{?}{=} y$	If x and y are strings, $x \stackrel{?}{=} y$ denotes comparing if $x = y$.
$\mathscr{A}$	Denotes a probabilistic, polynomial time adversary.
$\{\cdot\}_K$	Denotes the encryption of some message under some encryption key, K.
$[\cdot]_{K^{MAC}}$	Denote the computation of a MAC digest under some MAC key K^{MAC}.
$\sigma_{K^{Sign}}(\cdot)$	Denote the signature of some message under some signature key K^{Sign}.
$\oplus$	Denotes the bit-wise exclusive OR (XOR) operator.
$\Pr[\cdot]$	Denotes the probability that $p(\cdot)$ is true after ordered execution of the listed experiments.
pwd_{U_1,U_2}	Denotes some secret password shared between two users, U_1 and U_2.
$\mathscr{H}$ and $\mathscr{H}_i$	Denote some secure and independent cryptographic hash functions, where $i = 0,1,\ldots$.
$\mathbb{Z}_p^*$	Denotes the multiplicative group of non-zero integers modulo p where p is a sufficiently large prime p.
$\mathbb{Z}_q$	Denotes the group of integers modulo q where q is a prime such that $q\|p-1$.

Table 2.1 Summary of notations

Definition 2.1.2 *The number of elements in* $\mathbb{G}$, *denoted* $|\mathbb{G}|$, *is called the order of* $\mathbb{G}$. *A group* $\mathbb{G}$ *is finite if* $|\mathbb{G}|$ *is finite.*

$\mathbb{G}$ is said to be cyclic if there is an element $g \in \mathbb{G}$ such that for each $a \in \mathbb{G}$ there is an integer i with $a = g^i$. Such an element g is called a generator of $\mathbb{G}$.

In this book, we let $\mathbb{G} \subset \mathbb{Z}_p^*$ be a cyclic group of prime order q, where g is a generator of $\mathbb{G}$. The security parameters, p and q, are defined as the fixed form $q|p-1$ and $ord(g) = q$.

2.1.2 Bilinear Maps from Elliptic Curve Pairings

Using the notation of Boneh and Franklin [22], we let $\mathbb{G}_1$ be an additive group of prime order q and $\mathbb{G}_2$ be a multiplicative group of the same order q. We assume the existence of a map $\hat{e}$ from $\mathbb{G}_1 \times \mathbb{G}_1$ to $\mathbb{G}_2$ and that elements of $\mathbb{G}_1$ and $\mathbb{G}_2$ can be represented by bit strings of the appropriate lengths. Typically, $\mathbb{G}_1$ will be a subgroup of the group of points on an elliptic curve over a finite field, $\mathbb{G}_2$ will be a subgroup of the multiplicative group of a related finite field, and the map $\hat{e}$ will be derived from either the Weil or Tate pairing on the elliptic curve[1].

---

[1] Tate pairing appears to be more computationally efficient than Weil pairing [45, 59]. A more comprehensive description of how these groups, pairings and other parameters should be selected

The mapping $\hat{e}$ must be efficiently computable and has the following properties.

Bilinearity. For $Q, W, Z \in \mathbb{G}_1$, both

$$\hat{e}(Q, W + Z) = \hat{e}(Q, W) \cdot \hat{e}(Q, Z) \quad \text{and} \quad \hat{e}(Q + W, Z) = \hat{e}(Q, Z) \cdot \hat{e}(W, Z).$$

Non-Degeneracy. For some elements $P, Q \in \mathbb{G}_1$, we have $\hat{e}(P, Q) \neq 1_{\mathbb{G}_2}$.

Computability. For some elements $P, Q \in \mathbb{G}_1$, we have an efficient algorithm to compute $\hat{e}(P, Q)$.

A bilinear map, $\hat{e}$, is said to be an *admissible* bilinear map if it satisfies all three properties. Since $\hat{e}$ is bilinear, the map $\hat{e}$ is also symmetric.

2.1.3 Computational Problems and Assumptions

We introduce here several computational problems and assumptions, which are based on number theoretic problems. In other words, these cryptographic problems and assumptions exist within the framework of complexity theory. We recall the definitions for three frequently used complexity theory terms: the security parameter k, a *negligible function* (presented in Definition 2.1.3), and the definition of a *polynomial time algorithm* (presented in Definition 2.1.4).

In cryptographic algorithms, the security parameter, k, is important as negligibility of functions and complexity of algorithms are often parametised by k (e.g., the size of cryptographic groups and key lengths, within those algorithms). The larger the value of k is, the more computation is required to run an algorithm. The value k relates to the bounds on an adversary's success probability (i.e., k is often represented in unary notation as 1^k). All cryptographic algorithms in this book receive this value as input and the running time is measured in k.

Definition 2.1.3 (A Negligible Function [9]) *A function $\varepsilon(k) : \mathbb{N} \to \mathbb{R}$ in the security parameter k, is called negligible if it approaches zero faster than the reciprocal of any polynomial in k. That is, for every $c \in \mathbb{N}$ there is an integer k_c such that $\varepsilon(k) \leq k^{-c}$ for all $k \geq k_c$.*

Definition 2.1.4 (Polynomial Time Algorithm [9]) *A polynomial time algorithm (also called an efficient algorithm) is an algorithm whose worst-case running time function is of the form $O(k^c)$, where k is the input size and c is a constant.*

In defining assumptions, protocol designers have various degrees of freedom related to the concrete mathematical formulation of the assumption. For example, what kind of attackers are considered or over what values the probability spaces are defined.

---

in practice for efficiency and security is described by recent work of Barreto, Kim, Lynn, and Scott [8] and Galbraith [45].

In the following discussion, we will introduce the computational problems and assumptions that will form the basis of security for the schemes discussed in this book. The general structure of the problems is one of these two types.

Computational.   For a given problem instance, a probabilistic, polynomial time algorithm, $\mathscr{F}$, succeeds if and only if it can solve the problem instance.

Decisional.   For a given problem instance, another random problem instance is chosen with the same structure instance using the corresponding problem instance sampler and a random bit b. The probabilistic, polynomial time algorithm, $\mathscr{F}$, succeeds if, and only if, it can decide whether a given solution chosen randomly from the solution set of one of the two problem instances corresponds to the given problem instance.

The respective assumption states that no probabilistic, polynomial time algorithm has non-negligible advantage in k in solving the corresponding computational / decisional problem as described below for the given parameters. Let

- $x, y, z, a, b, c, d \in \mathbb{Z}_q^*$,
- $g, g^x, g^y, g^{xy}, g^z \in \mathbb{G}$,
- $P, aP, bP, cP, dP \in \mathbb{G}_1$, and
- $\hat{e}(P,P)^{abc}, \hat{e}(P,P)^d \in \mathbb{G}_2$.

Definition 2.1.5 (Computational Diffie-Hellman Problem [42])

$$Instance : (g, g^x, g^y)$$
$$Output : g^{xy}.$$

If we can solve the Discrete Logarithm Problem (DLP) [23][2] in $\mathbb{G}$, then we can also (immediately) solve the Computational Diffie-Hellman (CDH) problem although the converse is still an open research problem [23, 70, 79].

Definition 2.1.6 (Decisional Diffie-Hellman Problem)

$$Instance : (g, g^x, g^y, g^z)$$
$$Decide : g^z \stackrel{?}{=} g^{xy}.$$

Definition 2.1.7 (Bilinear Diffie-Hellman Problem [22])

$$Instance : (P, aP, bP, cP)$$
$$Output : \hat{e}(P,P)^{abc}.$$

The Bilinear Diffie-Hellman (BDH) problem is closely related to the Computational Diffie-Hellman (CDH) problem [22, 53]. For example, Horwitz and Lynn [53] show how the BDH problem (associated with a particular $\hat{e}$) can be obtained from the CDH problem with a simple game transformation. A recent survey by Joux [59] is

---

[2] The DLP forms the basis in the security of many cryptographic techniques [54, Chapter 3.6].

an excellent starting point for a detailed analysis of the relationship between BDH and other standard problems.

Definition 2.1.8 (Decisional Bilinear Diffie-Hellman Problem [21])

$$Instance : (P, aP, bP, cP, \hat{e}(P,P)^d)$$

$$Decide : d \stackrel{?}{=} abc \bmod q.$$

Note that the Decisional Bilinear Diffie-Hellma (DBDH) problem is easy in the group $\mathbb{G}_1$ [60] but is believed to be hard in the group $\mathbb{G}_2$.

Definition 2.1.9 (Gap Bilinear Diffie-Hellman Problem [84])

$$Instance : (P, aP, bP, cP)$$

$$Output : \hat{e}(P,P)^{abc} \in \mathbb{G}_2 \text{ with the help of a DBDH oracle.}$$

Boneh and Franklin [22] point out that the Gap Bilinear Diffie-Hellman (GBDH) parameter generators satisfying the GBDH assumption can be constructed from the Weil and Tate pairings associated with super-singular elliptic curves or abelian varieties.

Definition 2.1.10 (Bilinear Inverse Diffie-Hellman Problem)

$$Instance : (P, aP, cP)$$

$$Output : \hat{e}(P,P)^{a^{-1}c} \in \mathbb{G}_2.$$

Recent work of Zhang, Safavi-Naini, and Susilo [106] shows that the Bilinear Inverse Diffie-Hellman (BIDH) problem is polynomial time equivalent to the BDH problem.

2.1.4 Cryptographic Tools

Encryption schemes, signature schemes, message authentication codes, and cryptographic hash functions are functions which have many uses in cryptography. In order to obtain security arguments without compromising the efficiency of hash functions, such functions are hypothesized to behave like a random function. The security of the various encryption, signature, message authentication codes schemes is defined using an indistinguishability (IND) game. An example of the IND game is described in Definition 2.1.12.

2.1.4.1 Encryption Schemes: Asymmetric Setting

The classical goal of a secure encryption scheme is to preserve the privacy of messages. That is to allow one party to send a message to another such that the contents of the message remain hidden from anyone intercepting the communication. Any adversary, $\mathscr{A}$, should not be able to learn from a ciphertext information about its plaintext.

The standard definition for the security of encryption schemes (also known as *semantic security*) was first formulated by Goldwasser and Micali [47]. They consider privacy under indistinguishability of encryptions (IND) under chosen-plaintext attack (CPA)[3], and show that IND-CPA is equivalent to semantic security. The definition for an asymmetric encryption scheme [11] is given in Definition 2.1.11.

Definition 2.1.11 (An Asymmetric Encryption Scheme) *An asymmetric encryption scheme is given by a triple of algorithms, $\mathscr{PE} = (\mathscr{K},\mathscr{E},\mathscr{D})$, where*

- *$\mathscr{K}$, the key generation algorithm, is a probabilistic algorithm that takes a security parameter k and returns a pair (pk,sk) of matching public and secret keys.*
- *$\mathscr{E}$, the encryption algorithm, is a probabilistic algorithm that takes a public key pk and a message $x \in \{0,1\}^*$ to produce a ciphertext y.*
- *$\mathscr{D}$, the decryption algorithm, is a deterministic algorithm which takes a secret key sk and ciphertext y to produce either a message $x \in \{0,1\}^*$ or a special symbol $\perp$ to indicate that the ciphertext was invalid.*

We require that for all (pk,sk) which can be output by $\mathscr{K}(k)$, for all $x \in \{0,1\}^*$, and for all y that can be output by $\mathscr{E}_{pk}(x)$, we have that $\mathscr{D}_{sk}(y) = x$. We also require that $\mathscr{K}$, $\mathscr{E}$, and $\mathscr{D}$ can be computed in polynomial time.

Prior to discussing the basic notion of indistinguishability of encryptions for asymmetric (i.e., public-key) encryption, we describe the indistinguishability (IND) game. In the IND game, the attacker is asked to provide two messages, m_0 and m_1. The challenger picks one of these messages at random and encrypts it, giving the resulting ciphertext, y^*, back to the attacker. The attacker then guesses which message (i.e., m_0 or m_1) the challenger encrypted.

At first glance, this may seem trivial – the attacker can just encrypt both m_0 and m_1 to obtain y_0 and y_1 and compare whether

$$y_0 \stackrel{?}{=} y^* \text{ or } y_1 \stackrel{?}{=} y^*.$$

Recall that $\mathscr{E}$, the encryption algorithm, is probabilistic. In other words, encryption of the same message twice is unlikely to result in the same ciphertext, and knowing the encryption of a message may not help us recognise another encryption of the same message.

Definition 2.1.12 describes the indistinguishability (IND) game.

---

[3] In a chosen-plaintext attack (CPA), the adversary, $\mathscr{A}$, is allowed to encrypt plaintexts of $\mathscr{A}$'s choice. In the public-key setting, with the knowledge of the public key, $\mathscr{A}$ can compute a ciphertext for any plaintext desired. Hence, in the definitions of security under CPA, $\mathscr{A}$ is provided access to the public key.

Definition 2.1.12 (The Indistinguishability Game) *Let $\mathscr{PE} = (\mathscr{K}, \mathscr{E}, \mathscr{D})$ be the asymmetric encryption scheme described in Definition 2.1.11. The IND game for an attacker, $\mathscr{A} = (\mathscr{A}_1, \mathscr{A}_2)$, consists of four major steps, as described below.*

1. *A challenger generates a random key-pair (pk, sk) by running the key generation algorithm, $\mathscr{K}$.*
2. *The attacker, $\mathscr{A}$, runs $\mathscr{A}_1$ on the input k, which returns two messages m_0, m_1, as well as some state information s.*
3. *The challenger chooses a bit, $b \in \{0, 1\}$. It computes the challenge ciphertext $y^* = \mathscr{E}(m_b, pk)$.*
4. *$\mathscr{A}$ runs $\mathscr{A}_2$ on the input (y^*, pk, s). It returns a guess b' for b.*

$\mathscr{A}$ wins the game of $b' = b$, and its advantage in playing the IND game is defined to be

$$\mathsf{Adv}_{\mathscr{PE}, \mathscr{A}}(k) = |\Pr[b' = b] - \frac{1}{2}|$$

Definition 2.1.13 describes security for the asymmetric (i.e., public-key) encryption.

Definition 2.1.13 (Security under IND-CPA [11]) *$\mathscr{PE} = (\mathscr{K}, \mathscr{E}, \mathscr{D})$, an asymmetric encryption scheme, is secure in the sense of indistinguishability (equivalently [47], semantically secure) if for any probabilistic, polynomial time adversary $\mathscr{A} = (\mathscr{A}_1, \mathscr{A}_2)$, the following is negligible (in k):*

$$\mathsf{Adv}_{\mathscr{PE}, \mathscr{A}}(k) = 2 \times |\Pr[(pk, sk) \leftarrow \mathscr{K}(k); (m_0, m_1, s) \leftarrow \mathscr{A}_1(k, pk);$$
$$b \in_R \{0, 1\}; y \leftarrow \mathscr{E}_{pk}(m_b); b' \leftarrow \mathscr{A}_2(k, pk, y, s) : b = b']| - 1$$

2.1.4.2 Encryption Schemes: Symmetric Setting

The definition for a symmetric encryption scheme is given in Definition 2.1.14.

Definition 2.1.14 (A Symmetric Encryption Scheme [11]) *A symmetric encryption scheme is given by a triple of algorithms, $\mathscr{SE} = (\mathscr{K}, \mathscr{E}, \mathscr{D})$, where*

- *$\mathscr{K}$, the key generation algorithm, is a probabilistic algorithm that takes a security parameter k and returns a symmetric encryption key sk.*
- *$\mathscr{E}$, the encryption algorithm, is a deterministic algorithm that takes sk and a message $x \in \{0, 1\}^*$ to produce a ciphertext y.*
- *$\mathscr{D}$, the decryption algorithm, is a deterministic algorithm which takes sk and ciphertext y to produce either a message $x \in \{0, 1\}^*$ or a special symbol $\bot$ to indicate that the ciphertext was invalid.*

We require that for all sk which can be output by $\mathscr{K}(k)$, for all $x \in \{0, 1\}^*$, and for all y that can be output by $\mathscr{E}_{sk}(x)$, we have that $\mathscr{D}_{sk}(y) = x$. We also require that $\mathscr{K}$, $\mathscr{E}$, and $\mathscr{D}$ can be computed in polynomial time.

Security for symmetric encryption schemes is similar to that described for the asymmetric encryption scheme described in Definitions 2.1.12 and 2.1.13.

2.1.4.3 Digital Signature Schemes

Definition 2.1.15 describes the digital signature scheme.

Definition 2.1.15 (A Digital Signature Scheme) *A digital signature scheme is given by a triple of algorithms,* $\Sigma = (\mathcal{K}, \mathcal{G}, \mathcal{V})$, *where*

- $\mathcal{K}$, *the key generation algorithm, is a probabilistic algorithm that takes a security parameter k and returns a pair* (vk, sk) *of matching verification and signing keys.*
- $\mathcal{G}$, *the signature algorithm, is a probabilistic algorithm that takes a signing key, sk, and a message,* $x \in \{0,1\}^*$, *to produce a signature, S.*
- $\mathcal{V}$, *the verification algorithm, is a deterministic algorithm which takes a verification key, vk, and signature, S, to output a flag to indicate whether the signature is valid or invalid.*

We require that for all (pk, sk) *which can be output by* $\mathcal{K}(k)$, *for all* $x \in \{0,1\}^*$, *and for all S that can be output by* $\mathcal{G}_{sk}(x)$, *we have that* $\mathcal{V}_{pk}(S) = Valid$. *We also require that* $\mathcal{K}$, $\mathcal{E}$, *and* $\mathcal{V}$ *can be computed in polynomial time.*

The standard definition for the security of digital signature schemes was first given by Goldwasser, Micali, and Rivest [48] where they consider the *existential unforgeability*[4] under *adaptive chosen-message attack*[5] (ACMA).

Definition 2.1.16 (Security under ACMA [48]) $\Sigma = (\mathcal{K}, \mathcal{G}, \mathcal{V})$, *a signature scheme, is secure in the sense of adaptive chosen message attack (ACMA) if for any probabilistic, polynomial time forging algorithms* $\mathcal{F}$, *the following is negligible (in k):*

$$\Pr[(vk, sk) \leftarrow \mathcal{K}(k); = (x, s) \leftarrow \mathcal{F}^{\mathcal{G}_{sk}(\cdot)}(k, vk) : \mathcal{V}_{vk}(x, s) = Valid]$$

2.1.4.4 Message Authentication Codes

A message authentication code (MAC) allows two parties, who have shared a secret key in advance, to authenticate their subsequent communication. More formally, a MAC is a key-based algorithm which associates a tag with every valid message. The tag for a particular message may be efficiently verified by the party sharing the key. Furthermore, an adversary who sees many message/tag pairs is unable to forge a tag on a new message. We begin with a definition of a MAC algorithm as described in Definition 2.1.17.

Definition 2.1.17 (A MAC Scheme) *A MAC scheme is given by a triple of algorithms,* $\Pi = (\mathcal{K}, MAC, \mathcal{V})$, *where*

---

[4] Existential unforgeability is defined to be the property that the adversary, $\mathcal{A}$, is unable to forge the signature of one message that may not necessarily be the choice of $\mathcal{A}$.

[5] In an adaptive chosen-message attack, the adversary, $\mathcal{A}$, is allowed to ask the signer to sign a number of messages of $\mathcal{A}$'s choice. The choice of these messages may depend on previously obtained signatures.

- $\mathcal{K}$, the key generation algorithm, is a probabilistic algorithm that takes a security parameter k and returns sk.
- $\mathcal{G}$, the tagging algorithm, is a probabilistic algorithm that takes sk and a message $x \in \{0,1\}^*$ to produce a tag, T.
- $\mathcal{V}$, the verification algorithm, is a deterministic algorithm which takes a key sk, a message $x \in \{0,1\}^*$, and a tag T to indicate whether the tag is valid or invalid.

We require that for all k, all sk which can be output by $\mathcal{K}(k)$, all $x \in \{0,1\}^*$, and for all T that can be output by $\mathcal{G}_{sk}(x)$, we have that $\mathcal{V}_{sk}(x,T) = Valid$. We also require that $\mathcal{K}$, $\mathcal{G}$, and $\mathcal{V}$ can be computed in polynomial time.

We note that there are three types of attacks against MAC schemes [54], namely known text attack, chosen-message attack, and adaptive chosen-message attack. In this book, we only consider adaptive chosen-message attack, the strongest of the three attacks. The formal definitions of a MAC scheme and its security under adaptive chosen-message attack exactly parallel those given above for the digital signature scheme.

Definition 2.1.18 (Security under ACMA [48]) $\Pi = (\mathcal{K}, MAC, \mathcal{V})$, a MAC scheme, is secure in the sense of adaptive chosen message attack (ACMA) if for any probabilistic, polynomial time forging algorithms $\mathcal{F}$, the following is negligible (in k):

$$\Pr[(sk) \leftarrow \mathcal{K}(k); (x,s) \leftarrow \mathcal{F}^{\mathcal{G}_{sk}(\cdot)}(k) : \mathcal{V}_{sk}(x,T) = Valid]$$

2.1.4.5 Cryptographic Hash Functions

A hash function, $\mathcal{H}$, is an efficiently computable algorithm that maps an input x of arbitrary finite bit-length to an output $\mathcal{H}(x)$ of fixed bit-length n [54, Chapter 9]. In other words, hash functions are mappings which allow us to compress arbitrary long messages to fixed length values, and are often employed by cryptographic schemes.

We recall the definition of a Collision Resistant Hash Function (CRHF), $\mathcal{H}$, with inputs x, x' and outputs y, y' in the same manner which is given by Damgård [40, 41] and Preneel [85, Definition 2.2], as described in Definition 2.1.19.

Definition 2.1.19 (Collision Resistant Hash Function (CRHF)) A CRHF is a function $\mathcal{H}$ that satisfy the following underlying requirements:

- The description of $\mathcal{H}$ must be publicly known and should not require any secret information about its operation.
- **Preimage resistance:** for essentially all pre-specified outputs, it is computationally infeasible to find any input which hashes to that output (i.e., to find any preimage x' such that $\mathcal{H}(x') = y$ when given any y for which a corresponding input is unknown).
- **2nd-preimage resistance:** it is computationally infeasible to find any second input which has the same output as any specified input (i.e., given x, to find a 2nd-preimage $x' \neq x$ such that $\mathcal{H}(x) = \mathcal{H}(x')$.

- **Collision resistance:** *it is computationally infeasible to find any two distinct inputs x, x' which hash to the same output (i.e., such that $\mathcal{H}(x) = \mathcal{H}(x')$).*

Recent work of Rogaway and Shrimpton [87] formalizes the above requirements into seven different definitions. The implications and separations among these seven definitions within the concrete security and provable security framework are also presented.

2.1.4.6 Random Oracles

The definition of random oracle, first informally introduced by Fiat and Shamir [44] and later formalized by Bellare and Rogaway [15], represents an idealized view of hash functions. In other words, hash function is formalized by an oracle which produces a truly random value for each query. However, if the same query is asked more than once, identical answers are presented.

Some critics argue that in the real world, no single deterministic polynomial-time function can provide a good implementation of the random oracle. Consequently, it is argued that random oracles cannot be realized in practice [31, 65]. However, recent work of Coron, Dodis, Malinaud, and Puniya [39] shows how a provable secure arbitrary-size random oracle can be constructed from a compression function viewed as a fixed-length random oracle. Several constructions that can be implementable in practice are also presented.

The random oracle model is analogous to the ideal group model (also known as the generic group) introduced into cryptography by Shoup [95] and suffers from the same severe limitations as shown by Canetti, Goldreich, and Halevi [31]. Some might argue that a proof in the random oracle model is more of a heuristic proof than a real one. Despite the criticism, no one has yet provided a convincing contradiction to the practicality of the random oracle model. This model is still widely accepted by the cryptographic community[6]. In many applications, a very efficient protocol with a heuristic security proof is preferred over a much less efficient one with a complete security proof [32]. Moreover, as Black [17] observed, no scheme has yet to been proven secure in the random-oracle model and broken once instantiated with some hash function, unless that was the goal from the very beginning.

---

[6] In a recent work, Gentry, MacKenzie, and Ramzan [46] proposed the first practical and provable-secure oblivious transfer password-based protocol whose proof of security relies on the random oracle model.

2.2 Key Establishment Protocols and their Basis

Key establishment, a fundamental building block in cryptography, is defined to be any process whereby a shared secret key becomes available to two or more parties, for subsequent cryptographic use [54, Definition 12.2]. Such a scheme can be broadly classified into key agreement or key transport depending on the nature of the session key (whether input to the session key is required from only one party or all the participating parties) [27, 54].

The basis of many key establishment protocols relies on the Diffie–Hellman key exchange and RSA algorithm [86]. Some examples of such protocols are as follows.

Diffie–Hellman-based Protocols.

- The MQV protocol [73, 80].
- The HMQV protocol of Krawczyk [71] proven secure in the CK2001 model.
- The Unified Model protocol of Blake-Wilson, Johnson, and Menezes [18, Protocol 3] proven secure in the Bellare–Rogaway model.
- The OMDHKE protocol of Bresson, Chevassut, and Pointcheval [28] proven secure in the Bellare–Rogaway model.
- The "Twist-AUgmented" protocol of Chevassut, Fouque, Gaudry, and Pointcheval [35] proven secure in the Bellare–Rogaway model.
- The key exchange protocols of Katz, Ostrovsky, and Yung [63, 64] proven secure in the Bellare–Rogaway model.
- The password-based protocols, PPK, PAK, and PAK-Z, of MacKenzie [75] proven secure in the Bellare–Rogaway model.
- The password-based protocols, EKE and OPKeyX, of Abdalla, Chevassut, and Pointcheval [1] proven secure in the Bellare–Rogaway model.
- The password-based protocols, SPAKE-1 and SPAKE-2, of Abdalla and Pointcheval [2] proven secure in the Bellare–Rogaway model.

RSA-based Protocols Proven Secure in the Bellare–Rogaway Model.

- The password-authenticated key exchange protocols, SNAPI and SNAPI-X, of MacKenzie, Patel, and Swaminathan [76].
- The PEKEP and CEKEP protocols of Zhang [103].
- The QR-EKE protocol of Zhang [104].

However, in recent years, elliptic curve cryptography (ECC) [69, 82] has emerged as a promising branch of public-key cryptography due to its potential for offering similar security to established public-key cryptosystems at reduced key sizes. We observe an emerging trend in the use of identity-based cryptography, such as a large number of identity-based key agreement protocols based on pairings. Some examples of such protocols are as follows.

- The key agreement protocols of Sakai, Ohgishi, and Kasahara [89]; Smart [96]; Yi [101]; and Yi, Tan, Siew, and Syed [102].

- The multiple key agreement protocols of Kim, Huh, Hwang, and Lee [67]; and Kim, Ryu, and Yoo [68].
- The key agreement protocols of Boyd, Mao, and Paterson [26] proven secure in the CK2001 model.
- The key agreement protocol of Choi, Hwang, Lee, and Seo [36] proven secure in the Bellare–Rogaway model.
- The key agreement protocols of Chen and Kudla [33] proven secure in a restricted variant of the Bellare–Rogaway model.
- The key agreement protocols of Wang [99] proven secure in the Bellare–Rogaway model.
- The key agreement protocol of McCullagh and Barreto [81] proven secure in a restricted variant of the Bellare–Rogaway model.
- The key agreement protocol of Cheng, Chen, and Comley, and Tang [34] proven secure in the Bellare–Rogaway model.
- The key agreement protocol of Chow and Choo [37] proven secure in the Canetti–Krawczyk model.

Our recent survey of ID-based protocols [24], which examines their security and efficiency, revealed the following observations.

Observation 1.   The purported security of many existing identity-based protocols is either based on heuristic security arguments or the protocols are proven secure in a restricted model. This highlighted the need for more rigourously tested identity-based protocols.

Observation 2.   Some interesting similarities between several identity-based protocols and the Diffie–Hellman-based protocols. We then conjectured that these similarities may well extend to the security properties of these protocols.

It will be interesting if a generic proof approach for the mapping from Diffie–Hellman-based to identity-based protocols can be provided such that the security properties of the Diffie–Hellman-based protocols are preserved by the mapping. Consequently, we would be able to get two provable secure protocols for the price of one proof. However, this is beyond the scope of this book.

In this book, we will mainly be investigating Diffie–Hellman-based and identity-based key establishment protocols.

2.2.1 Protocol Architectures

We largely follow the general architectural criteria for classification of protocols proposed by Boyd and Mathuria [27, Chapter 1.3], as discussed in the following sections.

2.2.1.1 Existing Cryptographic Keys

Authentication is generally based on long-term keys which can be associated with identities. However, "long-term" covers all forms of information which can be linked to identities. This includes cryptographic keys such as RSA-based keys [86], passwords, and biometric information. We consider the following scenarios discussed by Boyd and Mathuria [27, Chapter 1.3].

1. The entities already share a secret (asymmetric or symmetric) key that can be used for cryptographic operations, such as encryption or message authentication code (MAC).

   - For example, the 3PKD protocol of Bellare and Rogaway [16] described in Protocol 3.1 assumes that the registered entities have a shared secret symmetric encryption key and MAC key with the trusted server. Both keys are independent of each other and are used to encrypt messages and compute MAC digests respectively.

2. An off-line server is used where the principals possess certified public keys. To verify the authenticity of a public key, it may be necessary to verify a chain of certificates. We may regard the use of public key certificates as equivalent to the use of an off-line server.

   - For example, the mutual authentication and key establishment protocol of Wong and Chan [100] described in Protocol 5.1 assumes that the registered entities have been issued a certificate that binds its public key to the entity's identity.

3. An on-line server is used (i.e., each principal shares a key with a trusted server). To pass information between parties, it may be necessary to pass it via a chain of on-line servers.

2.2.1.2 Method of Session Key Generation

As Menezes, van Oorschot, and Vanstone [54, Sections 1.11 and 1.63] and Boyd and Mathuria [27, Chapter 1.3] have pointed out, there are various ways that may be employed to generate session keys in a key establishment protocol.

Definition 2.2.1 (Key Transport Protocol) *In a key transport protocol, one user creates or obtains a secret value and securely transfers it to the other users.*

In a key transport protocol, the responder either trusts the originator for the session key establishment, or a third party for the session key generation and distribution. In both cases, the session key needs to be encrypted using either symmetric or asymmetric encryption schemes to prevent exposure. Protocol 2.1 presents a simple key transport protocol specified in the international standard ISO/IEC 11770 Part 3 [55] as ISO/IEC key transport mechanism 1.

$$A \hspace{10em} B$$

$N_A \in_R \{0,1\}^*$

$SK_{AB} \in_R \{0,1\}^k$

Encrypts message(A, SK_{AB}, N_A) with PK_B

$$\xrightarrow{\quad A, \{A, SK_{AB}, N_A\}_{PK_B}, N_A \quad}$$

$$\text{Decrypts } \{A, SK_{AB}, N_A\}_{PK_B}$$
$$\text{to obtain } SK_{AB}$$

Protocol 2.1: ISO/IEC key transport mechanism 1

Definition 2.2.2 (Key Agreement Protocol) *In a key agreement protocol, the session key is a function of inputs by all protocol users.*

A fundamental technique that can be used for key agreement was proposed by Diffie and Hellman [42]. It is based on the presumed intractability of the Diffie–Hellman problem as defined in Definition 2.1.5. Many key agreement protocols are built on the assumption of the difficulty of solving the Diffie-Hellman problem. One example is the authenticated key exchange protocol of Jeong, Katz, and Lee [57] described in Protocol 4.4.

Definition 2.2.3 (Hybrid Protocol) *In a hybrid protocol, the session key is a function of inputs by more than one principal, but not by all users (i.e., the protocol is a key agreement protocol from the viewpoint of some users, and a key transport protocol from the viewpoint of others).*

Protocol 2.2 describes a hybrid protocol of Gong [49]. In Protocol 2.2, N_A, N_B denote random nonces chosen by A and B respectively; N_S, and H_A, and H_B denote random nonces chosen by S; f denotes the one-way key derivation function used; and g denotes the one-way function used for authentication.

1. $A \longrightarrow B : A, B, N_A$
2. $B \longrightarrow S : A, B, N_A, N_B$
3. $S \longrightarrow B : N_S, f(N_S, N_B, A, K_{BS})$
   $\qquad \oplus (K_{AB}, H_A, H_B), g(SK_{AB}, H_A, H_B, K_{BS})$
4. $B \longrightarrow A : N_S, H_B$
5. $A \longrightarrow B : H_A$

Protocol 2.2: Gong's hybrid protocol

Only A and S have an input to the key derivation function, $f(N_S, N_B, A, K_{BS})$, and hence the protocol is a key agreement protocol from their viewpoints. To B, this protocol is a key transport protocol.

2.2.1.3 Number of Entities

Depending on situations, session keys for point-to-point communications might be established between two or more users, although two-party key establishment protocols are more general. Examples are as follows.

- a two-party key establishment protocol is the Diffie–Hellman-based protocol of Jeong, Katz, and Lee [57] described in Protocol 4.4,
- a three-party (tripartite) key establishment protocol is the one-round protocol of Joux [58], and
- a group-based protocol is the conference key agreement protocol due to Boyd and González Nieto [25] described in Protocol 8.1.

2.2.2 Protocol Goals and Attacks

The goals of a protocol can be defined as the properties that the protocol is trying to achieve. As Boyd and Mathuria [27, Chapter 2.1] suggested, "any attack on a protocol is only valid if it violates some property that the protocol was intended to achieve". Hence, we advocate that it is important for protocol designers to identify at an early stage the desirable properties / goals that a protocol offers. Without doing so, attacks can be discovered long after a protocol is proposed / published, only to have the original protocol designer claim that the attacks are invalid, as the protocol is not intended to provide such assurances against the properties being exploited.

2.2.2.1 Protocol Goals

Boyd and Mathuria [27, Chapter 2.1] and Roscoe [88] broadly define goals as *intensional* and *extensional* goals, as described below.

Intensional Specification.   The *intensional specification* of a protocol is highly dependent on the details of the protocol, as it must contain a detailed specification of what a correct protocol run is. The intensional specification can be used independently of the intended effect of the protocol and may be important for analysis of protocols.

Extensional Specification.   The *extensional specification* of a protocol is independent of the details of the protocol and would apply to any protocol that is designed to achieve the same effects. It reflects the external observable effect of the protocol rather than how the protocol is put together. It is used as a measure of success of an attack on a protocol and hence should always be achieved by all possible means.

The general concept is whether the protocol specifications take into consideration how the protocol operates, and not what each protocol principal gains from the protocol.

The fundamental goals of key establishment protocols [54, Definitions 12.6 – 12.8] are as follows:

Implicit Key Authentication.   The property whereby one party is assured that no other party aside from a specifically identified second party (and possibly additional identified trusted parties) may gain access to a particular secret key.

Key Confirmation.   The property whereby one party is assured that a second (possibly unidentified) party actually has possession of a particular secret key.

Explicit Key Authentication.   The property obtained when both implicit key authentication and key confirmation hold.

Authenticated key establishment protocols aim to generate a session key between only specified participants who have actually participated in a recent run of the protocol. The formal definition for an authenticated key establishment protocol is given in Definition 2.2.4 .

Definition 2.2.4 (Authenticated Key Establishment Protocol [54]) *An authenticated key establishment protocol is a key establishment protocol which provides implicit key authentication.*

Syverson and van Oorschot [97] identified some generic goals for authenticated key establishment protocols, which are summarised in Table 2.2.

Goals	Description
Far-end Operative	A believes B recently said something.
Entity Authentication	A believes B recently replied to a specific challenge.
Secure Key Establishment	A has a certain key, K, which A believes is good for communication with B.
Key Freshness	A believes a certain key, K, has not been used before.
Key Confirmation	In addition to secure key establishment, A has received evidence confirming that B knows K.
Mutual Understanding of Shared Key	A believes that B has recently confirmed that B has a certain key, K, which B believes is good for communication with A.

Table 2.2 Summary of generic formal goals

2.2.2.2 Additional Security Attributes

There are many additional properties that are required for security of any key establishment protocol. These properties have been well studied and have been discussed by many authors. One such example is the paper of Blake-Wilson and Menezes [20], which provides an excellent overview. The most basic property is that a passive adversary eavesdropping on the protocol should be unable to obtain the session key.

In a modern context we usually require that, far from obtaining the whole key, the adversary cannot even reliably distinguish between the session key and a randomly chosen string of the expected length. We also generally expect the adversary to be an active one, not only able to see all messages sent, but also able to alter, delete and fabricate messages – in short the adversary is in control of the communications on the network.

A number of typical attacks lead to additional security properties as follows.

Known (Session) Key Security. It is often reasonable to assume that the adversary will be able to obtain session keys from any session different from the one under attack. A protocol has known-key security if it is secure under this assumption. This is generally regarded as a standard requirement for key establishment protocols.

Unknown Key Share Security. Sometimes the adversary may be unable to obtain any useful information about a session key, but can deceive the protocol principals about the identity of the peer entity. Such an attack is first described by Diffie, van Oorschot, and Wiener in 1992 [43], and can result in principals giving away information to the wrong party or accepting data as coming from the wrong party.

As discussed by Boyd and Mathuria [27, Chapter 5.1.2], the adversary need not obtain the session key to profit from this attack. Consider the scenario whereby A will deliver some information of value (such as e-cash) to B. Since B believes the session key is shared with the adversary, the adversary can claim this credit deposit as his. Also, the adversary can exploit such an attack in a number of ways if the established session key is subsequently used to provide confidentality or integrity [61]. Consequently security against unknown key share attacks is regarded as a standard requirement.

Forward Secrecy. When the long-term key of an entity is compromised the adversary will be able to masquerade as that entity in any future protocol runs. However, the situation will be even worse if the adversary can also use the compromised long-term key to obtain session keys that were accepted before the compromise. Protocols that prevent this are said to provide forward secrecy. Since there is usually a computational cost in providing forward secrecy it is sometimes sacrificed in the interest of efficiency.

Forward secrecy for identity-based (ID-based) protocols is similar to conventional public key cryptography. However, there is an additional concern. A random value $s \in \mathbb{Z}_q$ plays the role of the *master secret* of the *Key Generation Centre* (KGC) in the ID-based system. The KGC distributes to each party P_i with identity ID_i a long-term key pair consisting of public key $Q_i = \mathscr{H}(ID_i)$ and private key $S_i = sQ_i$. Here $\mathscr{H}$ is a hash function mapping identities $ID_i \in \{0,1\}^*$ onto $\mathbb{G}_1$. The KGC also publishes the system parameters which include descriptions of the two groups $\mathbb{G}_1$ and $\mathbb{G}_2$, a point P that generates $\mathbb{G}_1$, and a master public key sP. In such a system, the master key of the KGC is another secret that could become compromised. When this happens it is clear that the long-term keys of all users will be compromised. It is possible that a protocol can provide forward secrecy in the usual sense but still give away old session keys if the master key becomes known. We say that a protocol that retains confidentiality of old session keys even when the master key is known provides *KGC forward secrecy.*

Security attributes!Key Compromise Impersonation Resistance. Another problem that may occur when the long-term key of an entity A is compromised is that the adversary may be able to masquerade not only *as A* but also *to A* as another party B. Such a protocol is said to allow key compromise impersonation. Resistance to such attacks is often seen as desirable.

(Joint) Key Control. In a key agreement protocol, it is usually desired that no principal is able to choose or influence the value of the shared (session) key. This prevents any principal from forcing the use of an old key or a non-uniform distribution for the session key.

Key Integrity. The key integrity property was first described by Janson and Tsudik [56]. Key integrity is the property that the key has not been modified by the adversary, or equivalently only has inputs from legitimate principals.

- For a key transport protocol, key integrity means that if the key is accepted by any principal it must be the same key as chosen by the key originator.
- For a key agreement protocol, key integrity means that if a key is accepted by any principal it must be a known function of only the inputs of the protocol principals.

Protocols with different sets of desirable properties have been proposed to satisfy the varying needs in particular scenarios. In this book, we demonstrate that a number of protocols do not provide known session key security and unknown key share security, as claimed.

2.2.2.3 Types of Attacks

An attack on a protocol occurs only when any goal of the protocol is violated. Attacks can exist in many forms, and can be broadly categorised as *passive* and *active*. In a passive attack, the communications of the legitimate principals are not being disturbed. In an active attack, interaction is required, for example modification, deletion, addition of the data stream. In theory, active attacks can be detected while passive attacks cannot be so readily detected and need to be prevented.

Compiling an exhaustive list of attacks is by no means easy and perhaps impossible. We shall introduce some common known types of attack on security protocols. Note that in the list of attacks [54, 78] mentioned below, eavesdropping is the only passive attack, while the rest are active attacks.

Eavesdropping. The adversary compromises the confidentiality of the protocol, when it captures the information (message) sent in the protocol. However, the adversary does not alter or disturb the information captured in any way, and acts as a faithful relaying station. This form of attack, known as *eavesdropping*, is almost impossible to detect. To address eavesdropping attacks, cryptography is usually adopted to encrypt (protect) the confidential information such as the session key or identity of a principal.

Modification Attack.   The adversary compromises the integrity of the protocol when it captures the information (message) sent in the protocol and modifies this captured information and then transmits the information. One thing to note is that the entire message as well as the individual message fields are vulnerable to *modification attack*. Modification can be in the form of splitting the captured message and reassembling the fields from different captured messages. To address this modification of information attack, cryptography is usually adopted to encrypt and maintain integrity for all parts of the message that must be kept together, besides the individual fields.

Information Replay Attack.   An *information replay attack* is often used in combination with other attack elements. An information replay attack can be thought of as an insertion of a message, or part of a message, that has been previously sent in a protocol run by the adversary. The replayed information can be either from part of a previous protocol run or a protocol run that is taking place in parallel with the attacking protocol run. To address an information replay attack, a fresh element is required in the design and implementation of the protocol. The fresh property offers the assurance that the unique freshness value has not been used before.

Reflection Attack.   A *reflection attack* is a variant of a replay attack. The adversary sends the protocol messages back to the originating principal in a setting where two principals are engaged in a shared key protocol. This attack is practical as some party might want to establish a secure channel with itself. For example, a mobile user that communicates with its desktop computer, while both the mobile device and the desktop have the same identity in the form of the same digital certificate, as described by Krawczyk [71].

Typing Attack.   A *typing attack* occurs when an adversary successfully replaces a message field of one type with a message field of another type in any protocol run, regardless of whether the message field being replaced or used for replacement is encrypted or not. Two examples are the type flaw attacks discovered by Basin, Mödersheim, and Viganò [6, 7] and Long [74] on the Yahalom protocol [29] and the amended Needham–Schroeder [83] protocol with conventional keys respectively. Proposed measures to address such attacks include ensuring that encryption keys are used once and only once, and changing the order of the message elements each time they are used.

Cryptanalysis Attack.   *cryptanalysis attack* occurs when an adversary learns some useful knowledge from the protocol that he/she can use in performing future cryptanalysis. For example, when sufficient evidence such as some values relating to the key-bits is in the hands of the adversary, the adversary can find or make an intelligent guess regarding some of the key-bits. Counter measures include the design and implementation of protocols that will hide the evidence needed to guess the keys. Examples include the leakage-resilient protocols of Shin, Kobara, and Imai [91, 92, 93, 94].

Protocol Interaction Attack.   A *protocol interaction attack* occurs when an adversary manages to choose a new protocol of his/her choice to interact with a known protocol. One proposed measure to address a protocol interaction attack is to include the protocol details in an authenticated part of the protocol messages [66].

Parallel Session Attack.   A *parallel session attack* occurs when an adversary executes two or more runs of the protocol concurrently. As we advocate in Chapter 3, it is normal to assume that a host can establish several concurrent sessions with many different parties in a real world setting. A "secure" protocol should ensure that individual sessions can be uniquely identified.

Oracle Attack.   In an *oracle attack*, an adversary tricks an honest principal into inadvertently revealing some information. In such an attack, the honest principal is used as a tool by the adversary to obtain information which otherwise she cannot possibly have obtained. One possible measure to address this attack is to explicitly state the roles of each individual of a protocol so that it is clear to which run of which protocol it belongs [3, 4].

2.2.2.4 A Need for Rigorous Treatment

There exist many protocols whose purported security is based on heuristic security arguments. The main problem with protocols with only heuristic security arguments is that they lack formal foundations and suffer from the following problems:

- Since this approach does not account for all possible attacks, the security guarantees are limited and often insufficient. In this book, previously unknown flaws are revealed on several protocols with only heuristic security arguments (see Sections 9.4 and 10.4.1).
- This approach does not provide a clear framework with a formal description of a "secure" protocol and what constitutes an "attack".

On the other hand, in the provable security approach for protocols, the security proofs make explicit the assumptions behind the protocols' security and the security goals provided by the protocols are formally defined. Therefore, we will know whether a proposed attack is valid and what it means to be secure. For example, Katz and Shin [62] present a number of claimed "insider attacks" on several provably secure protocols [90, 105] although those protocols were never claimed to be secure against such attacks.

2.3 The Computational Complexity Approach

We now present overview of the Bellare–Rogaway [13, 14, 16] and Canetti–Krawczyk [10, 30] computational complexity models. We mainly work in these models and several protocols proposed in this book are proven secure in one of these models.

For the remainder of this book,

- the Bellare and Rogaway 1993 model [14] is denoted as the BR93 model,
- the Bellare and Rogaway 1995 model [16] is denoted as the BR95 model,
- the Bellare, Pointcheval, and Rogaway 2000 model [13] is denoted as the BPR2000 model, and
- the Canetti and Krawczyk 2001 model [10, 30] is denoted as the CK2001 or the Canetti–Krawczyk model.

Collectively, the BR93 model, the BR95 model, and the BPR2000 model will also be referred to as the Bellare–Rogaway models.

2.3.1 Adversarial Powers

In the Bellare–Rogaway and Canetti–Krawczyk models, the adversary, $\mathscr{A}$, is defined to be a probabilistic, polynomial time (PPT) machine that is in control of all communications between a fixed set of protocol participants. Each protocol participant, P_i, can run multiple sessions with different partners concurrently. The action of U_u running a session, i, is modelled as an oracle.

The adversary, $\mathscr{A}$ controls the communications between the protocol participants by interacting with the set of oracles, Π_{U_u,U_v}^i, where Π_{U_u,U_v}^i is defined to be the ith instantiation of a protocol participant, U_u, in a specific protocol run and U_v is the principal with whom U_u wishes to establish a secret key. $\mathscr{A}$ controls the communication channels via the queries to the targeted oracles. A description of the oracle types is presented as follows.

Send(U_u,U_v,i,m) query. A Send(U_u,U_v,i,m) query to an oracle, Π_{U_u,U_v}^i, computes a response according to the protocol specification and decision on whether to accept or reject yet, and returns them to the adversary $\mathscr{A}$. If Π_{U_u,U_v}^i has either accepted with some session key or terminated, this will be made known to $\mathscr{A}$.

Session-Key Reveal(U_u,U_v,i) query. Any oracle, Π_{U_u,U_v}^i, upon receiving such a query and if Π_{U_u,U_v}^i has accepted and holds some session key, will send this session key back to $\mathscr{A}$.

This query is known as a Reveal(U_u,U_v,i) query in the Bellare–Rogaway model. As Blake-Wilson, Johnson and Menezes [18] have indicated, the Reveal query in the Bellare–Rogaway and Canetti–Krawczyk models is designed to capture the notion of known key security.

Session-State Reveal(U_u,U_v,i) query. The oracle, Π_{U_u,U_v}^i, upon receiving such a query and if Π_{U_u,U_v}^i has neither accepted nor held some session key, will return all its internal state to $\mathscr{A}$. This includes any ephemeral parameters but not long-term secret parameters.

Corrupt(U_u, K_E) query.   The Corrupt(U_u, K_E) query captures unknown key share attacks and insider attacks[7]. This query allows $\mathscr{A}$ to corrupt the principal U_u at will, and thereby learn the complete internal state of the corrupted principal. Notice that a Corrupt query does not result in the release of the session keys since $\mathscr{A}$ already has the ability to obtain session keys through Reveal queries.

In the BR95 model, the Corrupt query also gives $\mathscr{A}$ the ability to overwrite the long-lived key of the corrupted principal with any value of her choice. In the stronger Corrupt model of BPR2000, this query allows $\mathscr{A}$ the ability to install bogus passwords of her choice on the various servers.

Protocols proven secure in the Bellare–Rogaway or Canetti–Krawczyk models that allow the Corrupt query are also proven secure against the unknown-key share attack. That is, if a key is to be shared between some parties, U_1 and U_2, the corruption of some other (non-related) player in the protocol, say U_3, should not expose the session key shared between U_1 and U_2 as described in Chapter 8.

Test(U_u, U_v, i) query.   The Test(U_u, U_v, i) query is the only oracle query that does not correspond to any of $\mathscr{A}$'s abilities or any real-world event. This query allows us to define a notion of security. If $\Pi^i_{U_u, U_v}$ has accepted with some session key and is being asked a Test(U_u, U_v, i) query, then depending on a randomly chosen bit, b, $\mathscr{A}$ is given either the actual session key or a session key drawn randomly from the session key distribution. Informally, $\mathscr{A}$ succeeds if $\mathscr{A}$ can guess the bit b.

Table 2.3 provides a comparison of the types of queries allowed for the adversary in the various models.

Oracle Queries	BR93	BR95	BPR2000	CK2001
Send	Yes	Yes	Yes	Yes
Session-Key Reveal	Yes	Yes	Yes	Yes
Session-State Reveal	No	No	No	Yes
Corrupt	Yes	Yes	No	Yes
Test	Yes	Yes	Yes	Yes

Table 2.3 Summary of adversarial powers

Note that in the original BR93 model, the Corrupt query is not defined. However, we consider the BR93 model which allows the adversary access to a Corrupt query because later proofs of security in the BR93 model [5, 18, 19, 33, 77, 81, 100] allow the Corrupt query. The omission of such a (Corrupt) query may also allow a

---

[7] A formal and comprehensive model with an associated definition of security for group authenticated key establishment that encompasses insider attacks is recently presented by Katz and Shin [62].

protocol vulnerable to insider and unknown key share attacks to be proven secure in the model as described in Chapter 8.

2.3.2 Definition of Freshness

The notion of freshness of the oracle to whom the Test query is sent remains the same for the Bellare–Rogaway and Canetti–Krawczyk models. Freshness is used to identify the session keys about which $\mathscr{A}$ ought not to know anything because $\mathscr{A}$ has not revealed any oracles that have accepted the key and has not corrupted any principals knowing the key. Definition 2.3.1 describes freshness, which depends on the respective partnership definitions.

Definition 2.3.1 (Freshness) *Oracle $\Pi_{A,B}^{i}$ is fresh (or holds a fresh session key) at the end of execution if, and only if,*

1. *$\Pi_{A,B}^{i}$ has accepted with or without a partner oracle $\Pi_{B,A}^{j}$,*
2. *both $\Pi_{A,B}^{i}$ and $\Pi_{B,A}^{j}$ oracles have not been sent a* Reveal *query (or* Session-State Reveal *in the CK2001 model), and*
3. *A and B have not been sent a* Corrupt *query.*

The basic notion of freshness, which does not incorporate the notion of forward secrecy in the BPR2000 model, requires that no one in the model has been sent a Corrupt query. This effectively restricts $\mathscr{A}$ from asking any Corrupt query in the BPR2000 model.

2.3.3 Definition of Security

Security in the Bellare–Rogaway and Canetti–Krawczyk models is defined using the game $\mathscr{G}$, played between a malicious adversary $\mathscr{A}$ and a collection of Π_{U_u,U_v}^{i} oracles for players U_u, U_v and instances i. The adversary $\mathscr{A}$ runs the game $\mathscr{G}$, whose setting is explained as follows.

Stage 1: $\mathscr{A}$ is able to send any oracle queries at will.

Stage 2: At some point during $\mathscr{G}$, $\mathscr{A}$ will choose a fresh session on which to be tested and send a Test query to the fresh oracle associated with the test session. Note that the test session chosen must be fresh. Depending on a randomly chosen bit b, $\mathscr{A}$ is given either the actual session key or a session key drawn randomly from the session key distribution.

Stage 3: $\mathscr{A}$ continues making any oracle queries at will but cannot make Corrupt and/or Session-Key Reveal and/or Session-State Reveal queries (depending on the individual proof model) that trivially expose the test session key.

Stage 4: Eventually, $\mathscr{A}$ terminates the game simulation and outputs a bit b', which is its guess of the value of b.

A graphical illustration of the game $\mathscr{G}$ is presented in Figure 2.1.

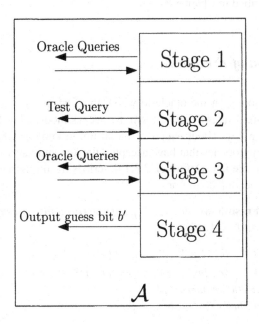

Fig. 2.1 Game simulation $\mathscr{G}$

In the original BR93 and BR95 models, Stage 3 of the game simulation, $\mathscr{G}$, is omitted and $\mathscr{A}$ is required to output the guess bit b' immediately after making a Test query. However, such a requirement is not strong enough, as discussed by Canetti and Krawczyk [30]. This stage has been included to address the problem, as proposed by Bellare, Petrank, Rackoff, and Rogaway in an unpublished paper [12].

The success of $\mathscr{A}$ in $\mathscr{G}$ is quantified in terms of $\mathscr{A}$'s advantage in distinguishing whether $\mathscr{A}$ receives the real key or a random value. $\mathscr{A}$ wins if, after asking a Test(U_u, U_v, i) query, where Π_{U_u, U_v}^i is fresh and has accepted, $\mathscr{A}$'s guess bit b' equals the bit b selected during the Test(U_u, U_v, i) query.

Let the advantage function of $\mathscr{A}$ be denoted by $\mathrm{Adv}^{\mathscr{A}}(k)$, where

$$\mathrm{Adv}^{\mathscr{A}}(k) = |2 \times Pr[b = b']| - 1.$$

2.3.4 The Bellare–Rogaway Models

An important difference between the three variants of the Bellare–Rogaway model is in the way partner oracles are defined (i.e., the definition of partnership). The definition of partnership is used in the definition of security to restrict the adversary's

Reveal and Corrupt queries to oracles that are not partners of the oracle whose key the adversary is trying to guess. In other words, the definition of security depends on the partnership mechanism and the notion of indistinguishability. These will be described in sections that follow.

2.3.4.1 The BR93 Model

The BR93 model defines partnership using the notion of matching conversations, where a conversation is defined to be the sequence of messages sent and received by an oracle. The sequence of messages exchanged only during the Send oracle queries is recorded in the transcript, T. At the end of a protocol run, T will contain the record of the Send queries and the responses as shown in Figure 2.2. Definition 2.3.2 gives a simplified definition of matching conversations for the case of the protocol shown in Figure 2.2.

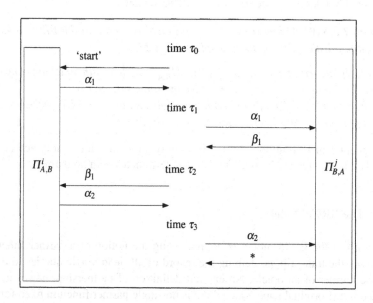

Fig. 2.2 Matching conversation

Definition 2.3.2 (Matching Conversations [14]) *Let n_S be the maximum number of sessions between any two parties in the protocol run. Run the protocol shown in Figure 2.2 in the presence of a malicious adversary $\mathscr{A}$ and consider an initiator oracle $\Pi_{A,B}^i$ and a responder oracle $\Pi_{B,A}^j$ who engage in conversations C_A and C_B respectively. $\Pi_{A,B}^i$ and $\Pi_{B,A}^j$ are said to be partners if they both have matching conversations, where*

$$C_A = (\tau_0, \text{'start'}, \alpha_1), (\tau_2, \beta_1, \alpha_2)$$
$$C_B = (\tau_1, \alpha_1, \beta_1), (\tau_3, \alpha_2, *), \text{ for } \tau_0 < \tau_1 < \ldots$$

This sequence encodes that

- *at time τ_0, oracle $\Pi_{A,B}^i$ was asked 'start' and responded with α_1.*
- *At a later time, $\tau_1 > \tau_0$, oracle $\Pi_{B,A}^j$ was asked α_1 and responded with β_1.*
- *Oracle $\Pi_{A,B}^i$ was asked β_1 and responded with α_2 at time $\tau_2 > \tau_1$.*
- *Finally, at time $\tau_3 > \tau_2$, oracle $\Pi_{B,A}^j$ was asked α_1 and responded with $*$.*

Note that the construction of the conversation shown in Definition 2.3.2 depends on the number of parties and the number of message flows. Informally, both $\Pi_{A,B}^i$ and $\Pi_{B,A}^j$ are said to be BR93 partners if each one responded to a message that was sent unchanged by its partner with the exception of perhaps the first and last messages.

Definition 2.3.3 describes security for the BR93 model.

Definition 2.3.3 (BR93 Security [14]) *A protocol is secure in the BR93 model if, for all probabilistic, polynomial time adversaries $\mathscr{A}$,*

Validity.   If uncorrupted oracles $\Pi_{A,B}^i$ and $\Pi_{B,A}^j$ complete with matching conversations, then both oracles accept and have the same session key.

Indistinguishability.   For all probabilistic, polynomial time adversaries, $\mathscr{A}$, the advantage of $\mathscr{A}$, $\mathsf{Adv}^{\mathscr{A}}(k)$, in game $\mathscr{G}$ is negligible.

Requirement 1 of Definition 2.3.3 implies entity authentication. Entity authentication is said to be violated if some fresh oracle terminates with no partner.

2.3.4.2 The BR95 Model

Partnership in the BR95 model is defined using the notion of a partner function, which uses the transcript containing the record of all Send oracle queries to determine the partner of an oracle. No explicit definition of partnership, however, was provided in the original paper since there is no single partner function fixed for any protocol. Instead, security is defined predicated on the existence of a suitable partner function. Definition 2.3.4 describes partnership for the BR95 model.

Definition 2.3.4 (BR95 Partner Function [16]) *A partner function f in the BR95 model is a polynomial-time mapping between an initiator oracle and a partnering responder oracle (if such a partner exists), which uses the transcript T to determine the partner of an oracle.*

Let A and B be some initiator and responder principals, and also i and j be some instances of A and B respectively. The notation $f_{A,B}^i(T) = j$ denotes that the partner oracle of $\Pi_{A,B}^i$ is $\Pi_{B,A}^j$. The initial values $f_{A,B}^i(T) = *$ and $f_{B,A}^j(T) = *$ mean that neither $\Pi^i_{A,B}$ nor $\Pi^j_{B,A}$ has a partner. Two oracles are BR95 partners if, and only if, the specific partner function in use says they are.

Such a partner definition can easily go wrong. One such example is the partner function described in the original BR95 paper for the 3PKD protocol [16], which was later found to be flawed as described in Chapter 3.

Definition 2.3.5 describes security for the BR95 model.

Definition 2.3.5 (BR95 Definition of Security [16]) *A protocol is secure in the BR95 model if both the following requirements are satisfied:*

Validity. *When the protocol is run between two oracles $\Pi^i_{A,B}$ and $\Pi^j_{B,A}$ in the absence of a malicious adversary, both $\Pi^i_{A,B}$ and $\Pi^j_{B,A}$ accept and hold the same session key, and*

Indistinguishability. *For all probabilistic, polynomial time adversaries, $\mathscr{A}$, the advantage of $\mathscr{A}$, $\mathrm{Adv}^{\mathscr{A}}(k)$, in game $\mathscr{G}$ is negligible.*

2.3.4.3 The BPR2000 Model

Partnership in the BPR2000 model is defined based on the notion of session identifiers (SIDs). In the BPR2000 model, the construction of SIDs is suggested to be the concatenation of messages exchanged during the protocol run. However, protocol designers can construct SIDs as they choose. We observe that the way SIDs are constructed can have an impact on the security of the protocol in the model as described in Chapter 5.

In this model, an oracle who has accepted will hold the associated session key, an SID and a partner identifier (PID). Definition 2.3.6 describes partnership in the BPR2000 model.

Definition 2.3.6 (BPR2000 Definition of Partnership [13]) *Two oracles, $\Pi^i_{A,B}$ and $\Pi^j_{B,A}$, are partners if, and only if, both oracles*

1. *have accepted the same session key with the same SID,*
2. *have agreed on the same set of principals (i.e., the initiator and the responder of the protocol), and*
3. *no other oracles besides $\Pi^i_{A,B}$ and $\Pi^j_{B,A}$ have accepted with the same SID.*

We now define security in the BPR2000 model as described in Definition 2.3.7.

Definition 2.3.7 (BPR2000 Definition of Security [13]) *A protocol is secure in the BPR2000 model if,*

Key Establishment *For all probabilistic, polynomial time adversaries, $\mathscr{A}$, the advantage of $\mathscr{A}$, $\mathrm{Adv}^{\mathscr{A}}(k)$, in game $\mathscr{G}$ is negligible.*

Entity Authentication Goal.   The advantage of any probabilistic, polynomial time adversaries, $\mathscr{A}$, has in violating entity authentication is negligible.

The notions of security for entity authentication are client-to-server authentication, server-to-client authentication, and mutual authentication. An adversary is said to violate client-to-server authentication if some fresh server oracle terminates with no partner. Similarly, an adversary is said to violate server-to-client authentication if some fresh client oracle terminates with no partner. An adversary is said to violate mutual authentication if some fresh oracle terminates with no partner.

2.3.5 The Canetti–Krawczyk Model

In the CK2001 model, there are two adversarial models, namely the unathenticated-links adversarial / real world model (UM) and the authenticated-links adversarial / ideal world model (AM). AM is the (ideal) world where messages are authenticated magically, and UM is the (real) world in which we want our protocols to be proven secure.

Let $\mathscr{A}_{UM}$ denote the (active) adversary in the UM, and $\mathscr{A}_{AM}$ denote the (passive) adversary in the AM.

AM. $\mathscr{A}_{AM}$ is allowed to invoke protocol runs, impersonate corrupted protocol participants, and reveal past session keys. However, $\mathscr{A}_{AM}$ is not allowed to fabricate any messages or send a message more than once.

UM. $\mathscr{A}_{UM}$ is allowed to do all the things that $\mathscr{A}_{AM}$ can. In addition, $\mathscr{A}_{UM}$ can fabricate any messages or send a message more than once.

Therefore, the difference between $\mathscr{A}_{AM}$ and $\mathscr{A}_{UM}$ lies in their powers. $\mathscr{A}_{AM}$ is restricted to only delay, delete, and relay messages but not to fabricate any messages or send a message more than once.

Prior to explaining how a provably secure protocol in the AM is translated to a provably secure protocol in the UM with the use of an authenticator, we require definitions of an emulator and an authenticator, as given in Definitions 2.3.8 and 2.3.9.

Definition 2.3.8 (Definition of an Emulator [10]) *Let π and π' be two protocols for n parties where π is a protocol in the AM and π' is a protocol in the UM. π' is said to emulate π if for any UM-adversary $\mathscr{A}_{UM}$ there exists an AM-adversary $\mathscr{A}_{AM}$, such that for all inputs, no polynomial time adversary can distinguish the cumulative outputs of all parties and the adversary between the AM and the UM with more than negligible probability.*

Definition 2.3.9 (Definition of an Authenticator [10]) *An authenticator is defined to be a mapping transforming a protocol π_{AM} in the AM to a protocol π_{UM} in the UM such that π_{UM} emulates π_{AM}.*

Figure 2.3 describes how an authenticator translates a provably secure protocol, π, in the AM to a provably secure protocol, π', in the UM. Such an authenticator can be constructed with a tool called a message transmission authenticator (MT-authenticator) [30].

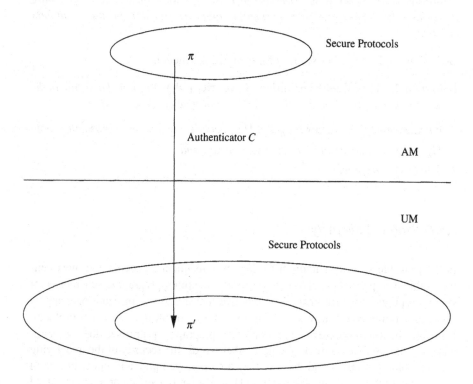

Fig. 2.3 Translating protocol in AM to UM

Security proofs for protocols in the UM depends on the security proofs of the underlying MT-authenticator used and that of the AM protocol. If any of these proofs break down, then the security proof for the UM protocol is invalid. One such example is presented in Chapter 8. In the example, we show how the flaw in the encryption-based MT-authenticator of Bellare, Canetti, and Krawczyk [10] invalidates security proofs of protocols that use the MT-authenticator by using protocol 2DHPE of Hitchcock, Tin, Boyd, González Nieto, and Montague [52] as a case study.

Partnership in the CK2001 model is defined using the notions of matching sessions and SIDs, as described in Definition 2.3.10. There is no formal definition of how SIDs should be defined in the CK2001 model and the values of SIDs are not specified. It is assumed that SIDs are known by protocol participants before the protocol begins. Such an assumption might not be practical as it requires some form of communication between the protocol participants prior to the start of the protocol. In practice, SIDs may be determined during protocol execution [30, 50, 51, 38, 98], as in the case of the BPR2000 model.

Definition 2.3.10 (Matching Sessions [30]) *Two sessions are said to be matching if they have the same session identifiers (SIDs) and corresponding partner identifiers (PIDs).*

Definition 2.3.11 describes security for the CK2001 model.

Definition 2.3.11 (CK2001 Definition of Security [30]) *A protocol is secure in the CK2001 model if for all probabilistic, polynomial time adversaries $\mathscr{A}$,*

1. *if two uncorrupted oracles $\Pi_{A,B}^{i}$ and $\Pi_{B,A}^{j}$ complete matching sessions, then both $\Pi_{A,B}^{i}$ and $\Pi_{B,A}^{j}$ must hold the same session key, and*
2. $\text{Adv}^{\mathscr{A}}(\text{k})$ *is negligible.*

2.3.6 Protocol Security

In the provable security paradigm for key establishment protocols, the most central problem in protocol design is to construct secure cryptographic schemes from strong cryptographic primitives. It is intuitive that the use of insecure or inappropriate cryptographic primitives will almost certainly result in an insecure protocol. However, the use of secure and appropriate cryptographic primitives does not automatically equate to a secure protocol. In other words, the security of the underlying cryptographic primitives and the way they are employed play an important role in the security of the cryptographic scheme. Thus, if a well-designed protocol is indeed secure, then one should be able to write down a proof of security[8], which says that the only way that the protocol is broken is if one can break its underlying cryptographic assumptions. Security of a protocol is proven by finding a reduction to some well known computational problem whose intractability is assumed as described in Chapter 2.1.3.

Now that the Bellare–Rogaway and CK2001 models have been defined, we can define the key replicating attack. The key replicating attack, first introduced by Krawczyk [71], will be referred to frequently in this book and is described in Definition 2.3.12.

Definition 2.3.12 (Key Replicating Attack [71]) *A key replicating attack is defined to be an attack whereby the adversary, $\mathscr{A}$, succeeds in forcing the establishment of a session, S_1, (other than the Test session or its matching session) that has*

---

[8] As Lakatos [72] suggested, writing a proof makes explicit the assumptions behind an idea whereby such assumptions may lead to counter-examples. The counter-examples may then in turn cause generalization and refinement of the original theorem.

the same key as the Test *session. In this case, $\mathscr{A}$ can distinguish whether the* Test-*session key is real or random by asking a* Reveal *query to the oracle associated with S_1.*

2.4 Summary

This chapter provided the notation used throughout the book, the necessary background, and definitions of the general architectural criteria for the classification of key establishment protocols, their goals and additional security attributes, and attacks. These discussions provided a solid background understanding of the informal protocol design that helps in understanding the formal (provable security) approach.

Descriptions of the Bellare–Rogaway [13, 14, 16] and the Canetti–Krawczyk approaches [10, 30] for the analysis of key establishment protocols were also presented. These approaches (or models) will be used as the underlying building blocks in subsequent chapters in this book.

References

1. Michel Abdalla, Olivier Chevassut & David Pointcheval 2005. One-time Verifier-based Encrypted Key Exchange, in Serge Vaudenay (ed), Proceedings of Public Key Cryptography - PKC 2005. Lecture Notes in Computer Science 3386/2005: 47–64
2. Michel Abdalla & David Pointcheval 2005. Simple Password-Based Authenticated Key Protocols, in Alfred John Menezes (ed), Proceedings of Cryptographers' Track at RSA Conference - CT-RSA 2005. Lecture Notes in Computer Science 3376/2005: 191–208
3. Martín Abadi & Roger Needham 1994. Prudent Engineering Practice for Cryptographic Protocols, in *Proceedings of IEEE Symposium on Research in Security and Privacy 1994*. IEEE Computer Society Press: 122–136
4. Martín Abadi & Roger Needham 1996. Prudent Engineering Practice for Cryptographic Protocols. *IEEE Transactions on Software Engineering* 22(1): 6–15
5. Sattam S Al-Riyami & Kenneth G Paterson 2003. Tripartite Authenticated Key Agreement Protocols from Pairings, in Kenneth G Paterson (ed), Proceedings of 9th IMA Conference on Cryptography and Coding. Lecture Notes in Computer Science 2898/2003: 332–359. Extended version available from http://eprint.iacr.org/2002/035/
6. David A. Basin and Sebastian Mödersheim and Luca Viganó 2003. An On-the-Fly Model-Checker for Security Protocol Analysis. *Technical report* no 404. Information Security Group, ETH Zentrum
7. David A. Basin and Sebastian Mödersheim and Luca Viganó 2003. An On-the-Fly Model-Checker for Security Protocol Analysis, in Einar Snekkenes & Dieter Gollmann (eds), Proceedings of 8th European Symposium on Research in Computer Security - ESORICS 2003. Lecture Notes in Computer Science 2808/2003: 253–270
8. Paulo S L M Barreto, Hae Yong Kim, Ben Lynn & Michael Scott 2002. Efficient Algorithms for Pairing-based Cryptosystems, in Moti Yung (ed), Proceedings of Advances in Cryptology - CRYPTO 2002. Lecture Notes in Computer Science 2442/2002: 354–368
9. Mihir Bellare 2002. A Note on Negligible Functions. *Journal of Cryptology* 15(4): 271–284

10. Mihir Bellare, Ran Canetti & Hugo Krawczyk 1998. A Modular Approach to The Design and Analysis of Authentication and Key Exchange Protocols, in Jeffrey Vitter (ed), Proceedings of 30th ACM Symposium on the Theory of Computing - ACM STOC 1998. ACM Press: 419–428

11. Mihir Bellare, Anand Desai, David Pointcheval & Phillip Rogaway 1998. Relations Among Notions of Security for Public-Key Encryption Schemes, in Hugo Krawczyk (ed), Proceedings of Advances in Cryptology - CRYPTO 1998. Lecture Notes in Computer Science 1462/2003: 26–45

12. Mihir Bellare, Erez Petrank, Charles Rackoff & Phillip Rogaway 1996. *Authenticated Key Exchange in the Public Key Model.* Unpublished Manuscript.

13. Mihir Bellare, David Pointcheval & Phillip Rogaway 2000. Authenticated Key Exchange Secure Against Dictionary Attacks, in Bart Preneel (ed), Proceedings of Advances in Cryptology - EUROCRYPT 2000. Lecture Notes in Computer Science 1807/2000: 139 – 155

14. Mihir Bellare & Phillip Rogaway 1993. Entity Authentication and Key Distribution, in Douglas R. Stinson (ed), Proceedings of Advances in Cryptology - CRYPTO 1993. Lecture Notes in Computer Science 773/1993: 110–125

15. Mihir Bellare & Phillip Rogaway 1993. Random Oracles Are Practical: A Paradigm For Designing Efficient Protocols, in *Proceedings of 1st ACM Conference on Computer and communications Security - ACM CCS 1993.* ACM Press: 62–73

16. Mihir Bellare & Phillip Rogaway 1995. Provably Secure Session Key Distribution: The Three Party Case, in F. Tom Leighton & Allan Borodin (eds), Proceedings of 27th ACM Symposium on the Theory of Computing - ACM STOC 1995. ACM Press: 57–66

17. John Black 2006. The Ideal-Cipher Model, Revisited: An Uninstantiable Blockcipher-Based Hash Function, in Serge Vaudenay (ed), Proceedings of Advances in Cryptology - EUROCRYPT 2006. Lecture Notes in Computer Science 4047/2006: 328–340. Extended version available from http://eprint.iacr.org/2005/210

18. Simon Blake-Wilson, Don Johnson & Alfred Menezes 1997. Key Agreement Protocols and their Security Analysis, in Michael Darnell (ed), Proceedings of 6th IMA International Conference on Cryptography and Coding. Lecture Notes in Computer Science 1335/1997: 30–45

19. Simon Blake-Wilson & Alfred Menezes 1997. Security Proofs for Entity Authentication and Authenticated Key Transport Protocols Employing Asymmetric Techniques, in Bruce Christianson, Bruno Crispo, T Mark, A Lomas & Michael Roe (eds), Proceedings of Security Protocols Workshop. Lecture Notes in Computer Science 1361/1997: 137–158

20. Simon Blake-Wilson & Alfred Menezes 1998. Authenticated Diffie–Hellman Key Agreement Protocols, in Stafford E Tavares & Henk Meijer (eds), Proceedings of Selected Areas in Cryptography - SAC 1998. Lecture Notes in Computer Science 1556/1998: 339–361

21. Dan Boneh 1998. The Decision Diffie–Hellman Problem, in Joe P Buhler (ed), Proceedings of 3rd Algorithmic Number Theory Symposium - ANTS-III. Lecture Notes in Computer Science 1423/1998: 48–63

22. Dan Boneh & M Franklin 2003. Identity-Based Encryption from the Weil Pairing. *SIAM Journal on Computing* 32(3): 585–615

23. Dan Boneh & Richard J Lipton 1996. Algorithms for Black-Box Fields and their Application to Cryptography, in Neal Koblitz (ed), Proceedings of Advances in Cryptology - CRYPTO 1996. Lecture Notes in Computer Science 1109/1996: 283–297

24. Colin Boyd & Kim-Kwang Raymond Choo 2005. Security of Two-Party Identity-Based Key Agreement, in Ed Dawson & Serge Vaudenay (eds), Proceedings of 1st International Conference on Cryptology in Malaysia - MYCRYPT 2005. Lecture Notes in Computer Science 3715/2005: 229–243

25. Colin Boyd & Juan Manuel González Nieto 2003. Round-optimal Contributory Conference Key Agreement, in Yvo Desmedt (ed), Proceedings of Public Key Cryptography - PKC 2003. Lecture Notes in Computer Science 2567/2003: 161–174

26. Colin Boyd, Wenbo Mao & Kenny Paterson 2004. Key Agreement using Statically Keyed Authenticators, in Markus Jakobsson, Moti Yung & Jianying Zhou (eds), Proceedings of Applied Cryptography and Network Security - ACNS 2004. Lecture Notes in Computer Science 3089/2004: 248–262

27. Colin Boyd & Anish Mathuria 2003. *Protocols for Authentication and Key Establishment.* Springer-Verlag

28. Emmanuel Bresson, Olivier Chevassut & David Pointcheval. New Security Results on Encrypted Key Exchange, in Feng Bao, Robert H Deng & Jianying Zhou (eds), Proceedings of Public Key Cryptography - PKC 2004. Lecture Notes in Computer Science 2947/2004: 145–158

29. Michael Burrows, Martín Abadi & Roger Needham 1990. A Logic of Authentication. *ACM Transactions on Computer Systems* 8(1): 18–36

30. Ran Canetti & Hugo Krawczyk 2001. Analysis of Key-Exchange Protocols and Their Use for Building Secure Channels, in Birgit Pfitzmann (ed), Proceedings of Advances in Cryptology - EUROCRYPT 2001. Lecture Notes in Computer Science 2045/2001: 453–474. Extended version available from http://eprint.iacr.org/2001/040/

31. Ran Canetti, Oded Goldreich & Shai Halevi 2004. The Random Oracle Methodology, Revisited. *Journal of the ACM* 51(4): 557–594. Extended version available from http://eprint.iacr.org/1998/011

32. Dario Catalano, David Pointcheval & Thomas Pornin 2007. Trapdoor Hard-to-Invert Group Isomorphisms and Their Application to Password-based Authentication. *Journal of Cryptology* 20(1): 115–149

33. Liqun Chen & Caroline Kudla 2003. Identity Based Authenticated Key Agreement Protocols from Pairings, in *Proceedings of IEEE Computer Security Foundations Workshop - CSFW 2003*. IEEE Computer Society Press: 219–233. Corrected version at http://eprint.iacr.org/2002/184/

34. Zhaohui Cheng, Liqun Chen, Richard Comley & Qiang Tang 2006. Identity-Based Key Agreement with Unilateral Identity Privacy Using Pairings, in Kefei Chen, Robert H Deng, Xuejia Lai & Jianying Zhou (eds), Proceedings of 2nd Information Security Practice and Experience Conference - ISPEC 2006. Lecture Notes in Computer Science 3903/2006: 202–213

35. Olivier Chevassut, Pierre-Alain Fouque, Pierrick Gaudry & David Pointcheval 2006. The Twist-Augmented Technique for Key Exchange, in Moti Yung, Yevgeniy Dodis, Aggelos Kiayias & Tal Malkin (eds), Proceedings of Public Key Cryptography - PKC 2006. Lecture Notes in Computer Science 3958/2006: 410–426

36. Kyu Young Choi, Jung Yeon Hwang, Dong Hoon Lee & In Seog Seo 2005. ID-based Authenticated Key Agreement for Low-Power Mobile Devices, in Colin Boyd & Juan Manuel González Nieto (eds), Proceedings of 10th Australasian Conference on Information Security and Privacy - ACISP 2005. Lecture Notes in Computer Science 3574/2005: 494–505

37. Sherman S M Chow & Kim-Kwang Raymond Choo 2007. Strongly-Secure Identity-Based Key Agreement and Anonymous Extension, in Juan A Garay, Arjen K Lenstra, Masahiro Mambo & Ren Peralta (eds), Proceedings of 10th International Conference on Information Security - ISC 2007. Lecture Notes in Computer Science 4779/2007: 203–220

38. Yvonne Cliff, Yiu-Shing Terry Tin & Colin Boyd 2006. Password Based Server Aided Key Exchange, in Jianying Zhou, Moti Yung & Feng Bao (eds), Proceedings of Applied Cryptography and Network Security - ACNS 2006. Lecture Notes in Computer Science 3989/2006: 146–161

39. Jean-Sebastien Coron, Yevgeniy Dodis, Cecile Malinaud & Prashant Puniya 2005. Merkle-Damgard Revisited: How to Construct a Hash Function, in Victor Shoup (ed), Proceedings of Advances in Cryptology - CRYPTO 2005. Lecture Notes in Computer Science 3621/2005: 430–448

40. Ivan Damgård 1987. Collision Free Hash Functions and Public Key Signature Schemes, in David Chaum & Wyn L Price (eds), Proceedings of Advances in Cryptology – EUROCRYPT 1987. Lecture Notes in Computer Science 304/1987: 203–216

41. Ivan Damgård 1989. A Design Principle for Hash Functions, in Gilles Brassard (ed), Proceedings of Advances in Cryptology - CRYPTO 1989. Lecture Notes in Computer Science 435/1990: 416–427

42. Whitfield Diffie & Martin Hellman 1976. New Directions in Cryptography. *IEEE Transaction on Information Theory* 22(6): 644–654

43. Whitfield Diffie, Paul C van Oorschot & Michael J Wiener 1992. Authentication and Authenticated Key Exchange. *Journal of Designs, Codes and Cryptography* 2(2): 107–125

44. Amos Fiat & Adi Shamir 1986. How to Prove Yourself: Practical Solutions to Identification and Signature Problems, in Andrew M Odlyzko (ed), Proceedings of Advances in Cryptology - CRYPTO 1986. Lecture Notes in Computer Science 263/1987: 186–194

45. Steven D Galbraith 2002. Implementing the Tate Pairing, in Claus Fieker & David R Kohel (eds), Proceedings of 5th International Symposium on Algorithmic Number Theory - ANTS-V 2002. Lecture Notes in Computer Science 2369/2002: 324–337

46. Craig Gentry, Philip MacKenzie & Zulfikar Ramzan 2005. Password Authenticated Key Exchange Using Hidden Smooth Subgroups, in *Proceedings of 12th ACM Conference on Computer and Communications Security - ACM CCS 2005*. ACM Press: 299–309

47. Shafi Goldwasser & S Micali 1984. Probabilisitic Encryption. *Journal of Computer and System Sciences* 28(3): 270–299. Available from http://people.csail.mit.edu/joanne/shafi-pubs.html

48. Shafi Goldwasser, S Micali & Ron L Rivest 1988. A Digital Signature Scheme Secure Against Adaptive Chosen-Message Attacks. *SIAM Journal on Computing* 17(2: 281 – 308

49. Li Gong 1989. Using One-Way Functions for Authentication. *ACM SIGCOMM Computer Communications Review* 8(11): 8–11

50. Yvonne Hitchcock, Colin Boyd & Juan Manuel González Nieto 2004. Tripartite Key Exchange in the Canetti-Krawczyk Proof Model, in Anne Canteaut & Kapaleeswaran Viswanathan (eds), Proceedings of 5th International Conference on Cryptology in India - INDOCRYPT 2004. Lecture Notes in Computer Science 3348/2004: 17–32

51. Yvonne Hitchcock, Colin Boyd & Juan Manuel González Nieto 2005. Modular Proofs for Key Exchange: Rigorous Optimizations in the Canetti-Krawczyk Model. *Applicable Algebra in Engineering, Communication and Computing Journal* 16(6): 405–438

52. Yvonne Hitchcock, Yiu-Shing Terry Tin, Colin Boyd, Juan Manuel González Nieto & Paul Montague 2003. A Password-Based Authenticator: Security Proof and Applications, in Thomas Johansson & Subhamoy Maitra (eds), Proceedings of 4th International Conference on Cryptology in India - INDOCRYPT 2003. Lecture Notes in Computer Science 2904/2003: 388–401

53. Jeremy Horwitz & Ben Lynn 2002. Toward Hierarchical Identity-Based Encryption, in Lars R Knudsen (ed), Proceedings of Advances in Cryptology - EUROCRYPT 2002. Lecture Notes in Computer Science 2332/2002: 466–481

54. Alfred J Menezes, Paul C van Oorschot & Scott A Vanstone 1997. *Handbook of Applied Cryptography*. CRC Press

55. ISO 1999. *Information Technology – Security Techniques – Key Management – Part 3: Mechanisms Using Asymmetric Techniques ISO/IEC 11770-3*. International Standard.

56. Phil Janson & Gene Tsudik 1995. Secure and Minimal Protocols for Authenticated Key Distribution. *Computer Communications* 18(9): 645–653

57. Ik Rae Jeong, Jonathan Katz & Dong Hoon Lee 2004. One-Round Protocols for Two-Party Authenticated Key Exchange, in Markus Jakobsson, Moti Yung & Jianying Zhou (eds), Proceedings of Applied Cryptography and Network Security - ACNS 2004. Lecture Notes in Computer Science 3089/2004: 220–232

58. Antoine Joux 2000. A One Round Protocol for Tripartite Diffie–Hellman, in Wieb Bosma (ed), Proceedings of 4th International Symposium on Algorithmic Number Theory - ANTS-IV. Lecture Notes in Computer Science 1838/2000: 385–394

59. Antoine Joux 2002. The Weil and Tate Pairings as Building Blocks for Public Key Cryptosystems, in Claus Fieker and David R Kohel (eds), Proceedings of 5th International Symposium on Algorithmic Number Theory - ANTS-V. Lecture Notes in Computer Science 2369/2002: 20–32

60. Antoine Joux & Kim Nguyen 2003. Separating Decision Diffie–Hellman from Computational Diffie–Hellman in Cryptographic Groups. *Journal of Cryptology* 16(4): 239–247

61. Burton S Kaliski 2001. An Unknown Key-Share Attack on the MQV Key Agreement Protocol. *ACM Transactions on Information and System Security (TISSEC)* 4(3): 275–288

62. Jonathon Katz & Ji Sun Shin 2005. Modeling Insider Attacks on Group Key-Exchange Protocols, in *Proceedings of 12th ACM Conference on Computer and Communications Security - ACM CCS 2005*. ACM Press: 180–189

63. Jonathan Katz, Rafail Ostrovsky & Moti Yung 2001. Efficient Password-Authenticated Key Exchange Using Human-Memorable Passwords, in Birgit Pfitzmann (ed), Proceedings of Advances in Cryptology - EUROCRYPT 2001. Lecture Notes in Computer Science 2045/2001: 475–494

64. Jonathan Katz, Rafail Ostrovsky & Moti Yung 2002. Forward Secrecy in Password-Only Key Exchange Protocols, in Stelvio Cimato, Clemente Galdi & Giuseppe Persiano (eds), roceedings of 3rd Conference on Security in Communication Networks - SCN 2002. Lecture Notes in Computer Science 2576/2003: 29–44

65. Jonathon Katz & Moti Yung 2003. Scalable Protocols for Authenticated Group Key Exchange, in Dan Boneh (ed), Proceedings of Advances in Cryptology - CRYPTO 2003. Lecture Notes in Computer Science 2729/2003: 110–125

66. John Kelsey, Bruce Schneier & David Wagner 1997. Protocol Interactions and the Chosen Protocol Attack, in Bruce Christianson, Bruno Crispo, T Mark, A Lomas & Michael Roe (eds), Proceedings of Security Protocols Workshop. Lecture Notes in Computer Science 1361/1998: 91–104

67. Young-Sin Kim, Eui-Nam Huh, Jun Hwang & Byung-Wook Lee 2004. ID-Based Authenticated Multiple-Key Agreement Protocol from Pairings, in Antonio Laganà, Marina L Gavrilova, Vipin Kumar, Youngsong Mun, Chih Jeng Kenneth Tan & Osvaldo Gervasi (eds), Proceedings of International Conference On Computational Science And Its Applications - ICCSA 2004. Lecture Notes in Computer Science 3046/2004: 672–680

68. Kee-Won Kim, Eun-Kyung Ryu & Kee-Young Yoo 2004. ID-Based Authenticated Multiple-Key Agreement Protocol from Pairings, in Antonio Laganà, Marina L Gavrilova, Vipin Kumar, Youngsong Mun, Chih Jeng Kenneth Tan & Osvaldo Gervasi (eds), Proceedings of International Conference On Computational Science And Its Applications - ICCSA 2004. Lecture Notes in Computer Science 3046/2004: 672–680

69. Neal Koblitz 1987. Elliptic Curve Cryptosystems. *Mathematics of Computation* 48(177): 203-209

70. Neal Koblitz & Alfred Menezes 2004. A Survey of Public-Key Cryptosystems. *SIAM Review* 46(4): 599–634

71. Hugo Krawczyk 2005. HMQV: A High-Performance Secure Diffie–Hellman Protocol, in Victor Shoup (ed), Proceedings of Advances in Cryptology - CRYPTO 2005. Lecture Notes in Computer Science 3621/2005: 546–566. Extended version available from http://eprint.iacr.org/2005/176/

72. Imre Lakatos 1976. *Proofs and Refutations : The Logic of Mathematical Discovery*. Cambridge University Press

73. Laurie Law, Alfred Menezes, Minghua Qu, Jerry Solinas & Scott Vanstone 2003. An Efficient Protocol for Authenticated Key Agreement. *Designs, Codes and Cryptography* 28(1): 119–134

74. Benjamin W Long 2005. Formal Verification of a Type Flaw Attack on a Security Protocol Using Object-Z, in Helen Treharne, Steve King, Martin C Henson & Steve Schneider (eds), Proceedings of 4th International Conference of B and Z Users: Formal Specification and Development in Z and B – ZB 2005. Lecture Notes in Computer Science 3455/2005: 319–333

75. Philip D MacKenzie 2002. The PAK Suite: Protocols for Password-Authenticated Key Exchange. *Technical report* no 2002-46. DIMACS Center, Rutgers University

76. Philip D MacKenzie, Sarvar Patel & Ram Swaminathan 2000. Password-Authenticated Key Exchange Based on RSA, in Tatsuaki Okamoto (ed), Proceedings of Advances in Cryptology - ASIACRYPT 2000. Lecture Notes in Computer Science 1976/2000: 599–613

77. Philip D MacKenzie & Ram Swaminathan 1999. Secure Network Authentication with Password Identification. Submitted to the IEEE P1363 Working Group

78. Wenbo Mao 2003. *Modern Cryptography: Theory and Practice*. Prentice Hall PTR

79. Ueli M Maurer & Stefan Wolf 1999. The Relationship Between Breaking the Diffie–Hellman Protocol and Computing Discrete Logarithms. *SIAM Journal on Computing* 28(5): 1689–1721

80. Alfred Menezes, Minqhua Qu & Scott A Vanstone 1995. Some Key Agreement Protocols Providing Implicit Authentication, in *Proceedings of 2nd Workshop on Selected Areas in Cryptography - SAC 1995*: 22–32

81. Noel McCullagh & Paulo S L M Barreto 2005. A New Two-Party Identity-Based Authenticated Key Agreement, in Alfred John Menezes (ed), Proceedings of Cryptographers' Track at RSA Conference - CT-RSA 2005. Lecture Notes in Computer Science 3376/2005: 262–274. Extended version available from http://eprint.iacr.org/2004/122/

82. Victor S Miller 1985. Use of Elliptic Curves in Cryptography, in Hugh C Williams (ed), Proceedings of Advances in Cryptology - CRYPTO 1985. Lecture Notes in Computer Science 218/1986: 417–426

83. R M Needham & M D Schroeder 1978. Using Encryption for Authentication in Large Networks of Computers. *ACM Journal of Communications* 21(12): 993–999

84. Tatsuaki Okamoto & David Pointcheval 2001. The Gap-Problems: a New Class of Problems for the Security of Cryptographic Schemes, in Kwangjo Kim (ed), Proceedings of Public Key Cryptography - PKC 2001. Lecture Notes in Computer Science 1992/2001: 104–118

85. Bart Preneel 1993. Analysis and design of Cryptographic Hash Functions. Ph.D. Thesis, Katholieke Universiteit Leuven

86. Ronald Rivest, Adi Shamir & Leonard Adleman 1978. A Method for Obtaining Digital Signatures and Public-Key Cryptosystems. *Communications of the ACM* 21(2): 120–126

87. Phillip Rogaway & Thomas Shrimpton 2004. Cryptographic Hash-Function Basics: Definitions, Implications, and Separations for Preimage Resistance, Second-Preimage Resistance, and Collision Resistance, in Bimal K Roy and Willi Meier (eds), Proceedings of Fast Software Encryption - FSE 2004. Lecture Notes in Computer Science 3017/2004: 371–388

88. A W Roscoe 1996. Intensional Specifications of Security Protocols, in *Proceedings of 9th IEEE Computer Security Foundations Workshop - CSFW 1996*. IEEE Computer Society Press: 28–38

89. Ryuichi Sakai, Kiyoshi Ohgishi & Masao Kasahara 2000. Cryptosystems Based on Pairing, *Proceedings of the 2000 Sympoium on Cryptography and Information Security - SCIS 2000*: 26–28

90. Kyungah Shim 2003. *Cryptanalysis of Al-Riyami-Paterson's Authenticated Three Party Key Agreement Protocols.* Cryptology ePrint Archive, Report 2003/122. http://eprint.iacr.org/2003/122

91. SeongHan Shin, Kazukuni Kobara & Hideki Imai 2003. Leakage-Resilient Authenticated Key Establishment Protocols, in Chi-Sung Laih (ed), Proceedings of Advances in Cryptology - ASIACRYPT 2003. Lecture Notes in Computer Science 2894/2003: 155–172

92. SeongHan Shin, Kazukuni Kobara & Hideki Imai 2005. A Simple Leakage-Resilient Authenticated Key Establishment Protocol, Its Extensions, and Applications. *IEICE Transactions* E85-A(3: 736–754

93. SeongHan Shin, Kazukuni Kobara & Hideki Imai 2005. A Simplified Leakage-Resilient Authenticated Key Exchange Protocol with Optimal Memory Size, in Pascal Lorenz & Petre Dini (eds), Proceedings of 4th International Conference on Networking – ICN 2005. Lecture Notes in Computer Science 3421/2005: 944–952

94. SeongHan Shin, Kazukuni Kobara & Hideki Imai 2005. Efficient and Leakage-Resilient Authenticated Key Transport Protocol Based on RSA, in Angelos Keromytis & Moti Yung (eds), Proceedings of Applied Cryptography and Network Security - ACNS 2005. Lecture Notes in Computer Science 3531/2005: 269–284

95. Victor Shoup 1997. Lower Bounds for Discrete Logarithms and Related Problems, in Walter Fumy (ed), Proceedings of Advances in Cryptology - EUROCRYPT 1997. Lecture Notes in Computer Science 1233/1993: 256–266

96. Nigel Smart 2002. An Identity based Authenticated Key Agreement Protocol based on the Weil Pairing. *IEE Electronics Letters* 38(13): 630–632

97. Paul F Syverson & Paul C van Oorschot 1994. On Unifying Some Cryptographic Protocol Logics, in *Proceedings of IEEE Symposium on Research in Security and Privacy 1994*. IEEE Computer Press: 14–28

98. Yiu Shing Terry Tin, Colin Boyd & Juan Manuel González Nieto 2003. Provably Secure Mobile Key Exchange: Applying the Canetti-Krawczyk Approach, in Reihaneh Safavi-Naini & Jennifer Seberry (eds), Proceedings of 8th Australasian Conference on Information Security and Privacy - ACISP 2003. Lecture Notes in Computer Science 2727/2003: 166–189

99. Yongge Wang 2005. *Efficient Identity-Based and Authenticated Key Agreement Protocol.* Cryptology ePrint Archive, Report 2005/108. http://eprint.iacr.org/2005/108/

100. Duncan S Wong & Agnes H Chan 2001. Efficient and Mutually Authenticated Key Exchange for Low Power Computing Devices, in Colin Boyd (ed), Proceedings of Advances in Cryptology - ASIACRYPT 2001. Lecture Notes in Computer Science 2248/2001: 172–289

101. Xun Yi 2003. Efficient ID-Based Key Agreement from Weil Pairing. *IEE Electronics Letters* 39(2): 206–208

102. Xun Yi, Chik How Tan, Chee Kheong Siew & M R Syed 2002. ID-Based Key Agreement for Multimedia Encryption. *IEEE Transactions on Consumer Electronics* 48(2): 298–303

103. Muxiang Zhang2004. New Approaches to Password Authenticated Key Exchange Based on RSA, in Pil Joong Lee (ed), Proceedings of Advances in Cryptology - ASIACRYPT 2004. Lecture Notes in Computer Science 3329/2004: 230–244

104. Muxiang Zhang 2004. Password Authenticated Key Exchange Using Quadratic Residues, in Markus Jakobsson, Moti Yung & Jianying Zhou (eds), Proceedings of Applied Cryptography and Network Security - ACNS 2004. Lecture Notes in Computer Science 3089/2004: 248–262

105. Fangguo Zhang & Xiaofeng Chen 2003. Attack on an ID-based Authenticated Group Key Agreement Scheme from PKC 2004. *Information Processing Letters* 91(4): 191–193

106. Fangguo Zhang, Reihaneh Safavi-Naini & Willy Susilo 2004. An Efficient Signature Scheme from Bilinear Pairings and Its Applications, in Feng Bao, Robert H Deng & Jianying Zhou (eds), Proceedings of Public Key Cryptography - PKC 2004. Lecture Notes in Computer Science 2947/2004: 277–290

Chapter 3
A Flawed BR95 Partnership Function

In a real world setting, it is normal to assume that a host can establish several concurrent sessions with many different parties. Sessions are specific to both the communicating parties. In the case of key distribution protocols, sessions are specific to both the initiator and the responder principals, where every session is associated with a unique session key. To model the real world implementation, the most recent definition of partnership based on session identifiers (SIDs) in the BPR2000 model seems most natural. SIDs enable unique identification of the individual sessions. Without such means, communicating hosts will have difficulty determining the associated session key for a particular session.

We consider the use of SIDs to establish partnership analogous to the use of sockets in establishing connections between an initiating client process and a responding server process in network service protocol architecture [7]. A socket [9, 8] is bound to a port number so that the TCP layer can identify the application to which that data is destined to be sent, analogous to a SID being bound to a particular session enabling communicating principals to determine to which session messages belong. Since the initial development of sockets in the early 1980s, the use of sockets has been prevalent in protocols such as TCP/IP and UDP. In fact, Bellare, Pointcheval, and Rogaway [3] recognised that SIDs are typically found in protocols such as SSL and IPSec.

We observe that an important difference between the various variants of the Bellare–Rogaway models is in the way partner oracles are defined (i.e., the definition of partnership). We examine partnering in the BR95 model and observe that the specific partner function defined in the proof of security for the 3PKD protocol is flawed. Consequently, the BR95 proof is invalidated, although not irreparably so. More interestingly, we also demonstrate that it does not seem possible to introduce a practical definition of partnership based on SIDs in the 3PKD protocol.

The inability to define a unique SID in the 3PKD protocol so that the communicating principals can uniquely distinguish messages from different sessions leads one to question the practicality and usefulness of the protocol in a real world setting. In our view, the design of any entity authentication and/or key establishment protocol should incorporate a secure means of uniquely identifying a particular communication session among the many concurrent sessions that a communicating party may have with many different parties. One outcome of this work is such a means of session identification.

Material presented in this chapter has appeared in the following publication:

- Kim-Kwang Raymond Choo, Colin Boyd, Yvonne Hitchcock, and Greg Maitland. On Session Identifiers in Provably Secure Protocols: The Bellare–Rogaway Three-Party Key Distribution Protocol Revisited. In Blundo Carlo and Stelvio Cimato, editors, 4th Conference on Security in Communication Networks - SCN 2004, volume 3352/2005 of Lecture Notes in Computer Science, pages 352–367. Springer-Verlag, 2004.

3.1 A Flaw in the Security Proof for 3PKD Protocol

In this section, we describe the 3PKD protocol and an execution of the protocol run in the presence of a malicious adversary, followed by an explanation of the specific partner function used in the BR95 proof. Using an execution of the protocol as a case study, we demonstrate that the specific partner function used in the BR95 proof enables a malicious adversary to reveal a session key at one oracle, where the same session key is considered fresh at a different, non-BR95 partner oracle.

3.1.1 The 3PKD Protocol

Protocol 3.1 involves three parties, a trusted server S and two principals, A and B, who wish to establish communication. The security goal of Protocol 3.1 is to distribute a session key between two communication principals (i.e., the key establishment goal), which is suitable for establishing a secure session. Forward-secrecy and mutual authentication are not considered in the protocol. However, concurrent executions of Protocol 3.1 are possible.

In Protocol 3.1, the encryption keys, K_{AS}^{enc} and K_{BS}^{enc}, and the MAC keys, K_{AS}^{MAC} and K_{BS}^{MAC}, are independent of each other.

1. Protocol 3.1 begins by having A randomly select a k-bit challenge R_A, where k is the security parameter. A then sends R_A to B with whom she desires to communicate.
2. Upon receiving the message R_A from A, B also randomly selects a k-bit challenge R_B and sends R_B together with R_A as a message (R_A, R_B) to the server S.

1. $A \longrightarrow B : R_A$
2. $B \longrightarrow S : R_A, R_B$
3a. $S \longrightarrow A : \{SK_{AB}\}_{K_{AS}^{enc}}, [A, B, R_A, \{SK_{AB}\}_{K_{AS}^{enc}}]_{K_{AS}^{MAC}}$
3b. $S \longrightarrow B : \{SK_{AB}\}_{K_{BS}^{enc}}, [A, B, R_B, \{SK_{AB}\}_{K_{BS}^{enc}}]_{K_{BS}^{MAC}}$

Protocol 3.1: 3PKD protocol

3. Upon receiving the message, S, runs the session key generator to obtain a session key SK_{AB}, which has not been used before. S then

- encrypts SK_{AB} with K_{AS}^{enc} and K_{BS}^{enc} to obtain ciphertexts α_A and α_B,
- computes the MAC digests of the strings $(A, B, R_A, \{SK_{AB}\}_{K_{AS}^{enc}})$ and $(A, B, R_B, \{SK_{AB}\}_{K_{BS}^{enc}})$ under the keys K_{AS}^{MAC} and K_{BS}^{MAC}, β_A and β_B respectively, and
- sends messages (α_A, β_A) and (α_B, β_B) to A and B respectively in Steps 3a and 3b of Protocol 3.1.

3.1.2 Key Replicating Attack on 3PKD Protocol

Attack 3.1 depicts an example execution of Protocol 3.1 in the presence of a malicious adversary, $\mathscr{A}$, which will be used to demonstrate a flaw. The specific partner function used in the BR95 proof enables a malicious adversary to reveal a session key at one oracle, where the same session key is considered fresh at a different, non partner oracle. Consequently, the BR95 proof will be shown to be invalid.

1. $A \longrightarrow B$ (intercepted by $\mathscr{A}$) : R_A
1($\mathscr{A}$). $\mathscr{A}$ (impersonating A) $\longrightarrow B : R_E$
2. $B \longrightarrow S$ (intercepted by $\mathscr{A}$) : R_E, R_B
2($\mathscr{A}$). $\mathscr{A}$ (impersonating B) $\longrightarrow S : R_A, R_B$
3a. $S \longrightarrow A :$ $\{SK_{A,B}\}_{K_{AS}^{enc}},$
                                          $[A, B, R_A, \{SK_{A,B}\}_{K_{AS}^{enc}}]_{K_{AS}^{MAC}}$
3b. $S \longrightarrow B :$ $\{SK_{A,B}\}_{K_{BS}^{enc}},$
                                          $[A, B, R_B, \{SK_{A,B}\}_{K_{BS}^{enc}}]_{K_{BS}^{MAC}}$

Attack 3.1: Key replicating attack on Protocol 3.1

1.   An active adversary, $\mathscr{A}$, intercepts and deletes the message R_A sent by A to B.
1($\mathscr{A}$). $\mathscr{A}$ then sends a fabricated message R_E to B impersonating A.
2.   Upon receiving the message R_E, and believing that this message originated from A, B also randomly selects a k-bit challenge R_B and sends R_B together with R_E as a message (R_E, R_B) to the server S.

$2(\mathscr{A})$. $\mathscr{A}$ then intercepts and deletes this message (R_E, R_B), and sends the fabricated message (R_A, R_B) to S impersonating B.

3. Upon receiving the message (R_A, R_B) from $\mathscr{A}$, and believing that this message originated from B, S runs the session key generator to obtain a unique session key SK_{AB}, which has not been used before. S then runs as per protocol specification.

Immediately after both A and B have verified and accepted with the session key SK_{AB}, $\mathscr{A}$ sends a Reveal query to A and obtains the session key SK_{AB} from A. This enables the adversary $\mathscr{A}$ to break the protocol. Such an attack is termed the key replicating attack as described in Definition 2.3.12.

Table 3.1 shows the oracle queries associated with Attack 3.1.

On query of q:	Return:	Append to T:
$\mathsf{SendClient}(A,B,i,*)$	R_A	$\langle q, R_A \rangle$
$\mathsf{SendClient}(B,A,j,R_E)$	(R_E, R_B)	$\langle q, (R_E, R_B) \rangle$
$\mathsf{SendServer}(A,B,s,(R_A,R_B))$	$((\alpha_{A,i},\beta_{A,i}), (\alpha_{B,j},\beta_{B,j}))$	$\langle q, ((\alpha_{A,i},\beta_{A,i}),$ $(\alpha_{B,j},\beta_{B,j}))\rangle$
$\mathsf{SendClient}(A,B,i,(\alpha_{A,i},\beta_{A,i}))$	$Accept_{A,i}$	$\langle q, Accept_{A,i}\rangle$
$\mathsf{SendClient}(B,A,j,(\alpha_{B,j},\beta_{B,j}))$	$Accept_{B,j}$	$\langle q, Accept_{B,j}\rangle$
$\mathsf{Reveal}(A,B,i)$	$SK_{A,B,i}$	

Table 3.1 Oracle queries associated with Attack 3.1

3.1.3 The Partner Function used in the BR95 Proof

We now present the specific partner function used in the BR95 proof. The partner function is defined in two parts, namely the partner of the responder oracle and the partner of the initiator oracle. Let f be the partner function defined in the BR95 proof, $\Pi^i_{A,B}$ be the initiator oracle, and $\Pi^j_{B,A}$ be the responder oracle. Both values $f^i_{A,B}(T)$ and $f^j_{B,A}(T)$ are initially set to $*$, which means that neither $\Pi^i_{A,B}$ nor $\Pi^j_{B,A}$ is BR95 partnered. The description of f is now given, where T is the transcript with which the adversary terminates the execution of the protocol run.

BR95 partner of the initiator oracle. The first two records of T associated with queries of the oracle $\Pi^i_{A,B}$ are examined. If the first record indicates that $\Pi^i_{A,B}$ had the role of an initiator oracle, was sent a $\mathsf{SendClient}(A,B,i,*)$ query and replied with R_A, and the second record indicates that $\Pi^i_{A,B}$'s reply to a $\mathsf{SendClient}(A,B,i,(\alpha_A,\beta_A))$ was the decision $Accept$, then T is examined to determine if some server oracle, $\Psi^k_{A,B}$, sent a message of the form (α_A, β'_A) for some β'_A. If so, determine if this message was in response to a $\mathsf{SendServer}(A,B,k,(R_A,R_B))$ query for some R_B, and if this is also true, determine if there is a unique j such that an oracle $\Pi^j_{B,A}$ generated a message (R_A,R_B).

If such an oracle $\Pi_{B,A}^{j}$ is found, then set $f_{A,B}^{i}(T) = j$, meaning that the BR95 partner of $\Pi_{A,B}^{i}$ is $\Pi_{B,A}^{j}$.

BR95 partner of the responder oracle.   The first two records of T associated with
queries of the oracle $\Pi_{B,A}^{j}$ are examined. If the first record indicates that $\Pi_{B,A}^{j}$
had the role of a responder oracle, and was sent a $\mathsf{SendClient}(B,A,j,R_A)$ query,
and the second record indicates that $\Pi_{B,A}^{j}$ accepted, then determine if there is a
unique i such that an oracle $\Pi_{A,B}^{i}$ generated a message R_A. If such an oracle $\Pi_{A,B}^{i}$
is found, then set $f_{B,A}^{j}(T) = i$, meaning that the BR95 partner of $\Pi_{B,A}^{j}$ is $\Pi_{A,B}^{i}$.

Suppose that the adversary terminates the execution of the protocol run in Attack 3.1
with some transcript T_1. According to the BR95 partner function f, $\Pi_{A,B}^{i}$ has no
BR95 partner because although there is a $\mathsf{SendServer}(A,B,k,(R_A,R_B))$ query for
some R_B, there does not exist a unique j such that an oracle $\Pi_{B,A}^{j}$ generated a message (R_A,R_B). Hence, $f_{A,B}^{i}(T_1) = *$.

For the execution of the protocol run in Attack 3.1, $\Pi_{B,A}^{j}$ has no BR95 partner because although $\Pi_{B,A}^{j}$ accepted, there does not exist a unique oracle $\Pi_{A,B}^{i}$ that it generated a message R_E (recall R_E is fabricated by $\mathscr{A}$). Hence, $f_{B,A}^{j}(T_1) = *$. Hence,
we have shown that the protocol state is not secure since $\mathscr{A}$ can reveal a fresh non
partner oracle, either $\Pi_{A,B}^{i}$ or $\Pi_{B,A}^{j}$, and find the session key accepted by $\Pi_{B,A}^{j}$ or
$\Pi_{A,B}^{i}$ respectively.

It is possible to fix the flawed partner function used in the BR95 model, as shown
below.

Fixed BR95 partner of the initiator oracle.   The first two records of T associated
with queries of the oracle $\Pi_{A,B}^{i}$ are examined. If the first record indicates that
$\Pi_{A,B}^{i}$ had the role of an initiator oracle, was sent a $\mathsf{SendClient}\,(A,B,i,*)$ query
and replied with R_A, and the second record indicates that $\Pi_{A,B}^{i}$'s reply to a
$\mathsf{SendClient}(A,B,i,(\alpha_A,\beta_A))$ was the decision *Accept*, then T is examined to
determine if some server oracle, $\Psi_{A,B}^{k}$ or $\Psi_{B,A}^{k}$, sent a message of the form
(α_A,β_A') for some β_A'. If so, determine if this message was in response to a
$\mathsf{SendServer}(A,B,k,(R_A,R_B))$ or $\mathsf{SendServer}(B,A,k,(R_B,R_A))$ query for some
R_B, and if this is also true, determine if there is a unique j such that an oracle
$\Pi_{B,A}^{j}$ generated a message (R_A',R_B) for any R_A'. If such an oracle $\Pi_{B,A}^{j}$ is found,
then set $f_{A,B}^{i}(T) = j$, meaning that the BR95 partner of $\Pi_{A,B}^{i}$ is $\Pi_{B,A}^{j}$.

Fixed BR95 partner of the responder oracle.   The first two records of T associated
with queries of the oracle $\Pi_{B,A}^{j}$ are examined. If the first record indicates that
$\Pi_{B,A}^{j}$ had the role of a responder oracle, was sent a $\mathsf{SendClient}\,(B,A,j,R_A')$
query and replied with (R_A',R_B), and the second record indicates that $\Pi_{B,A}^{j}$'s
reply to a $\mathsf{SendClient}(B,A,j,(\alpha_B,\beta_B))$ was the decision *Accept*, then T is examined to determine if some server oracle, $\Psi_{A,B}^{k}$ or $\Psi_{B,A}^{k}$, sent a message of the
form (α_B,β_B') for some β_B'. If so, determine if this message was in response to

a $\mathsf{SendServer}(A,B,k,(R_A,R_B))$ or $\mathsf{SendServer}(B,A,k,(R_B,R_A))$ query for some R_A, and if this is also true, determine if there is a unique i such that an oracle $\Pi_{A,B}^i$ generated a message R_A. If such an oracle $\Pi_{A,B}^i$ is found, then set $f_{B,A}^j(T) = i$, meaning that the BR95 partner of $\Pi_{B,A}^j$ is $\Pi_{A,B}^i$.

The only differences between the fixed definition of an initiator's partner and the original definition are that the server may think that the initiator and responder roles are swapped, and that the nonce output by B on behalf of A, R_A', need not be identical to the nonce output by A itself, R_A. The definition of a responder's partner has been made analogous to that of an initiator's partner. Using the fixed partner function in our example execution, $\Pi_{A,B}^i$'s partner is $\Pi_{B,A}^j$ and $\Pi_{B,A}^j$'s partner is $\Pi_{A,B}^i$.

3.2 A Revised 3PKD Protocol in Bellare–Rogaway Model

We now revisit the construction of SIDs in the BPR2000 model and demonstrate that it does not seem possible to define partnership based on SIDs in the 3PKD protocol. We then propose an improvement to the 3PKD protocol with a natural candidate for the SID. Consequently, the protocol is practical in a real world setting.

3.2.1 Defining SIDs in the 3PKD Protocol

Bellare, Pointcheval, and Rogaway [3] suggested that SIDs can be constructed on-the-fly using fresh unique contributions from the communicating participants. Uniqueness of SIDs is necessary since otherwise two parties may share a key but not be BPR2000 partners, and hence the protocol would not be considered secure. Within the 3PKD protocol, the only values that A and B can be sure are unique are R_A and R_B. However, the integrity of only one of R_A and R_B is preserved cryptographically for each party in the protocol. Since the integrity of a SID consisting of R_A and R_B is not preserved cryptographically, attacks such as the one proposed in Chapter 3.1 are possible. An alternative would be to use an externally generated SID, such as a counter, but the use of such a SID would be inconvenient. Hence, it does not seem possible to use SIDs to successfully define partnership in the 3PKD protocol.

3.2.2 An Improved Provably Secure 3PKD Protocol

In order for partnership to be defined using the notion of SIDs in Protocol 3.1, we propose an improvement to the protocol as shown in Protocol 3.2. In Protocol 3.2,

S binds both values composing the session identifier, R_A and R_B, to the session key for each party, using the MAC digests in message flows 3a and 3b.

---

1. $A \longrightarrow B: R_A$
2. $B \longrightarrow S: R_A, R_B$
3a. $S \longrightarrow A: \{SK_{AB}\}_{K_{AS}^{enc}}, [A, B, R_A, R_B, \{SK_{AB}\}_{K_{AS}^{enc}}]_{K_{AS}^{MAC}}, R_B$
3b. $S \longrightarrow B: \{SK_{AB}\}_{K_{BS}^{enc}}, [A, B, R_A, R_B, \{SK_{AB}\}_{K_{BS}^{enc}}]_{K_{BS}^{MAC}}$

Protocol 3.2: An Improved Provably Secure 3PKD Protocol

The primitives used in Protocol 3.2 are the notions of a secure encryption scheme and a secure message authentication scheme described in Chapter 2.1.4.

3.2.3 Security Proof for the Improved 3PKD Protocol

In this section, we present the proof for Protocol 3.2.

Theorem 3.2.1 *Protocol 3.2 is a secure key establishment protocol in the sense of Definition 2.3.7 if the underlying message authentication scheme is secure in the sense of existential unforgeability under adaptive chosen message attack (ACMA) as described in Definition 2.1.16 and the underlying encryption scheme is indistinguishable under chosen plaintext attack (IND-CPA) as described in Definition 2.1.13.*

The proof of Theorem 3.2.1 generally follows that of Bellare and Rogaway [4], but is adjusted to the different partnering function used. The validity of the protocol is straightforward to verify and we concentrate on the indistinguishability requirement.

The security of Protocol 3.2 is proved by finding a reduction to the security of the encryption scheme and the message authentication scheme. Let N_s be the maximum number of sessions between any two parties in the protocol run and N_p be the maximum number of players in the protocol run, where both N_s and N_p are polynomial in the security parameter k. Security is proved by finding a reduction to the security of the underlying message authentication scheme and the underlying encryption scheme.

The general notion of the proof is to assume that there exists an adversary $\mathscr{A}$ who can gain a non-negligible advantage in distinguishing the test key in game $\mathscr{G}$ (i.e., $\mathrm{Adv}^{\mathscr{A}}(k)$ is non-negligible), and use $\mathscr{A}$ to break the underlying encryption scheme or the message authentication scheme. In other words, we consider an adversary $\mathscr{A}$ that breaks the security of the protocol.

Using results of Bellare, Boldyreva and Micali [1], we may allow an adversary against an encryption scheme to obtain encryptions of the same plaintext under different independent encryption keys. Such an adversary is termed a multiple eavesdropper, $\mathcal{ME}$. In Protocol 3.2, upon receiving a message from the responder principal, the server sends out two ciphertexts derived from the encryption of the same plaintext under two independent encryption keys. Hence, we consider a multiple eavesdropper $\mathcal{ME}$ who is allowed to obtain encryptions of the same plaintext under two different independent encryption keys. The formal definition of $\mathcal{ME}$ is given by Definition 3.2.1.

Definition 3.2.1 ([1, 4]) *Let $\Omega = (\mathcal{K}, \mathcal{E}, \mathcal{D})$ be an encryption scheme with security parameter k, $\mathcal{SE}$ be the single eavesdropper and $\mathcal{ME}$ be the multiple eavesdropper, and $\mathcal{O}_{k_A}$ and $\mathcal{O}_{k_B}$ be two different independent encryption oracles associated with encryption keys k_A and k_B. We define the advantage functions of $\mathcal{SE}$ and $\mathcal{ME}$ to be:*

$$Adv^{\mathcal{SE}}(k) = 2 \times Pr[\mathcal{SE} \leftarrow \mathcal{O}_{k_A}; (m_0, m_1 \in_R \mathcal{SE}); \theta \in_R \{0,1\}; \gamma_A \in_R \mathcal{O}_{k_A}(m_\theta)$$
$$: \mathcal{SE}(\gamma_A) = \theta] - 1$$
$$Adv^{\mathcal{ME}}(k) = 2 \times Pr[\mathcal{ME} \leftarrow \mathcal{O}_{k_A}, \mathcal{O}_{k_B}; (m_0, m_1 \in_R \mathcal{ME}); \theta \in_R \{0,1\};$$
$$\gamma_A \in_R \mathcal{O}_{k_A}(m_\theta), \gamma_B \in_R \mathcal{O}_{k_B}(m_\theta) : \mathcal{ME}(\gamma_A, \gamma_B) = \theta] - 1$$

Lemma 3.2.1 ([1]) *Suppose the advantage function of $\mathcal{SE}$ against the encryption scheme is ε_k. Then the advantage function of $\mathcal{ME}$ is at most $2 \times \varepsilon_k$.*

As a consequence of Lemma 3.2.1, an encryption scheme secure against IND-CPA in the single eavesdropper setting will also be secure against IND-CPA in the multiple eavesdropper setting [1].

The proof is divided into two cases since the adversary $\mathcal{A}$ can either gain her advantage against the protocol while forging a MAC digest with respect to some user's MAC key or gain her advantage against the protocol without forging a MAC digest. The proof assumes that there exists an adversary $\mathcal{A}$ who has a non-negligible advantage against the protocol, and shows that this implies that either the encryption scheme or the message authentication scheme is insecure.

3.2.3.1 Adaptive MAC Forger $\mathcal{F}$

Following the approach of Bellare, Kilian and Rogaway [2], we quantify security of the MAC scheme in terms of the probability of a successful MAC forgery under adaptive chosen-message attack, which we denote by $Pr[Succ^{\mathcal{F}}(k)]$. For the MAC scheme to be secure under chosen-message attack, $Pr[Succ^{\mathcal{F}}(k)]$ must be negligible. In other words, the MAC scheme is considered broken if a forger $\mathcal{F}$ is able to produce a valid MAC forgery for a MAC key unknown to it.

For the first part of the proof, assume that at some stage $\mathcal{A}$ asks a SendClient$(B,$

$A, j, (\alpha_{B,j}, \beta_{B,j}))$ query to some fresh oracle, $\Pi_{B,A}^{j}$, such that $\Pi_{B,A}^{j}$ accepts, but the MAC digest value $\beta_{B,j}$ used in the SendClient$(B, A, j, (\alpha_{B,j}, \beta_{B,j}))$ query was not previously output by a fresh oracle. Hence, Pr[MACforgery] is non-negligible. We construct an adaptive MAC forger $\mathscr{F}$ against the security of the message authentication scheme using $\mathscr{A}$. We define an attack game $\mathscr{G}_{\mathscr{F}}$ as follows.

- **Stage 1:** $\mathscr{F}$ is provided permanent access to the MAC oracle $\mathscr{O}_{x'}$ associated with the MAC key x' throughout the game $\mathscr{G}_{\mathscr{F}}$.

  - $\mathscr{F}$ randomly chooses a principal $\overline{U}$, where $\overline{U} \in \{U_1, \ldots, U_{N_p}\}$. $\overline{U}$ is $\mathscr{F}$'s guess at which principal $\mathscr{A}$ will choose for the MAC forgery.
  - $\mathscr{F}$ randomly generates the list of MAC keys for the $\{U_1, \ldots, U_{N_p}\} \setminus \{\overline{U}\}$ principals.
  - $\mathscr{F}$ randomly generates the list of encryption keys of the $\{U_1, \ldots, U_{N_p}\}$ principals.

- **Stage 2:** $\mathscr{F}$ runs $\mathscr{A}$ and answers all oracle queries from $\mathscr{A}$. This can be done in a straightforward manner since $\mathscr{F}$ can respond to all oracle queries from $\mathscr{A}$ as required using the keys chosen in Stage 1 and $\mathscr{O}_{x'}$. In addition, $\mathscr{F}$ records all the MAC digests it receives from $\mathscr{O}_{x'}$. If, during its execution, $\mathscr{A}$ makes an oracle query that includes a forged MAC digest for $\overline{U}$, then $\mathscr{F}$ outputs the MAC forgery as its own, and halts. Otherwise, $\mathscr{F}$ halts when $\mathscr{A}$ halts.

The random choice of $\overline{U}$ by $\mathscr{F}$ means that the probability that $\overline{U}$ is the party for whom $\mathscr{A}$ generates a forgery (if $\mathscr{A}$ generates any forgery at all) is at least $1/N_p$. Hence, the success probability of $\mathscr{F}$ is

$$\Pr[\mathsf{Succ}^{\mathscr{F}}(k)] \geq \frac{\Pr[\mathsf{MACforgery}(k)]}{N_p}.$$

Hence

$$\Pr[\mathsf{MACforgery}] \leq N_p \cdot \Pr[\mathsf{Succ}^{\mathscr{F}}(k)].$$

Since we know that N_p is polynomial in the security parameter k and $\mathsf{Adv}^{\mathscr{F}}(k)$ is negligible by definition of the security of the message authentication scheme, Pr[MACforgery] is also negligible.

3.2.3.2 Multiple Eavesdropper Attacker $\mathscr{ME}$

The second part of the proof assumes that the adversary $\mathscr{A}$ gains her advantage without forging a MAC digest. We construct another algorithm $\mathscr{ME}$ that uses $\mathscr{A}$ against the security of the encryption scheme, whose behaviour is described by the attack game $\mathscr{G}_{\mathscr{ME}}$ shown below and in Figure 3.1. Recall that $\mathscr{ME}$ hands a pair of messages (m_0, m_1) to the challenger and receives $\gamma_A = \mathscr{E}_{k_A}(m_\theta)$ and $\gamma_B = \mathscr{E}_{k_B}(m_\theta)$, which are encryptions under two different keys of one of the messages. The objective of $\mathscr{ME}$ is to correctly predict the challenge bit θ in the game simulation $\mathscr{G}_{\mathscr{ME}}$ (i.e., have $\theta' = \theta$).

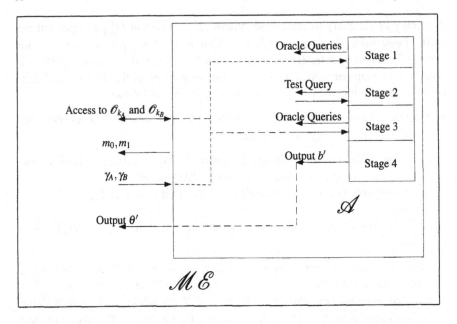

Fig. 3.1 Game $\mathcal{G}_{\mathcal{ME}}$

$\mathcal{ME}$ runs $\mathcal{A}$ to determine whether m_0 or m_1 was encrypted as γ_A and γ_B. By examining all oracle queries made by $\mathcal{A}$, $\mathcal{ME}$ outputs her prediction, θ'. The details of the game $\mathcal{G}_{\mathcal{ME}}$ in Figure 3.1 are explained as follows.

Stage 1: $\mathcal{ME}$ is provided permanent access to two different encryption oracles $\mathcal{O}_{k_A}$ and $\mathcal{O}_{k_B}$ associated with encryption keys k_A and k_B respectively.

Stage 2: $\mathcal{ME}$ chooses a pair of messages (m_0, m_1) of equal length and hands them to the challenger. The challenger then chooses a random challenge bit, θ (i.e., $\theta \in_R \{0, 1\}$), and returns the ciphertexts γ_A and γ_B to $\mathcal{ME}$, where $\gamma_A = \mathcal{E}_{k_A}(m_\theta)$ and $\gamma_B = \mathcal{E}_{k_B}(m_\theta)$. $\mathcal{ME}$ then randomly chooses the following:

- target initiator and responder principals, A and B, where $A, B \in_R \{U_1, \ldots, U_{N_p}\}$,
- target session between A and B whose instance at the server is u (i.e., the session of $\Psi_{A,B}^u$), where $u \in_R \{1, \ldots, N_s\}$,
- list of encryption keys (i.e., $K_{U_i}^{enc}$) for all participants except A and B, and list of MAC keys (i.e., $K_{U_i}^{MAC}$) for all participants.

Stage 3: $\mathcal{ME}$ runs $\mathcal{A}$ to determine whether m_0 or m_1 was encrypted as γ_A and γ_B. By examining all oracle queries made by $\mathcal{A}$, $\mathcal{ME}$ outputs her prediction, θ'. $\mathcal{A}$ makes a series of SendClient$(U_1, U_2, \imath, m)$, SendServer$(U_1, U_2, \imath, m)$, Reveal$(U, \imath)$, and Corrupt(U, K) oracle queries to $\mathcal{ME}$, which can be answered by $\mathcal{ME}$ as explained below. At some point during $\mathcal{G}_{\mathcal{ME}}$, $\mathcal{A}$ makes a Test$(U_1, U_2, \imath)$ query on some fresh oracle (in the sense of Definition 2.3.1), which $\mathcal{ME}$ must also answer.

On receipt of $\mathsf{SendClient}(U_1, U_2, \iota, m)$ queries:

- If U_1 = initiator, U_2 = responder, and $m = *$, then this will start a protocol run. This query can be successfully answered by $\mathscr{ME}$ and the outgoing message is some randomly chosen k-bit challenge R_{U_1}.

- If U_1 = responder, U_2 = initiator, and m is some k-bit challenge R_{U_1}, then $\mathscr{ME}$ will successfully answer with R_{U_1}, R_{U_2}, where R_{U_2} is some randomly chosen k-bit challenge.

- If U_I = initiator, U_R = responder (where $\{U_1, U_2\} = \{U_I, U_R\}$), and the message $m = \{SK_{U_1,U_2,\iota}\}_{K_{U_1}^{enc}}, [U_I, U_R, R_{U_I}, R_{U_R}, \{SK_{U_1,U_2,\iota}\}_{K_{U_1}^{enc}}]_{K_{U_1}^{MAC}}$. Since we assume that $\mathscr{A}$ is not able to produce any MAC forgeries, all session keys (if accepted) are known from the $\mathsf{SendServer}(U_1, U_2, \iota, m)$ queries. Hence, if the MAC digest verifies correctly, the MAC digest must be authentic (i.e., must have been generated by $\mathscr{ME}$ during a SendServer query) and in this case, $\mathscr{ME}$ will output the decision $\delta = accept$. Otherwise, $\mathscr{ME}$ will output the decision $\delta = reject$, as the protocol specification demands.

- If U_I = initiator, U_R = responder where $\{U_1, U_2\} = \{U_I, U_R\}$, and $m \in \{(\gamma_A, [U_I, U_R, R_{U_I}, R_{U_R}, \gamma_A]_{K_{U_1}^{MAC}}), (\gamma_B, [U_I, U_R, R_{U_I}, R_{U_R}, \gamma_B]_{K_{U_1}^{MAC}})\}$.

  $\mathscr{ME}$ will be given γ_A and γ_B as input, and hence known to $\mathscr{ME}$. With the assumption that $\mathscr{A}$ is not able to produce any MAC forgeries, if the MAC digest verifies correctly, then the MAC digest must have been generated by $\mathscr{ME}$ during a SendServer query. In this case, $\mathscr{ME}$ will output the decision $\delta = accept$, otherwise $\mathscr{ME}$ will output the decision $\delta = reject$, as the protocol specification demands.

- In all other cases the input to the SendClient query is invalid, so $\mathscr{ME}$ will randomly choose a bit θ' as its response and hand it to the challenger. Hence, SendClient queries can be correctly answered by $\mathscr{ME}$.

On receipt of $\mathsf{SendServer}(U_1, U_2, \iota, m)$ queries:
Message m must be of the form (R_{U_1}, R_{U_2}), where R_{U_1} and R_{U_2} are some k-bit challenges, otherwise $\mathscr{ME}$ will randomly choose a bit θ' as its response and hand it to the challenger.

- If this is the target session (i.e., $U_1 = A$, $U_2 = B$, and $\iota = u$), then $\mathscr{ME}$ will compute the MAC digest using the respective MAC keys and output $(\gamma_A, [U_1, U_2, R_{U_1}, R_{U_2}, \gamma_A]_{K_A^{MAC}})$ and $(\gamma_B, [U_1, U_2, R_{U_1}, R_{U_2}, \gamma_B]_{K_B^{MAC}})$ to U_1 and U_2 respectively.

- If this is not the target session, $\mathscr{ME}$ will compute the MAC digest using the respective MAC keys and output $(\alpha_{U_1}, [U_1, U_2, R_{U_1}, R_{U_2}, \alpha_{U_1})]_{K_{U_1}^{MAC}})$ and $(\alpha_{U_2}, [U_1, U_2, R_{U_1}, R_{U_2}, \alpha_{U_2})]_{K_{U_2}^{MAC}})$ to U_1 and U_2 respectively, where $\alpha_{U_1} = \mathscr{O}_{k_A}(SK_{U_1,U_2,\iota})$ if $U_1 = A$, $\alpha_{U_1} = \{SK_{U_1,U_2,\iota}\}_{K_{U_1}^{enc}}$ if $U_1 \neq A$, $\alpha_{U_2} = \mathscr{O}_{k_B}(SK_{U_2,U_1,\iota})$ if $U_2 = B$, and $\alpha_{U_2} = \{SK_{U_2,U_1,\iota}\}_{K_{U_2}^{enc}}$ if $U_2 \neq B$.

- In all other cases the input to the SendServer query is invalid, so $\mathcal{ME}$ will randomly choose a bit θ' as its response and hand it to the challenger. Hence, SendServer queries can be correctly answered by $\mathcal{ME}$.

On receipt of $\mathsf{Reveal}(U_1, U_2, \iota)$ queries:

- If $\Pi^\iota_{U_1,U_2}$ has accepted and it forms the target session (i.e., $\{U_1, U_2\} = \{A, B\}$) and the last flow that $\Pi^\iota_{U_1,U_2}$ received had the form (α, β), where $\alpha \in \{\gamma_A, \gamma_B\}$), then $\mathcal{ME}$ will randomly choose a bit θ' as its response and hand it to the challenger.
- If this session has accepted but it is not the target session, then $\mathcal{ME}$ will output the session key $SK_{U_1,U_2,\iota}$, since all session keys are known from the $\mathsf{SendServer}(U_1, U_2, \iota, m)$ queries.
- In all other cases the input to the Reveal query is invalid, so $\mathcal{ME}$ will randomly choose a bit θ' as its response and hand it to the challenger. Hence, Reveal queries can be correctly answered by $\mathcal{ME}$.

On receipt of $\mathsf{Corrupt}(U, K)$ queries:

- If $U \in \{A, B\}$ (i.e., $\mathcal{A}$ is trying to corrupt the initiator or responder principal of the target session), then $\mathcal{ME}$ will randomly choose a bit θ' as its response and hand it to the challenger.
- If $U \in \{U_1, \ldots, U_{N_p}\} \setminus \{A, B\}$, then $\mathcal{ME}$ will hand all internal information for U to $\mathcal{A}$, update U as corrupted and also update K^{enc}_U to be K.

On receipt of $\mathsf{Test}(U_1, U_2, \iota)$ query:

- If this is the target session (i.e., $\{U_1, U_2\} = \{A, B\}$ and the last flow that $\Pi^\iota_{U_1,U_2}$ received had the form (α, β), where $\alpha \in \{\gamma_A, \gamma_B\}$), then $\mathcal{ME}$ will answer the query with m_0, else $\mathcal{ME}$ will randomly choose a bit θ' as its response and hand it to the challenger. After making a Test query and getting an answer of the form $SK_{U_1,U_2,\iota}$ from $\mathcal{ME}$, $\mathcal{A}$ continues interacting with the protocol and eventually outputs a guess bit b', where $b' \in_R \{0, 1\}$. $\mathcal{ME}$ then outputs $\theta' = b'$ as its response and hands it to the challenger.

The random choices of A, B, and u by $\mathcal{ME}$ mean that the probability that the target session is the same as the session that $\mathcal{A}$ chooses as the Test session is $\frac{1}{N_p^2 N_s}$. We claim that if the target session and Test session are the same, and the Test session is fresh, then $\mathcal{ME}$ will succeed whenever $\mathcal{A}$ succeeds and fail whenever $\mathcal{A}$ fails. To see that this is true, suppose $\Pi^i_{A,B}$ and $\Pi^j_{B,A}$ receive γ_A and γ_B and both accept. If $\mathcal{A}$ attempts to reveal either of these oracles, then neither will be considered fresh. This can be seen since the valid MAC digests mean that both oracles have the same SID, and the random generation of both components of the SID implies that no other (honest) party will have accepted with the same SID, and thus $\Pi^i_{A,B}$ and $\Pi^j_{B,A}$ are partners (since it is easy to verify that the other partnership requirements are also met). We also observe that no other oracle apart from $\Pi^i_{A,B}$ and $\Pi^j_{B,A}$ accepts after receiving γ_A and γ_B since only one server instance outputs a valid MAC digest for this pair of ciphertexts, and this server instance only outputs a valid MAC digest for one pair of nonces.

It is easy to verify that when the target session and Test session are different, or when the Test session is not fresh, $\mathcal{ME}$ outputs a random bit, so has probability of $\frac{1}{2}$ of succeeding. Hence, $\mathcal{ME}$'s success probability is given by

$$\Pr[Succ^{\mathcal{ME}}(k)] = \frac{N_p^2 N_s - 1}{2N_p^2 N_s} + \frac{\Pr[b' = b|\overline{\text{MACforgery}}]}{N_p^2 N_s}$$

$$= \frac{N_p^2 N_s - 1}{2N_p^2 N_s} + \frac{(\text{Adv}^{\mathcal{A}}(k)|\overline{\text{MACforgery}}) + 1}{2N_p^2 N_s}$$

$$2 \cdot \Pr[Succ^{\mathcal{ME}}(k)] - 1 = \frac{N_p^2 N_s - 1}{N_p^2 N_s} + \frac{(\text{Adv}^{\mathcal{A}}(k)|\overline{\text{MACforgery}}) + 1}{N_p^2 N_s} - 1$$

$$\text{Adv}^{\mathcal{ME}}(k) = \frac{(\text{Adv}^{\mathcal{A}}(k)|\overline{\text{MACforgery}})}{N_p^2 N_s}$$

$$(\text{Adv}^{\mathcal{A}}(k)|\overline{\text{MACforgery}}) = N_p^2 N_s \cdot \text{Adv}^{\mathcal{ME}}(k) \quad ,$$

where $\Pr[b' = b|\overline{\text{MACforgery}}]$ is the probability that $\mathcal{A}$ succeeds given that $\mathcal{A}$ does not make any MAC forgeries and $(\text{Adv}^{\mathcal{A}}(k)|\overline{\text{MACforgery}})$ is the advantage of $\mathcal{A}$ given that $\mathcal{A}$ does not make any MAC forgeries. Since we know that both N_p and N_s are polynomial in the security parameter k and $\text{Adv}^{\mathcal{ME}}(k)$ is negligible by definition of the security of the encryption scheme, $(\text{Adv}^{\mathcal{A}}(k)|\overline{\text{MACforgery}})$ is also negligible.

3.2.3.3 Conclusion of Proof

The proof concludes by observing that:

$$\text{Adv}^{\mathcal{A}}(k) = (\text{Adv}^{\mathcal{A}}(k)|\text{MACforgery}) \times \Pr[\text{MACforgery}]$$

$$+ (\text{Adv}^{\mathcal{A}}(k)|\overline{\text{MACforgery}}) \times \Pr[\overline{\text{MACforgery}}]$$

$$\leq \Pr[\text{MACforgery}] + (\text{Adv}^{\mathcal{A}}(k)|\overline{\text{MACforgery}})$$

Hence, $\text{Adv}^{\mathcal{A}}(k)$ is negligible when the encryption scheme and message authentication scheme in use are secure against IND-CPA and secure against existential forgery under adaptive chosen-message attack respectively, and therefore the improved 3PKD protocol is also secure.

3.3 Summary

By making a small change to the 3PKD protocol we have allowed session identifiers (SIDs) to be defined in a natural way. This makes the improved protocol a more useful tool for practical applications since we have provided a simple way to identify which secure session key should be used on which communication channel. At the same time we would argue that the resulting definition of partnering is more intuitive, and consequently we believe that our proof of security is more straightforward than the one presented by Bellare and Rogaway in their original paper.

As a result of our findings in this chapter, we would recommend that all provably secure protocols should use partnering definitions based on SIDs. This situation is common for two-party protocols [3, 5, 6]; even if a session identifier is not explicitly used in the security definition, one can easily be defined from the fresh inputs of each principal.

References

1. Mihir Bellare, A. Boldyreva & Silvio Micali 2000. Public-key Encryption in a Multi-User Setting: Security Proofs and Improvements, in Bart Preneel (ed), Proceedings of Advances in Cryptology – EUROCRYPT 2000. Lecture Notes in Computer Science 1807/2000: 259 - 274
2. Mihir Bellare, Joe Kilian & Phillip Rogaway 2000. The Security of the Cipher Block Chaining Message Authentication Code. *Journal of Computer and System Sciences* 61(3): 362-399
3. Mihir Bellare, David Pointcheval & Phillip Rogaway 2000. Authenticated Key Exchange Secure Against Dictionary Attacks, in Bart Preneel (ed), Proceedings of Advances in Cryptology - EUROCRYPT 2000. Lecture Notes in Computer Science 1807/2000: 139 - 155
4. Mihir Bellare & Phillip Rogaway 1995. Provably Secure Session Key Distribution: The Three Party Case, in F. Tom Leighton & Allan Borodin (eds), Proceedings of 27th ACM Symposium on the Theory of Computing - ACM STOC 1995. ACM Press: 57–66
5. Simon Blake-Wilson & Alfred Menezes 1998. Authenticated Diffie–Hellman Key Agreement Protocols, in Stafford E Tavares & Henk Meijer (eds), Proceedings of Selected Areas in Cryptography - SAC 1998. Lecture Notes in Computer Science 1556/1998: 339-361
6. Ran Canetti & Hugo Krawczyk 2001. Analysis of Key-Exchange Protocols and Their Use for Building Secure Channels, in Birgit Pfitzmann (ed), Proceedings of Advances in Cryptology - EUROCRYPT 2001. Lecture Notes in Computer Science 2045/2001: 453–474. Extended version available from http://eprint.iacr.org/2001/040/
7. William Stallings 2003. *Data and Computer Communications – 7th Edition*. Prentice Hall
8. The Internet Engineering Task Force 1971. *RFC 0147 Definition of a Socket*. http://www.ietf.org/rfc/rfc0147.txt?number=0147
9. The Internet Engineering Task Force 1971. *RFC 0204 Sockets in Use*. http://tools.ietf.org/html/rfc204

Chapter 4
On The Key Sharing Requirement

The definitions of security in the Bellare–Rogaway and CK2001 models have two basic requirements; namely:

1. two parties who have completed matching sessions (i.e., partners) are required to accept the same session key, which we term a key sharing requirement, and
2. the key secrecy requirement (also known as implicit key authentication as described in Chapter 2.2.2.1) whereby no adversary or anyone other than the legitimate parties involved will learn about the session key at the end of a protocol run.

Although the key sharing requirement seems straight-forward, there are actually a number of possible variants of this requirement. We identify several variants of the key sharing requirement in this chapter.

We also revisit Protocol 3.1 and the authenticated key exchange protocol $\mathscr{TS}2$ due to Jeong, Katz, and Lee [15]. Protocol 3.1 was proven secure in the BR95 model and subsequently Tin, Boyd, and González Nieto [19] provided a claimed proof of security for the same protocol in the CK2001 model. Protocol $\mathscr{TS}2$ carries a claimed proof of security in the BR93 model, but uses a different definition of partnership than that given in the original model description.

We reveal previously unknown flaws in these protocols. We demonstrate that both protocols violate the definition of security in the CK2001 and BR93 models respectively. The attack we present on the 3PKD protocol proven secure by Tin, Boyd, and González Nieto is similar to the attack on the Otway–Rees key establishment protocol [16] revealed by Fabrega, Herzog, and Guttman [13]. It was shown that a malicious adversary is able to make the initiator and the responder agree on a different session key by asking a trusted third party, the server, to create multiple session keys in response to the same message. We present a new 3PKD protocol as an improvement with a proof of security in the Canetti and Krawczyk (2001) model and a simple improvement to the specification of protocol $\mathscr{TS}2$.

Material presented in this chapter has appeared in the following publication:

- Kim-Kwang Raymond Choo and Yvonne Hitchcock. Security Requirements for Key Establishment Proof Models: Revisiting Bellare–Rogaway and Jeong–Katz–Lee Protocols. In Colin Boyd and Juan Manuel González Nieto, editors, 10th Australasian Conference on Information Security and Privacy - ACISP 2005, volume 3574/2005 of Lecture Notes in Computer Science, pages 429–442. Springer-Verlag, 2005. [Received the Best Student Paper award]

4.1 Bellare–Rogaway 3PKD Protocol in CK2001 Model

In this section, we demonstrate that the 3PKD protocol is insecure in the CK2001 model, contradicting the claim by Tin, Boyd, and González Nieto [19]. We point out that the existing proof breaks down because the uniqueness of session identifiers (SIDs) is not ensured. We then describe the MAC-based MT-authenticator [8], and protocol AM-3PKD proven secure in the AM [19]. By applying the MT-authenticator on protocol AM-3PKD, we obtain a new provably-secure 3PKD protocol in the CK2001 model.

4.1.1 The 3PKD Protocol

Similarly to Protocol 3.1 described in Chapter 3.1.1, Protocol 4.1 involves three parties, a trusted server S and two principals A and B.

$$A \qquad\qquad S \qquad\qquad B$$

$$R_A \in_R \{0,1\}^k \xrightarrow{A,R_A} \quad \xleftarrow{B,R_B} \quad R_B \in_R \{0,1\}^k$$

Randomly generate SK_{AB}

$$\alpha_a = \{SK_{AB}\}_{K_{AS}^{enc}}$$
$$\beta_a = [A,B,R_A,\alpha_a]_{K_{AS}^{MAC}}$$
$$\alpha_b = \{SK_{AB}\}_{K_{BS}^{enc}}$$
$$\beta_b = [A,B,R_B,\alpha_b]_{K_{BS}^{MAC}}$$
$$\xleftarrow{\alpha_a,\beta_a} \quad \xrightarrow{\alpha_b,\beta_b}$$

Decrypt α_a Decrypt α_b

If β_a verifies true, then   If β_b verifies true, then

Accept SK_{AB} Accept SK_{AB}

Protocol 4.1: 3PKD protocol proven secure by Tin, Boyd, and González Nieto

- Protocol 4.1 begins by having A randomly select a k-bit challenge, R_A, where k is the security parameter. A then sends it to B with whom she desires to communicate.

- Upon receiving the message R_A from A, B also randomly selects a k-bit challenge R_B and sends R_B together with R_A as a message (R_A, R_B) to the server S.

- Upon receiving the message (R_A, R_B) from B, S runs the session key generator to obtain a session key SK_{AB}, which has not been used before. S then encrypts SK_{AB} with K_{AS}^{enc} and K_{BS}^{enc} to obtain ciphertexts α_A and α_B, and computes the MAC digests β_A and β_B of the strings $(A, B, R_A, \{SK_{AB}\}_{K_{AS}^{enc}})$ and $(A, B, R_B, \{SK_{AB}\}_{K_{BS}^{enc}})$ under the keys K_{AS}^{MAC} and K_{BS}^{MAC} respectively. S then sends messages (α_A, β_A) and (α_B, β_B) to A and B respectively.

4.1.2 New Attack on 3PKD Protocol

Attack 4.1 depicts an example execution of Protocol 4.1 in the presence of a malicious adversary $\mathscr{A}$. Let $\mathscr{A}_U$ denote $\mathscr{A}$ impersonating some user U. At the end of

Attack 4.1: Execution of Protocol 4.1 in the presence of a malicious adversary

Attack 4.1, both uncorrupted principals A and B have matching sessions according to Definition 2.3.10. However, A and B have accepted different session keys, SK_{AB} and $SK_{AB,2}$, in violation of Definition 2.3.11.

Tin, Boyd, and González Nieto [19] suggest that SIDs can be constructed on the fly using unique contributions from both the initiator and the responder (i.e., $sid_A = (R_A, R_B)$ and $sid_B = (R_A, R_B)$ respectively). However, we show that the current construction of SIDs does not guarantee uniqueness, which invalidates the existing proof. Our observation supports our earlier findings in Chapter 3 that it does not seem possible to define a unique SID in Protocol 4.1.

4.1.3 A New Provably-Secure 3PKD Protocol in CK2001 Model

A possible solution to prevent Attack 4.1 is to require the server to store every message processed and not issue different session keys for the same input message received. This is similar to the approach taken by Backes [2] in his proof of security for the Otway–Rees protocol in the cryptographic library [3, 4], which has a provably secure cryptographic implementation. We argue, however, that this assumption only works well within a confined implementation and will not scale well to a more realistic environment with a large number of participating parties and a substantial level of traffic to any one server.

Another possible solution would be to introduce two extra messages for key confirmation. This would ensure that both parties have assurance that the other (partner) party is able to compute the same session key. However, this would increase the computational load of both the initiator and the responder.

We present an improved provably-secure protocol in the CK2001 model by applying the Canetti–Krawczyk MAC-based MT-authenticator to the Tin–Boyd–González Nieto protocol AM-3PKD [19]. Figure 4.1 describes the MAC-based MT-authenticator [8].

$$
\begin{array}{lcr}
A & & B \\
& \xleftarrow{\quad N_B \quad} & \text{Choose nonce } N_B \\
\text{Choose message } m & \xrightarrow{\ m,\,[B,N_B,m]K_{AB}^{MAC}\ } &
\end{array}
$$

Fig. 4.1 Canetti–Krawczyk MAC-based MT-authenticator

Protocol 4.2 describes the protocol AM-3PKD which is proven secure in the AM.

$$
\begin{array}{ccc}
A & S & B \\
& \text{Randomly generate } SK_{AB} & \\
& \alpha_a = \{SK_{AB}\}_{K_{AS}^{enc}} & \\
\text{Decrypt } \alpha_a \xleftarrow{\ sid,\alpha_a,B\ } & \alpha_b = \{SK_{AB}\}_{K_{BS}^{enc}} & \xrightarrow{\ sid,\alpha_b,A\ } \text{Decrypt } \alpha_b
\end{array}
$$

Protocol 4.2: Tin–Boyd–González Nieto protocol AM-3PKD

Protocol 4.3 describes the resultant UM protocol[1].

---

[1] Protocol 4.3 is included in a submission to the IEEE 802.11, The Working Group Setting the Standards for Wireless LANs, by Agre, Chen, Refaei, Sonalker, Zhu, and Yuan [1] and in another

$$A \qquad\qquad\qquad S \qquad\qquad\qquad B$$

$$R_A \in_R \{0,1\}^k \quad \xrightarrow{\quad A, R_A \quad} \qquad \xleftarrow{\quad B, R_B \quad} \quad R_B \in_R \{0,1\}^k$$

$$\text{Randomly generate } SK_{AB}$$

$$R_S \in_R \{0,1\}^k$$

$$\alpha_A = \{SK_{AB}\}_{K_{AS}^{enc}}$$

$$\beta_A = [A, B, R_A, R_B, R_S, \alpha_A]_{K_{AS}^{MAC}}$$

$$\alpha_B = \{SK_{AB}\}_{K_{BS}^{enc}}$$

$$\beta_B = [A, B, R_A, R_B, R_S, \alpha_B]_{K_{BS}^{MAC}}$$

Decrypt α_a $\xleftarrow{\quad A, \alpha_A, \beta_A, R_B, R_S \quad}$ $\xrightarrow{\quad B, \alpha_B, \beta_B, R_A, R_S \quad}$ Decrypt α_b

If β_a verifies true, then   If β_b verifies true, then

$$SK_{AB} \qquad sid_A = (R_A, R_B, R_S) = sid_B \qquad SK_{AB}$$

Protocol 4.3: A new provably-secure 3PKD protocol in the CK2001 (UM)

In Protocol 4.3, S generates a random nonce R_S each time a session key is generated. R_S is sent along with the associated session key to both A and B and with the contributions of both A and B (i.e., R_A and R_B). Within Protocol 4.3, the only values that A and B can be sure are unique are R_A, R_B, and R_S. SIDs are constructed using these values and the uniqueness of SIDs is ensured.

Informally, Attack 4.1 is no longer valid, since a new nonce is generated each time a new session key is generated. Note that there is a subtle difference between Protocol 4.3 and Protocol 3.2. In the solution described by Protocol 3.2, S does not generate a random nonce R_S each time a session key is generated. Attack 4.1, therefore, is still valid against Protocol 3.2. Protocol 3.2 is, however, secure in the BPR2000 model, since the BPR2000 partnership (i.e., Definition 2.3.6) requires two parties to have matching SIDs, agreeing PIDs, and the same session key in order to be partners. In the context of our attack, the two oracles are not BPR2000 partners. The BPR2000 security, therefore, is not violated. A detailed discussion is presented in Chapter 5.1.5.

Table 4.1 presents a comparison of the computational loads between Protocol 4.3 and three similar server-based three-party key establishment protocols, namely the Yahalom protocol [7], the Bauer–Berson–Feiertag protocol [5] and the Otway-Rees protocol [16]. We observe that the three other protocols are unable to satisfy the key share requirement in the presence of a malicious adversary (without making some "impractical" assumption – requiring the server to store every message processed and not issuing different session keys for the same message). From Table 4.1, we also observe that the computational load of Protocol 4.3 is comparable to those of

independent submission to The Internet Engineering Task Force (IETF) / Network Working Group [14].

the other protocols, yet provides a tighter definition of security (i.e., secure in the sense of Definitions 2.3.3 and 2.3.11).

Computational Operation	Protocol 4.3			Yahalom protocol [7] / Otway-Rees protocol [16] / Bauer–Berson–Feiertag protocol [5]		
	A	B	S	A	B	S
Encryption and Decryption	1	1	2	2/2/1	3/2/1	3/4/2
MAC generation	0	0	2	0	0	0
Messages	4					
Proof of Security	Yes			No, except for the Otway-Rees protocol.		
Security Goal	KSR2			KSR1		

Table 4.1 Comparison of the computational loads

4.2 Jeong–Katz–Lee Protocol $\mathscr{JL}2$

In this section, we describe protocol $\mathscr{JL}2$ [15]. We demonstrate how protocol $\mathscr{JL}2$ is insecure in the BR93 model with an example execution of protocol $\mathscr{JL}2$. We then present an improvement to the protocol specification.

4.2.1 Protocol $\mathscr{JL}2$

Protocol 4.4 describes protocol $\mathscr{JL}2$, which uses a different partnering function described in Definition 4.2.1.

Definition 4.2.1 (Modified Definition of Partnership) *Two oracles, $\Pi_{A,B}^i$ and $\Pi_{B,A}^j$, are partners if, and only if, they have agreed on the same set of principals (i.e., the initiator and the responder of the protocol), and no other oracles besides $\Pi_{A,B}^i$ and $\Pi_{B,A}^j$ have accepted with the same SID.*

Both the initiator and responder principals, A and B, are assumed to have a public/private key pair (P_A, S_A) and (P_B, S_B) respectively. At the end of Protocol 4.4's execution, both A and B accept with the session key $SK_{AB} = \mathscr{H}_0(A||B||sid||g^{R_A R_B}||g^{S_A S_B}) = SK_{BA}$.

$A\,(P_A,S_A)$		$B\,(P_B,S_B)$
$R_A \in_R \mathbb{Z}_q$	$\xrightarrow{\;g^{R_A}\;}$	$R_B \in_R \mathbb{Z}_q$
$sid_A = g^{R_A}\|g^{R_B}$	$\xleftarrow{\;g^{R_B}\;}$	$sid_B = g^{R_A}\|g^{R_B}$

Protocol 4.4: Jeong–Katz–Lee protocol $\mathcal{JL}2$

4.2.2 New Attack on Protocol $\mathcal{JL}2$

Attack 4.2 describes the execution of Protocol 4.4 in the presence of a malicious adversary $\mathcal{A}$, where $\mathcal{A}$ intercepts both messages and sends fabricated messages $g^{R_A}\|1$ and $1\|g^{R_B}$ to both B and A respectively.

$A\,(P_A,S_A)$		$\mathcal{A}$		$B\,(P_B,S_B)$
$R_A \in_R \mathbb{Z}_q$	$\xrightarrow{\;g^{R_A}\;}$		$\xleftarrow{\;g^{R_B}\;}$	$R_B \in_R \mathbb{Z}_q$
$sid_A = g^{R_A}\|1\|g^{R_B}$	$\xleftarrow{\;1\|g^{R_B}\;}$		$\xrightarrow{\;g^{R_A}\|1\;}$	$sid_B = g^{R_A}\|1\|g^{R_B}$

Attack 4.2: Execution of Protocol 4.4 in the presence of a malicious adversary

At the end of Attack 4.2, both A and B have accepted with $sid_A = g^{R_A}\|1\|g^{R_B} = sid_B$. According to Definition 4.2.1, both $\Pi_{A,B}^{sid_A}$ and $\Pi_{B,A}^{sid_B}$ are partners since they have accepted with the same SID and $PID(A) = B$ and $PID(B) = A$. Both $\Pi_{A,B}^{sid_A}$ and $\Pi_{B,A}^{sid_B}$, however, have accepted with different session keys

$$SK_{AB} = \mathcal{H}_0(A\|B\|sid_A\|(1\|g^{R_B})^{R_A}\|g^{S_A S_B})$$
$$SK_{BA} = \mathcal{H}_0(A\|B\|sid_B\|(g^{R_A}\|1)^{R_B}\|g^{S_A S_B})$$
$$\neq SK_{AB},$$

in violation of Requirement 2 in Definition 2.3.3.

4.2.3 An Improved Protocol $\mathcal{JL}2$

A simple solution to prevent Attack 4.2 is to include validity checking of the received messages by the recipient, as shown in Protocol 4.5. Let $BL(\cdot)$ denote the bit length of some message.

The validity checking ensures that the messages received by each party are in the group and that the bit lengths of the messages received by each party are correct.

$$A\ (P_A, S_A) \qquad\qquad\qquad B\ (P_B, S_B)$$
$$R_A \in_R \mathbb{Z}_q \qquad\qquad\qquad R_B \in_R \mathbb{Z}_q$$

Zero pad g^{R_A} to $\lceil log_2(p-1) \rceil$ bits

$$\xrightarrow{\quad g^{R_A} \quad}$$

$2 \le g^{R_A} \le p-1, (g^{R_A})^q \ne 1, BL(g^{R_A}) \overset{?}{=} \lceil log_2(p-1) \rceil$

Zero pad g^{R_B} to $\lceil log_2(p-1) \rceil$ bits

$$\xleftarrow{\quad g^{R_B} \quad}$$

$2 \le g^{R_B} \le p-1, (g^{R_B})^q \ne 1, BL(g^{R_B}) \overset{?}{=} \lceil log_2(p-1) \rceil$

$$sid_A = g^{R_A}||g^{R_B} \qquad\qquad sid_B = g^{R_A}||g^{R_B}$$
$$SK_{AB} = \mathcal{H}_0(A||B||sid_A||g^{R_A R_B}||g^{S_A S_B}) = SK_{BA}$$

Protocol 4.5: An improved Protocol 4.4

Informally, the attack outlined in Attack 4.2 will no longer be valid since the fabricated messages sent by the adversary will fail the validity check.

We may speculate that if the protocol designers fail to spot this inadequacy in the specification of their protocols, the protocol implementers are also highly unlikely to spot this inadequacy. Flaws in security protocol proofs or protocol specifications themselves certainly will have a damaging effect on the credibility of provably-secure protocols in the real world [18].

4.3 The Key Sharing Requirement

The key sharing requirement varies between the Bellare–Rogaway and CK2001 models. In this section, we identify four possible variants of the key sharing requirement, KSR1 to KSR4, as shown in Table 4.2.

Fabrega, Herzog, and Guttman [13] have also observed the ambiguity surrounding key sharing requirements (which they term key authentication) in the context of the Otway–Rees protocol. Although they did not see this as a serious flaw, they did highlight the lack of understanding of the protocol and the need to identify exactly what goals a protocol achieves.

KSR1 is a completeness requirement, which ensures that a key establishment protocol is behaving correctly. We advocate that KSR2 is a practical functional requirement and, depending on the individual implementation, the KSR2 requirement can be as important as the key secrecy requirement. Consider the scenario of a real world implementation of a key establishment protocol that does not provide the KSR2 requirement: two partners, after completing matching sessions, are unable to share the same session key. From the protocol implementers' perspectives, the usefulness (or

Variant		Required in
KSR1	Two communicating parties completing matching sessions in the *absence* of a malicious adversary accept the same session key.	BR95 model.
KSR2	Two communicating parties completing matching sessions in the *presence* of a malicious adversary accept the same session key.	BR93, BPR2000, CK2001 models.
KSR3	One party is assured that a second (possibly unidentified) party *is able to compute* a particular secret session key.	Optional in any of the BR93, BR95, BPR2000, or CK2001 models.
KSR4	One party is assured that a second (possibly unidentified) party *actually has possession of* a particular secret session key.	Unlikely to be achieved in the Bellare–Rogaway and CK2001 models.

Table 4.2 Variants of key sharing requirement

practicality) of such a key establishment protocol will be questionable.

KSR3 is a weaker version of KSR4, where KSR4 is the key confirmation goal described in Chapter 2.2.2.1. KSR4 is generally not achievable in the setting of the indistinguishability-based proof approach for protocols for the following reason.

- In order for one party, A, to be assured that a second (possibly unidentified) party, B, actually has possession of the secret session key, A would need to send to B some information derived from the key, such as the encryption of some message with the secret session key, as shown in Protocol 4.6 (i.e., the Yahalom protocol [7]).

In Protocol 4.6, we observe that B is assured that A actually has possession of the same secret session key, $SK_{AB}{}^2$ since A encrypts the nonce chosen by B, N_B, with the session key, SK_{AB}.
- Recall that security in the indistinguishability-based BR93, BR95, BPR2000, and CK2001 models is defined using a game simulation, $\mathcal{G}$, played between the adversary, $\mathcal{A}$, and a collection of player oracles, as described in Chapter 2.3.3. Success of $\mathcal{A}$ in $\mathcal{G}$ is quantified in terms of $\mathcal{A}$'s advantage in distinguishing whether $\mathcal{A}$ receives a real key or a random value from the game simulator.
- However, in the context of the proof simulation, $\mathcal{A}$ can ask a Send query using the test session key obtained from a Test query, and determine whether the test session key it was given (by the simulator) was real or a random value.
- Such information, consequently, renders Protocol 4.6 insecure as $\mathcal{A}$ will have a non-negligible advantage in distinguishing the Test key received from the game simulator.

---

[2] We observe that protocols proposed using an automated tool search in the computer security approach [9, 11, 12, 10, 17] usually provide key confirmation in this fashion – KSR4 shown in Table 4.2.

1. $A \rightarrow B : N_A$
2. $B \rightarrow S : B, \{A, N_A, N_B\}_{K_{BS}^{enc}}$
3. $S \rightarrow A : \{B, SK_{AB}, N_A, N_B\}_{K_{AS}^{enc}}, \{A, SK_{AB}\}_{K_{BS}^{enc}}$
4. $A \rightarrow B : \{A, SK_{AB}\}_{K_{BS}^{enc}}, \{N_B\}_{SK_{AB}}$

Protocol 4.6: Yahalom protocol

Recommendation. We recommend that the proof models should allow different options for the key sharing requirement in their formulation. KSR2, a practical and functional requirement, is the minimum requirement as it ensures both parties who have completed matching sessions in the presence of a malicious adversary to accept the same session key. Furthermore, protocols proven secure in such a model must indicate which variant of the key sharing requirement is satisfied.

4.4 Summary

A detailed study of the 3PKD protocol of Bellare and Rogaway [6] and protocol $\mathscr{TS}2$ of Jeong, Katz, and Lee [15] was made. We demonstrated that both protocols fail to achieve the key sharing requirement in the presence of a malicious adversary, in violation of the definition of security in their respective models.

As an improvement, we presented a new 3PKD protocol with a proof of security in the CK2001 model. A comparison with three existing three-party server-based protocols reveals that the computational load of our new 3PKD protocol is no more than that of the three other protocols, yet ensures that a stronger version of the key sharing requirement is satisfied. The improved 3PKD protocol is included in a submission to the IEEE 802.11, the working group setting the standards for wireless LANs [1] and in another independent submission to The Internet Engineering Task Force (IETF) / Network Working Group [14]. We also proposed a simple improvement to the specification of protocol $\mathscr{TS}2$ and identified four possible variants of the key sharing requirement.

As a result of this work, we would recommend that the proof models for key establishment protocols allow the various options of the key sharing requirement, depending on the individual needs of the protocol implementations and applications.

References

1. Jonathan Agre, Wei-Peng Chen, Mohammed Refaei, Anuja Sonalker, Chenxi Zhu & Xun Yuan 2005. Secure NOmadic Wireless Mesh (SnowMesh). Submission to the IEEE 802.11, The Working Group Setting the Standards for Wireless LANs.

`http://www.flacp.fujitsulabs.com/publications.html`

2. Michael Backes 2004. A Cryptographically Sound Dolev-Yao Style Security Proof of the Needham–Schroeder–Lowe Public–Key Protocol. *IEEE Journal on Selected Areas in Communications* 22(10): 2075–2086

3. Michael Backes 2004. A Cryptographically Sound Dolev-Yao Style Security Proof of the Otway-Rees Protocol, in Samarati P & Gollmann D (eds), Proceedings of 9th European Symposium on Research in Computer Security - ESORICS 2004. Lecture Notes in Computer Science 3193/2004: 89–108

4. Michael Backes, Birgit Pfitzmann & Michael Waidner 2003. A Composable Cryptographic Library with Nested Operations, in *Proceedings of 10th ACM Conference on Computer and communications Security - ACM CCS 2003*. ACM Press: 220–230

5. R. K. Bauer, Thomas A. Berson & Richard J. Feiertag 1983. A Key Distribution Protocol Using Event Markers. *ACM Transactions on Computer Systems* 1(3): 249–255

6. Mihir Bellare & Phillip Rogaway 1995. Provably Secure Session Key Distribution: The Three Party Case, in F. Tom Leighton & Allan Borodin (eds), Proceedings of 27th ACM Symposium on the Theory of Computing - ACM STOC 1995. ACM Press: 57–66

7. Michael Burrows, Martín Abadi & Roger Needham 1990. A Logic of Authentication. *ACM Transactions on Computer Systems* 8(1): 18–36

8. Ran Canetti & Hugo Krawczyk 2001. Analysis of Key-Exchange Protocols and Their Use for Building Secure Channels, in Birgit Pfitzmann (ed), Proceedings of Advances in Cryptology - EUROCRYPT 2001. Lecture Notes in Computer Science 2045/2001: 453–474. Extended version available from `http://eprint.iacr.org/2001/040/`

9. Hao Chen, John A. Clark & Jeremy L. Jacob 2003. Automated Design of Security Protocols, in *Proceedings of Congress on Evolutionary Computation - CEC 2003*. IEEE Computer Society Press: 2181–2188

10. Hao Chen, John A. Clark & Jeremy L. Jacob 2004. Synthesising Efficient and Effective Security Protocols, in Alessandro Armando and Luca Viganó (eds), Proceedings of 2nd International Joint Conference on Automated Reasoning – ARSPA 2004. Electronic Notes in Theoretical Computer Science 125(1): 25–41

11. John A. Clark & Jeremy L. Jacob 2000. Searching for a Solution: Engineering Tradeoffs and the Evolution of Provably Secure Protocols, in *Proceedings of IEEE Symposium on Security and Privacy 2000*. IEEE Computer Society Press: 82–95

12. John A. Clark & Jeremy L. Jacob 2001. Protocols are Programs too: The Meta-Heuristic Search for Security Protocols. *Information & Software Technology* 43(14): 891–904

13. F. Javier Thayer Fabrega, Jonathan C. Herzog & Joshua D. Guttman 1999. Strand Spaces: Proving Security Protocols Correct. *Journal of Computer Security* 7(2/3): 191–230

14. Dan Harkins, Yoshihiro Ohba, Madjid Nakhjiri & Rafael Marin Lopez 2007. Problem Statement and Requirements on a 3-Party Key Distribution Protocol for Handover Keying. Submission to The Internet Engineering Task Force (IETF) / Network Working Group. Available from `http://tools.ietf.org/html/draft-ohba-hokey-3party-keydist-ps-01`

15. Ik Rae Jeong, Jonathan Katz & Dong Hoon Lee 2004. One-Round Protocols for Two-Party Authenticated Key Exchange, in Markus Jakobsson, Moti Yung & Jianying Zhou (eds), Proceedings of Applied Cryptography and Network Security - ACNS 2004. Lecture Notes in Computer Science 3089/2004: 220–232

16. Dave Otway & Owen Rees 1987. Efficient and Timely Mutual Authentication. *ACM Operating Systems Review* 21(1): 8–10

17. Adrian Perrig & Dawn Song 2000. Looking for Diamonds in the Desert: Extending Automatic Protocol Generation to Three-Party Authentication and Key Agreement Protocols, in *Proceedings of 13th IEEE Computer Security Foundation Workshop - CSFW 2000*. IEEE Computer Society Press: 64–76

18. Jacques Stern, David Pointcheval, John Malone-Lee & Nigel Smart 2002. Flaws in Applying Proof Methodologies to Signature Schemes, in Moti Yung (ed), Proceedings of Advances in Cryptology - CRYPTO 2002. Lecture Notes in Computer Science 2442/2002: 93–110

19. Yiu Shing Terry Tin, Colin Boyd & Juan Manuel González Nieto 2003. Provably Secure Key Exchange: An Engineering Approach, Proceedings of Australasian Information Security Workshop Conference on ACSW Frontiers 2003. Conferences in Research and Practice in Information Technology 21: 97–104

Chapter 5
Comparison of Bellare–Rogaway and Canetti–Krawczyk Models

In the previous chapters, we studied the Bellare–Rogaway and Canetti–Krawczyk models. We revealed the flawed BR95 partnership function and identified four possible variants of the key sharing requirement in the Bellare–Rogaway and Canetti–Krawczyk models. A natural progression will be to study the Bellare–Rogaway and Canetti–Krawczyk models in more detail and compare their features.

In this chapter, we identify several variants of these proof models and several subtle differences between these variants and models. These differences have a significant impact on the security of the models and are presented as follows.

1: The way partner oracles are defined.   Security in the models depends on the notions of partnership of oracles and indistinguishability of session keys. The BR93 model defines partnership using the notion of matching conversations, where a conversation is a sequence of messages exchanged between some instances of communicating oracles in a protocol run. Partnership in the BR95 model is defined using the notion of a partner function, which uses the transcript (the record of all Send oracle queries) to determine the partner of an oracle by providing a mapping between two oracles that should share a secret key on completion of the protocol execution. However, such a partner definition can easily go wrong. One such example is the partner function described in the original BR95 paper for the 3PKD protocol [4], which was later found to be flawed as described in Chapter 3.

The BPR2000 model and the CK2001 model define partnership using the notion of session identifiers (SIDs). Although in the BPR2000 model, the construction of SIDs is suggested to be the concatenation of messages exchanged during the protocol run, protocol designers can construct SIDs differently. There is no formal definition of how SIDs should be defined in the CK2001 model. Instead, SIDs are defined to be some unique values agreed upon by two communicating parties prior to the protocol execution. We observe that the way SIDs are constructed can have an impact on the security of the protocol in the model.

2: The powers of the probabilistic, polynomial-time (PPT) adversary.   The CK2001 model enjoys the strongest adversarial power (compared to the Bellare–Rogaway models) as the adversary is allowed to ask the Session-State Reveal query that will return all the internal state (including any ephemeral parameters but not long-term secret parameters) of the target session to the adversary. In contrast, most models only allow the adversary to reveal session keys for uncorrupted parties. In the original BR93 and BPR2000 models, the Corrupt query is not allowed. This restricts the adversary from corrupting any principal at will, and hence the adversary is unable to learn the internal state of the corrupted principal.

In this chapter, we consider the BR93 model which allows the adversary access to a Corrupt query as explained in Chapter 2.3.1. However, we consider the original BPR2000 model without Corrupt query because the basic notion of BPR2000 freshness restricts the adversary, $\mathscr{A}$, from corrupting anyone in the model (i.e., effectively restricting $\mathscr{A}$ from asking any Corrupt query) as described in Chapter 2.3.2. However, we show that the omission of such a (Corrupt) query in the BPR2000 model allows an insecure protocol to be proven secure in the model.

3: The modular approach adopted in the CK2001 model.   A major advantage of the CK2001 model is its modular approach whereby protocols may be proven secure in an ideal world (AM) model in which the passive adversary is prevented from fabricating messages coming from uncorrupted principals, and translating such a protocol proven secure in the AM into one that is secure in the more realistic real world model (the UM). As Boyd, Mao, and Paterson [5] have pointed out, the CK2001 modular approach facilitates an engineering approach to protocol design, where protocol components may be combined by "mix and match" to tailor to the application at hand. Such a mix and match approach is analogous to a Java API library.

4: The provable security goals provided by the models.   Both the BR93 and BPR2000 models provide provable security for entity authentication & key distribution, whilst the BR95 model provides provable security for only the key distribution. Intuitively, protocols that provide both entity authentication and key distribution are "stronger" than protocols that provide only key distribution. In this chapter, we refer to the BR93 and BPR2000 models that provide provable security for only key distribution as BR93 (KE) and BPR2000 (KE) respectively, and the BR93 and BPR2000 models that provide provable security for both entity authentication & key distribution as BR93 (EA+KE) and BPR2000 (EA+KE) respectively. To the best of our knowledge, no distinction has ever been made between the Bellare–Rogaway model and its variants shown in Figure 5.1.

We are motivated by the observations that no formal study has been devoted to the comparisons of relations and relative strengths of security between the Bellare–Rogaway and Canetti–Krawczyk models. Although Shoup [8] provides a brief discussion on the Bellare–Rogaway models and the Canetti–Krawczyk model, his discussion is restricted to an informal comparison between the Bellare–Rogaway model and his model, and between the Canetti–Krawczyk model and his model.

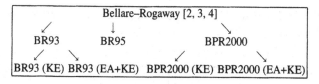

Fig. 5.1 The proof models and their variants

This work may ease the understanding of future security protocol proofs (protocols proven secure in one model may be automatically secure in another model), and protocol designers can make an informed decision when choosing an appropriate model in which to prove their protocols secure. Our main results are summarized in Figures 5.2 and 5.3.

The notation $x \rightarrow y$ (or $y \leftarrow x$) denotes that protocols proven secure in model x will also be secure in model y (i.e., implication relation where x implies y), $x \nrightarrow y$ (or $y \nleftarrow x$) denotes that protocols proven secure in model x do not necessarily satisfy the definition of security in model y. The numbers on the arrows represent the section in which the proof is provided, and the numbers in brackets on the arrows represent the sections in which the implication relation is proven.

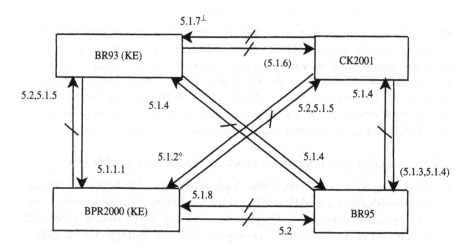

$\diamond$ holds if SIDs are constructed in the same manner in both models.
$\perp$ holds if SIDs are not defined to be the concatenation of messages exchanged during the protocol run.

Fig. 5.2 Notions of security

We observe that if SIDs in the CK2001 model are defined to be the concatenation of messages exchanged during the protocol run, then the implication CK2001 $\rightarrow$ BR93 holds, and the CK2001 model offers the strongest definition of security compared to the BR93 model.

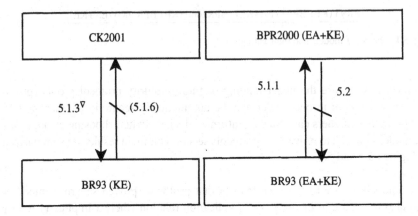

∇ holds if SIDs are defined to be the concatenation of messages exchanged during the protocol run.

Fig. 5.3 Additional comparisons

The proofs of the implication relations and counter-examples for non-implication relations shown in Figures 5.2 and 5.3 are presented in Chapter 5.1. In these counter-examples, we demonstrate that these protocols though secure in the existing proof model (in which they are proven secure) are insecure in another "stronger" proof model. Chapter 5.2 presents the drawback in the original formulation of the BPR2000 model by using a three-party password-based key exchange protocol (3PAKE) due to Abdalla and Pointcheval [1] as a case study.

Material presented in this chapter has appeared in the following publication:

- Kim-Kwang Raymond Choo, Colin Boyd, and Yvonne Hitchcock. Examining Indistinguishability-Based Proof Models for Key Establishment Protocols. In Bimal Roy, editor, Advances in Cryptology - Asiacrypt 2005, volume 3788/2005 of Lecture Notes in Computer Science, pages 585–604, Springer-Verlag, 2005.

5.1 Relating The Notions of Security

In our proofs for each of the implication relations shown in Figure 5.2, we construct a primary adversary, $\mathscr{P\!A}$, against the key establishment protocol in $\mathscr{P\!A}$'s model using a secondary adversary, $\mathscr{S\!A}$, against the same key establishment protocol in $\mathscr{S\!A}$'s model. $\mathscr{P\!A}$ simulates the view of $\mathscr{S\!A}$ by asking all queries of $\mathscr{S\!A}$ to the respective Send, Session-Key Reveal, Session-State Reveal, Corrupt, and Test oracles (to which $\mathscr{P}\mathscr{A}$ has access), and forwards the answers received from the oracles to $\mathscr{S}\mathscr{A}$. The specification of the simulation is given below.

Send. $\mathscr{P}\mathscr{A}$ is able to answer this query pertaining to any instance of a server or player by asking its Send oracle.

Session-Key Reveal. $\mathscr{P}\mathscr{A}$ is restricted from asking a Session-Key Reveal query to the target test oracle or its partner in its own game. Similarly, $\mathscr{S}\mathscr{A}$ faces the same restriction[R]. Hence, $\mathscr{P}\mathscr{A}$ is able to answer this query by asking its Reveal oracle and is able to simulate the Session-Key Reveal query perfectly.

Corrupt. $\mathscr{S}\mathscr{A}$ is disallowed from asking a Corrupt query to the principal of the target test session or whom the target test session thinks it is communicating with in its own game. Similarly, the $\mathscr{P}\mathscr{A}$ faces the same restriction. Hence, $\mathscr{P}\mathscr{A}$ is able to answer this query by asking its Corrupt oracle and simulates the Corrupt query perfectly.

Test.   If the following conditions are satisfied (under the assumption that both $\mathscr{P}\mathscr{A}$ and $\mathscr{S}\mathscr{A}$ choose the same Test session), then $\mathscr{P}\mathscr{A}$ queries its Test oracle. The Test oracle randomly chooses a bit, b_{Test}, and depending on b_{00}, the Test oracle either returns the actual session key or a random key. $\mathscr{P}\mathscr{A}$ then answers $\mathscr{S}\mathscr{A}$ with the answer received from its Test oracle. Let b_{SA} be the final output of $\mathscr{S}\mathscr{A}$, and $\mathscr{P}\mathscr{A}$ will output b_{SA} as its own answer. $\mathscr{P}\mathscr{A}$ succeeds and wins the game if $\mathscr{S}\mathscr{A}$ does.

The Test sessions in both $\mathscr{P}\mathscr{A}$'s and $\mathscr{S}\mathscr{A}$'s simulations have accepted, and must be fresh.

- Since $\mathscr{P}\mathscr{A}$ is able to answer all Send, Session-Key Reveal, and Corrupt queries asked by $\mathscr{S}\mathscr{A}$ as shown above, if the Test session in $\mathscr{S}\mathscr{A}$'s simulation has accepted, so does the same Test session in $\mathscr{P}\mathscr{A}$'s simulation.
- Since $\mathscr{P}\mathscr{A}$ faces the same restriction as $\mathscr{S}\mathscr{A}$ of not being able to reveal or corrupt an oracle or principal associated with the Test session, if the Test session in $\mathscr{S}\mathscr{A}$'s simulation is fresh, so is the same Test session in $\mathscr{P}\mathscr{A}$'s simulation.

The restrictions denoted as $\mathscr{R}$ are as follows:

$\mathscr{R}1$.   Non-partners in the simulation of $\mathscr{S}\mathscr{A}$ are also non-partners in the simulation of $\mathscr{P}\mathscr{A}$ so that whatever we can reveal in the simulation of $\mathscr{S}\mathscr{A}$, we can also reveal in the simulation of $\mathscr{P}\mathscr{A}$. Alternatively, we require that partners in the simulation of $\mathscr{P}\mathscr{A}$ are also partners in the simulation of $\mathscr{S}\mathscr{A}$ so that whatever we cannot reveal in the simulation of $\mathscr{P}\mathscr{A}$, we also cannot reveal in the simulation of $\mathscr{S}\mathscr{A}$.

$\mathscr{R}2$.   A fresh oracle in the simulation of $\mathscr{S}\mathscr{A}$ is also a fresh oracle the simulation of $\mathscr{P}\mathscr{A}$ so that whatever we cannot reveal in the simulation of $\mathscr{S}\mathscr{A}$, we also cannot reveal in the simulation of $\mathscr{P}\mathscr{A}$.

Note that Shoup [8, Remark 26] pointed out that an adversary $\mathscr{A}$ in the Bellare–Rogaway model wins the game if $\mathscr{A}$ is able to make two partner oracles accept different session keys without making any Reveal and Test queries. His findings are applicable to only the BR93 and CK2001 models where the definitions of security requires two partner oracles to accept with the same session key, as described in Definitions 2.3.3 and 2.3.11 respectively. However, this is not the case for the BR95 and BPR2000 models.

5.1.1 Proving BR93 (EA+KE) → BPR2000 (EA+KE)

Recall that the Corrupt query is not allowed in the BPR2000 model but is allowed in the BR93 model as shown in Table 2.3. Informally, the model with a greater adversarial power, especially one that allows the adversary access to the entire internal state of a player via the Corrupt query, has a tighter definition of security than the model with a weaker adversarial power.

5.1.1.1 Proof for the key establishment goal

Let the advantage of some probabilistic, polynomial time adversary, $\mathscr{A}_{00}$, in the BPR2000 (EA+KE) model be $\mathrm{Adv}^{\mathscr{A}_{00}}$, and the advantage of some probabilistic, polynomial time adversary, $\mathscr{A}_{93}$, in the BR93 (EA+KE) model be $\mathrm{Adv}^{\mathscr{A}_{93}}$.

Lemma 5.1.1 *For any key establishment protocol, for any $\mathscr{A}_{00}$, there exists an $\mathscr{A}_{93}$, such that* $\mathrm{Adv}^{\mathscr{A}_{00}} = \mathrm{Adv}^{\mathscr{A}_{93}}$.

An adversary $\mathscr{A}_{93}$ against the key establishment protocol in the BR93 (EA+KE) model is constructed using an adversary $\mathscr{A}_{00}$ against the same key establishment protocol in the BPR2000 (EA+KE) model. In other words, let $\mathscr{A}_{93}$ be the primary adversary and $\mathscr{A}_{00}$ be the secondary adversary where $\mathscr{A}_{93}$ simulates the view of $\mathscr{A}_{00}$. $\mathscr{A}_{93}$ asks all queries by $\mathscr{A}_{00}$ to the respective Send oracles, Session-Key Reveal oracles, and Test oracle (to which $\mathscr{A}_{93}$ has access), and forwards the answers received from the oracles to $\mathscr{A}_{00}$. Eventually, $\mathscr{A}_{00}$ outputs a guessed bit b_{00} and $\mathscr{A}_{93}$ will output b_{00} as its own answer. $\mathscr{A}_{93}$ succeeds and wins the game if $\mathscr{A}_{00}$ does.

In order to demonstrate that the primary adversary, $\mathscr{A}_{93}$, is able to answer the queries asked by the secondary adversary, $\mathscr{A}_{00}$, we need to satisfy $\mathscr{R}1$ and $\mathscr{R}2$. Using the example protocol execution shown in Figure 5.4, B is said to have a matching conversation with A if, and only if, message m'_A received is the same message m_A sent by A, and A is said to have matching conversation (in the BR93 model) with B if, and only if, message m'_B received is the same message m_B sent by B. In the context of Figure 5.4, $sid_A = m_A || m'_B$ and $sid_B = m'_A || m_A$ (in the BPR2000 model), and $sid_A = sid_B$ if message m'_A received by B is the same message m_A sent by A, and message m'_B received by A is the same message m_B sent by B. Hence, if both A and B have matching conversations, then $sid_A = m_A || m'_B = m'_A || m_A = sid_B$. If A and B are BR93-secure protocols, then A and B will also accept with the same session key.

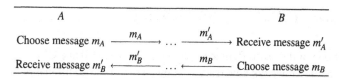

Fig. 5.4 An example protocol execution

Recall that the BPR2000 definition of partnership requires two oracles to accept with the same SID, corresponding PID, and the same key, in order to be considered partners. Now, if A and B do not have matching conversations, then A and B are not BR93 partners. This also implies that A and B are not BPR2000 partners since $sid_A \neq sid_B$. Since non-partners in the simulation of the secondary adversary, $\mathscr{A}_{00}$, are also non-partners in the simulation of the primary adversary, $\mathscr{A}_{93}$, $\mathscr{R}1$ is satisfied.

An oracle is considered fresh in the BPR2000 model if it (or its associated partner, if such a partner exists) has not been asked a Reveal query. An oracle is considered fresh in the BR93 model if it (or its associated partner, if such a partner exists) has not been asked either a Reveal or a Corrupt query. It follows easily that a fresh oracle in the BPR2000 model is also fresh in the BR93 model. Both $\mathscr{R}1$ and $\mathscr{R}2$, therefore, are satisfied.

To analyse $\mathrm{Adv}^{\mathscr{A}_{93}}$, we first consider the case in which the Test oracle associated with $\mathscr{A}_{93}$ returns a random key. The probability of $\mathscr{A}_{00}$ guessing the correct b_{00} bit is $\frac{1}{2}$ since it cannot gain any information about the hidden b_{93} bit. We then consider the case where the Test oracle associated with $\mathscr{A}_{93}$ returns the actual session key. In this case, the proof simulation of $\mathscr{A}_{00}$ is perfect and $\mathscr{A}_{93}$ runs $\mathscr{A}_{00}$ exactly in the game defining the security of $\mathscr{A}_{00}$. Therefore, if $\mathscr{A}_{00}$ has a non-negligible advantage, so does $\mathscr{A}_{93}$. This is in violation of our assumption and Lemma 5.1.1 follows.

5.1.1.2 Proof for the entity authentication goal

By inspection of Definitions 2.3.3 and 2.3.7, the definitions for entity authentication in both the BR93 and BPR2000 models are equivalent. Entity authentication is said to be violated if some fresh oracle terminates with no partner. Following from our earlier proofs in Chapter 5.1.1.1, we define $\mathscr{A}_{93}$ to simulate the view of $\mathscr{A}_{00}$; that is, $\mathscr{A}_{93}$ does anything that $\mathscr{A}_{00}$ does. Since non-partners in the simulation of $\mathscr{A}_{00}$ are also non-partners in the simulation of $\mathscr{A}_{93}$, therefore if $\mathscr{A}_{00}$ has a non-negligible probability in violating mutual authentication, so does $\mathscr{A}_{93}$. This is in violation of our assumption. The proof for entity authentication follows.

5.1.2 Proving CK2001 → BPR2000 (KE)

Recall that one of the key differences between the BPR2000 and CK2001 models is that the Canetti–Krawczyk adversary is allowed to ask the additional Session-State Reveal and Corrupt queries, as shown in Table 2.3. Intuitively, the model with a greater adversarial power has a tighter definition of security than the model with a weaker adversarial power. To support our observation, let the advantage of some probabilistic, polynomial time adversary in the BPR2000 (KE) model be $\mathrm{Adv}^{\mathscr{A}_{00KE}}$, and the advantage of some probabilistic, polynomial time adversary in the CK2001 model be $\mathrm{Adv}^{\mathscr{A}_{01}}$.

Lemma 5.1.2 *For any key establishment protocol and for any $\mathscr{A}_{00KE}$, there exists an $\mathscr{A}_{01}$, such that* $\mathrm{Adv}^{\mathscr{A}_{00KE}} = \mathrm{Adv}^{\mathscr{A}_{01}}$.

An adversary $\mathscr{A}_{01}$ against the security of a key establishment protocol in the CK2001 (UM) model is constructed using an adversary $\mathscr{A}_{01}$ against the security of the same key establishment protocol in the BPR2000 (EA+KE) model. The primary adversary, $\mathscr{A}_{01}$, runs the secondary adversary, $\mathscr{A}_{00KE}$, and has access to its Send oracles, Session-State Reveal oracles, Session-Key Reveal oracles, Corrupt oracles, and Test oracle.

Recall that we assume in Figure 5.2 that this relation holds if, and only if, SIDs for both the BPR2000 (KE) and CK2001 model are constructed in the same manner. If A and B are BPR2000 partners, then $sid_A = sid_B$ and A and B will also be partners in the CK2001 model, since $sid_A = sid_B$ implies that both A and B will have matching sessions. Hence, all CK2001 partners are also BPR2000 partners under the assumption that SIDs for both the BPR2000 (KE) and CK2001 model are constructed in the same manner. All partners of CK2001-secure protocols are also BPR2000 partners (recall that in CK2001 security as described in Definition 2.3.11, two partners within a secure protocol must accept the same session key). This implies $\mathscr{R}1$ is satisfied.

An oracle is considered fresh in the BPR2000 model if it (or its associated partner, if such a partner exists) has not been asked a Reveal query and an oracle is considered fresh in the CK2001 model if it (or its associated partner, if such a partner exists) has not been asked either a Reveal or a Corrupt query. Hence, it follows easily that a fresh oracle in the BPR2000 model is also fresh in the CK2001 model. Hence, both $\mathscr{R}1$ and $\mathscr{R}2$ are satisfied.

To analyse $\mathrm{Adv}^{\mathscr{A}_{01}}$, we first consider the case in which the Test oracle associated with $\mathscr{A}_{01}$ returns a random key. The probability of $\mathscr{A}_{00KE}$ guessing the correct b_{01} bit is $\frac{1}{2}$ since it cannot gain any information about the hidden b_{01} bit. We then consider the case where the Test oracle associated with $\mathscr{A}_{01}$ returns the actual session key. In this case, the proof simulation of $\mathscr{A}_{00KE}$ is perfect and $\mathscr{A}_{01}$ runs $\mathscr{A}_{00KE}$ exactly in the game defining the security of $\mathscr{A}_{00KE}$. Therefore, if $\mathscr{A}_{00KE}$ has a non-negligible advantage, so does $\mathcal{A}_{01}$. In other words, if such an adversary, $\mathcal{A}_{00KE}$, exists, so does $\mathcal{A}_{01}$. This is in violation of our assumption and Lemma 5.1.2 follows.

5.1.3 Proving CK2001 → BR93 (KE)

Recall that one of the key differences between the BR93 and CK2001 models is that the BR93 adversary is not allowed to ask any Session-State Reveal query whilst the CK2001 adversary is allowed to ask such a query, as shown in Table 2.3. Intuitively, the model with a greater adversarial power, especially one that allows the adversary access to the internal state of player oracles (i.e., Session-State Reveal query), has a tighter definition of security than the model with a weaker adversarial power.

This proof follows on from Chapter 5.1.2. Let the advantage of some probabilistic, polynomial time adversary in the BR93 (KE) model, $\mathcal{A}_{93KE}$, be $\text{Adv}^{\mathcal{A}_{93KE}}$.

Lemma 5.1.3 *For any key establishment protocol and for any $\mathcal{A}_{93KE}$, there exists an $\mathcal{A}_{01}$, such that $\text{Adv}^{\mathcal{A}_{93KE}} = \text{Adv}^{\mathcal{A}_{01}}$.*

We construct an adversary $\mathcal{A}_{01}$ against the security of a key establishment protocol in the CK2001 model using an adversary $\mathcal{A}_{93KE}$ against the security of the same key establishment protocol in the BR93 model. Since we assume that SIDs in the CK2001 model are defined to be the concatenation of messages exchanged during the protocol run (similar to how SIDs are defined in the proof that appears in Chapter 5.1.1), the discussion on the notion of partnership between the BPR2000 and BR93 models applies to the discussion on the notion of partnership between the CK2001 and BR93 models. Hence, all BR93 partners are also CK2001 partners, and all CK2001 partners are also BR93 partners (under the assumption that SIDs in the CK2001 model are defined to be the concatenation of messages sent and received during the protocol execution). Therefore, $\mathcal{A}_{01}$ is able to simulate the view of $\mathcal{A}_{93KE}$. Note that since $\mathcal{A}_{93KE}$ is not allowed to ask any Session-State Reveal in the BR93 model, $\mathcal{A}_{93KE}$ will not be asking any such queries in the simulation.

To analyse $\text{Adv}^{\mathcal{A}_{01}}$, we first consider the case in which the Test oracle associated with $\mathcal{A}_{01}$ returns a random key. The probability of $\mathcal{A}_{93KE}$ guessing the correct b_{01} bit is $\frac{1}{2}$ since it cannot gain any information about the hidden b_{01} bit. We then consider the case where the Test oracle associated with $\mathcal{A}_{01}$ returns the actual session key. In this case, the proof simulation of $\mathcal{A}_{93}$ is perfect and $\mathcal{A}_{01}$ runs $\mathcal{A}_{93KE}$ exactly in the game defining the security of $\mathcal{A}_{93KE}$. If $\mathcal{A}_{93KE}$ has a non-negligible advantage, so does $\mathcal{A}_{01}$ (i.e., $\text{Adv}^{\mathcal{A}_{01}} = \text{Adv}^{\mathcal{A}_{93KE}}$ is also negligible), which in violation of our assumption. Lemma 5.1.3 follows.

5.1.4 BR93 (KE) → BR95 and BR93 (KE), CK2001 ↤ BR95

In key establishment protocols proven secure in the BR93 and CK2001 models, two parties in the same session must accept the same session key in the presence of a malicious adversary (i.e., KSR2 in Table 4.2). However, such a requirement is not required in the BPR2000 and the BR95 models. Consider the scenario of an example execution of a BR95 provably-secure protocol in the presence of a malicious adversary that resulted in two partner oracles accepting different session keys. This scenario does not violate BR95 security as described in Definition 2.3.5. This protocol, therefore, is still secure in the BR95 model. When two partner oracles, however, accept two different session keys, both the BR93 security and the CK2001 security are violated. In other words, KSR2 described in Table 4.2 is not satisfied. This same protocol, therefore, is not secure in the BR93 (KE) and CK2001 models. One such example protocol is the Bellare–Rogaway 3PKD protocol proven secure in the BR95 model [4], described in Protocol 3.1.

Attack 5.1 depicts an example execution of Protocol 3.1 in the presence of a malicious adversary. At the end of Attack 5.1, both uncorrupted principals A and B accept different session keys, SK_{AB} and $SK_{AB,2}$. Both A and B, however, are BR93 partners since they have matching conversations. The BR93 security is violated since A and B accept different session keys. Protocol 3.1, therefore, is not secure in the BR93 model.

Similarly, CK2001 security is violated in the sense of Definition 2.3.11. Both uncorrupted principals A and B have matching sessions, according to Definition 2.3.10, but accept different session keys, SK_{AB} and $SK_{AB,2}$. Protocol 3.1, therefore, is also not secure in the CK2001 model.

---

1. $A \longrightarrow B: \quad R_A$
2. $B \longrightarrow S: \quad R_A, R_B$
3a. $S \longrightarrow A: \quad \{SK_{AB}\}_{K_{AS}^{enc}}, [A, B, R_A, R_B, \{SK_{AB}\}_{K_{AS}^{enc}}]_{K_{AS}^{MAC}}, R_B$
3b. $S \longrightarrow B: \quad \{SK_{AB}\}_{K_{BS}^{enc}}, [A, B, R_A, R_B, \{SK_{AB}\}_{K_{BS}^{enc}}]_{K_{BS}^{MAC}}$

    $\mathscr{A}$ intercepts and deletes $\{SK_{AB}\}_{K_{BS}^{enc}}, [A, B, R_B, \{SK_{AB}\}_{K_{BS}^{enc}}]_{K_{BS}^{MAC}}$.

2. $\mathscr{A}_B \longrightarrow S: \quad R_A, R_B$
3a. $S \longrightarrow A: \quad \{SK_{AB,2}\}_{K_{AS}^{enc}}, [A, B, R_A, R_B, \{SK_{AB,2}\}_{K_{AS}^{enc}}]_{K_{AS}^{MAC}}, R_B$

    $\mathscr{A}$ intercepts and deletes $\{SK_{AB,2}\}_{K_{AS}^{enc}}, [A, B, R_A, \{SK_{AB,2}\}_{K_{AS}^{enc}}]_{K_{AS}^{MAC}}, R_B$.

3b. $S \longrightarrow B: \quad \{SK_{AB,2}\}_{K_{BS}^{enc}}, [A, B, R_A, R_B, \{SK_{AB,2}\}_{K_{BS}^{enc}}]_{K_{BS}^{MAC}}$

Attack 5.1: Execution of Protocol 3.1 in the presence of a malicious adversary

The attack we present on Protocol 3.1 is similar to the attack on the Otway–Rees key establishment protocol revealed by Fabrega, Herzog, and Guttman [7]. It was shown that a malicious adversary is able to make the initiator and the responder agree on a different session key by asking a trusted third party (i.e., server) to create multiple session keys in response to the same message. Although Fabrega, Herzog, and Guttman were perhaps the first to reveal that two communicating parties in a protocol might not agree on the same key in the presence of a malicious adversary, they did not see this as a serious flaw. This, however, is a flaw in the BR93 and CK2001 models where the definitions of security require two partner oracles to accept with the same session key, as explained in Chapter 4.

5.1.5 BR93 (KE) / CK2001 ↮ BPR2000 (KE)

As a counter-example, we revisit and use Protocol 3.2 which has a proof of security in the BPR2000 (KE) model. We then demonstrate that Protocol 3.2 fails to satisfy KSR2 described in Chapter 4. Therefore, Protocol 3.2 is also insecure in the BR93 (KE) and CK2001 models.

Attack 5.2 depicts an example execution of Protocol 3.2 in the presence of a malicious adversary. At the end of Attack 5.2, both uncorrupted prinicpals A and B have matching sessions according to Definition 2.3.10. However, they have accepted different session keys (i.e., A accepts session key SK_{AB} and B accepts session key $SK_{AB,2}$). This violates Definitions 2.3.3 and 2.3.11 which implies that Protocol 3.2 is not secure under the BR93 (KE) and the CK2001 models. According to Definition 2.3.6 however, both A and B are not BPR2000 partners since they do not agree on the same session key and, hence, the protocol does not violate the BPR2000 security (i.e., Definition 2.3.7).

---

1. $A \longrightarrow B: \ R_A$

2. $B \longrightarrow S: \ R_A, R_B$

3a. $S \longrightarrow A: \ \{SK_{AB}\}_{K_{AS}^{enc}}, [A, B, R_A, R_B, \{SK_{AB}\}_{K_{AS}^{enc}}]_{K_{AS}^{MAC}}, R_B$

3b. $S \longrightarrow B: \ \{SK_{AB}\}_{K_{BS}^{enc}}, [A, B, R_A, R_B, \{SK_{AB}\}_{K_{BS}^{enc}}]_{K_{BS}^{MAC}}$

   $\mathscr{A}$ intercepts and deletes $\{SK_{AB}\}_{K_{BS}^{enc}}, [A, B, R_B, \{SK_{AB}\}_{K_{BS}^{enc}}]_{K_{BS}^{MAC}}$.

2. $\mathscr{A}_B \longrightarrow S: R_A, R_B$

3a. $S \longrightarrow A: \ \{SK_{AB,2}\}_{K_{AS}^{enc}}, [A, B, R_A, R_B, \{SK_{AB,2}\}_{K_{AS}^{enc}}]_{K_{AS}^{MAC}}, R_B$

   $\mathscr{A}$ intercepts and deletes $\{SK_{AB,2}\}_{K_{AS}^{enc}}, [A, B, R_A, \{SK_{AB,2}\}_{K_{AS}^{enc}}]_{K_{AS}^{MAC}}$.

3b. $S \longrightarrow B: \ \{SK_{AB,2}\}_{K_{BS}^{enc}}, [A, B, R_A, R_B, \{SK_{AB,2}\}_{K_{BS}^{enc}}]_{K_{BS}^{MAC}}$

Attack 5.2: Execution of Protocol 3.2 in the presence of a malicious adversary

5.1.6 CK2001 ↮ BR93 (EA+KE)

We use the mutual authentication and key establishment protocol (MAKEP) due to Wong and Chan [9], which was proven secure in the BR93 (EA+KE) model. There are two communicating principals in MAKEP, namely the server B and the client of limited computing resources, A. A and B are each assumed to know the public key of the other party. At the end of Protocol 5.1's execution, both A and B accept with session keys $SK_{AB} = \mathcal{H}(\sigma) = SK_{BA}$.

$$A\ (a, g^a) \qquad\qquad\qquad\qquad B\ (SK_B, PK_B)$$
$$r_A \in_R \{0,1\}^k, x = \{r_A\}_{PK_B}$$
$$b \in_R \mathbb{Z}_q \setminus \{0\}, \beta = g^b \quad \xrightarrow{\ Cert_A, \beta, x\ } \quad \text{Decrypt } x$$
$$\sigma = (r_A \oplus r_B) \qquad\qquad\qquad\qquad r_B \in \{0,1\}^k$$
$$ID_B, y = a\mathcal{H}(\sigma) + b \bmod q \quad \xleftarrow{\ \{r_B, ID_B\}_{r_A}\ } \quad g^y \overset{?}{=} (g^a)^{\mathcal{H}(\sigma)} \beta$$
$$SK_{AB} = \mathcal{H}(\sigma) \qquad \xrightarrow{\quad y \quad} \quad SK_{BA} = \mathcal{H}(\sigma)$$

Protocol 5.1: Wong–Chan MAKEP

Attack 5.3 depicts an example execution of Protocol 5.1 in the presence of a malicious adversary, $\mathcal{A}$.

- The adversary, $\mathcal{A}$, intercepts the message sent by A and sends a fabricated message, $Cert_{\mathcal{A}}, \beta \cdot g^e, x$, claiming the message originated from itself ($\mathcal{A}$).
- Upon receiving the message, B thinks that $\mathcal{A}$ (and not A) wants to establish a session and will respond as per protocol specification.
- $\mathcal{A}$ is then able to send a Session-State Reveal query to B, and knows the values of both r_A and r_B.

Subsequently, A completes the protocol execution and accepts session-key, $SK_{AB} = \mathcal{H}(\sigma_A)$, thinking that the key is being shared with B, when in fact, B knows nothing about this session. Since $\mathcal{A}$ obtains the values of r_B, $\mathcal{A}$ is able to compute $\mathcal{H}(r_A \oplus r_{\mathcal{A}})||ID_B) = SK_{AB}$, in violation of the key establishment goal (i.e., Definition 2.3.11).

Hence, Protocol 5.1 though secure in the BR93 (EA+KE) model, is insecure in the CK2001 model.

5.1.7 BR93 (KE) ↤ CK2001

Canetti and Krawczyk prove the basic Diffie–Hellman protocol secure in the UM [6]. In order to prove BR93 (KE) ↤ CK2001, we modified the (Canetti–Krawczyk) Diffie–Hellman protocol to include a redundant nonce N_{BA}, as shown in Protocol 5.2. The modified Diffie–Hellman protocol does not authenticate the redundant nonce N_{BA}. Although N_{BA} is not authenticated, addition of N_{BA} does not affect the security of the protocol.

$$A \qquad\qquad \mathscr{A} \qquad\qquad B$$

$$\xrightarrow{\quad Cert_A,\beta,x \quad} \text{Fabricate} \qquad\qquad\qquad \xrightarrow{\quad Cert_{\mathscr{A}},\beta\cdot g^e,x \quad}$$

$$\xleftarrow{\quad \{r_B,ID_B\}_{r_A} \quad} \text{Intercept} \qquad\qquad\qquad \xleftarrow{\quad \{r_B,ID_B\}_{r_A} \quad}$$

$$\xrightarrow{\qquad\qquad} \text{Session} - \text{State Reveal}$$

$$\xleftarrow{\quad \{r_{\mathscr{A}},ID_B\}_{r_A} \quad} \text{Fabricate} \qquad\qquad\qquad \xleftarrow{\quad r_A,r_B \quad}$$

$$\sigma_A = (r_A \oplus r_{\mathscr{A}})||ID_B$$
$$y = a\mathscr{H}(\sigma_A)+b \bmod q$$
$$SK_{AB} = \mathscr{H}(\sigma_A) \xrightarrow{\quad y \quad}$$
$$SK_{AB} = \mathscr{H}(\sigma_A) \text{ with knowledge of } r_A \text{ and } r_{\mathscr{A}}$$

Attack 5.3: Execution of Protocol 5.1 in the presence of a malicious adversary

$$A \qquad\qquad\qquad\qquad\qquad\qquad\qquad\qquad B$$

$$x \in \mathbb{Z}_q \qquad \xrightarrow{\quad A,sid,g^x \quad} \qquad y \in \mathbb{Z}_q$$

$$\text{Verify Signature} \xleftarrow{\quad B,sid,g^y,Sig_{d_B}(B,sid,g^y,g^x,A),N_{BA} \quad} \quad y,N_{BA} \in \mathbb{Z}_q$$

$$SK_{AB} = g^{xy} \xrightarrow{\quad A,sid,g^y,Sig_{d_A}(A,sid,g^y,g^x,B),N_{BA} \quad} SK_{AB} = g^{xy}$$

Protocol 5.2: A modified (Canetti–Krawczyk) Diffie–Hellman protocol

Attack 5.4 depicts an example execution of Protocol 5.2 in the presence of a malicious adversary. Recall that we assume that the non-implication relation: BR93 (KE) $\nleftarrow$ CK2001 holds if, and only if, SIDs in the CK2001 model are not defined to be the concatenation of messages exchanged during the protocol run, as shown in Figure 5.2. Let $\mathscr{A}_U$ denote $\mathscr{A}$ intercepting the message and sending a fabricated message impersonating U.

$$A \qquad\qquad\qquad\qquad\qquad \mathscr{A} \qquad\qquad\qquad\qquad\qquad B$$

$$\xrightarrow{\quad A,sid,g^x \quad} \qquad\qquad\qquad\qquad \xrightarrow{\quad A,sid,g^x \quad}$$

$$\xleftarrow{B,sid,g^y,Sig_{d_B}(B,sid,g^y,g^x,A),N_{\mathscr{A}}} \;\Big|\; \mathscr{A}_A \;\Big|\; \xleftarrow{B,sid,g^y,Sig_{d_B}(B,sid,g^y,g^x,A),N_{BA}}$$

$$\xrightarrow{A,sid,g^y,Sig_{d_A}(A,sid,g^y,g^x,B),N_{\mathscr{A}}} \;\Big|\; \mathscr{A}_B \;\Big|\; \xrightarrow{A,sid,g^y,Sig_{d_A}(A,sid,g^y,g^x,B),N_{BA}}$$

Attack 5.4: Execution of Protocol 5.2 in the presence of a malicious adversary

At the end of Attack 5.4, both A and B are partners according to Definition 2.3.10, since they have matching SIDs and corresponding PIDs (i.e., $PID_A = B$ and $PID_B = A$). In addition, both uncorrupted A and B accept the same session key, $SK_{AB} = g^{xy} = SK_{BA}$. The CK2001 definition of security is not violated (in the sense of Definition 2.3.11). Both A and B, however, did not receive all of each other's messages (recall that the last two messages are fabricated by $\mathscr{A}$) and neither A's nor B's replies were all in response to genuine messages by B and A respectively. Both A and B are not BR93 partners. $\mathscr{A}$, however, can obtain a fresh session key of either A or B by revealing non-partner instances of B or A respectively, in violation of BR93 security (Definition 2.3.3) – key replicating attack as described in Definition 2.3.12.

5.1.8 BPR2000 (KE) ↤ BR95

Recall that security in the models depend on the notion of partnership. No explicit definition of partnership, however, was provided in the BR95 model and there is no single partner function fixed for any protocol in the BR95 model. The flawed partner function for the 3PKD protocol described in the original BR95 paper was fixed in Chapter 3.1.3. As we have pointed out, there is no way to securely define a SID for the 3PKD protocol that will preserve the proof of security. Protocols that are secure in the BR95 model, therefore, may not necessarily be able to be proven secure in the BPR2000 (KE) model.

5.2 A Drawback in the BPR2000 Model

In this section, we reveal a drawback with the original formulation of the BPR2000 model using protocol 3PAKE due to Abdalla and Pointcheval [1] as a case study. In this section, we reveal a drawback with the original formulation of the BPR2000 model using protocol 3PAKE due to Abdalla and Pointcheval [1] as a case study.

5.2.1 Case Study: Abdalla–Pointcheval 3PAKE

Protocol 5.3 describes the three-party authenticated key establishment (3PAKE) protocol of Abdalla and Pointcheval [1], which carries a proof of security in the BPR2000 model. Let A and B be two clients who wish to establish a shared session key, SK; S be a trusted server; pwd_A (and pwd_B) denote the passwords shared between A and S (B and S respectively); $\mathscr{G}_1, \mathscr{G}_2$, and $\mathscr{H}$ denote random oracles; and l_r and l_k denote security parameters.

$A\ (pwd_A)$	$S\ (pwd_A, pwd_B)$	$B\ (pwd_B)$
$x \in_R \mathbb{Z}_p, X = g^x$	$r \in_R \mathbb{Z}_p$	$y \in_R \mathbb{Z}_p, Y = g^y$
$pw_{A,1} = \mathscr{G}_1(pwd_A)$	$R \in_R \{0,1\}^{l_R}$	$pw_{B,1} = \mathscr{G}_1(pwd_B)$
$X^* = X \cdot pw_{A,1}$	$pw_{A,1} = \mathscr{G}_1(pwd_A)$	$Y^* = Y \cdot pw_{B,1}$
$\xrightarrow{\ A,B,X^*\ }$		$\xleftarrow{\ B,A,Y^*\ }$

$$pw_{B,1} = \mathscr{G}_1(pwd_B)$$
$$X = X^*/pw_{A,1}, Y = Y^*/pw_{B,1}$$
$$\overline{X} = X^r, \overline{Y} = Y^r$$
$$pw_{A,2} = \mathscr{G}_2(R, pwd_A, X^*)$$
$$pw_{B,2} = \mathscr{G}_2(R, pwd_B, Y^*)$$
$$\overline{X}^* = \overline{X} \cdot pw_{B,2}, \overline{Y}^* = \overline{Y} \cdot pw_{A,2}$$

$\xleftarrow{\ S,B,R,Y^*,\overline{Y}^*\ }$		$\xrightarrow{\ S,A,R,X^*,\overline{X}^*\ }$
$pw_{A,2} = \mathscr{G}_2(R, pwd_A, X^*)$		$pw_{B,2} = \mathscr{G}_2(R, pwd_B, Y^*)$
$\overline{Y} = \overline{Y}^*/pw_{A,2}$		$\overline{X} = \overline{X}^*/pw_{B,2}$
$K = \overline{Y}^x = g^{xry}$		$K = \overline{Y}^x = g^{xry}$

$$T = (R, X^*, Y^*, \overline{X}^*, \overline{Y}^*)$$
$$SK_A = \mathscr{H}(A, B, S, T, K) = SK_B$$

Protocol 5.3: Abdalla–Pointcheval 3PAKE

5.2.2 Unknown Key Share Attack on 3PAKE

Attack 5.5 describes an execution of Protocol 5.3 in the presence of a malicious adversary, $\mathscr{A}$. Let C be another client who has a shared password, pwd_C, with the server, S. Prior to the start of the communication initiated by A, $\mathscr{A}$ corrupts a non-related player, C (i.e., static corruption), thereby learning all internal states of C (including the shared password with S, pwd_C).

- In Attack 5.5, $\mathscr{A}$ corrupts a third player, C, before the protocol execution starts (i.e., static corruption).
- $\mathscr{A}$ intercepts the first message from A and changes the identity field in the message from A, B to A, C.
- $\mathscr{A}$ impersonates A and sends the fabricated message A, C, X^* to S.
- $\mathscr{A}$ impersonates C and sends another fabricated message C, A, E^* to S.
- Upon receiving both messages, S will respond as per protocol specification.

At the end of Attack 5.5, A believes that the session key, $SK_A = \mathscr{H}(A, B, S, T, K)$, is being shared with B. However, B is still waiting for S's reply, which will never arrive, since $\mathscr{A}$ has intercepted and deleted the message from the network. However, $\mathscr{A}$ is able to compute the fresh session key of A, as $\mathscr{A}$ is able to decrypt and obtain $K = g^{xre}$ and $SK_A = \mathscr{H}(A, B, S, T, K)$, since parameters $A, B, S,$ and T are public. Note that T is the transcript of the protocol execution.

$A\ (pwd_A)$ $\qquad \mathscr{A} \qquad$ $S\ (pwd_A, pwd_B, pwd_C)$ $\qquad \mathscr{A} \qquad$ $B\ (pwd_B)$

$\mathscr{A}$ corrupt C and obtain all internal states of C, including pwd_C

$\xrightarrow{\quad A,B,X^* \quad}$ Intercept $\qquad\qquad\qquad\qquad$ Intercept $\xleftarrow{\quad B,A,Y^* \quad}$

$$e \in_R \mathbb{Z}_p, E = g^e \text{ s.t. underlying value } E \neq 1$$
$$E^* = E \cdot \mathscr{G}_1(pwd_C)$$

$\xrightarrow{\quad A,C,X^* \quad}$ $\qquad\qquad\qquad\qquad\qquad$ $\xleftarrow{\quad C,A,E^* \quad}$

$$pw_{A,1} = \mathscr{G}_1(pwd_A)$$
$$pw_{C,1} = \mathscr{G}_1(pwd_C)$$
$$X = X^*/pw_{A,1}, E = E^*/pw_{C,1}$$
$$\overline{X} = X^r, \overline{E} = E^r$$
$$pw_{A,2} = \mathscr{G}_2(R, pwd_A, X^*)$$
$$pw_{C,2} = \mathscr{G}_2(R, pwd_C, E^*)$$
$$\overline{X}^* = \overline{X} \cdot pw_{C,2}, \overline{E}^* = \overline{E} \cdot pw_{A,2}$$

Intercept $\qquad\qquad\qquad \xleftarrow{\quad S,C,R,E^*,\overline{E}^* \quad}$

$\xleftarrow{\quad S,B,R,E^*,\overline{E}^* \quad}$ $\qquad\qquad$ $\xrightarrow{\quad S,A,R,X^*,\overline{X}^* \quad}$

$$pw_{A,2} = \mathscr{G}_2(R, pwd_A, X^*) \qquad\qquad pw_{C,2} = \mathscr{G}_2(R, pwd_C, E^*)$$
$$\overline{E} = \overline{E}^*/pw_{A,2}, K = \overline{E}^x = g^{xre} \qquad \overline{X} = \overline{X}^*/pw_{C,2}, K = \overline{E}^x = g^{xre}$$
$$T = (R, X^*, E^*, \overline{X}^*, \overline{E}^*) \qquad\qquad T = (R, X^*, E^*, \overline{X}^*, \overline{E}^*)$$
$$SK_A = \mathscr{H}(A,B,S,T,K) \qquad\qquad SK_C = \mathscr{H}(A,B,S,T,K)$$

Attack 5.5: Unknown key share attack on Protocol 5.3

Consequently, Protocol 5.3 is insecure. This attack[1], however, cannot be detected in the existing BPR2000 model since the Corrupt query is not allowed. Protocols proven secure in a proof model that allows the Corrupt query (in the proof simulation) ought to be secure against the unknown key share attack. If a key is to be shared between some parties, U_1 and U_2, the corruption of some other (non-related) player in the protocol, say U_3, should not expose the session key shared between U_1 and U_2. Protocol 5.3, therefore, will be insecure in the BR93, BR95, and CK2001 models, since $\mathscr{A}$ is able to trivially expose a fresh session key (i.e., $\text{Adv}^{\mathscr{A}}(k)$ is non-negligible) by corrupting a non-partner player.

---

[1] Informally, it appears that this attack can be avoided by including the identities of both A and B when computing $pw_{A,2}$ and $pw_{B,2}$.

5.3 Summary

The Bellare–Rogaway and Canetti–Krawczyk proof models were examined. We analysed some non-intuitive gaps in the relations and the relative strengths of security between both models and their variants. We then provided a detailed comparison of the relative strengths of the notions of security between the Bellare–Rogaway and Canetti–Krawczyk proof models. We also revealed a drawback with the BPR2000 model and a previously unpublished flaw in the Abdalla–Pointcheval protocol 3PAKE [1]. Such an attack, however, would not be captured in the model due to the omission of Corrupt queries. In this chapter, we demonstrated that

1. if the session identifier (SID) in the CK2001 model is defined to be the concatenation of messages exchanged during the protocol run, then the CK2001 model offers the strongest definition of security compared to the Bellare–Rogaway model and its variants, and
2. the BPR2000 model is the weakest model.

As a result of this work, we make the following recommendations.

1. The CK2001 model should preferably be used since it appears to offer the strongest definition of security compared to the Bellare–Rogaway model and its variants (under the assumption that session identifier is defined to be the concatenation of messages exchanged during the protocol run). One caveat of proving protocols in the CK2001 model is that these protocols might be computationally inefficient due to the stronger CK2001 security requirement.
2. However, as a minimum, protocols should be proven secure in a model that allows static corruption whereby the adversary is allowed to corrupt some non-related participant and learn all internal states of the corrupted participant prior to the start of the protocol execution.

References

1. Michel Abdalla & David Pointcheval 2005. Interactive Diffie–Hellman Assumptions with Applications to Password-based Authentication, in Andrew Patrick & Moti Yung (eds), Proceedings of 9th International Conference on Financial Cryptography - FC 2005. Lecture Notes in Computer Science 3570/2005: 341–356
2. Mihir Bellare, David Pointcheval & Phillip Rogaway 2000. Authenticated Key Exchange Secure Against Dictionary Attacks, in Bart Preneel (ed), Proceedings of Advances in Cryptology - EUROCRYPT 2000. Lecture Notes in Computer Science 1807/2000: 139 – 155
3. Mihir Bellare & Phillip Rogaway 1993. Entity Authentication and Key Distribution, in Douglas R. Stinson (ed), Proceedings of Advances in Cryptology - CRYPTO 1993. Lecture Notes in Computer Science 773/1993: 110–125
4. Mihir Bellare & Phillip Rogaway 1995. Provably Secure Session Key Distribution: The Three Party Case, in F. Tom Leighton & Allan Borodin (eds), Proceedings of 27th ACM Symposium on the Theory of Computing - ACM STOC 1995. ACM Press: 57–66

5. Colin Boyd, Wenbo Mao & Kenny Paterson 2004. Key Agreement using Statically Keyed Authenticators, in Markus Jakobsson, Moti Yung & Jianying Zhou (eds), Proceedings of Applied Cryptography and Network Security - ACNS 2004. Lecture Notes in Computer Science 3089/2004: 248–262

6. Ran Canetti & Hugo Krawczyk 2001. Analysis of Key-Exchange Protocols and Their Use for Building Secure Channels, in Birgit Pfitzmann (ed), Proceedings of Advances in Cryptology - EUROCRYPT 2001. Lecture Notes in Computer Science 2045/2001: 453–474. Extended version available from http://eprint.iacr.org/2001/040/

7. F. Javier Thayer Fabrega, Jonathan C. Herzog & Joshua D. Guttman 1999. Strand Spaces: Proving Security Protocols Correct. *Journal of Computer Security* 7(2/3): 191–230

8. Victor Shoup 1999. On Formal Models for Secure Key Exchange (Version 4). *Technical report* no RZ 3120 (#93166). IBM Research, Zurich

9. Duncan S Wong & Agnes H Chan 2001. Efficient and Mutually Authenticated Key Exchange for Low Power Computing Devices, in Colin Boyd (ed), Proceedings of Advances in Cryptology - ASIACRYPT 2001. Lecture Notes in Computer Science 2248/2001: 172–289

Chapter 6
An Extension to the Bellare–Rogaway Model

Gong [13] has shown that protocols using timestamps require fewer messages and rounds than protocols using nonce-based challenge-response. Boyd [8] proposed a novel method of achieving key freshness which does not require both participants' nonces to be passed to the server, thus reducing the number of messages and rounds to the same as that required for timestamp-based protocols. However, a known weakness of the protocol of Boyd is that if a user's long-term key is compromised, then an attacker can masquerade as that user even after the compromised key is replaced with a new one. Moreover, the original protocol of Boyd does not have a proof of security and suffers from the problems described in earlier Chapter 2.2.2.4.

In this chapter, we prove a protocol closely based on one originally proposed by Boyd [8] secure in the BR93 model. However, this protocol also suffer from the same known weakness of the protocol by Boyd. In other words, if a user's long-term key is compromised, then an attacker can masquerade as that user even after the compromised key is replaced with a new one. Since there is no notion of resetting in the BR93 model, there is no way to observe such a possibility. The BR93 model is extended to allow more realistic adversary capabilities, under which the proven secure protocol becomes insecure.

We then propose an equally efficient alternative protocol that provides protection against the compromise of long-term keys without taking recourse to revocation lists. We prove this alternative protocol secure in the extended BR93 model. We remark that protocols proven secure in the extended model will also be secure in the original model. An extension to this alternative protocol allows session keys to be renewed in subsequent sessions without the server's further involvement even in the event that the long-term key or the earlier session key have been compromised. A comparative summary is also presented.

Material presented in this chapter has appeared in the following publication:

- Colin Boyd and Kim-Kwang Raymond Choo and Anish Mathuria. An Extension to Bellare and Rogaway (1993) Model: Resetting Compromised Long-Term

Keys. In Lynn Margaret Batten and Reihaneh Safavi-Naini, editors, 11th Australasian Conference on Information Security and Privacy - ACISP 2006, volume 4058/2006 of Lecture Notes in Computer Science, pages 371–382, Springer-Verlag, 2006.

6.1 A Provably-Secure Revised Protocol of Boyd

Prior to defining the protocol that we shall prove secure, we define the authenticated encryption scheme that will be employed.

6.1.1 Secure Authenticated Encryption Schemes

A *symmetric encryption scheme* $\mathscr{SE} = (\mathscr{K}, \mathscr{E}, \mathscr{D})$ consists of three algorithms, namely: the *key generation* algorithm $\mathscr{K}$, the *encryption* algorithm $\mathscr{E}$, and the *decryption* algorithm $\mathscr{D}$ as described below.

- $\mathscr{K}$ is a probabilistic algorithm which, on input 1^k, outputs a key K.
- $\mathscr{E}$ is a probabilistic algorithm which takes a key K and a message M drawn from a message space $\mathscr{M}$ associated to K and returns a ciphertext C. This is denoted by $C \in_R \mathscr{E}_K(M)$.
- $\mathscr{D}$ is a deterministic algorithm which takes a key K and a ciphertext C and returns the corresponding plaintext M or the symbol $\bot$ which indicates an illegal ciphertext. This is denoted as $x \leftarrow \mathscr{D}_K(C)$. We require that $\mathscr{D}_K(\mathscr{E}_K(M)) = M$ for every $K \leftarrow \mathscr{K}(1^k)$.

For security we use the definitions of Bellare and Namprempre [3]. We require that the symmetric encryption scheme provides confidentiality in the sense of indistinguishability under chosen plaintext attacks (*IND-CPA security*) and provides integrity in the sense of preserving integrity of plaintexts (*INT-PTXT security*). We note that each of these is the weakest of the properties defined by Bellare and Namprempre and are provided by either encrypt-then-MAC or by MAC-then-encrypt constructions. Therefore there are many practical ways of implementing our protocol which can reasonably be expected to satisfy these assumptions. We now define these concepts more precisely.

For any efficient (probabilistic, polynomial time) adversary $\mathscr{X}$, the confidentiality security is defined in terms of the following game, which we call $\mathscr{G}_1$.

1. The challenger chooses a key $K \leftarrow \mathscr{K}(1^k)$.
2. Given access to the encryption oracle, the adversary outputs two messages of equal length $M_0, M_1 \in \mathscr{M}$ of her choice.
3. The challenger computes $C_b \in_R \mathscr{E}_K(M_b)$ where $b \in_R \{0,1\}$. The bit b is kept secret from the adversary.

4. The adversary is then given C_b and has to output a guess b' for b.

We define the advantage of the adversary $\mathscr{X}$ playing the above game as

$$\text{Adv}_{\mathscr{X}}^{\text{ind}-\text{cpa}}(k) = |2 \cdot \text{Pr}[b' = b]| - 1.$$

Definition 6.1.1 *The encryption scheme $\mathscr{SE}$ is IND-CPA secure if the advantage of all efficient adversaries playing game $\mathscr{G}_1$ is negligible.*

For any efficient adversary $\mathscr{F}$, the integrity security is defined in terms of the following game, which we call $\mathscr{G}_2$.

1. Choose a key $K \leftarrow \mathscr{K}(1^k)$.
2. The adversary $\mathscr{F}$ is given access to the encryption oracle and also a *verification oracle* which on input a ciphertext C outputs 0 if $\mathscr{D}_K(C) = \perp$ and outputs 1 if C is a legitimate ciphertext.
3. The adversary wins if it can find a legitimate ciphertext C^* such that the plaintext $M = \mathscr{D}_K(C^*)$ was never used as a query to the encryption oracle. In this case we say the event **forgery** has occurred.

We define the advantage of the adversary playing the above game as

$$\text{Adv}_{\mathscr{F}}^{\text{int}-\text{ptxt}}(k) = |2 \cdot \text{Pr}[\text{forgery}]| - 1.$$

Definition 6.1.2 *The encryption scheme $\mathscr{SE}$ is INT-PTXT secure if the advantage of all efficient adversaries playing game $\mathscr{G}_2$ is negligible.*

6.1.2 Revised Protocol of Boyd

Now that the authenticated encryption scheme to be employed in the protcol has been defined, we can define the protocol that we shall prove secure. All parameter choices depend on a security parameter k. In Protocol 6.1, the following notations are used: $\mathscr{H}$ denotes some secure cryptographic hash function; $\{m\}_K$ denotes an encryption of some message m under symmetric key K; S denotes a server who shares long-term symmetric keys K_{AS} and K_{BS} with A and B, respectively; N_A, N_B, and K_S denote nonces generated by A, B and S, respectively.

Protocol 6.1 is a server-based protocol in which users A and B as well as the server S contribute to the key value. The session key obtained by A and B at the end of the protocol execution is denoted as K_{AB}. We refer the protocol message fields that are encrypted using the long-term symmetric keys, K_{AS} and K_{BS}, as tickets. As Boyd and Mathuria [9] pointed out, such protocols which employ tickets to re-establish session keys are often known as repeated authentication protocols in the literature. Protocol 6.1 is very similar to that proposed by Boyd [8]. Differences are as follows.

1. In the earlier protocol of Boyd, the session key is determined by a MAC function so that the session key is $K_{AB} = MAC_{K_S}(N_A, N_B)$.

A	S	B
$N_A \in_R \{0,1\}^k$	$\xrightarrow{\;A,B,N_A\;}$ $K_S \in_R \{0,1\}^k$	
	$\xrightarrow{\{A,B,K_S\}_{K_{AS}},\{A,B,K_S\}_{K_{BS}},N_A}$	
		$N_B \in_R \{0,1\}^k$
	$\xleftarrow{\{A,B,K_S\}_{K_{AS}},N_B}$	Decrypt $\{A,B,K_S\}_{K_{BS}}$
Decrypt $\{A,B,K_S\}_{K_{AS}}$		
$SID_A = N_A \parallel N_B$		$SID_B = N_A \parallel N_B$
$K_{AB} = \mathscr{H}(K_S \parallel SID_A)$		$K_{AB} = \mathscr{H}(K_S \parallel SID_B)$
Status: ACCEPTED		Status: ACCEPTED

Protocol 6.1: A revised key agreement protocol of Boyd

2. There is no partnering mechanism (e.g., session identifiers) specified in the earlier protocol of Boyd. Message exchanges in the real world are seldom conducted over secure channels. Therefore, it is realistic to assume that any adversary is able to modify messages at will, which is the case in the Bellare–Rogaway style models [1, 4, 5, 6, 7]. As Goldreich and Lindell [11, Section 1.3] have pointed out, such an adversary capability means that the adversary is able to conduct concurrent executions of the protocol (one with each party). Therefore, without such partnering mechanism, communicating parties will be unable to uniquely distinguish messages from different sessions. Hence, in Protocol 6.1, we define partnership using the notion of session identifiers, SID[1].

3. The key confirmation messages have been removed, which consist of a handshake using the shared secret. These can easily be added in a standard way [4]. The session key itself must not be used to authenticate the key confirmation messages, otherwise the adversary can use them to easily distinguish the session key.

6.1.3 Security Proof

The proof follows that of Bellare and Rogaway [5] quite closely; differences include the use of a combined authenticated encryption scheme (as opposed to separate encryption and MAC functions) and the different partnering function used. The general idea of the security proof is to assume that the protocol adversary can gain an advantage and use this to break the assumptions about the security of the encryption algorithm. Since the adversary relies on its oracles to run we simulate the oracles so

---

[1] We remark that the security proof of Protocol 6.1 does not hinge on the difficulty of predicting a valid session identifier. In fact, we may assume that session identifiers are made publicly available when the status of the principal becomes "ACCEPTED". In other words, anyone (including the adversary, $\mathscr{A}$) knows what the value of a particular session identifier after the associated oracle has accepted the session key associated with the particular session identifier.

that we can supply the answers to all the queries the adversary might ask. We cannot supply answers which rely on knowledge of the encryption keys that we are trying to break, so we use the integrity of plaintexts to show that these queries would, almost certainly, not be answered by any oracle running the protocol. As long as the simulation works with non-negligible probability the assumption about the encryption scheme fails.

Following Bellare and Rogaway [5] we need to extend the definition of a secure encryption scheme to allow the adversary to obtain multiple encryptions of the same ciphertext under many different independent encryption keys. Such an adversary is termed a *multiple eavesdropper*. A multiple eavesdropper, $\mathcal{ME}$, is allowed to obtain encryptions of the same plaintext under two different independent encryption keys. We can bound the advantage of a multiple eavesdropper by considering it as a special case of the multi-user setting analysed by Bellare, Boldyreva and Micali [2]. In their notation we have the case of $q_e = 1$, meaning that the adversary can only obtain one encryption for each encryption key. Specialising their main theorem gives the following.

Lemma 6.1.1 *Suppose that an adversary has advantage at most $\varepsilon(k)$ for encryption scheme $(\mathcal{E}, \mathcal{D})$. Then a multiple eavesdropper has advantage not more than $n \cdot \varepsilon(k)$.*

Notice that since an authenticated encryption scheme is also a secure encryption scheme in the sense defined by this result, it also holds for an authenticated encryption scheme. This allows us to define a variant of game $\mathcal{G}_1$ which we call $\mathcal{G}_1'$. The only difference between these is that in $\mathcal{G}_1'$ the adversary is given access to two encryption oracles for two independently generated keys, and its challenge consists of two encryptions of either m_0 or m_1 under the two keys.

The idea of the proof is to consider the situation when the adversary at some stage *forges* a message successfully. When this occurs we can use the adversary to break the integrity of the authenticated encryption scheme. When this does not occur we use the adversary to break the confidentiality. More formally, define **forge** to be the event that the protocol adversary, $\mathcal{A}$ produces a ciphertext C associated with a uncorrupted entity U such that $\mathcal{D}_K(C) \neq \perp$ where K is the long term key of entity U. Noting that

$$\Pr(\text{success}) \leq \Pr(\text{forge}) + \Pr(\text{success}|\overline{\text{forge}})$$

we can split the proof up by showing that each of the two terms on the right is negligible.

6.1.3.1 Integrity attacker

Assume that $\mathcal{A}$ is an adversary against the protocol. We use $\mathcal{A}$ to construct a forger $\mathcal{F}$ for the authenticated encryption scheme $\mathcal{SE}$ described in Definition 6.1.1. We will say that the event $\text{success}_{\mathcal{F}}$ occurs if $\mathcal{F}$ wins game $\mathcal{G}_2$ against $\mathcal{SE}$.

Lemma 6.1.2 *There is an efficient algorithm $\mathscr{F}$ defined using $\mathscr{A}$ such that if* forge *occurs with non-negligible probability then* success$_\mathscr{F}$ *occurs with non-negligible probability*.

In order to prove Lemma 6.1.2 we describe how $\mathscr{F}$ is constructed. When $\mathscr{F}$ runs it receives access to the encryption and verification oracles of the authenticated encryption scheme $\mathscr{SE}$. Its output must be a forged ciphertext for a message m which was not previously input to the encryption oracle.

In order to obtain the forgery $\mathscr{F}$ runs $\mathscr{A}$ by first choosing a user U_i for $i \in_R [1,Q]$. This user will be simulated as though its long-term key is the one used in $\mathscr{SE}$. For all other $j \in [1,Q]$ with $j \neq i$, $\mathscr{F}$ generates the long-term shared key using the key generation algorithm $\mathscr{K}_k$. This allows $\mathscr{F}$ to answer all the oracle queries from $\mathscr{A}$ as follows.

Send(U,s,M) For any well-formed queries to S, $\mathscr{F}$ can reply with valid ciphertexts, by choosing the session key and forming the ciphertexts, either directly using the known key or using the encryption oracle in the case of U_i. For queries to initiate a protocol run, $\mathscr{F}$ can generate a random nonce and answer appropriately. Finally, consider a query to either an initiator or responder oracle including a claimed server message (corresponding to protocol messages 2 or 3). The relevant ciphertext can be verified either directly using the known key or using the verification oracle. If the ciphertext is verified correctly then the oracle accepts and this information is returned to $\mathscr{A}$.

Reveal(U,s) Since all session keys are known from running the Send(U,s,M) queries the query can be trivially answered with the correct session key (if accepted).

Corrupt(U) As long as $U \neq U_i$ all the private information is available and the query can be answered. In the case $U = U_i$ then the query cannot be answered and $\mathscr{F}$ will abort and fail.

Test(U,s) Since all the accepted session keys are known from running the Send queries the query can be trivially answered by identifying the correct session key.

$\mathscr{F}$ continues the simulation until a forgery event against $\mathscr{SE}$ occurs, or until $\mathscr{A}$ halts. Note that as long as $\mathscr{F}$ does not abort then the simulation is perfect. If forge occurs then the probability that the user involved is U_i equals $1/Q$. In this case the event success$_\mathscr{F}$ occurs. Futhermore, in this case $\mathscr{F}$ does not abort since U_i cannot be corrupted before the forge event. Therefore we arrive at the following upper bound.

$$\Pr(\text{forge}) \leq Q \cdot \Pr(\text{success}_\mathscr{F}) \tag{6.1}$$

6.1.3.2 Confidentiality attacker

Now assume that $\mathscr{A}$ gains an advantage without producing a forgery. This time we use $\mathscr{A}$ to form an algorithm $\mathscr{X}$ which has a non-negligible advantage in the encryption scheme.

Lemma 6.1.3 *There is an efficient algorithm $\mathscr{X}$ defined using $\mathscr{A}$ such that if* success *occurs but* forge *does not occur, then $\mathscr{X}$ wins game $\mathscr{G}_1'$.*

Two random keys K and K' are chosen by the challenger for $\mathscr{S\!E}$ and $\mathscr{X}$ is given access to the encryption oracles for these keys. First $\mathscr{X}$ chooses two users U_i and U_j for $i, j \in_R [1, Q]$. For all other $k \in [1, Q]$, $\mathscr{X}$ generates the long-term key using the key generation algorithm $\mathscr{K}_k$. Next $\mathscr{A}$ chooses two random session keys K_0 and K_1. The two messages that $\mathscr{X}$ asks of the challenger for $\mathscr{S\!E}$ are $M_0 = (U_i, U_j, K_0)$ and $M_1 = (U_i, U_j, K_1)$. The challenger responds with a ciphertext pair C_b, C_b' which are the authenticated encryptions of either M_0 or M_1 under the two keys K and K'. Suppose that Q_S is the maximum number of Send queries that $\mathscr{A}$ will ask of the server and Q_H is the maximum number of hash queries that $\mathscr{A}$ will ask of the server. $\mathscr{X}$ chooses a value s_0 randomly in $[1, Q_S]$. The idea is that $\mathscr{X}$ will inject the ciphertexts C_b, C_b' into a random server $\mathrm{Send}(U, s, M)$ query. $\mathscr{X}$ proceeds to simulate responses for $\mathscr{A}$ as follows.

$\mathscr{H}(K \| SID_i^k)$ For queries $\mathscr{H}(K \| SID_i^k)$, if this query was asked before, then return the previous answer. Otherwise, return a random value, $v \in_R \{0, 1\}^k$. In addition, store this answer together with the query in a list of DH-tuples.

$\mathrm{Send}(U, s, M)$ First consider Send queries to the server. $\mathscr{X}$ must simulate responses from the server with ciphertexts for two users A and B. There are three cases:

- Neither A nor B is equal to U_i. The session key K_S is chosen randomly by $\mathscr{X}$ and the required tickets can be generated by $\mathscr{X}$ using the long-term keys chosen.
- One of A or B is equal to U_i and the other is not equal to U_j. $\mathscr{X}$ chooses the session key randomly and obtains the ticket for U_i using the encryption oracle and generates the ticket for the other user with the known long-term key.
- One of A or B is equal to U_i and the other is equal to U_j. If $s = s_0$ then $\mathscr{A}$ uses C_b and C_b' as the two tickets for U_i and U_j. Otherwise $\mathscr{X}$ chooses the session key randomly and obtains the tickets for U_i and U_j using the encryption oracles.

Now consider Send queries sent to users. Queries to initiate a protocol run are trivially simulated. Queries that include ciphertexts must be answered by either accepting or rejecting depending on whether the ciphertext is valid. Because forge does not occur we know that $\mathscr{A}$ cannot form a valid ciphertext unless it was output as a result of a Send query to the server. Therefore $\mathscr{X}$ has seen every valid ciphertext before and can respond with acceptance when these are seen. Ciphertexts that $\mathscr{X}$ has not seen are rejected.

$\mathrm{Reveal}(U, s)$ $\mathscr{X}$ knows all session keys that have been accepted, with the possible exception of the one that has been injected in C_b and C_b'. If $\mathscr{A}$ asks for the key for this special case then $\mathscr{X}$ aborts with failure. Otherwise $\mathscr{X}$ can return the correct key.

Corrupt(U) $\mathscr{X}$ generated all the long-term keys except for those of U_i and U_j. If either of these two parties is corrupted then $\mathscr{X}$ aborts with failure. Otherwise $\mathscr{X}$ can return the correct long-term key.

Test(U, s)   Suppose that the two tickets C_b and C_b' were accepted by oracles $\Pi_{U_i}^{s_i}$ and $\Pi_{U_j}^{s_j}$. If $(U, s) \notin \{(U_i, s_i), (U_j, s_j)\}$ then $\mathscr{X}$ halts and fails. Otherwise, $\mathscr{X}$ returns the key or a random value.

Eventually $\mathscr{A}$ halts and outputs a bit b. $\mathscr{X}$ returns that same bit to the challenger.

This completes the description of $\mathscr{X}$. Let lucky be the event that $\mathscr{X}$ does not fail during the Test query. When lucky occurs, $\mathscr{X}$ wins game $\mathscr{G}_1'$ whenever $\mathscr{A}$ is successful. This means that $\Pr(\text{success}_{\mathscr{X}} | \text{lucky}) \geq \Pr(\text{success}_{\mathscr{A}} | \overline{\text{forge}})$. We also have $\Pr(\text{lucky}) \geq 1/(Q^2 \cdot Q_S)$. Putting these together we obtain:

$$\Pr(\text{success}_{\mathscr{A}} | \overline{\text{forge}}) \leq Q^2 \cdot Q_S \cdot Q_H \cdot \Pr(\text{success}_{\mathscr{X}}). \qquad (6.2)$$

6.1.3.3 Conclusion of Security Proof

We know that N, Q_S, and Q_H are polynomial in the security parameter k and ε is negligible by definition. combining equations 6.1 and 6.2 we obtain the following result, which shows that if the authenticated encryption algorithm used in the protocol is secure, then the protocol is also secure.

Theorem 6.1.1 *Let $\mathscr{A}$ be any polynomial time adversary against the security of the protocol and $\mathscr{H}$ is modelled as a random oracle. Then there is an integrity adversary, $\mathscr{F}$, and a confidentiality adversary, $\mathscr{X}$ against the encrypted authentication algorithm such that:*

$$\Pr(\text{success}_{\mathscr{A}}) \leq Q \cdot \Pr(\text{success}_{\mathscr{F}}) + Q^2 \cdot Q_S \cdot Q_H \cdot \Pr(\text{success}_{\mathscr{X}}).$$

6.2 An Extension to the BR93 Model

As acknowledged by Boyd [8], there is a significant weakness in his protocol (and similarly in Protocol 6.1) in a realistic setting. It is inevitable that from time to time long-term keys of users will be compromised. For example, this could be through theft of a device containing the key. It seems natural that in such a case the user should be re-issued with a new long-term key and then allowed to continue using the protocol. For many server-based protocols this procedure will not influence the protocol security. However, for Protocol 6.1, this is not the case. It is easy to see that an adversary who obtains a long-term key of a user can continue to use it to masquerade as that user even after a new long-term key has been issued.

Despite Theorem 6.1.1 being proven in the previous section, the (significant) weakness in Protocol 6.1 discussed cannot be captured. The reason that this attack is possible even though we have proven the protocol secure, is that there is no notion of replacing a long-term key in the BR93 model: once a party has been corrupted it must remain so. In other words, once a party, say U_1, is corrupted and its long-term key revealed to the adversary, $\mathscr{A}$, U_1 is no longer considered fresh in the sense of Definition 2.3.1.

One of the motivations for this work is to remove a known weakness of the protocol of Boyd [8] under the effect of a compromise of a long-term key. That is, even if the adversary, $\mathscr{A}$, has corrupted some party, say U_1, $\mathscr{A}$ should not be able to impersonate U_1 using the compromised long-term key (of U_1) after a new long-term key has been issued to U_1. In order to take into account this sort of attack we add a new query called **Reset** to the list of actions that an adversary is allowed to perform and adjust the definition of freshness.

Reset Query. The Reset(U_i, K_{New}) query captures the notion of replacement for a compromised long-term key of principal U_i with a new randomly distributed key, K_{New}. When a corrupted U_i is being asked such a Reset query,

- player U_i is re-considered fresh in the sense of Definition 2.3.1,
- any oracle(s) $U_i^1, \ldots, U_i^{\delta-1}$ that were activated before the Reset query are unfresh in the sense of Definition 2.3.1, and
- subsequent oracles $U_i^\delta, U_i^{\delta+1}, \ldots$ are considered fresh in the sense of Definition 2.3.1 (unless U_1 is corrupted again).

An adversary $\mathscr{A}$ who has access to this new query can always defeat Protocol 6.1 as follows.

1. $\mathscr{A}$ uses Send queries to run the protocol between A and B.
2. Then $\mathscr{A}$ issues a Corrupt(A) query to obtain the long-term key of A. This enables $\mathscr{A}$ to decrypt the ticket $\{A, B, K_S\}_{K_{AS}}$ sent to A during a previous protocol run with B, and hence obtain the key K_S contained in it.
3. $\mathscr{A}$ now resets A and masquerades as S, replaying the ticket originally sent to B together with any random value for N_A. This activates a fresh oracle Π_B^s, that will choose a nonce N_B and accept the session key $\mathscr{H}(K_S \| N_A \| N_B)$.
4. Consequently, $\mathscr{A}$ knows the value of this accepted key, in violation of Definition 2.3.3.

In order to avoid the problem, one method is to introduce a validity period for tickets and to issue a blacklist for tickets that have been compromised. This is the method suggested by Crispo, Popescu, and Tanenbaum [10] whereby they show that a large number of users can be accommodated in a practical system. It is easily checked that this prevents the above attack, since revoked tickets cannot be replayed by the adversary. However, such an approach entails a considerable infrastructure (not unlike a public key infrastructure) and might not scale well to a more realistic environment with a large number of participating entitites.

6.3 An Efficient Protocol in Extended Model

We now describe an alternative protocol and provides a proof of its security in the extended model.

6.3.1 An Efficient Protocol

Protocol 6.2 describes our proposed key agreement protocol with key confirmation. The notation used in Protocol 6.2 follows that of Table 2.1: $\mathcal{H}_0$ and $\mathcal{H}_1$ denote two independent secure cryptographic hash functions, $[\cdot]_{MK}$ denotes the computation of some MAC digest using MAC key, MK, $\{\cdot\}_{K_{US}}$ denotes the encryption of some message using encryption key, K_{US}, that is being shared by some user and the server, and $\|$ denotes the concatenation of messages. We assume that $G, q, g, \mathcal{H}_0, \mathcal{H}_1$ are fixed in advance and known to the entire network, and that each party P_i has a long-term symmetric key, K_{P_iS}, shared with the server, S.

A	S	B

$N_A \in_R \{0,1\}^k \xrightarrow{\{A,B,g^{N_A}\}_{K_{AS}}}$

$\{A,B,g^{N_A}\}_{K_{BS}}$

$N_B \in_R \{0,1\}^k$

$SID_B = g^{N_A}\|g^{N_B}$

$MK_{AB} = \mathcal{H}_1(A\|B\|SID_B\|(g^{N_A})^{N_B})$

$K_{AB} = \mathcal{H}_0(A\|B\|SID_B\|(g^{N_A})^{N_B})$

Delete N_B

$\xleftarrow{g^{N_B}, [\text{"1"},B,A,SID_B]_{MK_{AB}}}$

$SID_A = g^{N_A}\|g^{N_B}$

$MK_{AB} = \mathcal{H}_1(A\|B\|SID_A\|(g^{N_B})^{N_A})$

Verify received MAC digest, $[\text{"1"},B,A,SID_B]_{MK_{AB}}$

$K_{AB} = \mathcal{H}_0(A\|B\|SID_A\|(g^{N_B})^{N_A})$

Delete N_A

$\xrightarrow{[\text{"2"},A,B,SID_A]_{MK_{AB}}}$

Verify $[\text{"2"},A,B,SID_A]_{MK_{AB}}$

Status: ACCEPTED   Status: ACCEPTED

Protocol 6.2: A new key agreement protocol

Informally, Protocol 6.2 removes the known weakness of Protocol 6.1, as described below.

1. Upon completion of an execution of Protocol 6.2, both A and B have accepted session keys of the same value, $K_{AB} = \mathcal{H}_0(A\|B\|g^{N_A}\|g^{N_B}\|g^{N_BN_A})$.

2. Suppose the adversary, $\mathscr{A}$, compromises the long-term key of A, K_{AS}. With knowledge of K_{AS}, $\mathscr{A}$ can decrypt the earlier message, $\{A, B, g^{N_A}\}_{K_{AS}}$, and learn g^{N_A}. $\mathscr{A}$ also knows g^{N_B} from observing the Protocol 6.2's execution. However, finding $g^{N_B N_A}$ is equivalent to solving the CDH problem (recall that N_A has been deleted from the internal state of A upon completion of the execution of Protocol 6.2). Moreover, this implies that Protocol 6.2 provides *forward secrecy* since the knowledge of the compromised long-term keys, K_{AS} or K_{BS}, does not allow the adversary to find the session key, $K_{AB} = \mathscr{H}_0(A||B||g^{N_A}||g^{N_B}||g^{N_B N_A})$.

6.3.2 Security Proof

Theorem 6.3.1 *Assuming the Computational Diffie-Hellman (CDH) assumption is satisfied in* $\mathbb{G}$, *Protocol 6.2 is a secure key agreement protocol providing key confirmation and forward secrecy when* $\mathscr{H}_0$ *and* $\mathscr{H}_1$ *are modeled as random oracles and if the underlying message authentication scheme and encryption scheme are secure in the sense of existential unforgeability under adaptive chosen-message attack and indistinguishable under chosen-plaintext attack respectively.*

The validity of Protocol 6.2 is straightforward to verify and we concentrate on the indistinguishability requirement. The security is proved by finding a reduction to the security of the underlying message authentication scheme and the underlying encryption scheme.

The security of Protocol 6.2 is based on the CDH problem in the random oracle model. An adversary, $\mathscr{A}$, can get information about a particular session key $K_{ij} = \mathscr{H}_0(i||j||SID_i^k||g^{N_i N_j})$ if $\mathscr{A}$ has queried the random oracle on the point $i||j||SID_i^k||g^{N_i N_j}$. This will allows us to solve the CDH problem with probability related to that of $\mathscr{A}$'s success probability.

The general notion follows that of the proof presented in Chapter 6.1.3. For consistency, let Q be the upper bound of the number of parties in $\mathscr{G}$, Q_S be the maximum number of **Send** queries that $\mathscr{A}$ will ask of the server, and Q_H be the maximum number of hash queries that $\mathscr{A}$ will ask of the server. The proof is divided into two parts since the adversary, $\mathscr{A}$, can either gain her advantage against Protocol 6.2 while forging a MAC digest or gain her advantage against Protocol 6.2 without forging a MAC digest.

The proof then concludes by observing that $\text{Adv}^{\mathscr{A}}(k)$ is negligible when $\mathscr{H}_0$, and $\mathscr{H}_1$ are modeled as random oracles and if the underlying message authentication scheme and encryption scheme are secure in the sense of existential unforgeability under adaptive chosen-message attack and indistinguishable under chosen-plaintext attack respectively, and therefore Protocol 6.2 is also secure.

6.3.2.1 Integrity Breaker

We assume that there exists an adversary, $\mathscr{A}$, against Protocol 6.2. We then construct an integrity breaker, $\mathscr{F}_1$, that make use of $\mathscr{A}$ to break the underlying message authentication scheme. Let Forge be the event that, for some instance Π_i^k with partner P_j, the adversary queries $\text{Send}(i,k,m)$ and (1) neither P_i nor P_j were ever corrupted; (2) m was never sent by P_j and (3) Π_i^k computes a valid session key.

Lemma 6.3.1 *There is an efficient algorithm $\mathscr{F}_1$ defined using $\mathscr{A}$ such that if* Forge *occurs with non-negligible probability then* $\text{success}_{\mathscr{F}_1}$ *occurs with non-negligible probability.*

The integrity breaker, $\mathscr{F}_1$, is able to simulate the view of $\mathscr{A}$ and answers all the oracle queries of $\mathscr{A}$. $\mathscr{F}_1$ will continue the simulation until either the event that Forge occurs or until $\mathscr{A}$ halts.

Let $\text{Pr}(\text{Forge}_{i,j})$ be the probability that Forge occurs for a specific pair of parties i, j. Clearly, we have $\text{Pr}(\text{Forge}) \leq N^2 \cdot \text{Pr}(\text{Forge}_{i,j})$ since we can embed an instance of the CDH problem within the one-time MAC key. Now, if we replace the key, $K_{ij} = g^{U_1 U_2}$ by a random element from $\mathbb{G}$, this does not affect $\text{Pr}(\text{Forge}_{i,j})$ by more than a factor loss of ε. However, the probability that $\text{Pr}(\text{Forge}_{i,j})$ occurs when K_{ij} is truly random is at most ε' by the security of the MAC. Therefore, we arrive at the upper bound

$$\text{Pr}(\text{Forge}) \leq N^2(\varepsilon + \varepsilon').$$

All queries by the adversary, $\mathscr{A}$, can be answered normally by $\mathscr{F}_1$. $\mathscr{F}_1$ continues the simulation until $\text{Pr}(\text{Forge})$ happens or until $\mathscr{A}$ terminates. Thus, the simulation is perfect so long $\mathscr{F}_1$ does not terminate. We then arrive at the following upper bound.

$$\text{Pr}(\text{Forge}) \leq Q \cdot N^2(\varepsilon + \varepsilon') \cdot \text{Pr}(\text{success}_{\mathscr{F}_1}). \tag{6.3}$$

6.3.2.2 Confidentiality Breaker

We construct a confidentiality breaker, $\mathscr{X}_1$, using $\mathscr{A}$, as shown in the attack game, $\mathscr{G}_{\mathscr{X}_1}$. The idea underlying this proof follows that presented in Chapter 6.1.3.2. $\mathscr{X}_1$ is given access to the encryption oracles associated with the two random keys K and K'. $\mathscr{X}_1$ then generates the long-term key for all users, except two randomly selected users, U_i and U_j.

Let $\text{Pr}(\text{Success}_{\mathscr{A}}|\overline{\text{Forge}_{i,j}})$ be the probability that the adversary, $\mathscr{A}$, manages to gain an advantage without forging a MAC digest for a specific pair of parties i, j. Clearly, we have $\text{Pr}(\text{Success}_{\mathscr{A}}) \leq N^2 \cdot \text{Pr}(\text{Success}_{\mathscr{A}}|\overline{\text{Forge}_{i,j}})$ since we can embed an instance of the CDH problem. Now, if we replace the key, $K_{ij} = g^{U_1 U_2}$ by a random element from $\mathbb{G}$, this does not affect $\text{Pr}(\text{Forge}_{i,j})$ by more than a factor loss of ε. However, the probability that $\text{Pr}(\text{Forge}_{i,j})$ occurs when K_{ij} is truly random is at most ε' by the security of the MAC. Therefore, we arrive at the upper bound

$$\Pr(\text{Forge}) \leq N^2(\varepsilon + \varepsilon').$$

$\mathcal{X}_1$ runs $\mathcal{A}$ and answers all oracle queries from $\mathcal{A}$, as follows:

- For queries $\mathcal{H}_0(i||j||SID_i^k||Z)$, if this query was asked before, then return the previous answer. Otherwise, return a random value, $v \in_R \{0,1\}^k$. In addition, store this answer together with the query in a list of DH-tuples.
- For Send, Reveal, Corrupt, and Test queries, $\mathcal{X}_1$ answer them honestly.
- In the event that a Reset(U) query is asked, $\mathcal{X}_1$ is also able to answer this correctly by returning a new random long-term key generated using the key generation algorithm $\mathcal{K}_k$. $\mathcal{X}_1$ has to maintain a table containing the internal state associated with U.

  1. If U has been corrupted, then the status of U is updated to be fresh. Otherwise, $\mathcal{X}_1$ halts the simulation.
  2. Then any oracle(s) $U_i^1, \ldots, U_i^{\delta-1}$ that were activated before the Reset query are considered unfresh, while subsequent oracles $U_i^{\delta}, U_i^{\delta+1}, \ldots$ are considered fresh.

- At the conclusion of the game simulation if $\mathcal{X}_1$ has not terminated, $\mathcal{X}_1$ randomly chooses a tuple, (U_a, U_b, U_{ab}), from its list of DH-tuples, finds a and b such that $U_a = U_1 g^a$ and $U_b = U_2 g^b$, and outputs $\frac{U_{ab}}{U_2^a U_1^b g^{ab}}$.

Let

- event1 be the event that, for some $i, j \in [q_p]$, $\mathcal{A}$ at some point queries the random oracle at a point $i||j||SID_i^k||g^w$, whereby both P_i and P_j are fresh (i.e., not corrupted) in the entire course of $\mathcal{G}$, and $W = g^{N_i N_j}$.
- event2 be the event that, for some $i, j \in [q_p]$, $\mathcal{A}$ at some point queries the random oracle at a point $i||j||SID_i^k||g^x$ for some k, $SID_i^k = U||V = g^{N_i} g^{N_j}$ and $X = g^{N_i N_j}$.

The probability that $\mathcal{X}_1$ returns the correct answer is at least $\frac{Pr_{\mathcal{A}}[\text{event1} \wedge \text{corrupted}]}{Q_H \cdot N^2 \cdot \varepsilon}$, since the simulation of $\mathcal{G}_{\mathcal{X}_1}$ is perfect until the point, if any, that event1 or event2 occurs. In the event that event2 occurs, with probability $\frac{1}{Q_H}$, $\mathcal{X}_1$ selects a tuple, (U_a, U_b, U_{ab}), from its list of DH-tuples, for which $U_{ab} = g^{\alpha_1 \alpha_2}$ where $\alpha_1 := \log_g U_a$ and $\alpha_2 := \log_g U_b$. In other words, this tuple, (U_a, U_b, U_{ab}), selected by $\mathcal{X}_1$ is a DH-tuple. Then $\mathcal{X}_1$ has outputed a correct solution to the CDH instance. Thus,

$$Pr_{\mathcal{A}}(\text{event2}) \leq Q_H \cdot \varepsilon.$$

Since we have shown that both $Pr_{\mathcal{A}}[\overline{\text{event1} \wedge \text{corrupted}}] \leq Q_H \cdot N^2 \cdot \varepsilon$ and $Pr_{\mathcal{A}}[\text{event2}] \leq Q_H \cdot \varepsilon$, we have

$$\Pr(\text{success}_{\mathcal{A}}|\overline{\text{Forge}}) \leq (Q_H \cdot N^2 \cdot \varepsilon + Q_H \cdot \varepsilon) \cdot \Pr(\text{success}_{\mathcal{X}_1}). \qquad (6.4)$$

6.3.2.3 Conclusion of Security Proof

We know that N, Q_S, and Q_H are polynomial in the security parameter k and ε is negligible by definition. Therefore, by combining equations 6.3 and 6.4 we conclude the proof of Theorem 6.3.1.

6.4 Comparative Security and Efficiency

Similar to the work of Gong [13] and Boyd [8], our motivation is to design protocols efficient in both messages and rounds. Therefore, we present a comparative summary of Protocols 6.1 and 6.2 with other similar server-based key establishment protocols of Gong [12, 13] as described in Table 6.1. In particular, we compare Protocols 6.1 and 6.2 with the protocol classes defined by Gong where both users contribute to the session key.

	Protocols	Messages/Rounds	Security proof?
	The following three protocols do not provide key confirmation (KC). However, key confirmation can be provided at the cost of an extra message.		
1.	Protocol 6.1	3 (+1 for KC)	Proven secure in the BR93 model.
2.	Timestamp-based protocol of Gong [13]	4 (+1 for KC)	No.
3.	Nonce-based protocol of Gong [13]	5 (+1 for KC)	No.
	The following three protocols provide key confirmation.		
4.	Alternative protocol of Gong using uncertified keys [13]	5	No.
5.	Hybrid protocol of Gong [12]	5	No.
6.	Protocol 6.2	4	
	Proven secure in the extended BR93 model. Protocols proven secure in the extended BR93 model will also be secure in the BR93 model. Moreover, Protocol 6.2 provides both key confirmation and forward secrecy.		

Table 6.1 A comparative summary

In terms of both messages and rounds, we observe that

- Protocol 6.1 is as efficient as that obtained by Gong [13] for server-based protocols with similar goals using timestamps.
- Protocol 6.2, which provides key confirmation, breaks Gong's lower bound of four since an extra round is required for providing key confirmation in the first three protocols described in described in Table 6.1.

Moreover, Protocol 6.2 removes the known weakness of Protocol 6.1 under the effect of a compromise of a long-term key as described in Chapter 6.3.1 at the expense of computational overhead (i.e., Protocol 6.2 is more computational expensive due to the use of Diffie–Hellman exponentation).

We also remark that another attractive feature of Protocol 6.2 is the extension which allows session keys to be renewed in subsequent sessions without the server's further involvement. The extension to Protocol 6.2 that allows the session key to be renewed is described in Protocol 6.3. This entails A and B exchanging new nonces N'_A and N'_B and computing the new session key as $K'_{AB} = \mathcal{H}_1(A||B||S||N'_A||N'_B||g^{N_A N_B}) = K'_{BA}$.

$$A \hspace{11cm} B$$

$$N'_A \in_R \{0,1\}^k \xrightarrow{\quad A, N'_A \quad} \xleftarrow{\quad B, N'_B \quad} N'_B \in_R \{0,1\}^k$$

$$SID_{A'} = (N'_A||N'_B) = SID_{B'}$$

$$K'_{AB} = \mathcal{H}_1(A||B||S||SID_{A'}||g^{N_A N_B}) = \mathcal{H}_1(A||B||S||SID_{B'}||g^{N_A N_B}) = K'_{BA}$$

Protocol 6.3: An extension to Protocol 6.2

Recall from our earlier discussion in Chapter 6.3.1 that exposing the long-term key will not enable the adversary to learn the CDH key, $g^{N_A N_B}$. Neither will the adversary be able to learn the CDH key, $g^{N_A N_B}$, by exposing an earlier agreed session key, K_{AB}. If the adversary is able to learn $g^{N_A N_B}$ by exposing K_{AB}, then we will be able to make use of such an adversary to break the underlying CDH problem. Therefore, the extension presented in Protocol 6.3 is still possible even if the long-term key or the earlier session key have been compromised. However, this is not the case for the other server-based three-party key establishment protocols described in Table 6.1.

6.5 Summary

We proved the security of another protocol example, revised protocol of Boyd [8] – Protocol 6.1, in the BR93 model. Although Protocol 6.1 is known to be insecure under reasonable assumptions, this does not show up in the original BR93 model because there is no capability for the adversary to reset corrupted principals.

We then extended the BR93 model so that it allows more realistic adversary capabilities, which allows us to detect a known weakness of Protocol 6.1 that cannot be captured in the original (BR93) model. We also presented another protocol (i.e., Protocol 6.2) that is efficient in both messages and rounds, and proved Protocol 6.2 secure in the extended BR93 model. This work also allowed us to detect a known weakness of the Boyd key agreement protocol [8] that cannot be captured in the original BR93 model.

References

1. Michel Abdalla, Pierre-Alain Fouqu & David Pointcheval 2005. Password-Based Authenticated Key Exchange in the Three-Party Setting, in Serge Vaudenay (ed), Proceedings of Public Key Cryptography - PKC 2005. Lecture Notes in Computer Science 3386/2005: 65-84

2. Mihir Bellare, A Boldyreva & Silvio Micali 2000. Public-key Encryption in a Multi-User Setting: Security Proofs and Improvements, in Bart Preneel (ed), Proceedings of Advances in Cryptology – EUROCRYPT 2000. Lecture Notes in Computer Science 1807/2000: 259–274

3. Mihir Bellare & Chanathip Namprempre 2000. Authenticated Encryption: Relations Among Notions and Analysis of the Generic Composition Paradigm, in Tatsuaki Okamoto (ed), Proceedings of Advances in Cryptology - ASIACRYPT 2000. Lecture Notes in Computer Science 1976/2000: 531–545

4. Mihir Bellare, David Pointcheval & Phillip Rogaway 2000. Authenticated Key Exchange Secure Against Dictionary Attacks, in Bart Preneel (ed), Proceedings of Advances in Cryptology - EUROCRYPT 2000. Lecture Notes in Computer Science 1807/2000: 139 - 155

5. Mihir Bellare & Phillip Rogaway 1995. Provably Secure Session Key Distribution: The Three Party Case, in F. Tom Leighton & Allan Borodin (eds), Proceedings of 27th ACM Symposium on the Theory of Computing - ACM STOC 1995. ACM Press: 57–66

6. Simon Blake-Wilson & Alfred Menezes 1997. Security Proofs for Entity Authentication and Authenticated Key Transport Protocols Employing Asymmetric Techniques, in Bruce Christianson, Bruno Crispo, T Mark, A Lomas & Michael Roe (eds), Proceedings of Security Protocols Workshop. Lecture Notes in Computer Science 1361/1997: 137–158

7. Simon Blake-Wilson & Alfred Menezes 1998. Authenticated Diffie–Hellman Key Agreement Protocols, in Stafford E Tavares & Henk Meijer (eds), Proceedings of Selected Areas in Cryptography - SAC 1998. Lecture Notes in Computer Science 1556/1998: 339–361

8. Colin Boyd 1996. A Class of Flexible and Efficient Key Management Protocols, in *Proceedings of 9th IEEE Computer Security Foundations Workshop - CSFW 1996*. IEEE Computer Society Press: 2–8

9. Colin Boyd & Anish Mathuria 2003. *Protocols for Authentication and Key Establishment*. Springer-Verlag

10. Bruno Crispo, Bogdan C Popescu & Andrew S Tanenbaum 2004. Symmetric Key Authentication Services Revisited, in Huaxiong Wang, Josef Pieprzyk & Vijay Varadharajan (eds), Proceedings of 9th Australasian Conference on Information Security and Privacy - ACISP 2004. Lecture Notes in Computer Science 3108/2004: 248–261

11. Oded Goldreich & Yehuda Lindell 2001. Session-Key Generation using Human Passwords Only, in Joe Kilian (ed), Proceedings of Advances in Cryptology – CRYPTO 2001. Lecture Notes in Computer Science 2139/2001: 408–432. Updated Version available from http://eprint.iacr.org/2000/057/

12. Li Gong 1989. Using One-Way Functions for Authentication. *ACM SIGCOMM Computer Communications Review* 8(11): 8–11

13. Li Gong 1993. Lower Bounds on Messages and Rounds for Network Authentication Protocols, in *Proceedings of 1st ACM Conference on Computer and Communications Security - ACM CCS 1993*. ACM Press: 26–37

Chapter 7
A Proof of Revised Yahalom Protocol

Although the Yahalom protocol, proposed by Burrows, Abadi, and Needham in 1990 [10], is one of the most prominent key establishment protocols analyzed by researchers from the computer security community (using automated proof tools), the protocol does not possess a security proof within a computational complexity framework. We note that in a recent work of Backes and Pfitzmann [2], a simplified version of this protocol is proven in the cryptographic library that corresponds to a slightly extended Dolev–Yao model [15].

In this chapter, we present a protocol for key establishment that is closely based on the Yahalom protocol. We then present a security proof in the Bellare–Rogaway model and the random oracle model. We hope that by providing such a proof for a slightly modified Yahalom protocol, this will be of interest to the researchers, in particular to researchers from the computer security community. We also observe that no partnering mechanism is specified within the Yahalom protocol (as in the case for many other key establishment protocols). In a real world setting, it is normal to assume that a host can establish several concurrent sessions with many different parties. Sessions are specific to both the communicating parties. In the case of key distribution protocols, sessions are specific to both the initiator and the responder principals, where every session is associated with a unique session key. Session identifiers (SIDs) enable unique identification of the individual sessions. We then present a brief discussion on the role and the possible construct of session identifiers as a form of partnering mechanism, which allows the right session key to be identified in concurrent protocol executions. We recommend that SIDs should be included within protocol specification rather than consider SIDs as artefacts in protocol proof.

Material presented in this chapter has appeared in the following publication:

- Kim-Kwang Raymond Choo. A Proof of Revised Yahalom Protocol in the Bellare and Rogaway (1993) Model. The Computer Journal, 50(5):591–601, 2007. [Received the Wilkes Award for the best paper published in the 2007 volume of *The Computer Journal*]

7.1 The Yahalom Protocol and its Simplified Version

We now revisit the Yahalom protocol [10] described in Protocol 7.1. At the end of Protocol 7.1's execution, both users A and B will accept the session key (SK_{AB}) generated by the trusted server, S. Other notation in Protocol 7.1 is as follows: $\mathscr{E}(m)_K$ denotes an encryption of some message m under symmetric key K; S denotes a server who shares long-term symmetric keys K_{AS} and K_{BS} with A and B respectively; N_A and N_B denote nonces generated by A and B respectively.

---

1. $A \rightarrow B : N_A$
2. $B \rightarrow S : B, \mathscr{E}(A, N_A, N_B)_{K_{BS}^{enc}}$
3. $S \rightarrow A : \mathscr{E}(B, SK_{AB}, N_A, N_B)_{K_{AS}^{enc}}, \mathscr{E}(A, SK_{AB})_{K_{BS}^{enc}}$
4. $A \rightarrow B : \mathscr{E}(A, SK_{AB})_{K_{BS}^{enc}}, \mathscr{E}(N_B)_{SK_{AB}}$

Protocol 7.1: The Yahalom protocol

Protocol 7.1 provides key confirmation – B is assured that A actually has possession of the same secret session key, SK_{AB}, since A sends to B the encryption of the nonce chosen by B, N_B, using SK_{AB}.

Choo and Hitchcock [13] pointed out informally that it does not appear possible to prove Protocol 7.1 secure in the BR93 model due to the encryption of the nonce using the established session key (i.e., $\mathscr{E}(N_B)_{SK_{AB}}$) in the last message (from A to B). In an independent yet related work, Backes and Pfitzmann [2] raise similar observation. In the simplified version proposed by Backes and Pfitzmann [2], the encryption of the nonce using the established session key (i.e., $\mathscr{E}(N_B)_{SK_{AB}}$) in message 4 is removed from the protocol for the following reason.

- Recall that security in the BR93 model is defined using a game simulation, $\mathscr{G}$, played between the adversary, $\mathscr{A}$, and a collection of player oracles, as described in Chapter 2.3.3 and success of $\mathscr{A}$ in $\mathscr{G}$ is quantified in terms of $\mathscr{A}$'s advantage in distinguishing whether $\mathscr{A}$ receives a real key or a random value from the game simulator.
- In the context of the proof simulation for Protocol 7.1, $\mathscr{A}$ can perform the follow set of actions.

  Stage 1. Asks a series of Send queries that model the above simulation of Protocol 7.1. For example, the adversary, $\mathscr{A}$, obtains nonce N_A after asking a Send$(A, B, *)$ query. $\mathscr{A}$ then proceed to choose nonce N_B and ask a Send$(B, A, (N_A, N_B))$ query where the game simulator will respond as per protocol specification.

  Stage 2. Decides that this particular session is the Test session, and then asks a Test query. The game simulator returns the key, SK_b.

  Stage 3. Skipped.

Stage 4.   Using the response from the Test query in stage 2, the adversary is able to determine whether the test session key given by the simulator was real or a random value as shown below. Recall that N_B is chosen by $\mathscr{A}$ in Stage 1 and let $\mathscr{D}(\cdot)_{SK}$ denotes the decryption of some message using the decryption key SK.

$$\mathscr{D}(\mathscr{E}(N_B)_{SK_{AB}})_{SK_b} \stackrel{?}{=} N_B$$

This, consequently, renders Protocol 7.1 insecure as $\mathscr{A}$ will have a non-negligible advantage in distinguishing the Test key received from the game simulator. This is in violation of Definition 2.3.3.

7.2 A New Provably-Secure Protocol

We will use the authenticated encryption scheme presented in Chapter 6 in the security proof for our proposed protocol.

Now that the authenticated encryption scheme to be employed in the protocol has been defined, we can define the protocol that we shall prove secure. New notation introduced here in Protocol 7.2 are:

- $\mathscr{H}$ and $\mathscr{H}_1$ denote two secure and independent cryptographic hash functions;
- $\{m\}_K$ denotes an authenticated encryption of some message m under symmetric key K;
- $\|$ denotes concatenation of messages;
- sid denotes the session identifier[1];
- $N_U \in_R \{0,1\}^w$ denotes a random w-bit nonce; and
- $SK_{AB} \in_R \{0,1\}^k$ denotes the random k-bit key generated by the server, S, for some session.

Protocol 7.2 is very similar to Protocol 7.1 and differences include (but not limited to) the following:

1. In Protocol 7.1, the session key (SK_{AB}) is contributed by the server, S, whilst for Protocol 7.2, users A and B as well as the server S contribute to the key value ($MK_{AB} = \mathscr{H}(sid\|0\|SK_{AB})$).
2. In Protocol 7.1's specification, there is no partnering mechanism (e.g., sid) specified. Without such partnering mechanism, communicating parties will be unable to uniquely distinguish messages from different sessions. This is further discussed in Chapter 7.3.
3. Due to the use of an authenticated encryption scheme in Protocol 7.2, the computational overhead is slightly more expensive than that of Protocol 7.1.

---

[1] Note that sid is made public upon protocol completion, and the security of the protocol does not hinge on the difficulty of predicting a valid sid. In other words, anyone (including the adversary, $\mathscr{A}$) knows what a particular sid is.

A	S	B

$N_A \in_R \{0,1\}^w$ $\xrightarrow{\quad A, N_A \quad}$ $N_B \in_R \{0,1\}^w$

$$sid_B = A||B||S||N_A||N_B$$

$$\xleftarrow{\quad \{sid_B\}_{K_{BS}}, B \quad}$$

$$SK_{AB} \in_R \{0,1\}^k$$

$$\xleftarrow{\quad \{SK_{AB}, sid_B\}_{K_{BS}}, \{SK_{AB}, sid_B, N_B\}_{K_{AS}} \quad}$$

Decrypt $\{SK_{AB}, sid_B, N_B\}_{K_{AS}}$

$sid_B \stackrel{?}{=} A||B||S||N_A||N_B$

$EK_A = \mathscr{H}_1(sid_B||1||SK_{AB})$

Session key, $MK_A = \mathscr{H}(sid_B||0||SK_{AB})$

STATUS: Accepted $\xrightarrow{\quad \{SK_{AB}, sid_B\}_{K_{BS}}, \{N_B\}_{EK_A} \quad}$ Decrypt $\{SK_{AB}, sid_B\}_{K_{BS}}$

Verify sid_B; $EK_B = \mathscr{H}_1(sid_B||1||SK_{AB})$

Decrypt $\{N_B\}_{EK_A}$ and obtain N_B'

$$N_B' \stackrel{?}{=} N_B$$

Session key, $MK_B = \mathscr{H}(sid_B||0||SK_{AB})$

STATUS: Accepted

Protocol 7.2: A revised Yahalom protocol

Informally, the inclusion of the

- Identities of the participants[2] and role asymmetry within the session key construction effectively ensures some sense of direction. If the role of the participants or the identities of the (perceived) partner change, the session keys will also be different. Hence, this provides resilience against unknown key share and reflection attacks.
- Unique session identifier (*sid*) within the session key construction ensures that session keys will be fresh. Moreover, it appears that the publication of *sid* upon protocol completion results in $\mathscr{A}$ being unable to get B to accept nonce pair (which is part of the published *sid*) as the session key. Recall a different *sid* also mean a different session key. Hence, it appears that the type flaw attack revealed on Protocol 7.1 by Basin, Mödersheim, and Viganò [3, 5] is thwarted.

7.2.1 Proof for Protocol 7.2

Theorem 7.2.1 *Protocol 7.2 is a secure key establishment protocol if the underlying authenticated encryption scheme is INT-PTXT secure as described in Definition 6.1.1 and both $\mathscr{H}$ and $\mathscr{H}_1$ are modelled as independent random oracles.*

---

[2] Such an approach is also recommended by National Institute of Standards and Technology (NIST) [6]

The proof follows the approach described in Chapter 6.1.3.

7.2.1.1 Integrity attacker

We now construct a forger $\mathscr{F}$ against the security of the authenticated encryption scheme, $\mathscr{SE}$, described in Definition 6.1.1, using an adversary against Protocol 7.2, $\mathscr{A}$. We will say that the event success$_{\mathscr{F}}$ occurs if $\mathscr{F}$ wins game $\mathscr{G}_2$ against $\mathscr{SE}$.

Lemma 7.2.1 *There is an efficient algorithm $\mathscr{F}$ defined using $\mathscr{A}$ such that if* forge *occurs with non-negligible probability then* success$_{\mathscr{F}}$ *occurs with non-negligible probability*.

In order to prove Lemma 6.1.2 we describe how $\mathscr{F}$ is constructed. When $\mathscr{F}$ runs it receives access to the encryption and verification oracles of the authenticated encryption scheme $\mathscr{SE}$. Its output must be a forged ciphertext for a message m which was not previously input to the encryption oracle.

In order to obtain the forgery $\mathscr{F}$ runs $\mathscr{A}$ by first choosing a user U_i for $i \in_R [1,Q]$. This user will be simulated as though its long-term key is the one used in $\mathscr{SE}$. For all other $j \in [1,Q]$ with $j \neq i$, $\mathscr{F}$ generates the long-term shared key using the key generation algorithm $\mathscr{K}_k$. This allows $\mathscr{F}$ to answer all the oracle queries from $\mathscr{A}$ as follows.

Send(U_1, s, M)   For any well-formed queries to S, $\mathscr{F}$ can reply with valid ciphertexts, by choosing the session key and forming the ciphertexts, either directly using the known key or using the encryption oracle in the case of U_i. For queries to initiate a protocol run, $\mathscr{F}$ can generate a random nonce and answer appropriately. Finally, consider a query to either an initiator or responder oracle including a claimed server message (corresponding to protocol messages 3 or 4). The relevant ciphertext can be verified either directly using the known key or using the verification oracle. If the ciphertext is verified correctly then the oracle accepts and this information is returned to $\mathscr{A}$.

Reveal(U, s)   Since all session keys are known from running the Send(U, s, M) queries the query can be trivially answered with the correct session key (if accepted).

Corrupt(U)   As long as $U \neq U_i$ all the private information is available and the query can be answered. In the case $U = U_i$ then the query cannot be answered and $\mathscr{F}$ will abort and fail.

Test(U, s)   Since all the accepted session keys are known from running the Send queries the query can be trivially answered by identifying the correct session key.

$\mathscr{F}$ continues the simulation until a forgery event against $\mathscr{SE}$ occurs, or until $\mathscr{A}$ halts. Note that as long as $\mathscr{F}$ does not abort then the simulation is perfect. If forge occurs then the probability that the user involved is U_i equals $1/Q$. In this case the event success$_\mathscr{F}$ occurs. Futhermore, in this case $\mathscr{F}$ does not abort since U_i cannot be corrupted before the forge event. Therefore we arrive at the following upper bound.

$$\Pr(\text{forge}) \leq Q \cdot \Pr(\text{success}_\mathscr{F}) \qquad (7.1)$$

7.2.1.2 Confidentiality attacker

For the second part of the proof, we assume that $\mathscr{A}$ gains an advantage without producing a forgery. We construct an attacker with a non-negligible advantage against the encryption scheme, $\mathscr{X}$, using the adversary, $\mathscr{A}$, as described in Chapter 6.1.3.2. Two random keys K and K' are chosen by the challenger for $\mathscr{SE}$ and $\mathscr{X}$ is given access to the encryption oracles for these keys. First $\mathscr{X}$ chooses two users U_i and U_j for $i, j \in_R [1, Q]$. For all other $k \in [1, Q]$, $\mathscr{X}$ generates the long-term key using the key generation algorithm $\mathscr{K}_k$. Next $\mathscr{A}$ chooses two random session keys K_0 and K_1. Suppose that Q_S is the maximum number of Send queries that $\mathscr{A}$ will ask of the server and Q_H is the maximum number of hash queries that $\mathscr{A}$ will ask of the server. $\mathscr{X}$ chooses a value s_0 randomly in $[1, Q_S]$. The idea is that $\mathscr{X}$ will inject the ciphertexts C_b, C_b' into a random SendServer query. $\mathscr{X}$ proceeds to simulate responses for $\mathscr{A}$ as follows. Let U_I and U_R denote the initiator and the responder respectively.

Note that we also require two separate lists of tuples, $L_{\mathscr{H}}$ and $L_{\mathscr{H}_1}$ to be maintained. If we are asked queries of the form $\mathscr{H}(SID_i^k||0||SK)$ and $\mathscr{H}_1(SID_i^k||1||SK)$, we check to see if the queries have been previously asked. If so, then the previous answer stored in the respective list will be returned (to maintain consistency). Otherwise, return a random value, $v \in_R \{0,1\}^k$. In addition, store this answer together with the query in the respective list.

SendClient: In the case of $U_1 = U_I$, $U_2 = U_R$, and $m = *$, then this will start a protocol run. This query can be successfully answered by $\mathscr{X}$ and the outgoing message is some randomly chosen k-bit challenge N_{U_1}.

SendClient: In the case of $U_1 = U_R$, $U_2 = U_I$, and m is some k-bit challenge, then $\mathscr{X}$ will choose a unique k-bit challenge, N_{U_2}; computes the session identitifer, $sid = U_1||U_2||S||m||N_{U_2}$ and the respective ciphertext; and successfully answer this query.

SendServer: In the case of $U_1 = \{U_I, U_R\}$, $U_2 = S$, and m is of the right format (as per message 2 in protocol specification), then S will run the session key generator and output a session key not previously output and generates the respective ciphertexts as the protocol specification demands.

SendClient: In the case of $U_1 = U_I$, $U_2 = U_R$, and m is of the right format (as per message 3 in protocol specification). Since we assume that $\mathscr{A}$ is not able to produce any MAC forgeries, all session keys (if accepted) are known from the SendServer(U_1, U_2, ι, m) queries. Hence, if the received ciphertext (MAC digest) verifies correctly, the message must have been generated by $\mathscr{X}$ during a SendServer query and in this case, $\mathscr{X}$ will output the decision $\delta = accept$. Otherwise, $\mathcal{X}$ will output the decision $\delta = reject$, as the protocol specification demands.

SendClient: If $U_1 = U_I$, $U_2 = U_R$, and m is of the right format (as per message 4 in protocol specification). Again under the assumption that $\mathcal{A}$ is not able to produce any MAC forgeries, all session keys (if accepted) are known from the SendServer(U_1, U_2, ι, m) queries. Since we also know the keying materials for both the session key and the one-time encryption/MAC key EK (used to encrypt the nonce of U_R) are the same and if received ciphertext (MAC digest) verifies correctly, the message must have been generated by $\mathcal{X}$ during a SendServer query. Therefore, $\mathcal{X}$ will output the decision $\delta = accept$. Otherwise, $\mathcal{X}$ will output the decision $\delta = reject$, as the protocol specification demands.

In all other cases the input to the SendClient or SendServer is invalid, $\mathcal{X}$ will terminate and halt the simulation. Hence, SendClient and SendServer queries can be correctly answered by $\mathcal{X}$.

This completes the description of $\mathcal{X}$. Since all the accepted session keys are known from running the SendClient and SendServer queries, the Test query can be trivially answered by identifying the correct session key.

Let lucky be the event that $\mathcal{X}$ does not fail during the Test query. When lucky occurs, $\mathcal{X}$ wins game $\mathcal{G}'_1$ whenever $\mathcal{A}$ is successful. This means that

$$\Pr(\text{success}_{\mathcal{X}} | \text{lucky}) \geq \Pr(\text{success}_{\mathcal{A}} | \overline{\text{forge}}).$$

We also have $\Pr(\text{lucky}) \geq 1/(Q^2 \cdot Q_S)$. Putting these together we obtain:

$$\Pr(\text{success}_{\mathcal{A}} | \overline{\text{forge}}) \leq Q^2 \cdot Q_S \cdot \Pr(\text{success}_{\mathcal{X}}). \tag{7.2}$$

7.2.1.3 Conclusion of Proof for Theorem 7.2.1

Since N, Q_S, and Q_H are polynomial in the security parameter k and ε is negligible by definition. Therefore, by combining equations 7.1 and 7.2 completes the proof for Theorem 7.2.1.

7.2.2 An Extension to Protocol 7.2

In addition to the basic Protocol 7.2, there is an extension which allows the session key to be renewed in subsequent sessions without the server's further involvement (i.e., re-authentication). This entails A and B exchanging new nonces N'_A and N'_B and computing the new session key as $MK'_A = \mathcal{H}(sid_{A'} || SK_{AB}) = \mathcal{H}(sid_{B'} || SK_{AB}) = MK'_B$ where $sid_{A'} = sid_{B'} = (A || B || S || N'_A || N'_B)$ as described by Protocol 7.3. Protocol 7.3 can also be enhanced with key confirmation, which consists of a handshake using the shared secret.

A	B

$$N'_A \in_R \{0,1\}^w \xrightarrow{\ A, N'_A\ } \xleftarrow{\ B, N'_B\ } N'_B \in_R \{0,1\}^w$$

$$sid_{A'} = (A||B||S||N'_A||N'_B) = sid_{B'}$$

$$MK'_A = \mathcal{H}(sid_{A'}||SK_{AB}) = \mathcal{H}(sid_{B'}||SK_{AB}) = MK'_B$$

Protocol 7.3: An extension to Protocol 7.2 (i.e., re-authentication)

Remark. We are unable to prove Protocol 7.3 secure in the current model we are using. To prove Protocol 7.3 secure, we would have to modify the definitions of freshness (described in Definition 2.3.1) and partnership (described in Definition 2.3.6). This is to restrict the adversary from exposing session key agreed by both A and B in their previous session (i.e., SK_{AB}) without rendering the session key unfresh.

7.3 Partnering Mechanism: A Brief Discussion

In Protocol 7.1, partnering mechanism does not form part of its specification. Message exchanges in the real world are seldom conducted over secure channels. Therefore, it is realistic to assume that any adversary is able to modify messages at will, which is the case in the Bellare–Rogaway style models. As Goldreich and Lindell [17, Section 1.3] have pointed out, such an adversary capability means that the adversary is able to conduct concurrent executions of the protocol (one with each party).

For protocols proven secure in the Bellare–Rogaway style models or the Canetti–Krawczyk model [11], session identifiers as partnering mechanism are not explicitly part of the protocol specification but rather embedded within the partnership definition (e.g., it is stated that the correctness of session identifiers can be omitted from the formal protocol specification [19]). We also observe that in the Canetti–Krawczyk model, the values of the session identifiers are not specified. Instead, it is assumed that session identifiers are known by protocol participants before the protocol begins. Such an assumption might not be practical as it requires some forms of communication between the protocol participation prior to the start of the protocol. Furthermore, by assuming that session identifiers are known by protocol participants before the protocol begins indicates that session identifiers do not form part of the protocol specification.

We advocate that session identifiers play a significant role in protocol security as they bind together incoming and outgoing messages, and uniquely identify a particular session. In other words, attacks against protocol is also predicated on the constructions of SIDs chosen as shown by Bohli, González Vasco, and Steinwandt

[9] and Choo and Hitchcock [13].

In practice, it seems more intuitive to include session identifiers within the protocol specification since implementation of such protocols (e.g., SSL and IPSec) should allow applications to distinguish between the various concurrent sessions between one or many other applications. In other words, protocol on its own (without the session identifiers component) does not allow concurrent executions since oracles have no means of uniquely identifying one session from another. Moreover, not all protocols are proven secure in the Bellare–Rogaway style models and the Canetti–Krawczyk model or carry any security proofs.

How to Construct SIDs? In practice, session identifiers may be determined during protocol execution [11, 14, 20], as in the case of the Bellare, Pointcheval, and Rogaway model [7] and recent work of Krawczyk [21] whereby session identifiers are defined to be the concatentation of all incoming and outgoing messages. However, this might not be achievable in some protocols where the protocol participants do not have full view of the messages exchanged (e.g., the inability to define session identifiers in the Bellare–Rogaway 3PKD protocol [8] pointed out by Choo *et al.* [12]). As a bare minimum, session identifiers constructed in this context, should contain some unique contributions from each participant (e.g., random nonces, timestamps) and the identities of the peers (which is the case for Protocol 7.2).

Recommendations. Therefore, we suggest consider the construction of session identifiers or some forms of partnering mechanism within the protocol specification. Otherwise, this will result in the inability of communicating principals to uniquely distinguish messages from different sessions. Consequently, this leads one to question the practicality and usefulness of the protocol in a real world setting. Moreover, including session identifiers in the key derivation function ensures that entities who have completed matching sessions, partners, will accept the same session key.

Word of Caution. We do not claim that including session identifiers or some forms of partnering mechanism within protocol specifications is the panacea to the design of secure protocols. The security of the protocol is based on many other factors, such as the underlying cryptographic primitives used. However, in our view, the design of any entity authentication and/or key establishment protocol should incorporate a secure means of uniquely identifying a particular communication session among the many concurrent sessions that a communicating party may have with many different parties.

7.4 Summary

Table 7.1 presents a comparative summary of our proven secure protocol, Protocol 7.2, with two other similar server-based three-party key establishment protocols, namely the Bauer–Berson–Feiertag protocol [4] and the Otway-Rees protocol [22].

Protocols	Computational	Security proof?
Protocol 7.2	Slightly more expensive due to use of authenticated encryption scheme	BR93 model
Extensions to Protocol 7.2 allows session key to be renewed in subsequent sessions without invoking the server (see Protocol 7.3). Moreover, Protocol 7.2 ensures that entities who have completed matching sessions, partners, will accept the same session key (recall that *sid* is included in the key derivation function) without requiring the server to store every message processed and not issue different session keys for the same input message received.		
Otway-Rees [22]	cheap	Dolev–Yao style model [1]
In the approach taken by Backes [1], the server is required to store every message processed and not issue different session keys for the same input message received. Without this assumption, a malicious adversary is able to make the initiator and the responder agree on a different session key by asking a trusted third party (i.e., server) to create multiple session keys in response to the same message, as revealed by Fabrega, Herzog, and Guttman [16]. However, it has been pointed out that this assumption only works well within a confined implementation and will not scale well to a more realistic environment with a large number of participating parties and a substantial level of traffic to any one server [13].		
Bauer–Berson–Feiertag [4]	cheap	No

Table 7.1 A comparative summary

In conclusion, we proved the security of another protocol example (a revised protocol based on the Yahalom protocol [10]) in the BR93 model. In terms of both messages and rounds, we observe from Table 7.1 that all three protocols satisfy the lower bound of four messages obtained by Gong [18] for server-based protocols with similar goals using timestamps. However, an extension to Protocol 7.2 allows session key to be renewed in subsequent sessions without invoking the server (as described in Chapter 7.2.2), which makes it more attractive than the other two protocols (in a realistic setting). As mentioned in Chapter 7.2.2, we are unable to prove Protocol 7.3 secure in the current model we are using. To prove Protocol 7.3 secure, we would have to modify the definitions of freshness (described in Definition 2.3.1) and partnership (described in Definition 2.3.6). This is to restrict the adversary from exposing session key agreed by both A and B in their previous session (i.e., SK_{AB}) without rendering the session key unfresh.

We then briefly discussed the role of session identifiers as a form of partnering mechanism and concluded with the recommendation that session identifiers should be included within protocol specification. This will allow concurrent executions and a mean of uniquely identifying one session from another. Furthermore, by including session identifiers in the key derivation function, ensures that entities who have completed matching sessions, partners, will accept the same session key.

As a result of this work, we recommended that session identifiers should be included within protocol specification rather than considering session identifiers as artefacts in protocol proof, even for protocols proven secure in the computational complexity framework.

References

1. Michael Backes 2004. A Cryptographically Sound Dolev-Yao Style Security Proof of the Otway-Rees Protocol, in Samarati P & Gollmann D (eds), Proceedings of 9th European Symposium on Research in Computer Security - ESORICS 2004. Lecture Notes in Computer Science 3193/2004: 89–108

2. Michael Backes & Birgit Pfitzmann 2006. On the Cryptographic Key Secrecy of the Strengthened Yahalom Protocol, in Simone Fischer-Hübner, Kai Rannenberg, Louise Yngström & Stefan Lindskog (eds), Proceedings of IFIP TC-11 21st International Information Security Conference - SEC 2006. IFIP International Federation for Information Processing Series 201/2006: 233–245

3. David A. Basin and Sebastian Mödersheim and Luca Viganó 2003. An On-the-Fly Model-Checker for Security Protocol Analysis. *Technical report* no 404. Information Security Group, ETH Zentrum

4. R. K. Bauer, Thomas A. Berson & Richard J. Feiertag 1983. A Key Distribution Protocol Using Event Markers. *ACM Transactions on Computer Systems* 1(3): 249–255

5. David A. Basin and Sebastian Mödersheim and Luca Viganó 2003. An On-the-Fly Model-Checker for Security Protocol Analysis, in Einar Snekkenes & Dieter Gollmann (eds), Proceedings of 8th European Symposium on Research in Computer Security - ESORICS 2003. Lecture Notes in Computer Science 2808/2003: 253–270

6. Elaine Barker, Don Johnson, & Miles Smid 2006. Recommendation for Pair-Wise Key Establishment Schemes Using Discrete Logarithm Cryptography. *Special Publication (SP 800-56A)*. National Institute of Standards and Technology

7. Mihir Bellare, David Pointcheval & Phillip Rogaway 2000. Authenticated Key Exchange Secure Against Dictionary Attacks, in Bart Preneel (ed), Proceedings of Advances in Cryptology - EUROCRYPT 2000. Lecture Notes in Computer Science 1807/2000: 139 – 155

8. Mihir Bellare & Phillip Rogaway 1995. Provably Secure Session Key Distribution: The Three Party Case, in F. Tom Leighton & Allan Borodin (eds), Proceedings of 27th ACM Symposium on the Theory of Computing - ACM STOC 1995. ACM Press: 57–66

9. Jens-Matthias Bohli, Maria Isabel González Vasco & Rainer Steinwandt 2005. Secure Group Key Establishment Revisited. *Cryptology ePrint Archive, Report 2005/395*. http://eprint.iacr.org/2005/395

10. Michael Burrows, Martín Abadi & Roger Needham 1990. A Logic of Authentication. *ACM Transactions on Computer Systems* 8(1): 18–36

11. Ran Canetti & Hugo Krawczyk 2001. Analysis of Key-Exchange Protocols and Their Use for Building Secure Channels, in Birgit Pfitzmann (ed), Proceedings of Advances in Cryptology - EUROCRYPT 2001. Lecture Notes in Computer Science 2045/2001: 453–474. Extended version available from http://eprint.iacr.org/2001/040/

12. Kim-Kwang Raymond Choo, Colin Boyd, Yvonne Hitchcock & Greg Maitland 2004. On Session Identifiers in Provably Secure Protocols: The Bellare-Rogaway Three-Party Key Distribution Protocol Revisited, in Blundo Carlo & Stelvio Cimato (eds), Proceedings of 4th Conference on Security in Communication Networks - SCN 2004. Lec-

ture Notes in Computer Science 3352/2005: 352–367. Extended version available from http://eprint.iacr.org/2004/345

13. Kim-Kwang Raymond Choo & Yvonne Hitchcock 2005. Security Requirements for Key Establishment Proof Models: Revisiting Bellare–Rogaway and Jeong–Katz–Lee Protocols, in Colin Boyd & Juan Manuel González Nieto (eds), Proceedings of 10th Australasian Conference on Information Security and Privacy - ACISP 2005. Lecture Notes in Computer Science 3574/2005: 429–442. Received the Best Student Paper award

14. Yvonne Cliff, Yiu-Shing Terry Tin & Colin Boyd 2006. Password Based Server Aided Key Exchange, in Jianying Zhou, Moti Yung & Feng Bao (eds), Proceedings of Applied Cryptography and Network Security - ACNS 2006. Lecture Notes in Computer Science 3989/2006: 146–161

15. Danny Dolev & Andrew C Yao 1983. On the Security of Public Key Protocols. *IEEE Transaction of Information Technology* 29(2): 198–208

16. F. Javier Thayer Fabrega, Jonathan C. Herzog & Joshua D. Guttman 1999. Strand Spaces: Proving Security Protocols Correct. *Journal of Computer Security* 7(2/3): 191–230

17. Oded Goldreich & Yehuda Lindell 2001. Session-Key Generation using Human Passwords Only, in Joe Kilian (ed), Proceedings of Advances in Cryptology – CRYPTO 2001. Lecture Notes in Computer Science 2139/2001: 408–432. Updated Version available from http://eprint.iacr.org/2000/057/

18. Li Gong 1993. Lower Bounds on Messages and Rounds for Network Authentication Protocols, in *Proceedings of 1st ACM Conference on Computer and Communications Security - ACM CCS 1993*. ACM Press: 26–37

19. Yvonne Hitchcock, Colin Boyd & Juan Manuel González Nieto 2004. Tripartite Key Exchange in the Canetti-Krawczyk Proof Model, in Anne Canteaut & Kapaleeswaran Viswanathan (eds), Proceedings of 5th International Conference on Cryptology in India - INDOCRYPT 2004. Lecture Notes in Computer Science 3348/2004: 17–32

20. Yvonne Hitchcock, Colin Boyd & Juan Manuel González Nieto 2005. Modular Proofs for Key Exchange: Rigorous Optimizations in the Canetti-Krawczyk Model. *Applicable Algebra in Engineering, Communication and Computing Journal* 16(6): 405–438

21. Hugo Krawczyk 2005. HMQV: A High-Performance Secure Diffie–Hellman Protocol, in Victor Shoup (ed), Proceedings of Advances in Cryptology - CRYPTO 2005. Lecture Notes in Computer Science 3621/2005: 546–566. Extended version available from http://eprint.iacr.org/2005/176/

22. Dave Otway & Owen Rees 1987. Efficient and Timely Mutual Authentication. *ACM Operating Systems Review* 21(1): 8–10

Chapter 8
Errors in Computational Complexity Proofs for Protocols

We have presented several examples of flawed computational proofs of protocol security in the earlier chapters. Flaws in security proofs certainly will have a damaging effect on the trustworthiness and the credibility of provably-secure protocols in the real world. Despite the difficulties in obtaining correct security proofs, we advocate the importance of proofs for arguing about protocol security.

In this chapter, we identify some situations where errors in proofs arise and hope that similar structural mistakes can be avoided in future security proofs. As case studies, we use several protocols with claimed proofs in the Bellare–Rogaway model, namely the conference key agreement protocol due to Boyd and González Nieto [5], the mutual authentication and key establishment protocols (JP-MAKEP) due to Jakobsson and Pointcheval [15], and WC-MAKEP due to Wong and Chan [26]. These protocols are presented in Sections 8.1, 8.2, and 8.3 respectively. New attacks on these protocols are demonstrated and flaws in their existing security proofs are revealed. Ways of preventing the attacks are also proposed. We remark that the improved protocols are not proven secure, and are presented mainly to provide a better insight into the proof failures.

We also examine an encryption-based MT authenticator due to Bellare, Canetti, and Krawczyk [3] in Chapter 8.4. The flaw in the encryption-based MT-authenticator is revealed and an improved MT-authenticator is presented. The revealed flaw supports an earlier observation of Rogaway [22] who pointed out the importance of robust and detailed definitions in concrete security. In fact, specifications adopted in the computer security approach are expected to be precise (without ambiguity) and detailed, as such specifications are subjected to automated checking using formal tools. Boyd and Mathuria [6] also pointed out that it is the responsibility of the protocol designers and not the protocol implementers to define the details of protocol specifications. Protocol implementers (usually non-specialists and/or industrial practitioners) will usually plug-and-use existing provably-secure protocols without reading the formal proofs of the protocols [18, 19].

We then demonstrate how this revealed flaw in the MT-authenticator [3] invalidates security proofs of protocols that use the MT-authenticator by using protocol 2DHPE of Hitchcock, Tin, Boyd, González Nieto, and Montague [13] as a case study.

Material presented in this chapter has appeared in the following publication:

- Kim-Kwang Raymond Choo, Colin Boyd, and Yvonne Hitchcock. Errors in Computational Complexity Proofs for Protocols. In Bimal Roy, editor, Advances in Cryptology - Asiacrypt 2005, volume 3788/2005 of Lecture Notes in Computer Science, pages 624–643. Springer-Verlag, 2005.

8.1 Boyd–González Nieto Protocol

The conference key agreement protocol[1] Protocol 8.1 [5] carries a claimed proof of security in the BR93 model, but uses a different definition of partnership than that given in the original model description. Recall the notation introduced in Table 2.1: (e_U, d_U) denotes the encryption and signature keys of principal U respectively; $\{\cdot\}_{e_U}$ denotes the encryption of some message under key e_U; $\sigma_{d_U}(\cdot)$ denotes the signature of some message under the signature key d_U; N_U denotes the random nonce chosen by principal U; $\mathscr{H}$ denotes some cryptographic hash function; and SK_U denotes the session key accepted by U. Protocol 8.1 involves a set of p users, $\mathscr{U} = \{U_1, U_2, \ldots, U_p\}$. The session identifier (SID) in Protocol 8.1 is defined to be the concatenation of messages received and sent.

---

1. $U_1 \rightarrow *: \mathscr{U} = \{U_1, U_2, \ldots, U_p\}, \sigma_{d_{U_1}}(\mathscr{U}, \{N_1\}_{e_{U_2}}, \ldots, \{N_1\}_{e_{U_p}})$
2. $U_1 \rightarrow *: \{N_1\}_{e_{U_i}}$ for $1 < i \leq p$
3. $U_i \rightarrow *: U_i, N_i$

The session key is $SK_{U_i} = \mathscr{H}(N_1 || N_2 || \ldots || N_p)$.

Protocol 8.1: Boyd–González Nieto conference key agreement protocol

1 and 2. The initiator, U_1, randomly selects a k-bit challenge N_1, where k is the security parameter. U_1 then encrypts N_1 under the public keys of the other participants in the protocol, signs the encrypted nonces $\{N_1\}_{e_{U_2}}, \ldots, \{N_1\}_{e_{U_p}}$ and broadcasts these messages in protocol flows 1 and 2 of Protocol 8.1.

3. The other principals, upon receiving the broadcast messages, will respond with their identity and a random nonce. All principals are then able to compute the shared session key

$$SK_{U_i} = \mathscr{H}(N_1 || N_2 || \ldots || N_p).$$

---

[1] Although this protocol was proposed fairly recently, it has already been widely cited and used as a benchmark [2, 7, 9, 10, 11, 16, 17].

8.1.1 Unknown Key Share Attack on Protocol

Attack 8.1 shows the execution of Protocol 8.1 in the presence of a malicious adversary, $\mathscr{A}$. For simplicity, let $\mathscr{U} = \{U_1, U_2, U_3\}$ and $\mathscr{U}_\mathscr{A} = \{\mathscr{A}, U_2, U_3\}$, which denote two different sessions.

1.	$U_1 \rightarrow U_2, U_3:$	$\mathscr{U} = \{U_1, U_2, U_3\}$
		$\sigma_{d_{U_1}}(\mathscr{U}, \{N_1\}_{e_{U_2}}, \{N_1\}_{e_{U_3}})$
2.	$U_1 \rightarrow U_2, U_3:$	$\{N_1\}_{e_{U_2}}, \{N_1\}_{e_{U_3}}$
		Both messages intercepted by $\mathscr{A}$
1($\mathscr{A}$).	$\mathscr{A} \rightarrow U_2, U_3:$	$\mathscr{U}_\mathscr{A} = \{\mathscr{A}, U_2, U_3\}$
		$\sigma_{d_\mathscr{A}}(\mathscr{U}_\mathscr{A}, \{N_1\}_{e_{U_2}}, \{N_1\}_{e_{U_3}})$
2($\mathscr{A}$).	$\mathscr{A} \rightarrow U_2, U_3:$	$\{N_1\}_{e_{U_2}}, \{N_1\}_{e_{U_3}}$ for $1 < i \leq p$
3.	$U_i \rightarrow *:$	$U_i, N_i,$ for $i = 2, 3$

The session key is $SK_{U_i} = \mathscr{H}(N_1 \| N_2 \| N_3)$.

Attack 8.1: Unknown key share attack on Protocol 8.1

In Attack 8.1, the actions of the entities are as follows:

1 and 2. The initiator, U_1, encrypts N_1 under the public keys of the other participants in the protocol (i.e., $\mathscr{U} \setminus U_1$), signs the encrypted nonces $\{N_1\}_{e_{U_2}}$, $\{N_1\}_{e_{U_3}}$ together with $\mathscr{U}$, and broadcasts these messages in protocol flows 1 and 2.

1($\mathscr{A}$) and 2($\mathscr{A}$). A malicious adversary, $\mathscr{A}$, intercepts the broadcast messages sent by U_1; that is, the broadcast messages sent by U_1 never reach the intended recipients, U_2 and U_3.

- $\mathscr{A}$ then signs the intercepted encrypted nonces $\{N_1\}_{e_{U_2}}$, $\{N_1\}_{e_{U_3}}$ together with $\mathscr{U}_\mathscr{A}$ (instead of $\mathscr{U}$) under $\mathscr{A}$'s signing key.
- $\mathscr{A}$ now acts as the **initiator** in a **different session** and broadcasts these messages in protocol flows 1 and 2.

3. U_2 and U_3 upon receiving the broadcast messages, reply to $\mathscr{A}$ with their identities and random nonces.

$\mathscr{A}$ impersonates U_2 and U_3 and forwards the messages from U_2 and U_3 to U_1. U_1, U_2, and U_3 are then able to compute the shared session key

$$SK_{U_i} = \mathscr{H}(N_1 \| N_2 |, | \ldots \| N_n).$$

Table 8.1 describes the internal states of players U_1, U_2, and U_3 at the end of Attack 8.1. We observe that U_1 is not partnered with either U_2 or U_3 according to Definition 2.3.6, since U_1 does not have matching SIDs or agreeing PIDs. Such an attack is also termed the key replicating attack as described in Definition 2.3.12. In this case, $\mathscr{A}$ can distinguish whether the Test-session key is real or a random value by asking a Reveal query to the oracle associated with S_1).

U_1 believes that the session key SK_{U_1} is being shared with U_2 and U_3, but U_2 (and U_3 respectively) believes the key $SK_{U_2} = \mathscr{H}(N_1 \| N_2 \| N_3) = SK_{U_3} = SK_{U_1}$ is being

U	sid_U	pid_U
U_1	$\mathcal{U}, \sigma_{d_{U_1}}(\mathcal{U}, \{N_1\}_{e_{U_2}}, \{N_1\}_{K_{U_3}}),$ $\{N_1\}_{e_{U_2}}, \{N_1\}_{e_{U_3}}, U_2, N_2, U_3, N_3$	$\{U_2, U_3\}$
U_2	$\mathcal{U}_{\mathscr{A}}, \sigma_{d_{\mathscr{A}}}(\mathcal{U}_{\mathscr{A}}, \{N_1\}_{e_{U_2}}, \{N_1\}_{e_{U_3}}),$ $\{N_1\}_{e_{U_2}}, \{N_1\}_{e_{U_3}}, U_2, N_2, U_3, N_3$	$\{\mathscr{A}, U_3\}$
U_3	$\mathcal{U}_{\mathscr{A}}, \sigma_{d_{\mathscr{A}}}(\mathcal{U}_{\mathscr{A}}, \{N_1\}_{e_{U_2}}, \{N_1\}_{e_{U_3}}),$ $\{N_1\}_{e_{U_2}}, \{N_1\}_{e_{U_3}}, U_2, N_2, U_3, N_3$	$\{\mathscr{A}, U_2\}$

Table 8.1 Internal states of players U_1, U_2, and U_3

shared with $\mathscr{A}$ and U_3 (and U_2 respectively), when in fact, the key is being shared among U_1, U_2, and U_3. However, $SK_{U_1} = SK_{U_2} = SK_{U_3} = \mathscr{H}(N_1||N_2||N_3)$. Although the adversary, $\mathscr{A}$, does not know the value of the session key as $\mathscr{A}$ does not know the value of N_1, $\mathscr{A}$ is able to send a Reveal query to the session associated with either U_2 or U_3 and obtain $SK_{U_2} = \mathscr{H}(N_1||N_2||N_3) = SK_{U_3}$, which has the same value as SK_{U_1}. Protocol 8.1 is not secure in the BR93 model since $\mathscr{A}$ is able to obtain the fresh session key of the initiator U_1 by revealing non-partner oracles of U_1, namely U_2 or U_3, in violation of the security definition given in Definition 2.3.3.

8.1.2 An Improved Conference Key Agreement Protocol

It would appear that by changing the order of the application of the signature and encryption schemes, Attack 8.1 can be avoided. At first glance, however, this may appear to contradict the result of An, Dodis, and Rabin [1] that no matter what order signature and encryption schemes are applied, the result can still be secure. A closer inspection reveals that our observation actually supports the findings of An *et al.*, since the protocol operates in a multi-user setting. Although An *et al.* found that signature and encryption schemes can be applied in either order in the two user setting, they found some further restrictions in the multi-user setting. These restrictions are that the sender's identity must be included in every encryption and the recipient's identity must be included in every signature. In this case, swapping the order of the encryption and signature schemes happens to cause Protocol 8.1 to fulfil these requirements.

An alternative way to prevent Attack 8.1 is to include the session identifier, *sid*, in the key derivation function. We use the same construct for *sid* as used by Boyd and González Nieto, which is the concatenation of all messages received. In the improved protocol, the adversary $\mathscr{A}$ will not be able to "claim" ownership of the encrypted message $\{N_1, U_1\}_{e_{U_i}}$ since the identity of the initiator is included in the encryption. Since the construct of the session key in the improved protocol comprises the associated *sid*, a different *sid* will imply a different session key. Hence, Attack 8.1 will no longer be valid against this improved protocol. Protocol 8.2 describes the improved protocol.

---

1. $U_1 \rightarrow * : \mathcal{U} = \{U_1, U_2, \ldots, n\}, \sigma_{d_{U1}}(\mathcal{U}, \{N_1, U_1\}_{K_{U_2}}, \ldots, \{N_1, U_1\}_{K_{U_n}})$
2. $U_1 \rightarrow * : \{N_1, U_1\}_{e_{U_i}}$ for $1 < i \leq n$
3. $U_i \rightarrow * : U_i, N_i$

The session key is $SK_{U_i} = \mathcal{H}(N_1 \| sid)$.

Protocol 8.2: An improved Protocol 8.1

8.1.3 Limitations of Existing Proof

In the existing proof, the security of Protocol 8.1 is proven by finding a reduction to the security of the encryption and signature schemes used. The number of protocol participants in the proof simulation, p, is assumed to be equal to the number of players allowed in the model, n, where n is polynomial in the security parameter k. In its reductionist approach, the proof assumes that there exists an adversary $\mathcal{A}$ who can gain a non-negligible advantage, $\mathrm{Adv}^{\mathcal{A}}(k)$, in distinguishing the test key from a random one. An attacker is then constructed that uses $\mathcal{A}$ to break either the underlying encryption scheme or the digital signature scheme.

In the context of Attack 8.1, assume that the number of protocol participants in the proof simulation is three. The proof then assumes that the number of parties in the model is also three. However, in order to carry out the attack, we have to corrupt a fourth player, U_4, to obtain the signature key of U_4. Note that U_4 is an outsider as shown in Figure 8.1.

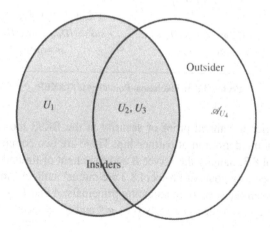

Fig. 8.1 Insiders vs outsider

In the proof simulation of the protocol execution shown in Attack 8.1, $\mathcal{A}$ corrupts U_4, an outsider in the target session, and assumes U_4's identity. Since U_4 does not exist in the model assumed by the proof, the attacker against the encryption and signature schemes cannot simulate the $\text{Corrupt}(U_4)$ query for $\mathscr{A}$. Thus the proof fails since, although $\mathscr{A}$ succeeds, it cannot be used to break either the encryption or signature schemes. Our observation[2] is consistent with the above results of An *et al.*, which highlight the underlying cause of the proof breakdown – the proof environment effectively did not allow a multi-user setting in which to analyse the signature and encryption schemes.

8.2 Jakobsson–Pointcheval MAKEP

Protocol 8.3 describes the published version of JP-MAKEP [15], which was designed for low power computing devices[3]. Protocol 8.3 is extremely efficient due to the employment of the Schnorr signature scheme [23]. All expensive computations can be precomputed by the protocol initiator, A. In other words, no on-line computation is required of the protocol initiator, A.

$$\text{Client } A \ (x_A, g^{x_A}) \hspace{4cm} \text{Server } B \ (x_B, g^{x_B})$$

$$a, t \in_R \mathbb{Z}_q, c = g^a, T = g^t, K = (g^{x_B})^a$$

$$r = \mathscr{H}_1(T, g^{x_B}, c, K), A' = \mathscr{H}_2(g^{x_B}, c, K) \xrightarrow{\quad ID_B, c, r \quad}$$

$$\hspace{6cm} K = c^{x_B}, A = \mathscr{H}_2(g^{x_B}, c, K)$$

$$A' \stackrel{?}{=} A \hspace{2cm} \xleftarrow{\quad A, e \quad} \hspace{1cm} 0 \le e < 2^k$$

$$d = t - e x_A \bmod q \hspace{1cm} \xrightarrow{\quad ID_A, d \quad}$$

$$\hspace{5cm} r \stackrel{?}{=} \mathscr{H}_1(g^d(g^{x_A})^e, g^{x_B}, c, K)$$

$$sid = (ID_B, c, r, A, e, ID_A, d) \hspace{2cm} sid = (ID_B, c, r, A, e, ID_A, d)$$

$$sk = \mathscr{H}_0(g^{x_B}, c, K) \hspace{3cm} sk = \mathscr{H}_0(g^{x_B}, c, K)$$

Protocol 8.3: Jakobsson–Pointcheval MAKEP

Protocol 8.3 carries a claimed proof of security in the BR93 model but uses the notion of SIDs in the definition of partnership. There are two communicating principals in Protocol 8.3, namely the server B and the client of limited computing resources, A. The security goals of Protocol 8.3 are mutual authentication and key establishment between the two communicating principals. A and B are each assumed to know the public key of the other party (i.e., g^{x_B} and g^{x_A} respectively).

---

[2] The author would like to acknowledge Dr. Juan Manuel González Nieto's insightful discussions on Protocol 8.1 and confirmation of our observation on the proof.

[3] The original version (i.e., Protocol 10.1) appeared in the unpublished pre-proceedings of Financial Crypto 2001 with a claimed proof of security in the BR93 model. Nevertheless, a flaw in the protocol was discovered by Wong and Chan [26]. In this published version, the flaw found by Wong and Chan in the original version has been fixed.

8.2.1 Unknown Key Share Attack on JP-MAKEP

Attack 8.2 depicts an example execution of Protocol 8.3 in the presence of a malicious adversary $\mathscr{A}$.

$A\,(x_A, g^{x_A})$	$\mathscr{A}\,(x_{\mathscr{A}}, g^{x_{\mathscr{A}}})$	$B\,(x_B, g^{x_B})$
ID_B, c, r	ID_B, c, r	
$\xleftarrow{\hspace{1.5cm}}$	$\xrightarrow{\hspace{1.5cm}}$	
$A, e' = 0$		A, e
$\xleftarrow{\hspace{1.5cm}}$	Fabricate	$\xleftarrow{\hspace{1.5cm}}$
$ID_A, d = t$		$ID_{\mathscr{A}}, d - ex_{\mathscr{A}} \bmod q$
$\xrightarrow{\hspace{1.5cm}}$	Fabricate	$\xrightarrow{\hspace{1.5cm}}$

$$r \overset{?}{=} \mathscr{H}_1(g^{d-ex_{\mathscr{A}}}(g^{x_{\mathscr{A}}})^e, g^{x_B}, c, K)$$

$$sid_{B\mathscr{A}} = (ID_B, c, r, A, e, ID_{\mathscr{A}}, d - ex_{\mathscr{A}} \bmod q)$$

$$sid_{AB} = (ID_B, c, r, A, e', ID_A, d) \neq sid_{B\mathscr{A}}$$

$$sk_{AB} = \mathscr{H}_0(g^{x_B}, c, K) \qquad\qquad sk_{B\mathscr{A}} = \mathscr{H}_0(g^{x_B}, c, K)$$

Attack 8.2: Unknown key attack on Protocol 8.3

At the end of Attack 8.2, B believes he shares a session key, $sk_{B\mathscr{A}} = \mathscr{H}_0(g^{x_B}, c, K)$, with the adversary $\mathscr{A}$, when in fact the key is being shared with A (i.e., unknown key share attack). A and B are not partners since they have different SIDs, $sid_{B\mathscr{A}} = (ID_B, c, r, A, e, ID_{\mathscr{A}}, d - ex_{\mathscr{A}} \bmod q) \neq sid_{AB}$, and different perceived partners (i.e., $PID_A = A$ and $PID_B = \mathscr{A}$).

From Attack 8.2, we observe that A has terminated the protocol without any partners, in violation of the server-to-client authentication goal. The server, B, has terminated the protocol with the adversary, $\mathscr{A}$, as its partner. The client-to-server authentication, therefore, is not violated. Protocol 8.3 is not secure since the adversary is able to obtain a fresh session key of A by revealing a non-partner oracle of A (i.e., an oracle of B), in violation of Definition 2.3.3. A possible solution to prevent Attack 8.2 is to change $0 \leq e < 2^k$ in the protocol specification to $0 < e < 2^k$.

8.2.2 Flaws in Existing Security Proof for JP-MAKEP

In the proof simulation of Protocol 8.3, let P be another client where $P \neq A, B$. P is clearly the "outsider" in the target session of Attack 8.2 that $\mathscr{A}$ is attacking. $\mathscr{A}$ then corrupts P, the outsider, and assumes P's identity. This is allowed in the existing proof [15, Lemma 3] for the server-to-client authentication, since it is claimed that Protocol 8.3 provides partial forward-secrecy whereby corruption of the client may not help to recover the session keys.

The proof assumes that the probability of $\mathscr{A}$ violating the server-to-client authentication is negligible. In the context of Attack 8.2, $\mathscr{A}$ managed to violate the server-to-client authentication by corrupting a non-partner player, P. By violating the server-to-client authentication, $\mathscr{A}$ is then able to distinguish a real key or a random value by asking a Reveal query to a non-partner server oracle of A. This violates the server-to-client authentication with non-negligible probability. The discrete logarithm breaker $\mathscr{A}_{\mathscr{DL}}$ (which is constructed using $\mathscr{A}$) is unable to obtain a non-negligible probability of breaking the discrete logarithm problem, contradicting the underlying assumption in the proof. Consequently, the proof simulation fails (the result of Reveal and Corrupt queries were not adequately considered in the simulation).

8.3 Wong–Chan MAKEP

Protocol 8.4 describes WC-MAKEP [26], which was proposed as an improvement to the original unpublished version of Protocol 8.3. Note that Protocol 8.4 describes the corrected version of WC-MAKEP, where the computation of $\sigma = (r_A \oplus r_B)$ by A is replaced by $\sigma = (r_A \oplus r_B)||ID_B$.

$$
\begin{array}{lll}
A\,(a,g^a) & & B\,(SK_B,PK_B) \\
r_A \in_R \{0,1\}^k, x = \{r_A\}_{PK_B} & & \\
b \in_R \mathbb{Z}_q \setminus \{0\}, \beta = g^b & \xrightarrow{\;Cert_A,\beta,x\;} & \text{Decrypt } x \\
\sigma = (r_A \oplus r_B)||ID_B & & \\
y = a\mathscr{H}(\sigma) + b \bmod q & \xleftarrow{\;\{r_B,ID_B\}_{r_A}\;} & r_B \in \{0,1\}^k \\
SK_{AB} = \mathscr{H}(\sigma) & \xrightarrow{\quad y \quad} & g^y \overset{?}{=} (g^a)^{\mathscr{H}(\sigma)}\beta, SK_{BA} = \mathscr{H}(\sigma)
\end{array}
$$

Protocol 8.4: Wong–Chan MAKEP

8.3.1 A New Attack on WC-MAKEP

Attack 8.3 depicts an example execution of Protocol 8.4, where at the end of Attack 8.3, A and B accept with the same session key, $SK_{AB} = \mathscr{H}(\sigma) = SK_{BA}$.

According to Definition 2.3.2, however, both A and B are not partners as B's replies are not in response to genuine messages sent by A. Therefore, both A and B will not have matching conversations given in Definition 2.3.2. This is known as a key replicating attack described in Definition 2.3.12 since two non-partner oracles, $\Pi_{A,B}$ and $\Pi_{B,A}$, have accepted session keys of the same value. The adversary, $\mathscr{A}$, is then allowed to reveal a fresh non-partner oracle, $\Pi_{B,A}$, and find the session key accepted by $\Pi_{A,B}$. This violates Definition 2.3.3.

A	$\mathcal{A}$	B
$\xrightarrow{\;Cert_A,\beta,x\;}$	Fabricate message	$\xrightarrow{\;Cert_A,\beta\cdot g^e,x\;}$
$\xleftarrow{\;\{r_B,ID_B\}_{r_A}\;}$		$\xleftarrow{\;\{r_B,ID_B\}_{r_A}\;}$
$\xrightarrow{\;y\;}$	$y' = y + e \bmod q$.	$g^{y'} \stackrel{?}{=} (g^a)^{\mathcal{H}(\sigma)}(\beta \cdot g^e)$
$SK_{AB} = \mathcal{H}(\sigma)$	$\xrightarrow{\;y'\;}$	$SK_{BA} = \mathcal{H}(\sigma)$

Attack 8.3: Key replicating attack on Protocol 8.4

Moreover, both oracles, $\Pi_{A,B}$ and $\Pi_{B,A}$, have terminated the protocol without any partners, in violation of the mutual authentication goal. Protocol 8.4, therefore, is insecure in the BR93 model since at the end of Attack 8.3, both the key establishment and mutual authentication goals are violated.

8.3.2 Preventing the Attack

In order to prevent Attack 8.3, we propose to change the construction of the session key to $SK = \mathcal{H}(A,B,\beta,x,y,\sigma)$. The inclusion of the sender's and responder's identities and messages (β,x,y) in the key derivation function effectively binds the session key to all messages sent and received by both A and B [8]. If the adversary changes any of the messages in the transmission, the session key will also be different. Informally, Attack 8.3 will no longer be valid against Protocol 8.4.

8.3.3 Flaws in Existing Security Proof for WC-MAKEP

The existing sketchy security proof for Protocol 8.4 fails to provide a proof simulation. In the absence of a game simulation in the existing proof, we may only speculate that the proof fails to adequately consider the simulation of Send and Reveal queries in the same sense as outlined in Chapter 8.2.2.

For the flaws in the AMP protocol [21] and EPA protocol [14] revealed by Wan and Wang [25], both proofs fail to provide any proof simulations. These examples highlight the importance of detailed proof simulations, as the omission of such simulations could potentially result in protocols claimed to be secure being, in fact, insecure.

8.4 An MT-Authenticator

In this section, we reveal an inadequacy in the specification of the encryption based MT-authenticator proposed by Bellare, Canetti, and Krawczyk [3] and identify a flaw in its proof simulation. We then demonstrate with an example protocol (the protocol 2DHPE [13]) how the flaw in the security proof for the encryption-based MT-authenticator results in the violation of the key establishment goal in the protocol 2DHPE where a malicious adversary is able to learn a fresh session key. The attack we reveal on the protocol 2DHPE also applies to protocol 14 that appears in the full version of [12]. Surprisingly, the inadequacy in the specification was not spotted in the proof simulation of the MT-authenticator, and has not previously been spotted in other protocols [12, 13] using this MT-authenticator.

We speculate that if protocol designers fail to spot this inadequacy in the specification of their protocols, the protocol implementers are also highly unlikely to spot this inadequacy until specific attacks have been demonstrated, as suggested by Bleichenbacher [4].

Having identified the flaw in the security proof for the MT-authenticator, we provide a revised MT-authenticator. As a result, protocols using the revised encryption based MT-authenticator will no longer be flawed due to their use of this MT-authenticator. The notation used throughout this section is as follows: the notation $\{\cdot\}_{K_U}$ denotes an encryption of some message m under U's public key, K_U; and $MAC_K(m)$ denotes the computation of MAC digest of some message m under key K.

8.4.1 Encryption-Based MT-Authenticator

Figure 8.2 describes the encryption based MT-authenticator, which is based on a public-key encryption scheme indistinguishable under chosen-ciphertext attack and the authentication technique used by Krawczyk [20]. Note that the specification of the encryption-based MT-authenticator does not specify the deletion of the received nonce v_A from B's internal state before sending out the last message. Note that v_A is also the one-time MAC key.

A		B
Choose nonce v_A	$\xleftarrow{\quad sid,m \quad}$	Choose message m
	$\xrightarrow{\quad sid,m,\{v_A\}_{K_B} \quad}$	Decrypt $\{v_A\}_{K_B}$
Verify $MAC_{v_A}(m,A)$	$\xleftarrow{\quad sid,m,MAC_{v_A}(m,A) \quad}$	Compute $MAC_{v_A}(m,A)$

Fig. 8.2 Bellare–Canetti–Krawczyk encryption-based MT-authenticator

8.4.2 Flaw in Existing Security Proof Revealed

In the usual tradition of reductionist proofs, the existing MT-authenticator proof [3] assumes that there exists an adversary $\mathscr{A}$ who can break the MT-authenticator. An encryption-aided *MAC* forger, $\mathscr{F}$, is constructed using such an adversary, $\mathscr{A}$, against the unforgeability of the underlying *MAC* scheme. Subsequently, the encryption-aided *MAC* forger, $\mathscr{F}$, can be used to break the encryption scheme. The *MAC* forger, $\mathscr{F}$, who has access to a *MAC* oracle, is easily constructed as follows:

- guess at random an index i,
- for all but the i-th session, generate a key v_k and answer queries as expected,
- if $\mathscr{A}$ calls a Session-State Reveal[4] on any session other than the i-th session, the response can easily be simulated,
- if $\mathscr{A}$ calls a Session-State Reveal on the i-th session, $\mathscr{F}$ aborts.

The assumption is that if $\mathscr{A}$ has a non-negligible advantage against the underlying protocol, then $\mathscr{F}$ has a non-negligible probability of forging a *MAC* digest.

Consider the scenario shown in Attack 8.4. When $\mathscr{A}$ asks for the one-time *MAC* key, v_k, with a Session-State Reveal query, it is perfectly legitimate since this session with SID of sid_j is not the i-th session with SID of sid_i. Recall that sessions with non-matching SIDs (i.e., $sid_i \neq sid_j$) are non-partners.

Attack 8.4: An example execution of encryption-based MT-authenticator

$\mathscr{F}$ is unable to answer such a query since v_A is a secret key. Note that the *MAC* oracle to which $\mathscr{F}$ has access is associated with v_A, but $\mathscr{F}$ does not know v_A. Hence, the proof simulation is aborted and $\mathscr{F}$ fails. $\mathscr{F}$ does not have a non-negligible probability of forging a *MAC* digest (since it fails), although $\mathscr{A}$ has a non-negligible

---

[4] Note that in the original paper of Bellare, Canetti, and Krawczyk [3], a Session-State Reveal is known as a Session-Corruption query.

advantage against the security of the underlying protocol, in violation of the underlying assumption in the proof.

We note that in a later independent yet related work by Tian and Wong [24],the same flaw in the security proof for the encryption-based MT-authenticator described in Attack 8.4 was presented.

8.4.3 Addressing the Flaw

We propose that the party concerned in the encryption-based MT-authenticator described in Figure 8.2 to delete the received nonce from its internal state before sending out the *MAC* digest computed using the received nonce, as described in Figure 8.3.

A		B
Choose nonce v_A	$\xleftarrow{\quad sid,m \quad}$	Choose message m
	$\xrightarrow{sid,m,\{v_A\}_{K_B}}$	Decrypt $\{v_A\}_{K_B}$
		Compute $MAC_{v_A}(m,A)$
Verify $MAC_{v_A}(m,A)$	$\xleftarrow{sid,m,MAC_{v_A}(m,A)}$	**Delete** v_A

Fig. 8.3 A revised encryption-based MT-authenticator

As a result, the adversary, $\mathscr{A}$, will not be able to obtain the value of v_A using a Session-State Reveal query. In the proof of the security of the MT-authenticator, therefore, the encryption-aided *MAC* forger, $\mathscr{F}$, will be able to answer such a query because $\mathscr{F}$ is no longer required to return the value of v_A. Attack 8.4 will no longer be valid, since $\mathscr{A}$ will no longer be able to obtain the value of v_A and fabricate a *MAC* digest.

8.4.4 An Example Protocol as a Case Study

Protocol 8.5 describes a password-based protocol 2DHPE due to Hitchcock, Tin, Boyd, González Nieto, and Montague [13]. Using Protocol 8.5 as an example, we demonstrate that as a result of the flaw in the security proof for the encryption-based MT-authenticator, the security proof for Protocol 8.5 is also invalid.

In Protocol 8.5, both A and B are assumed to share a secret password, $pwd_{A,B}$, and the public keys of both A and B (i.e., K_A and K_B respectively) are known to all participants in the protocol. Protocol 8.5 uses the encryption-based MT-authenticator to authenticate the message B, sid, g^y from B.

Protocol 8.5: Hitchcock–Tin–Boyd–González Nieto–Montague protocol 2DHPE

Attack 8.5 describes an example execution of Protocol 8.5 in the presence of a malicious adversary $\mathscr{A}$ (in the UM). We assume that $\mathscr{A}$ has a shared password, $pwd_{\mathscr{A},B}$, with B. At the end of Attack 8.5, oracle $\Pi_{A,B}^{sid}$ has accepted a shared session key $SK_{A,B} = g^{xz}$ with $\Pi_{B,A}^{sid}$. However, such an oracle (i.e., $\Pi_{B,A}^{sid}$) does not exist. By sending a Session-State Reveal query to oracle $\Pi_{B,\mathscr{A}}^{sid_{\mathscr{A}}}$, $\mathscr{A}$ learns the internal state of $\Pi_{B,\mathscr{A}}^{sid_{\mathscr{A}}}$, which includes v'_A. With v'_A, $\mathscr{A}$ can fabricate and send a MAC digest to A. Hence, the adversary is able to obtain a fresh session key of $\Pi_{A,B}^{sid}$ (i.e., $SK_{A,B} = g^{xz}$) since $\mathscr{A}$ knows z (in fact, z is chosen by $\mathscr{A}$).

Attack 8.5: Execution of Protocol 8.5 in the presence of a malicious adversary

If the encryption-based MT-authenticator requires B to delete the received nonce v'_A from B's internal state before sending out message 3, then $\mathscr{A}$ will not be able to obtain the value of v'_A with a Session-State Reveal query and fabricate $MAC_{v'_A}(B, sid, g^y, A)$. Attack 8.5 will no longer work.

8.5 Summary

Through a detailed study of several protocols and an authenticator with claimed proofs of security, we revealed the following.

In the Boyd–González Nieto Protocol.   An inappropriate proof model environment is one of the likely areas where protocol proofs might go wrong. In the existing security proof for the Boyd–González Nieto conference key agreement protocol [5], we observed that the proof model environment has the same number of parties in the model as in the protocol. This effectively does not allow a multi-user setting in which to analyse the signature and encryption schemes. Consequently, this shortcoming fails to include the case where $\mathscr{A}$ is able to corrupt a player that does not participate in the particular key agreement protocol session, and obtains a fresh key of any initiator principal by causing disagreement amongst parties about who is participating in the key exchange.

The attack we reveal on Boyd–González Nieto conference key agreement protocol is an unknown key share attack described in Chapter 2.2.2.2. In the attack on Boyd–González Nieto protocol, $\mathscr{A}$ is able to reveal the key of a non-partner oracle whose key is the same as the initiator principal, thus violating the key establishment goal.

The existence of this attack means that the security proof for Boyd–González Nieto's protocol is invalid, since the proof model allows Corrupt queries. Protocols proven secure in a proof model that allows the "Corrupt" query (in the proof simulation) ought to be secure against the unknown key share attack, since if a key is to be shared between some parties, U_1, U_2, and U_3, the corruption of some other (non-related) player in the protocol, say U_4, should not expose the session key shared between U_1, U_2, and U_3. A similar observation was presented in Chapter 5.2.2. In the proof simulations of the protocols on which we perform an unknown key share attack, $\mathscr{A}$ does not corrupt the owner or the perceived partners of the target Test session, but instead corrupts some other (non-related) player in the protocol that is not associated with the target Test session or a member of the "attacked" protocol session.

In the Jakobsson–Pointcheval MAKEP.   We also described an unknown key share attack on the Jakobsson–Pointcheval MAKEP which breaks the reduction of the proof from JP-MAKEP to the discrete logarithm problem. Similarly to the Boyd–González Nieto protocol, the proof model allows Corrupt queries for clients, and hence secure protocols ought to be immune to unknown key share attacks.

In the Wong–Chan MAKEP.   An attack against Wong–Chan MAKEP is described where an adversary $\mathscr{A}$ is able to obtain a fresh key of an initiator oracle by revealing a non-partner server oracle sharing the same session key. The proof was sketchy and failed to provide any simulation.

In the Encryption-Based Authenticator.   We demonstrated that an adversary, $\mathscr{A}$, is able to use a Session-State Reveal query to find the one-time MAC key and use it to authenticate a fraudulent message. We identified the problem (in its proof) to be due to an incomplete proof specification (Session-State Reveal queries not adequately considered). This resulted in the failure of the proof simulation where the adversary has a non-negligible advantage. However, the *MAC* forger, $\mathscr{F}$, does not have a non-negligible probability of forging a *MAC* digest since it fails. This violates the underlying assumption in the proof. We also demonstrated how the flaw in this MT authenticator invalidates the security proofs for protocols that use the MT-authenticator using protocol 2DHPE [13] as a case study.

In summary, we have identified the following areas where protocol proofs are likely to fail.

1. An inappropriate proof model environment.
2. Send, Session-State Reveal, Session-Key Reveal, and Corrupt queries that are not adequately considered in the proof simulations.
3. Omission of proof simulations.

We also observe that certain constructions of session keys may contribute to the security of the key establishment protocol. This observation supports our findings described in the next chapter.

References

1. Jee Hea An, Yevgeniy Dodis & Tal Rabin 2002. On the Security of Joint Signature and Encryption, in Lars R Knudsen (ed), Proceedings of Advances in Cryptology - EUROCRYPT 2002. Lecture Notes in Computer Science 2332/2002: 83–107
2. Daniel Augot, Raghav Bhaskar, Valerie Issarny & Daniele Sacchetti 2005. An Efficient Group Key Agreement Protocol for Ad Hoc Networks, in *Proceedings of 1st International IEEE WoWMoM Workshop on Trust, Security and Privacy for Ubiquitous Computing - TSPUC 2005*. IEEE Computer Society Press: 576–580
3. Mihir Bellare, Ran Canetti & Hugo Krawczyk 1998. A Modular Approach to The Design and Analysis of Authentication and Key Exchange Protocols, in Jeffrey Vitter (ed), Proceedings of 30th ACM Symposium on the Theory of Computing - ACM STOC 1998. ACM Press: 419–428
4. Daniel Bleichenbacher 2005. Breaking a Cryptographic Protocol with Pseudoprimes in Serge Vaudenay (ed), Proceedings of Public Key Cryptography - PKC 2005. Lecture Notes in Computer Science 3386/2005: 9–15
5. Colin Boyd & Juan Manuel González Nieto 2003. Round-optimal Contributory Conference Key Agreement, in Yvo Desmedt (ed), Proceedings of Public Key Cryptography - PKC 2003. Lecture Notes in Computer Science 2567/2003: 161–174
6. Colin Boyd & Anish Mathuria 2003. *Protocols for Authentication and Key Establishment*. Springer-Verlag
7. Kyu Young Choi, Jung Yeon Hwang & Dong Hoon Lee 2003. Efficient ID-based Group Key Agreement with Bilinear Maps, in Feng Bao, Robert H Deng & Jianying Zhou (eds), Proceedings of Public Key Cryptography - PKC 2004. Lecture Notes in Computer Science 2497/2004: 130–144
8. Kim-Kwang Raymond Choo, Colin Boyd & Yvonne Hitchcock 2005. On Session Key Construction in Provably Secure Protocols, in Ed Dawson & Serge Vaudenay (eds), Proceedings of 1st International Conference on Cryptology in Malaysia - MYCRYPT 2005.

Lecture Notes in Computer Science 3715/2005: 116–131. Extended version available from
http://eprint.iacr.org/2005/206

9. Ratna Dutta & Rana Barua 2005. Constant Round Dynamic Group Key Agreement, in Jianying Zhou, Javier Lopez, Robert H Deng & Feng Bao (eds), Proceedings of 8th Information
   Security Conference - ISC 2005. Lecture Notes in Computer Science 3650/2005: 74–88

10. Ratna Dutta, Rana Barua & Palash Sarkar 2004. Provably Secure Authenticated Tree Based
    Group Key Agreement Protocol, in Javier Lopez, Sihan Qing & Eiji Okamoto (eds), Proceed-
    ings of 6th International Conference on Information and Communications Security - ICICS
    2004. Lecture Notes in Computer Science 3269/2004: 494–503

11. Javier Herranz & Jorge L Villar 2004. An Unbalanced Protocol for Group Key Exchange, in
    Sokratis Katsikas, Javier Lopez & Gnther Pernul (eds), Proceedings of Trust and Privacy in
    Digital Business - TrustBus 2004. Lecture Notes in Computer Science 3184/2004: 172–180

12. Yvonne Hitchcock, Colin Boyd & Juan Manuel González Nieto 2004. Tripartite Key
    Exchange in the Canetti-Krawczyk Proof Model, in Anne Canteaut & Kapaleeswaran
    Viswanathan (eds), Proceedings of 5th International Conference on Cryptology in India -
    INDOCRYPT 2004. Lecture Notes in Computer Science 3348/2004: 17–32

13. Yvonne Hitchcock, Yiu-Shing Terry Tin, Colin Boyd, Juan Manuel González Nieto &
    Paul Montague 2003. A Password-Based Authenticator: Security Proof and Applications, in
    Thomas Johansson & Subhamoy Maitra (eds), Proceedings of 4th International Conference
    on Cryptology in India - INDOCRYPT 2003. Lecture Notes in Computer Science 2904/2003:
    388–401

14. Yong Ho Hwang, Dae Hyun Yum & Pil Joong Lee 2003. EPA: An Efficient Password-Based
    Protocal for Authenticated Key Exchange, in Reihaneh Safavi-Naini & Jennifer Seberry (eds),
    Proceedings of 48th Australasian Conference on Information Security and Privacy - ACISP
    2003. Lecture Notes in Computer Science 2727/2003: 452–463

15. Markus Jakobsson & David Pointcheval 2001. Mutual Authentication and Key Exchange
    Protocol for Low Power Devices, in Paul F Syverson (ed), Proceedings of 5th Interna-
    tional Conference on Financial Cryptography - FC 2001. Lecture Notes in Computer Science
    2339/2002: 169–186

16. Ik Rae Jeong, Jonathan Katz & Dong Hoon Lee 2004. One-Round Protocols for Two-Party
    Authenticated Key Exchange, in Markus Jakobsson, Moti Yung & Jianying Zhou (eds), Pro-
    ceedings of Applied Cryptography and Network Security - ACNS 2004. Lecture Notes in
    Computer Science 3089/2004: 220–232

17. Jonathon Katz & Moti Yung 2003. Scalable Protocols for Authenticated Group Key Ex-
    change, in Dan Boneh (ed), Proceedings of Advances in Cryptology - CRYPTO 2003. Lecture
    Notes in Computer Science 2729/2003: 110–125

18. Neal Koblitz & Alfred Menezes 2004. Another Look at "Provable Security". *Technical re-
    port* no CORR 2004-20. Centre for Applied Cryptographic Research, University of Waterloo,
    Canada. Available from http://eprint.iacr.org/2004/152/

19. Neal Koblitz & Alfred Menezes 2006. Another Look at "Provable Security". *Journal of Cryp-
    tology* 20(1): 3– 37

20. Hugo Krawczyk 1996. SKEME: A Versatile Secure Key Exchange Mechanism for Internet, in
    Proceedings of ISOC Network and Distributed System Security - NDSS 1996. Internet Society
    Press: 114–127

21. Taekyoung Kwon 2001. Authentication and Key Agreement via Memorable Passwords, in
    Proceedings of ISOC Networks and Distributed Security Systems - NDSS 2001. Internet So-
    ciety Press

22. Phillip Rogaway 2004. MOn the Role Definitions in and Beyond Cryptography, in Michael J
    Maher (ed), Proceedings of 9th Asian Computing Science Conference - ASIAN 2004. Lecture
    Notes in Computer Science 3321/2004: 13–32

23. CP Schnorr 1989. Efficient Identification and Signature for Smart Cards, in Gilles Brassard
    (ed), Proceedings of Advances in Cryptology - CRYPTO 1989. Lecture Notes in Computer
    Science 435/1990: 235–251

24. Xiaojian Tian & Duncan S Wong 2006. Session Corruption Attack and Improvements on Encryption Based MT-Authenticators, in David Pointcheval (ed), Proceedings of Cryptographers' Track at RSA Conference - CT-RSA 2006. Lecture Notes in Computer Science 3860/2006: 34–51

25. Zhiguo Wan & Shuhong Wang 2004. Cryptanalysis of Two Password-Authenticated Key Exchange Protocols, in Huaxiong Wang, Josef Pieprzyk & Vijay Varadharajan (eds), Proceedings of 9th Australasian Conference on Information Security and Privacy - ACISP 2004. Lecture Notes in Computer Science 3108/2004: 164–175

26. Duncan S Wong & Agnes H Chan 2001. Efficient and Mutually Authenticated Key Exchange for Low Power Computing Devices, in Colin Boyd (ed), Proceedings of Advances in Cryptology - ASIACRYPT 2001. Lecture Notes in Computer Science 2248/2001: 172–289

Chapter 9
On Session Key Construction

There is neither a formal definition of session key construction in any of the proof models nor the existence of a rule of thumb on how session keys in key establishment protocols should be constructed. This chapter uses two case studies to illustrate that the way session keys are constructed can have an impact on the security of the protocol in the model. It appears that certain ways of constructing a session key may contribute to the security of a key establishment protocol. Moreover, using a key agreement protocol of Lee, Kim, and Yoo [12], we demonstrate that making similar changes to the way session key is constructed in the protocol prevents our revealed reflection attack.

Our case studies are an ID-based key establishment protocol due to Chen and Kudla [4] and an ID-based protocol 2P-IDAKA due to McCullagh and Barreto [13]. Both protocols are role-symmetric and carry proofs of security in the BR93 model. However, the existing proofs of both protocols restrict the adversary from asking any Reveal query. Their arguments follow on from earlier work of Blake-Wilson, Johnson, and Menezes [2] who pointed out that it does not seem possible for role-symmetric protocols to be secure in the BR93 model if the Reveal query is allowed. In recent work, Jeong, Katz, and Lee [7] present two protocols $\mathcal{TS}1$ and $\mathcal{TS}2$, both with proofs of security in the BR93 model. This work contradicts the claim of Blake-Wilson, Johnson, and Menezes [2] as both protocols $\mathcal{TS}1$ and $\mathcal{TS}2$ are similar to the protocols analysed by Blake-Wilson, Johnson, and Menezes in the BR93 model, but without restricting the adversary from asking the Reveal query.

We examine the existing arguments on the restriction of the Reveal query. We then demonstrate that by making a simple change to the construction of the session key (and not changing the protocol details), we are able to prove Chen and Kudla's protocol secure in an intermediate variant of the BR93 model whereby the adversary, $\mathcal{A}$, is allowed to ask all the queries available in the model except asking Reveal queries to the sessions owned by the partner of the target Test session. Although we are unable to prove the improved protocol secure in the BR93 model without restricting $\mathcal{A}$ from asking the Reveal query due to some technicality, the improved protocol does not appear to suffer from any insecurities even if we allow $\mathscr{A}$ to ask any Reveal queries to the perceived partner of the target Test session. Furthermore, allowing $\mathscr{A}$ to ask Reveal queries directed at the owner of the Test session in our proof, effectively means that the improved Chen and Kudla's protocol is secure against reflection attacks. We reveal some errors in the existing proof of protocol 2P-IDAKA [13] as well as the observation that the proof is in a restricted BR93 model whereby $\mathscr{A}$ does not generate the input to the Test session, which is not a normal assumption in the Bellare–Rogaway model. Similar findings on the existing proof of protocol 2P-IDAKA were presented in a later independent yet related work by Cheng and Chen [5].

Surprisingly, no one has pointed out the importance of session key construction despite its significance to the security of key establishment protocols. Of course, we do not claim that session keys constructed in our proposed fashion will necessarily result in a provably-secure protocol as the security of the protocol is based on many other factors, such as the underlying cryptographic primitives used. However, we do claim that having a sound construction of session keys will reduce the number of possible attacks on the key establishment protocol. The key agreement protocol of Lee, Kim, and Yoo [12] is used as a case study to demonstrate that sich an approach can prevent a reflection attack.

Material presented in this chapter has appeared in the following publications:

- Kim-Kwang Raymond Choo, Colin Boyd, and Yvonne Hitchcock. On Session Key Construction in Provably Secure Protocols. In Ed Dawson and Serge Vaudenay, editors, 1st International Conference on Cryptology in Malaysia - Mycrypt 2005, volume 3715/2005 of Lecture Notes in Computer Science, pages 116–131. Springer-Verlag, 2005.
- Kim-Kwang Raymond Choo. Revisit Of McCullagh–Barreto Two-Party ID-Based Authenticated Key Agreement Protocols (Preliminary version available from http://eprint.iacr.org/2004/343/). *International Journal of Network Security*, 1(3):154–160, 2005.
- Kim-Kwang Raymond Choo. Revisiting Lee, Kim, and Yoo Authenticated Key Agreement Protocol. *International Journal of Network Security*, 2(1):64–68, 2006.

9.1 Chen–Kudla ID-Based Protocol

In this section, we revisit the Chen–Kudla ID-based key establishment protocol [4] as described by Protocol 9.1. We present the arguments of the existing proof on why the Reveal query is not allowed, and present an improved protocol. We then explain why the Reveal query cannot be answered if the adversary $\mathscr{A}$ ask any Reveal queries to the partner player of the target Test session. We conclude this section with a security proof for the improved protocol.

9.1.1 The ID-Based Protocol

Protocol 9.1 describes ID-based authenticated key establishment protocol 2 of Chen and Kudla. The notation used in Protocol 9.1 follows that of Table 2.1:

- $\mathcal{H}$ denotes some secure hash function,
- $Q_A = \mathcal{H}(ID_A)$ and $Q_B = \mathcal{H}(ID_B)$ denote the public keys of A and B respectively,
- $S_A = sQ_A$ and $S_B = sQ_B$ denote the private keys of A and B respectively,
- $W_A = aQ_A$ and $W_B = bQ_B$ denote the ephemeral public keys of A and B respectively, and
- a and b are the ephemeral private keys of A and B respectively.

$$
\begin{array}{ccc}
A & & B \\
a \in_R \mathbb{Z}_q^* & \xrightarrow{\ W_A = aQ_A\ } & b \in_R \mathbb{Z}_q^* \\
K_{AB} = \hat{e}(S_A, W_B + aQ_B) & \xleftarrow{\ W_B = bQ_B\ } & K_{BA} = \hat{e}(W_A + bQ_A, S_B) \\
\multicolumn{3}{c}{K_{AB} = K_{BA} = \hat{e}(Q_A, Q_B)^{s(a+b)}} \\
\multicolumn{3}{c}{SK_{AB} = \mathcal{H}(K_{AB}) = SK_{BA} = \mathcal{H}(K_{BA})}
\end{array}
$$

Protocol 9.1: Chen–Kudla Protocol 2

At the end of Protocol 9.1's execution, both A and B accept the respective session keys, SK_{AB} and SK_{BA}.

$$
\begin{aligned}
SK_{AB} &= \mathcal{H}(\hat{e}(S_A, W_B + aQ_B)) \\
SK_{BA} &= \mathcal{H}(\hat{e}(W_A + bQ_A, S_B)) \\
&= SK_{AB}.
\end{aligned}
$$

9.1.2 Existing Arguments on Restriction of Reveal Query

In the existing proof by Chen and Kudla [4, Proof of Theorem 1], they indicate that no Reveal query is allowed due to the description provided in Attack 9.1. Attack 9.1 describes the execution of Protocol 9.1 in the presence of a malicious adversary, $\mathcal{A}$. Let $\mathcal{T}_A$ and $\mathcal{T}_B$ denotes the transcripts of A and B respectively.

At the end of Attack 9.1, neither A nor B have matching conversations. Therefore, according to Definition 2.3.2 in Chapter 2.3.4.1, they are not partners. However, both A and B accept the same session key $K_{AB} = K_{BA} = \hat{e}(Q_A, Q_B)^{s(a+b+c)}$. $\mathcal{A}$, therefore, is able to trivially expose a fresh session key by asking a Reveal query to a non-partner oracle. This is known as a key replicating attack described in Definition 2.3.12. Protocol 9.1 is, therefore, not secure if $\mathcal{A}$ is allowed access to a

A	$\mathscr{A}$	B
$a \in_R \mathbb{Z}_q^*$ $\xrightarrow{\;W_A = aQ_A\;}$	Intercept	
	$c \in_R \mathbb{Z}_q^* \xrightarrow{\;W_A + cQ_A\;}$	
$\xleftarrow{\;W_B + cQ_B\;}$	Intercept $\xleftarrow{\;W_B = bQ_B\;}$	$b \in_R \mathbb{Z}_q^*$

$$K_{AB} = \hat{e}(S_A, W_B + cQ_B + aQ_B) \qquad K_{BA} = \hat{e}(W_A + bQ_A + cQ_A, S_B)$$
$$\mathscr{T}_A = (W_A, W_B + cQ_B) \qquad\qquad \mathscr{T}_B = (W_A + cQ_A, W_B)$$
$$K_{AB} = K_{BA} = \hat{e}(Q_A, Q_B)^{s(a+b+c)}$$
$$SK_{AB} = \mathscr{H}(K_{AB}) = SK_{BA} = \mathscr{H}(K_{BA})$$

Attack 9.1: Key replicating attack on Protocol 9.1

Reveal query. Similar arguments apply for the remaining three protocols of Chen and Kudla [4].

9.1.3 Improved Chen–Kudla Protocol

Consider the scenario whereby session keys of A and B (denoted as SK_{AB} and SK_{BA} respectively) are constructed as

$$SK_{AB} = \mathscr{H}(K_{AB}) = \mathscr{H}(A||B||\mathscr{T}_A||\hat{e}(S_A, W_B + aQ_B))$$
$$= \mathscr{H}(A||B||\mathscr{T}_A||\hat{e}(Q_A, Q_B)^{s(a+b)}),$$
$$SK_{BA} = \mathscr{H}(K_{BA}) = \mathscr{H}(A||B||\mathscr{T}_B||\hat{e}(W_A + bQ_A, S_B)$$
$$= \mathscr{H}(A||B||\mathscr{T}_B||\hat{e}(Q_A, Q_B)^{s(a+b)}) = SK_{AB}$$

instead. The attack outlined in Attack 9.1 will no longer work since a non-matching conversation (i.e., $\mathscr{T}_A \neq \mathscr{T}_B$) will also mean that the session key is different, as shown below:

$$SK_{AB} = \mathscr{H}(K_{AB}) = \mathscr{H}(A||B||aQ_A||(b+c)Q_B||\hat{e}(S_A, W_B + aQ_B)),$$
$$SK_{BA} = \mathscr{H}(K_{BA}) = \mathscr{H}(A||B||(a+c)Q_A||bQ_B||\hat{e}(W_A + bQ_A, S_B)) \neq SK_{AB}.$$

Similarly, a reflection attack or an unknown key share attack would not work against the protocol since the construction of the session key introduces role asymmetry and the identities of the participants. Session keys will be different when the roles of the same principal switch. $\mathscr{A}$, therefore, appears to be unable to gain information about such fresh session key(s).

9.1.4 Security Proof for Improved Chen–Kudla Protocol

At first glance, it would seem that by fixing the attack outlined in Chapter 9.1.2, we have addressed the reasons why no Reveal query was allowed that was outlined in the existing proofs. We would, therefore, be able to prove the improved protocol secure in the unrestricted BR93 model. We demonstrate, however, that this is not possible unless we restrict the adversary from asking any Reveal queries to the partner of the Test session, as explained in Figure 9.1. By allowing the adversary to ask Reveal queries directed at the owner of the Test session (in our proof), however, we effectively prove the improved protocol secure against reflection attacks.

Recall that the general notion of the proof is to assume that there exists an adversary, $\mathscr{A}$, who can gain a non-negligible advantage in distinguishing the test key in the game described in Figure 2.1, and use $\mathscr{A}$ to break the underlying BDH problem described in Definition 2.1.7. We build an adversary, $\mathscr{A}_{\mathscr{BDH}}$, against the BDH problem using $\mathscr{A}$. The objective of $\mathscr{A}_{\mathscr{BDH}}$ is to compute and output the value $\hat{e}(P,P)^{xyz} \in \mathbb{G}_2$ when given a bilinear map $\hat{e}$, a generator of P of $\mathbb{G}_1$, and a triple of elements $xP, yP, zP \in \mathbb{G}_1$ with $x, y, z \in \mathbb{Z}_q^*$, where q is the prime order of the distinct groups $\mathbb{G}_1$ and $\mathbb{G}_2$.

Let oracle $\Pi_{A,B}^u$ be the initiator associated with the target Test session, and oracle $\Pi_{B,A}^v$ be the responder partner to $\Pi_{A,B}^u$. $\mathscr{A}_{\mathscr{BDH}}$ needs to simulate all responses to queries from $\mathscr{A}$, including the random oracle, $\mathscr{H}$. The proof specifies that $\mathscr{A}_{\mathscr{BDH}}$ can create all public/private key pairs for all players, except a randomly chosen player J. Let (Q_U, S_U) denote the public/private keys of players U other than J where $S_U = xQ_U$. $\mathscr{A}_{\mathscr{BDH}}$ is unable to compute the private key of J because $\mathscr{A}_{\mathscr{BDH}}$ is trying to solve the BDH problem, which is embedded in the public key of J.

Figure 9.1 shows a possible sequence of adversary actions and the responses generated by $\mathscr{A}_{\mathscr{BDH}}$. It can be seen that $\mathscr{A}$ will be able to distinguish between the simulation provided by $\mathscr{A}_{\mathscr{BDH}}$ and the actual protocol if it carries out this sequence of actions, since with overwhelming probability, $v \neq SK_{BC}$ (recall that v is randomly chosen). Hence, $\mathscr{A}_{\mathscr{BDH}}$ cannot answer any Reveal directed at the partner of the target Test session.

Theorem 9.1.1 *The improved Chen–Kudla protocol 2 is a secure authenticated key establishment protocol in the sense of Definition 2.3.3 if the Bilinear Diffie-Hellman (BDH) problem is hard, the hash function, $\mathscr{H}$, is a random oracle, and the adversary $\mathscr{A}$ does not ask any Reveal queries to any sessions owned by the partner player associated with the Test session.*

The proof for Theorem 9.1.1 generally follows that of Chen and Kudla [4, Proof of Theorem 1], except that we allow $\mathscr{A}$ to ask Reveal queries (but not to the partner player of the Test session). The details of the game simulation remain unchanged to that presented by Chen and Kudla [4, Proof of Theorem 1], except that we allow $\mathscr{A}$

$\mathcal{A}_{\mathcal{BDH}}$ $\mathcal{A}$

$b \in_R \mathbb{Z}_r^*$ $\xleftarrow{\text{Send}(B,C,j,cQ_C)}$ $c \in_R \mathbb{Z}_r^*$

$\xrightarrow{\quad bQ_B \quad}$

$\xleftarrow{\text{Reveal}(B,C,j)}$

$\mathcal{A}_{\mathcal{BDH}}$ is supposed to respond with $\mathcal{H}(B||C||j||e(cQ_C + bQ_C, S_B))$, but $\mathcal{A}_{\mathcal{BDH}}$ does not know S_B, and thus cannot know the input for its simulation of $\mathcal{H}$.

$v \in_R \{0,1\}^k$ $\xrightarrow{\quad v \quad}$

$\xleftarrow{\text{Corrupt}(C)}$

$\mathcal{A}_{\mathcal{BDH}}$ returns all internal states of C, including $S_C = sQ_C$.

$\xrightarrow{\quad S_C \quad}$

Compute $SK_{BC} = \mathcal{H}(C||B||i||\hat{e}(S_C, bQ_B + cQ_B))$

Verify whether $v \overset{?}{=} SK_{BC}$

Fig. 9.1 An example simulation of Protocol 9.1

to ask Reveal queries (but not to the partner player of the Test session), as given in Table 9.1.

Queries	Actions
Send(U_1, U_2, i)	$\mathcal{A}_{\mathcal{BDH}}$ answers all Send queries in the same fashion as the proof simulation presented by Chen and Kudla.
Corrupt(U, K)	$\mathcal{A}_{\mathcal{BDH}}$ answers all Corrupt queries in the same fashion as the proof simulation presented by Chen and Kudla.
Test(U_1, U_2, i)	$\mathcal{A}_{\mathcal{BDH}}$ answers the Test query in the same fashion as the proof simulation presented by Chen and Kudla.
$\mathcal{H}(U_1||U_2||i||te(m))$	$\mathcal{A}_{\mathcal{BDH}}$ returns a random value, $v \in_R \{0,1\}^k$ where k is the security parameter, and stores m in a list of tuples.
Reveal(U_1, U_2, i)	If oracle Π_{U_1,U_2}^i is not an oracle associated with the test session (or partner of such an oracle), and U_1 is not player J where $\mathcal{A}_{\mathcal{BDH}}$ did not generate the contents of the Send query to Π_{U_1,U_2}^i, then $\mathcal{A}_{\mathcal{BDH}}$ returns the associated session key. Otherwise $\mathcal{A}_{\mathcal{BDH}}$ terminates and halts the simulation. We observe that if $\mathcal{A}_{\mathcal{BDH}}$ halts because $U_1 = J$, the Test session chosen by $\mathcal{A}$ must be different to that desired by $\mathcal{A}_{\mathcal{BDH}}$, so even if the simulation had not halted here, it would have halted later.

Table 9.1 $\mathcal{A}_{\mathcal{BDH}}$ simulating the view of $\mathcal{A}$

$\mathcal{A}_{\mathcal{BDH}}$ is able to simulate the view of $\mathcal{A}$ perfectly by answering all oracle queries of $\mathcal{A}$. Upon the conclusion of the game (i.e., $\mathcal{A}$ is done), $\mathcal{A}_{\mathcal{BDH}}$ chooses a random element in the list of tuples and outputs it. The probability that $\mathcal{A}_{\mathcal{BDH}}$ did not abort at some stage and produces the correct output remains non-negligible. This concludes the proof of the theorem.

9.2 McCullagh–Barreto 2P-IDAKA Protocol

In this section, we revisit the McCullagh–Barreto protocol 2P-IDAKA [13]. Similarly to Chapter 9.1, we present the arguments of the existing proof on why the Reveal query is not allowed. We also identify some errors in the existing proof of the protocol. We then present an improved protocol.

9.2.1 The 2P-IDAKA Protocol

Protocol 9.2 describes the 2P-IDAKA protocol, which carries a proof of security in a weaker variant of the BR93 model whereby the adversary is not allowed to ask Reveal queries. Notation used in Protocol 9.2 is as follows:

- $(s+a)P$ and $(s+b)P$ denote the public key of A and B, and
- $A_{pri} = ((s+a))^{-1}P$ and $B_{pri} = ((s+b))^{-1}P$ denote the private key of A and B.

A		B
	$A_{KA} = x_a(s+b)P$	
$x_a \in_R Z_r^*$	$\xrightarrow{\hspace{2cm}}$	$x_b \in_R Z_r^*$
	$B_{KA} = x_b(s+a)P$	
$\hat{e}(B_{KA}, A_{pri})^{x_a} = \hat{e}(P,P)^{x_a x_b}$	$\xleftarrow{\hspace{2cm}}$	$\hat{e}(A_{KA}, B_{pri})^{x_b} = \hat{e}(P,P)^{x_a x_b}$

Protocol 9.2: McCullagh–Barreto 2P-IDAKA protocol

At the end of Protocol 9.2's execution, both A and B accept session keys

$$SK_{AB} = \hat{e}(B_{KA}, A_{pri})^{x_a} = \hat{e}(P,P)^{x_a x_b} = SK_{BA}.$$

9.2.2 Why Reveal Query is Restricted

No Reveal query is allowed on Protocol 9.2 due to the description provided in Attack 9.2 [6].

At the completion of Attack 9.2, both A and B have accepted the same session key (i.e., $SK_A = SK_B$). However, both A and B are non-partners since they do not have matching conversations as A's transcript is $(A_{KA}, B_{KA} \cdot x_E)$ whilst B's transcript is $(A_{KA} \cdot x_E, B_{KA})$. By sending a Reveal query to either A or B, $\mathscr{A}$ is able to trivially expose a fresh session key. Protocol 9.2, therefore, is not secure since $\mathscr{A}$ is able to obtain the session key of a fresh oracle of a non-partner oracle by revealing a

$$A \qquad\qquad \mathcal{A} \qquad\qquad B$$

$$x_a \in_R \mathbb{Z}_r^* \quad \xrightarrow{\ A_{KA} = x_a(s+b)P\ } \quad \text{Intercept}$$

$$x_E \in_E \mathbb{Z}_r^*$$

$$\text{Impersonate } A \quad \xrightarrow{\ A_{KA} \cdot x_E\ } \quad x_b \in_R \mathbb{Z}_r^*$$

$$\xleftarrow{\ B_{KA} = x_b(s+a)P\ }$$

$$\text{Intercept}$$

$$\xleftarrow{\ B_{KA} \cdot x_E\ } \quad \text{Impersonate } B$$

$$SK_A = \hat{e}(x_b(s+a)P \cdot x_E, A_{pri})^{x_a} = \hat{e}(P,P)^{x_a x_b x_E} = SK_B$$

Attack 9.2: Key replicating attack on Protocol 9.2

non-partner oracle holding the same key (i.e., key replicating attack as outlined in Definition 2.3.12). This violates the key establishment goal and the key integrity property outlined in Chapter 2.2.2.2 [6].

9.2.3 Errors in Existing Proof for 2P-IDAKA Protocol

The general notion of the existing proof of McCullagh and Barreto [13, Proof of Theorem 1], is to assume that there exists an adversary, $\mathcal{A}$, who can gain a non-negligible advantage in distinguishing the test key in the game described in Figure 2.1, and to use $\mathcal{A}$ to break the underlying Bilinear Inverse Diffie–Hellman Problem (BIDHP). An adversary, $\mathcal{A}_{\mathcal{BIDHP}}$, against the BIDHP is constructed using $\mathcal{A}$. The objective of $\mathcal{A}_{\mathcal{BIDHP}}$ is to compute and output the value $\hat{e}(P,P)^{\alpha^{-1}\beta}$ when given $P, \alpha P, \beta P$ for $x, y, z \in \mathbb{Z}_r^*$.

9.2.3.1 Error 1

In the existing proof, the public and private key pairs for some player, U_i, are selected as $((u-s)P, u^{-1}P)$, in contradiction to their description in the protocols where $((s+u)P, (s+u)^{-1}P)$ is given instead. The adversary, $\mathcal{A}$, is then able to tell that the public and private key pairs do not match by simply corrupting any player, as shown in Figure 9.2.

$$\mathcal{A}_{\mathcal{BIDHP}} \qquad\qquad\qquad \mathcal{A}$$

$$\xleftarrow{\ \text{Corrupt}(U)\ }$$

$$\text{Return all internal state of } U,$$

$$\text{including } (u)^{-1}P \quad \xrightarrow{\ u^{-1}P\ } \quad \text{Compute } \hat{e}(uP - sP, (u)^{-1}P)$$

Fig. 9.2 Illustration of error 1

We can check whether a public and private key pair match by computing

$$\begin{aligned}\hat{e}((s+u)P,(s+u)^{-1}P) &= \hat{e}((P,P)^{(s+u)(s+u)^{-1}} \\ &= \hat{e}(P,P).\end{aligned}$$

As outlined in Figure 9.2, however, when $\mathcal{A}$ computes the public and private key pair of U,

$$\begin{aligned}\hat{e}(uP-sP,(u)^{-1}P) &= \hat{e}((u-s)P,u^{-1}P) \\ &= \hat{e}(P,P)^{(u-s)u^{-1}} \\ &= \hat{e}(P,P)^{1-su^{-1}} \\ &\neq \hat{e}(P,P).\end{aligned}$$

$\mathcal{A}$ trivially knows that the public and private key pairs of U do not match. The existing proof is thus invalidated.

9.2.3.2 Error 2

We observed that the parameter $\beta P = x_j \alpha P$ given in the existing proof should be $\beta P = x_j(y_i - s)P$, as explained in Figure 9.3. In Figure 9.3, we assume that error 1 has been fixed. The public/private key pair of I (the partner player associated with the Test session is $((y_i-s)P,(y_i-s)^{-1}P)$, the public key of J (the owner of the Test session) is αP, and the private key of J (i.e., $\alpha^{-1}P$)) is unknown to both $\mathcal{A}_{\mathcal{BIDHP}}$ and $\mathcal{A}$.

$\mathcal{A}_{\mathcal{BIDHP}}$		$\mathcal{A}$
$x_i \in_R \mathbb{Z}_r^*$	$\xleftarrow{\mathsf{Send}(J,I,i,'start')}$	
	$\xrightarrow{x_iP}$	$\mathcal{A}$ is given $\beta P = x_j \alpha P$ as input from j
$x_iP = x_t(\alpha P)$	$\xleftarrow{\mathsf{Send}(I,J,j,\beta P)}$	

Fig. 9.3 Illustration of error 2

It is obvious from Figure 9.3 that we cannot have the values of both x_iP and x_jP computed using the public key of J, αP (at least one of x_iP and x_jP have to be computed using the public key of I). Let $x_t \in_R \mathbb{Z}_q^*$. To check, we compute

$$\begin{aligned}\hat{e}(P,P)^{x_t x_j} &= \hat{e}(P,P)^{x_i \alpha^{-1} \beta \alpha^{-1}} \\ &\neq \hat{e}(P,P)^{\alpha^{-1}\beta},\end{aligned}$$

which is what $\mathscr{A}_{\mathscr{BJGHP}}$ is trying to solve. The correct value for $\beta P = x_j \alpha P$ given in the existing proof should be $\beta P = x_j(y_i - s)P$, as explained below.

$$\widehat{e}(P,P)^{x_i x_j} = \widehat{e}(P,P)^{x_i \alpha^{-1} \beta (y_i - s)^{-1}}$$
$$= \widehat{e}(P,P)^{\alpha^{-1} \beta}.$$

We observe that for the existing proof to work, we would have to assume that the inputs to the Test session originated with the simulator, $\mathscr{A}_{\mathscr{BJGHP}}$, and not the adversary, $\mathscr{A}$. This is not, however, a normal assumption and resricts the BR93 model. If a slightly different assumption were made in the security proof for the improved Chen and Kudla's protocol in Chapter 9.1.4 (namely that if B is the partner of the Test session, then all Send query inputs to sessions of B that are later revealed were generated by $\mathscr{A}_{\mathscr{BGH}}$), then the proof in Chapter 9.1.4 would not have to restrict Reveal queries to B.

Consequences of errors in security proofs: Protocol implementers (usually non-specialists and/or industrial practitioners) will usually plug-and-use existing provably-secure protocols without reading the formal proofs of the protocols [8, 9]. Errors in security proofs or specifications themselves will certainly undermine the credibility and trustworthiness of provably-secure protocols in the real world [15], as we have mentioned in Chapter 8.

9.2.4 Improved 2P-IDAKA Protocol

Let A's transcript be denoted by $\mathscr{T}_A$ and B's transcript be denoted by $\mathscr{T}_B$. Consider the scenario whereby session keys of A and B are constructed as

$$SK_{AB} = \mathscr{H}(A||B||\mathscr{T}_A||\widehat{e}(B_{KA}, A_{pri})^{x_a}) = \mathscr{H}(A||B||\mathscr{T}_A||\widehat{e}(P,P)^{x_a x_b}),$$
$$SK_{BA} = \mathscr{H}(A||B||\mathscr{T}_B||\widehat{e}(A_{KA}, B_{pri})^{x_b}) = \mathscr{H}(A||B||\mathscr{T}_B||\widehat{e}(P,P)^{x_a x_b}) = SK_{AB}$$

instead. The attack outlined in Attack 9.2 will no longer be valid since a non-matching conversation (i.e., $\mathscr{T}_A \neq \mathscr{T}_B$) will also mean that the session key is different, as shown below:

$$SK_{AB} = \mathscr{H}(A||B||x_a(s+b)P||(x_b \cdot x_E)(s+a)P||\widehat{e}(B_{KA}, A_{pri})^{x_a}),$$
$$SK_{BA} = \mathscr{H}(A||B||(x_a \cdot x_E)(s+b)P||x_b(s+a)P||\widehat{e}(A_{KA}, B_{pri})^{x_b}) \neq SK_{AB}.$$

$\mathscr{A}$ is unable to gain information about any fresh session key(s). Figure 9.4 illustrates why Reveal queries directed at the owner of the Test session cannot be answered by $\mathscr{A}_{\mathscr{BGH}}$. Note that $\Pi^j_{J,C}$ is not the target Test session.

$\mathcal{ABSDHP}$ $\mathcal{A}$

$x_b \in_R \mathbb{Z}_{r}*$ $\xleftarrow{\quad \text{Send}(J,C,j,(x_c(s+b)P)) \quad}$

$x_c \in_R \mathbb{Z}_{r}*$

$\xrightarrow{\quad (x_b(s+b)P) \quad}$

$\xleftarrow{\quad \text{Reveal}(J,C,j) \quad}$

$\mathcal{ABSDHP}$ is supposed to respond with $\mathcal{H}(J||C||j||\hat{e}(x_c(s+b)P,J_{pri}))$, but $\mathcal{ABSDHP}$ does not know J_{pri}, and thus cannot know the input for its simulation of $\mathcal{H}$.

$v \in_R \{0,1\}^k$ $\xrightarrow{\qquad v \qquad}$

$\xleftarrow{\quad \text{Corrupt}(C) \quad}$

$\mathcal{ABSDHP}$ returns all internal states of C, including $C_{pri} = (s+c)^{-1}P$.

$\xrightarrow{\quad C_{pri} \quad}$

$SK_{BC} = \mathcal{H}(C||B||i||\hat{e}(x_c(s+b)P,C_{pri}))$

Verify if $v \overset{?}{=} SK_{BC}$

Fig. 9.4 An example simulation of Protocol 9.2

From Figure 9.4, it can be seen that $\mathcal{A}$ will be able to distinguish between the simulation provided by $\mathcal{ABSDHP}$ and the actual protocol if it carries out this sequence of actions, since with overwhelming probability, $v \neq SK_{BC}$ (recall that v is randomly chosen). Hence, $\mathcal{ABSDHP}$ cannot answer any Reveal directed at the owner of the target Test session, J, unless we make a similar type of assumption in the existing proof outlined in Chapter 9.2.3 that all Send query inputs to sessions of J that are later revealed were generated by $\mathcal{ABSDHP}$.

9.3 A Proposal for Session Key Construction

In this section, we present our proposal on how session keys should be constructed. Although we do not claim that session keys constructed in this fashion will result in a secure protocol (as the security of the protocol is based on many other factors, such as the underlying cryptographic primitives used), we do claim that having a sound construction of session keys may reduce the number of possible attacks on the protocol.

We propose that session keys in key establishment protocols should be constructed[1] as shown in Table 9.2.
The features of the keys are as follows.

- Inclusion of the identities of the participants and their roles in the key derivation function provides resilience against unknown key share attacks and reflection at-

---

[1] Our observation on the session key construction is cited in a special publication (SP 800-56A) – Recommendation for Pair-Wise Key Establishment Schemes Using Discrete Logarithm Cryptography by National Institute of Standards and Technology (NIST) [1].

Session key input	Properties
Identities of the participants and their roles	Resilience against unknown key share attacks [3, Chapter 5.1.2] and reflection attacks [10].
Unique session identifiers (SIDs)	Freshness and data origin authentication (assuming SIDs defined to be the concatenation of exchanged messages).
Ephemeral shared secrets and/or long-term (static) shared secrets	If the identities of the (perceived) partner participants change, the session keys will also be different.

Table 9.2 Construction of session key in key establishment protocols

tacks since the inclusion of both the identities of the participants and role asymmetry effectively ensures some sense of direction. If the role of the participants or the identities of the (perceived) partner participants change, the session keys will also be different.

- Inclusion of the unique session identifiers (SIDs) in the key derivation function ensure that session keys will be fresh. If SIDs are defined as the concatenation of messages exchanged during the protocol execution, messages altered during the transmission will result in different session keys (providing data origin authentication). Moreover, including session identifiers in deriving the session key would also prevent the key replication attack as shown in both this chapter and the earlier chapter.
- Inclusion of some other ephemeral shared secrets and/or long-term (static) shared secrets depending on individual protocols in the key derivation function , ensure that the session key is only known to the protocol participants.

9.4 Another Case Study

In this section, we revealed a new flaw (i.e., reflection attack) in the key agreement protocol of Lee, Kim, and Yoo [12] and demonstrate that the inclusion of the identities of the participants and their roles in the key derivation function thwarts the reflection attack. Note that the key agreement protocol of Lee, Kim, and Yoo does not have a proof of security.

Protocol 9.3 describes the key agreement protocol of Lee, Kim, and Yoo [12]. There are two communicating principals in Protocol 9.3, namely A and B. Both A and B are assumed to share a secret password, pwd_{AB}, and integers, $Q \bmod n$ and $Q^{-1} \bmod n$, are computed in some predetermined manner from pwd_{AB}. The system parameters are n and g, where n is a large prime and g is a generator of order $n-1$ of $GF(n)$. In the protocol, the notation $a \in_R \mathbb{Z}_q$ denotes that a is randomly drawn from $\mathbb{Z}_q$. At the end of Protocol 9.3's execution, both A and B will share a common secret session key, $SK_A = g^{ab} \bmod n = SK_B$.

$$A\ (pwd_{AB}, Q, Q^{-1}) \qquad\qquad B\ (pwd_{AB}, Q, Q^{-1})$$

$$a \in_R \mathbb{Z}_q \qquad\qquad b \in_R \mathbb{Z}_q$$

$$X_1 = g^{aQ} \oplus Q \bmod n \xrightarrow{\quad X_1 \quad} Y_1 = g^{bQ} \oplus Q \bmod n$$

$$\xleftarrow{\quad Y_1 \quad}$$

$$SK_A = (Y_1 \oplus Q)^{aQ^{-1}} = g^{ab} \bmod n = (X_1 \oplus Q)^{bQ^{-1}} = SK_B$$

Protocol 9.3: Lee, Kim, and Yoo (2005) authenticated key agreement protocol

9.4.1 Reflection Attack on Lee–Kim–Yoo Protocol

Attack 9.3 describes the execution of Protocol 9.3 in the presence of a malicious adversary, $\mathscr{A}$. Let $\mathscr{A}_U$ denotes the adversary impersonating some user, U.

$$A \qquad\qquad\qquad\qquad\qquad\qquad \mathscr{A}_B$$

$$a \in_R \mathbb{Z}_q \quad \xrightarrow{\quad X_1 = g^{aQ} \oplus Q \bmod n \quad}$$

Intercept message meant for B

Reflect message back to A and start concurrent session

$$a_{S2} \in_R \mathbb{Z}_q \quad \xleftarrow{\quad S2 : X_1 \quad}$$

$$\xrightarrow{\quad S2 : X_2 = g^{a_{S2}Q} \oplus Q \bmod n \quad}$$

Intercept message meant for B

Reflect message back to A

$$\xleftarrow{\quad X_2 \quad}$$

$$SK_A = (X_1 \oplus Q)^{a_{S2}Q^{-1}}$$

$$SK_{A(S2)} = (X_2 \oplus Q)^{aQ^{-1}}$$

Attack 9.3: Execution of Protocol 9.3 in the presence of a malicious adversary

At the end of Protocol 9.3's execution shown in Attack 9.3, A has accepted two session keys, SK_A and $SK_{A(S2)}$, which A believes that both keys are shared with B in different sessions, as explained below:

- SK_A is being used in the session where A is the initiator and
- $SK_{A(S2)}$ is being used in the session (S2) where A is the responder.

We observe that both session keys accepted by A, SK_A and $SK_{A(S2)}$, are of the same value, as shown below:

$$SK_A = (X_1 \oplus Q)^{a_{S2}Q^{-1}}$$
$$= g^{aa_{S2}} \bmod n$$
$$SK_{A(S2)} = (X_2 \oplus Q)^{aQ^{-1}}$$
$$= g^{aa_{S2}} \bmod n$$
$$= SK_A.$$

However, B is unaware of any of these sessions, and the adversary, $\mathcal{A}$, is able to trivially expose any of this key to obtain the other fresh session key (i.e., reflection attack).

9.4.2 Preventing the Attack

We propose to include the sender's and responder's identities and transcripts, $\mathcal{T}_U$ (i.e., concatenation of all messages sent and received), in the key derivation function, which will (effectively) bind the session key to all messages sent and received by both A and B, as shown below:

$$SK_{A(Fixed)} = \mathcal{H}(A||B||\mathcal{T}_A||(Y_1 \oplus Q)^{aQ^{-1}})$$
$$SK_{B(Fixed)} = \mathcal{H}(A||B||\mathcal{T}_B||(X_1 \oplus Q)^{bQ^{-1}})$$
$$= SK_{A(Fixed)},$$

where $\mathcal{H}$ denotes a secure hash function and $||$ denotes the concatenation of messages.

Informally, the reflection attack outlined in Attack 9.3 is no longer valid, since

$$SK_{A(Fixed)} = \mathcal{H}(A||B||\mathcal{T}_A||((X_1 \oplus Q)^{a_{S2}Q^{-1}}))$$
$$= \mathcal{H}(A||B||\mathcal{T}_A||(g^{aa_{S2}} \bmod n))$$
$$SK_{A(S2)(Fixed)} = \mathcal{H}(B||A||\mathcal{T}_B||((X_2 \oplus Q)^{aQ^{-1}}))$$
$$= \mathcal{H}(B||A||\mathcal{T}_B||(g^{aa_{S2}} \bmod n))$$
$$\neq SK_{A(Fixed)}.$$

9.5 Summary

By making a small change to the way session keys are constructed in the Chen–Kudla protocol 2, McCullagh–Barreto protocol 2P-IDAKA, and Lee–Kim–Yoo key agreement protocol, we demonstrated that the existing attacks no longer work. In addition, the security proofs of the Chen–Kudla protocol 2 and the McCullagh–

Barreto protocol 2P-IDAKA were improved to be less restrictive with regard to the Reveal queries allowed. The technicality of not being able to answer Reveal queries outlined in Sections 9.1.4 and 9.2.4 can be resolved using GAP assumption [14]. We note that in a later independent yet related work by Kudla and Paterson [11], the GAP assumption is also used to prove protocol 4 of Blake-Wilson, Johnson, and Menezes [2] secure in the BR93 model. We also found some errors in the McCullagh–Barreto proof, as well as observing that it is in a restricted version of the BR93 model that assumes that the adversary does not generate the input to the Test session.

As a result of our findings, we recommend that all provably secure protocols should construct session keys using materials comprising the identities of the participants and roles, unique session identifiers (SIDs), and some other ephemeral shared secrets and/or long-term (static) shared secrets.

References

1. Elaine Barker, Don Johnson, & Miles Smid 2006. Recommendation for Pair-Wise Key Establishment Schemes Using Discrete Logarithm Cryptography. *Special Publication (SP 800-56A)*. National Institute of Standards and Technology
2. Simon Blake-Wilson, Don Johnson & Alfred Menezes 1997. Key Agreement Protocols and their Security Analysis, in Michael Darnell (ed), Proceedings of 6th IMA International Conference on Cryptography and Coding. Lecture Notes in Computer Science 1335/1997: 30–45
3. Colin Boyd & Anish Mathuria 2003. *Protocols for Authentication and Key Establishment*. Springer-Verlag
4. Liqun Chen & Caroline Kudla 2003. Identity Based Authenticated Key Agreement Protocols from Pairings, in *Proceedings of IEEE Computer Security Foundations Workshop - CSFW 2003*. IEEE Computer Society Press: 219–233. Corrected version at http://eprint.iacr.org/2002/184/
5. Zhaohui Cheng & Liqun Chen 2007. On Security Proof of McCullagh-Barreto's Key Agreement Protocol and its Variants. *International Journal of Security and Networks* 2(3/4): 251–259
6. Kim-Kwang Raymond Choo 2005. Revisit Of McCullagh–Barreto Two-Party ID-Based Authenticated Key Agreement Protocols. *International Journal of Network Security* 1(3): 154–160. Preliminary version appears in http://eprint.iacr.org/2004/343/
7. Ik Rae Jeong, Jonathan Katz & Dong Hoon Lee 2004. One-Round Protocols for Two-Party Authenticated Key Exchange, in Markus Jakobsson, Moti Yung & Jianying Zhou (eds), Proceedings of Applied Cryptography and Network Security - ACNS 2004. Lecture Notes in Computer Science 3089/2004: 220–232
8. Neal Koblitz & Alfred Menezes 2004. Another Look at "Provable Security". *Technical report* no CORR 2004-20. Centre for Applied Cryptographic Research, University of Waterloo, Canada. Available from http://eprint.iacr.org/2004/152/
9. Neal Koblitz & Alfred Menezes 2006. Another Look at "Provable Security". *Journal of Cryptology* 20(1): 3–37
10. Hugo Krawczyk 2003. SIGMA: The 'SIGn-and-MAc' Approach to Authenticated Diffie–Hellman and Its Use in the IKE-Protocols, in Dan Boneh (ed), Proceedings of Advances in Cryptology - CRYPTO 2003. Lecture Notes in Computer Science 2729/2003: 400–425

11. Caroline Kudla & Kenneth G Paterson 2005. Modular Security Proofs for Key Agreement Protocols, in Bimal Roy (ed), Proceedings of Advances in Cryptology - ASIACRYPT 2005. Lecture Notes in Computer Science 3788/2005: 549–569

12. Sung-Wong Lee, Hyun-Sung Kim & Kee-Young Yoo 2005. Improvement of Lee and Lee's Authenticated Key Agreement Scheme. *Journal of Applied Mathematics and Computation* 162: 1049–1053

13. Noel McCullagh & Paulo S L M Barreto 2005. A New Two-Party Identity-Based Authenticated Key Agreement, in Alfred John Menezes (ed), Proceedings of Cryptographers' Track at RSA Conference - CT-RSA 2005. Lecture Notes in Computer Science 3376/2005: 262–274. Extended version available from http://eprint.iacr.org/2004/122/

14. Tatsuaki Okamoto & David Pointcheval 2001. The Gap-Problems: a New Class of Problems for the Security of Cryptographic Schemes, in Kwangjo Kim (ed), Proceedings of Public Key Cryptography - PKC 2001. Lecture Notes in Computer Science 1992/2001: 104–118

15. Jacques Stern, David Pointcheval, John Malone-Lee & Nigel Smart 2002. Flaws in Applying Proof Methodologies to Signature Schemes, in Moti Yung (ed), Proceedings of Advances in Cryptology - CRYPTO 2002. Lecture Notes in Computer Science 2442/2002: 93–110

Chapter 10
Complementing Computational Protocol Analysis

In recent years a number of researchers recognized the disparity in the two different approaches to protocol analysis outlined in Sections 1.2.1 and 1.2.2. Previous efforts in unifying the two domains have been devoted towards providing abstract models of cryptographic primitives which are suitable for machine analysis and yet can be proven to be functionally equivalent (in some well-defined sense) to the real cryptographic primitives that they model. Abadi and Rogaway [1, 2] started this trend. More recently, comprehensive efforts have been under way in several independent yet related projects by Canetti [11, 12], by Backes *et al.* [4, 5, 6, 7], and by Blanchet [8].

In this chapter we take a different, more pragmatic, approach to the problem. We are motivated by the observation that so far no researchers have tried to utilize the communication and adversary model from computational proofs in a machine specification and analysis. Although we cannot capture the complexity-based definitions for security and cryptographic primitives, we can ensure that the same protocol and adversary capabilities are specified in both the human-generated proofs and the machine analysis. Rather than trying to unify the two approaches, we treat them as complementary. We ensure that, as far as possible, they are analysing the same objects. Our concept is that the human proof will take care of the cryptographic details lacking in the machine analysis, while the machine analysis will help to ensure that human error resulting in basic structural mistakes is avoided.

We provide a formal specification and machine analysis of the adversary model from the BPR2000 model. The Bellare–Rogaway model is the most widely used model for human-generated security proofs of protocols. As a case study we analyse the protocol of Jakobsson and Pointcheval. The original version appeared in the unpublished pre-proceedings of Financial Cryptography 2001 with a claimed proof of security in the BR93 model. A flaw in the protocol was discovered by Wong and Chan [21]. In the published paper [15], the flaw in the protocol has been fixed as mentioned in Chapter 8.2. We also use tripartite key exchange protocols 8 and 9 of Hitchcock, Boyd, and González Nieto [14], which carry claimed security proofs, as case studies.

Our choice of formalism for this work is Asynchronous Product Automata (APA), a universal state-based formal method [20]. APA is supported by the Simple Homomorphism Verification Tool (SHVT) for analysis and verification of cooperating systems and communicating automata. Once the possible state transitions of each automaton have been specified, SHVT can be used to automatically search the state space of the model. SHVT provides a reachability graph of the explored states. In our APA specification, the abstract communication model captures the representation of the protocol, the message transmission, and the communication channels. The automated state space analyses performed with SHVT reveal the known attack on the Jakobsson-Pointcheval protocol and also two other previously unpublished attacks. This work differs significantly from related earlier work of Boyd and Viswanathan [10], as their formal specification did not capture the entire Bellare–Rogaway model. In addition, no automatic searching was performed and no new attack was revealed in their earlier work. The automated state space analyses performed with SHVT also reveal previously unpublished attacks on tripartite key exchange protocols 8 and 9 of Hitchcock, Boyd, and González Nieto.

Material presented in this chapter has appeared in the following publications:

- Kim-Kwang Raymond Choo, Colin Boyd, Yvonne Hitchcock, and Greg Maitland. Complementing Computational Protocol Analysis with Formal Specifications. In Theo Dimitrakos and Fabio Martinelli, editors, IFIP TC1 WG1.7 2nd International Workshop on Formal Aspects in Security and Trust - FAST 2004, volume 173/2005 of IFIP International Federation for Information Processing Series, pages 129–144. Springer-Verlag, 2004.
- Kim-Kwang Raymond Choo, Colin Boyd, and Yvonne Hitchcock. The Importance of Proofs of Security for Key Establishment Protocols: Formal Analysis of Jan–Chen, Yang–Shen–Shieh, Kim–Huh–Hwang–Lee, Lin–Sun–Hwang, & Yeh–Sun Protocols. *Computer Communications*, 29(15):2788–2797, 2006.
- Kim-Kwang Raymond Choo. Refuting Security Proofs for Tripartite Key Exchange with Model Checker in Planning Problem Setting. In 19th IEEE Computer Security Foundations Workshop - CSFW-19, pages 297–308. IEEE Computer Society, 2006.

10.1 The Formal Framework

In our formal framework using the APA specification, protocol principals are modelled as a family of elementary automata. The various state spaces of the principals are modelled as a family of state sets. The channel through which the elementary automaton communicates is modelled by the addition and removal of messages from the shared state component Network, which is initially empty. Each of the elementary automata only has access to the particular state components to which it is connected. In addition to the regular protocol principals, we specify an adversary $\mathscr{A}$, which has access to the shared state component Network, but no access to the internal states of the principals.

Adopting the adversary formalism from the BPR2000 model, we consider an adversary $\mathscr{A}$ who is able to intercept messages in the Network, swap data components in the intercepted messages to form new messages, remove messages from the Network, or fabricate new messages. $\mathscr{A}$ is then able to send these messages to the client or server oracles via the Network (corresponding to SendClient and SendServer queries in the BPR2000 model). Once an oracle, Π_U^i, has accepted and holds a session key, the (SID, PID) pair associated with that oracle becomes visible to the adversary $\mathscr{A}$ via the shared state component Transcript. If $\mathscr{A}$ so chooses, $\mathscr{A}$ is then able to obtain the session key of Π_U^i via a Reveal query or a Corrupt query. The shared state component Transcript also contains a log of all sent messages and is equivalent to a transcript in the Bellare–Rogaway model. The advantage of $\mathscr{A}_{BR}$ is not explicitly modelled in our specification due to its probabilistic nature. Instead of modelling the attack to distinguish between the real key and a random value, we simplify the game defined in Chapter 2.3.3 by assuming that $\mathrm{Adv}^{\mathscr{A}_{BR}} = 1$ if $\mathscr{A}_{BR}$ can obtain a fresh session key, otherwise $\mathrm{Adv}^{\mathscr{A}_{BR}} = 0$. Some attacks might be left out while analysing the game $\mathscr{G}$. Since our aim is to leave computational matters to the human-generated proof, this does not present an obstacle to our protocol analysis.

When using formal specification tools, insecurity is commonly specified in terms of the unreachability of the desired states or reachability of insecure states. A "secure" protocol in a formal specification does not necessarily imply that the protocol is secure. We find it more natural, therefore, to define insecurity in our formal framework as given in Definition 10.1.1. Protocols proven insecure in our formal specification model will also be insecure in the BPR2000 model. Definition 10.1.1 depends on the notions of partnership in Definition 2.3.7 and freshness in Definition 2.3.1.

Definition 10.1.1 *A protocol is insecure in our formal framework if:*

1. *two fresh non-partner oracles accept the same key, or*
2. *some fresh oracle accepts some key, which has been exposed (i.e., is known to $\mathscr{A}$), or*
3. *some fresh oracle accepts and terminates with no partner.*

10.2 Analysing a Provably-Secure Protocol

In this section, using the original version of Protocol 8.3 [15] as described in Protocol 10.1 as a case study, we specify Protocol 10.1 using APA. We demonstrate that SHVT can be used to find the hijacking attack first mentioned by Wong and Chan, and two previously unknown flaws in Protocol 10.1.

Client A (a, g^a)		Server B (b, g^b)

$$r_A, t_A \in_R \mathbb{Z}_q, K = y_B^{r_A} = g^{br_A}$$
$$k = h_0(g^b, g^{r_A}, K), r = h_1(g^{t_A})$$

$$k_2 = h_2(g^b, g^{r_A}, K) \qquad \xrightarrow{\quad g^{r_A}, r \quad} \qquad K = (g^{r_A})^b, k_2' = h_2(g^b, g^{r_A}, K)$$

$$k_2 \overset{?}{=} k_2' \qquad \xleftarrow{\quad k_2', e \quad} \qquad e \in_R \{0, 1\}^k$$

$$d = t_A - ae \bmod q \qquad \xrightarrow{\quad d \quad} \qquad r \overset{?}{=} h_1(g^d (g^a)^e),$$
$$k = h_0(g^b, g^{r_A}, K) \qquad\qquad\qquad\qquad k = h_0(g^b, g^{r_A}, K)$$

Protocol 10.1: Original unpublished version of Protocol 8.3

There are two communicating principals in Protocol 10.1; namely the server and the client of limited computing resources, A. The security goals of Protocol 10.1 are mutual authentication and key agreement between the two communicating principals. A and B are each assumed to know the public key of the other party. Prior to the protocol run, A can pre-compute the session key k (which is a hash of the shared secret with B) using Diffie-Hellman key exchange, the value r used for client authentication and B's public key (i.e., $k = h_0(g^b, g^{r_A}, K)$).

10.2.1 Protocol Specification

The first phase of our formal specification is to specify the basic types and the functions as shown in Figure 10.1. In order to increase run-time efficiency, and to overcome storage restrictions, we replace each unique data item in any message with a unique numeric message identifier (MID) in our specification. For example, the message in message flow 1 sent by A consists of two data items, g^{r_A} and r, whose message identifiers are $MID = 1$ and $MID = 2$ respectively. SID is the concatenation of these unique $MIDs$ (e.g. $SID = [1, 2, \ldots]$) instead of the concatenation of messages from the BPR2000 model. Note that due to the limitation on character fonts in the tool, E denotes the adversary in the APA specification.

10.2.1.1 Initial State of Protocol 10.1

The initial state of Protocol 10.1 is shown in Figure 10.2. The left-hand column shows the SHVT specification of the various initial states. An explanation is given in the right-hand column.

Examples of some basic types	
Agents	::= set of all the principals (i.e., A, B) and $\mathscr{A}$ (i.e., E)
A_State	::= A's internal state
A_Keys	::= set of A's public and private keys
Accepted	::= set of all oracles who had accepted (visible to $\mathscr{A}$)
Examples of some functions	
gFunction(g,m)	::= denotes g^m, where m is some value (e.g., gFunction(g,rA) denotes g^{rA} shown in Protocol 10.1)
verifyGFun(m1,m2)	::= the verification function used to verify if $g^{m1'} \stackrel{?}{=} g^{m2'}$ for some $m1'$ and $m2'$. (e.g., verifyGFun(gFunction(gFunction(g,a),b), gFunction(gFunction(g,b),a)) will return true)

Fig. 10.1 Examples of basic types and functions

A_State:=	{(B,server),(start,B), (publicK,gFunction(b),B)};	A knows that B is a server, can start a protocol session run with B (indicated by the keyword *start*), and knows the public key of B (i.e., g^b).
A_Keys:=	{(publicK,gFunction(a)),(privateK,a)};	A owns a key pair (a, g^a).
B_State:=	{(A,agent),(respond,A), (publicK,gFunction(a),A)};	B knows that A is an agent, can respond to a protocol run initiated by A (indicated by the keyword *respond*), and knows the public key of A (i.e., g^a).
B_Keys:=	{(publicK,gFunction(b)),(privateK,b)};	B owns a key pair (b, g^b).
E_State:=	{(publicK,gFunction(a),A),publicK, gFunction(b),B)};	$\mathscr{A}$ (Eve) knows the public keys of A and B.
Network:=	$\emptyset$;	Network is initially empty.
Transcript:=	$\emptyset$;	Transcript is initially empty.

Fig. 10.2 Initial state of Protocol 10.1

10.2.1.2 Step 1 of Protocol 10.1

Starting from the initial state shown in Figure 10.2, SHVT computes all reachable states. The first state transition of the initiator client A is explained in Figure 10.3. To ensure uniqueness of the values r_A, t_A and MID in the APA specification, once these values are assigned, they are removed from the pre-defined sets *new_random_nonce* and *MIDs*. We assume that (SID_A, PID_A) cannot be modified by the adversary. The (SID_A, PID_A) tuple is required to enable the SHVT analysis to define partnership.

10.2.1.3 A Malicious State Transition

An active adversary $\mathscr{A}$ is able to intercept message (g^{r_A}, r) meant for B from A, to fabricate a new message (g^{r_E}, r) and to send the fabricated message (g^{r_E}, r) to B via the Network. This state transition as shown in Figure 10.4 is equivalent to a SendServer query in the BPR2000 model.

def_trans_pattern A step_1	Definition of a state transition
B,gb,rA,tA,rAA,r,k,k2,K,SIDA,PIDA,MID	Variables used in this step
['start',B] ? A_State,	Precondition: A can start protocol run with B.
[B,'server'] ? A_State,	Precondition: A knows B is the server.
['publicK',gb,B] ? A_State,	Precondition: A knows B's public key gb. (gb is a variable that takes the value $gFunction(b)$.)
rAA << new_random_nonce,	Random unique nonce values are drawn
rA := head(rAA),	from the pre-defined set
tA := head(tail(rAA)),	*new_random_nonce* and assigned to r_A
tail(tail(rAA)) >> new_random_nonce,	and t_A respectively.
MID << SIDs,	Random unique *MIDs* are drawn from the
tail(tail(MID)) >> SIDs,	pre-defined set *SIDs* are assigned to g^{r_A} and r respectively.
SIDA := [head(MID),head(tail(MID))],	*SID* is the concatenation of these unique *MIDs*.
PIDA := B,	*PID* of A is set to B.
K := ['KFunction',gb,rA],	A computes a new $K = (g^b)^{r_A}$.
k := ['hash0',gb,['gFunction',g,rA],K],	A computes the new shared secret k using the hash function h_0 (i.e., $k = h_0(g^b, g^{r_A}, K)$).
r := ['hash1',['gFunction',g,tA]],	A computes $r = h_1(g^{t_A})$.
k2 := ['hash2',gb,['gFunction',g,rA],K],	A computes $k_2 = h_2(g^b, g^{r_A}, K)$.
['start',B] << A_State,	A initiated one session with B, so one tuple enabling a session to start is removed from A's state.
[SIDA,PIDA,[tA,k,k2,K]] >> A_State,	A stores the information that she shares with B for this protocol run.
(A,B, [head(SIDA1), head(tail(SIDA1))], ['gFunction',g, rA], r]) >> Network;	A sends message g^{r_A}, r to the Network.

Fig. 10.3 State transition - step 1 of Protocol 10.1

10.2.2 Protocol Analysis

Having formally specified Protocol 10.1 in APA, we analyse Protocol 10.1's specification using SHVT as shown in the following sections. The analyses were run on a Pentium IV 2.4 GHz computer with 512 Mb of RAM. The resulting analysis statistics are given in Figure 10.5. We set the break condition to terminate the SHVT analysis if any of the requirement(s) in Definition 10.1.1 are violated. The attack sequence and the internal states can be examined by viewing the reachability graph produced by SHVT.

For run-time efficiency, and to avoid enormous branching factors in the search space, we restrict the actions of the adversary so that certain actions are possible for only some message types. Running SHVT with adversaries having various restrictions and also restricting A to only two protocol runs results in SHVT finding the attacks shown in Attacks 10.1, 10.2, and 10.3.

def trans pattern E SendServer	Definition of a state transition
(ga,gb,A,B,M,SIDE,S,rE)	Variables used in this step
['publicK',ga,A] ? E_State,	Precondition: $\mathscr{A}$ knows A's public key.
('publicK',gb,B) ? E_State,	Precondition: $\mathscr{A}$ knows B's public key.
[A,'agent'] ? E_State,	Precondition: $\mathscr{A}$ knows A exists.
[B,'server'] ? E_State,	Precondition: $\mathscr{A}$ knows B exists.
A ≠ B,	Precondition: A and B are two different principals.
(A,B,S,M) ? Network,	Precondition: Checks if there exists any message from A intended for B in the network.
rAA << new_random_nonce,	Random unique nonce values are drawn
rA := head(rAA),	from the pre-defined set
tA := head(tail(rAA)),	*new_random_nonce* and assigned to r_A
tail(tail(rAA)) >> new_random_nonce,	and t_A respectively.
SIDE << SIDs,	Random unique *MIDs* are drawn from the
tail(tail(SIDE)) >> SIDs,	pre-defined set *SIDs* and assigned to *grE* and *rE* respectively.
['fabricated','mf1',[head(SIDE),elem(2,S)],	$\mathscr{A}$ stores information in her internal state.
['[gFunction',g, head(rE)]] >> E_State,	
(A,B,[head(SIDE),elem(2,S)],	$\mathscr{A}$ sends a fabricated message to B via the Network.
[['gFunction', g,head(rE)], elem(2,M)]) >> Network;	

Fig. 10.4 A malicious state transition

Protocol Analysis	# Players	# Runs	# Nodes	Run-Time	Flaws?
Hijacking Attack	2	1	34	2 secs	Yes
New Attack 1	2	2	144	3 secs	Yes
New Attack 2	2	2	1538	79 secs	Yes

Fig. 10.5 Analysis statistics

10.2.2.1 Hijacking Attack

State space analysis performed in the SHVT analysis reveals that both requirements 2 and 3 of Definition 10.1.1 can be violated. This attack was first mentioned by Wong and Chan [21] as shown in Attack 10.1.

10.2.2.2 New Attack 1

State space analysis in SHVT reveals that Requirement 1 of Definition 10.1.1 is violated. The internal state of the final node in the reachability graph reveals that the following four oracles have accepted some session key:

- $\Pi_A^{[1,2,7,10,12]}$ belonging to A and having $SID = [1,2,7,10,12]$ accepted session key, $h_0(g^{rA1}, g^{tA1}, (g^{rA1})^{tA1})$,
- $\Pi_A^{[3,4,9,8,11]}$ belonging to A and having $SID = [3,4,9,8,11]$ accepted session key, $h_0(g^{rA1}, g^{tA2}, (g^{rA1})^{tA2})$,

$A\,(a,g^a)$	$\mathscr{A}$	$B\,(b,g^b)$
$r_A,t_A \in_R \mathbb{Z}_q$		
$K = y_B^{r_A} = g^{br_A}$		
$k = h_0(g^b,g^{r_A},K)$		
$r = h_1(g^{t_A})$		
$k_2 = h_2(g^b,g^{r_A},K) \xrightarrow{\;g^{r_A},r\;}$		$K_1 = (g^{r_A})^b$
$\xrightarrow{\;g^{r_E},r\;}$		$K_2 = (g^{r_E})^b$
	$\xleftarrow{k_{2,1},e_1}$	
		$k_{2,1} = h_2(g^b,g^{r_A},K_1)$
		$e_1 \in_R \{0,1\}^k$
	$\xleftarrow{k_{2,2},e_2}$	
		$k_{2,2} = h_2(g^b,g^{r_E},K_2)$
		$e_2 \in_R \{0,1\}^k$
$k_2 \overset{?}{=} k_{2,1}$	$\xleftarrow{k_{2,1},e_2}$	
$d = t_A - ae_2 \bmod q \xrightarrow{\;d\;}$	$\xrightarrow{\;d\;}$	
		$r \overset{?}{=} h_1(g^d(g^a)^{e_2})$
$k_{AB} = h_0(g^b,g^{r_A},(g^b)^{r_A})$		$k_{BA} = h_0(g^b,g^{r_E},(g^{r_E})^b)$

Attack 10.1: A hijacking attack on Protocol 10.1

- $\Pi_B^{[1,4,7,8,11]}$ belonging to B and having $SID = [1,4,7,8,11]$ accepted session key, $h_0(g^{t_{A1}},g^{r_{A1}},(g^{t_{A1}})^{r_{A1}})$, and
- $\Pi_B^{[3,2,9,10,12]}$ belonging to B and having $SID = [3,2,9,10,12]$ accepted session key, $h_0(g^{t_{A1}},g^{r_{A2}},(g^{t_{A2}})^{r_{A1}})$.

None of these oracles have any partner oracles since their $SIDs$ are different. However, we observe that the pairs ($\Pi_A^{[1,2,7,10,12]}$, $\Pi_B^{[1,4,7,8,11]}$) and ($\Pi_A^{[3,4,9,8,11]}$, $\Pi_B^{[3,2,9,10,12]}$) have accepted with the same session keys as shown in Attack 10.2. This implies that by revealing one oracle in any pair, the adversary $\mathscr{A}$ is able to distinguish the session key held by the other oracle in the same pair. The protocol state is not secure since the adversary $\mathscr{A}$ can find a fresh session key. Mutual authentication is violated since both the client and server oracles terminate without a partner.

The attack sequence, shown in Attack 10.2, is revealed by following the reachability graph to the insecure state. The attack sequence is as follows:

1. The adversary $\mathscr{A}$ intercepts and removes the two original messages from the Network, swaps the components in these two messages to form two new messages, and sends these two modified messages to B impersonating A via the Network.
2. B, upon receiving these two messages, responds as per the protocol specification.
3. $\mathscr{A}$ intercepts the messages in protocol flow 2 sent by B to A, swaps the components in these two messages to form new messages and again sends these two modified messages back to the Network, impersonating B.

$A\ (a, g^a)$	$\mathscr{A}$	$B\ (b, g^b)$

$$r_{A,1}, t_{A,1} \in_R \mathbb{Z}_q$$
$$K_{A,1} = y_B^{r_{A,1}} = g^{br_{A,1}}$$
$$k_{A,1} = h_0(g^b, g^{r_{A,1}}, K_{A,1})$$
$$r_1 = h_1(g^{t_{A,1}})$$
$$k_{2(S1(A))} = h_2(g^b, g^{r_{A,1}}, K_{A,1}) \xrightarrow{\ g^{r_{A,1}}, r_1\ }$$

$$r_{A,2}, t_{A,2} \in_R \mathbb{Z}_q$$
$$K_{A,2} = y_B^{r_{A,2}} = g^{br_{A,2}}$$
$$k_{A,2} = h_0(g^b, g^{r_{A,2}}, K_{A,2})$$
$$r_2 = h_2(g^{t_{A,2}})$$

$$k_{2(S2(A))} = h_2(g^b, g^{r_{A,2}}, K_{A,2}) \xrightarrow{\ g^{r_{A,2}}, r_2\ } \xrightarrow{\ g^{r_{A,1}}, r_2\ } \quad K_1 = (g^{r_{A(1)}})^b$$

$$\xrightarrow{\ g^{r_{A,2}}, r_1\ } \quad K_2 = (g^{r_{A(2)}})^b$$

$$\xleftarrow{\ k_{2,1}, e_1\ } \quad k_{2,1} = h_2(g^b, g^{r_{A,1}}, K_1)$$
$$e_1 \in_R \{0,1\}^k$$

$$\xleftarrow{\ k_{2,2}, e_2\ } \quad k_{2,2} = h_2(g^b, g^{r_{A,2}}, K_2)$$

$$k_{2(S1(A))} \overset{?}{=} k_{2,1} \quad \xleftarrow{\ k_{2,1}, e_2\ } \quad e_2 \in_R \{0,1\}^k$$

$$k_{2(S2(A))} \overset{?}{=} k_{2,2} \quad \xleftarrow{\ k_{2,2}, e_1\ }$$

$$d_1 = t_{A,1} - ae_2 \bmod q \quad \xrightarrow{\ d_1\ } \xrightarrow{\ d_1\ } \quad r_2 \overset{?}{=} h_1(g^{d_1}(g^a)^{e_2})$$

$$d_2 = t_{A,2} - ae_1 \bmod q \quad \xrightarrow{\ d_2\ } \xrightarrow{\ d_2\ } \quad r_1 \overset{?}{=} h_1(g^{d_2}(g^a)^{e_1})$$

$$k_{AB_{(1)}} = h_0(g^b, g^{r_{A,1}}, (g^b)^{r_{A,1}}) \qquad\qquad k_{BA_{(1)}} = h_0(g^b, g^{r_{A,1}}, (g^{r_{A,1}})^b)$$
$$k_{AB_{(2)}} = h_0(g^b, g^{r_{A,2}}, (g^b)^{r_{A,2}}) \qquad\qquad k_{BA_{(2)}} = h_0(g^b, g^{r_{A,2}}, (g^{r_{A,2}})^b)$$

Attack 10.2: New attack 1 on Protocol 10.1

4. If A authenticates the server, she will respond with some value d as per the protocol specification. B receives the messages d_1 and d_2 in protocol flow 3.
5. Once some oracle has accepted and holds some session key, the particular (SID, PID) pair will be made visible to the adversary via the shared state component Transcript. $\mathscr{A}$ is then able to send Reveal queries to the oracles of B, and receive the session keys held by the associated fresh oracles of A.

10.2.2.3 New Attack 2

State space analysis in SHVT reveals that requirements 2 and 3 of Definition 10.1.1 are violated. The internal state of the final node in the reachability graph reveals that fresh oracles of B, $\Pi_B^{[3,2,5,6,9]}$ and $\Pi_B^{[5,2,7,8,16]}$, have accepted with no partner. The adversary $\mathscr{A}$ is able to compute both the session keys accepted by B since both session keys are computed based on the random number g^{r_E} chosen by the adversary $\mathscr{A}$. $\mathscr{A}$ is thus able to decrypt all messages sent by B to A encrypted with these session keys. The attack sequence is shown in Attack 10.3, and is revealed by following the reachability graph to the insecure state.

$$A\ (a, g^a) \qquad\qquad \mathscr{A} \qquad\qquad B\ (b, g^b)$$

$$r_{A,1}, t_{A,1} \in_R \mathbb{Z}_q, K_{A,1} = y_B^{r_{A,1}} = g^{b r_{A,1}}$$
$$k_{A,1} = h_0(g^b, g^{r_{A,1}}, K_{A,1}), r_1 = h_1(g^{t_{A,1}})$$
$$k_{2(S1(A))} = h_2(g^b, g^{r_{A,1}}, K_{A,1}) \xrightarrow{\ g^{t_{A,1}}, r_1\ }$$
$$r_{A,2}, t_{A,2} \in_R \mathbb{Z}_q$$
$$K_{A,2} = y_B^{r_{A,2}} = g^{b r_{A,2}}$$
$$k_{A,2} = h_0(g^b, g^{r_{A,2}}, K_{A,2})$$
$$r_2 = h_2(g^{t_{A,2}})$$
$$k_{2(S2(A))} = h_2(g^b, g^{r_{A,2}}, K_{A,2}) \xrightarrow{\ g^{t_{A,2}}, r_2\ } \xrightarrow{\ g^{r_{A,1}}, r_E\ } \quad K_1 = (g^{r_{A,1}})^b$$
$$\xrightarrow{\ g^{r_E}, r_1\ } \quad K_2 = (g^{r_E})^b$$
$$\xrightarrow{\ g^{r_E}, r_2\ } \quad K_3 = (g^{r_E})^b$$
$$\xrightarrow{\ g^{r_{A,2}}, r_E\ } \quad K_4 = (g^{r_{A,2}})^b$$
$$\xleftarrow{\ k_{2,1}, e_1\ } \quad k_{2,1} = h_2(g^b, g^{r_{A,1}}, K_1)$$
$$e_1 \in_R \{0,1\}^k$$
$$\vdots \qquad\qquad \vdots$$
$$\xleftarrow{\ k_{2,4}, e_4\ } \quad k_{2,4} = h_2(g^b, g^{r_{A,2}}, K_4)$$

$$k_{2(S1(A))} \overset{?}{=} k_{2,1} \qquad \xleftarrow{\ k_{2,1}, e_2\ } \qquad\qquad e_4 \in_R \{0,1\}^k$$
$$k_{2(S2(A))} \overset{?}{=} k_{2,4} \qquad \xleftarrow{\ k_{2,4}, e_3\ }$$
$$d_1 = t_{A,1} - a e_2 \bmod q \qquad \xrightarrow{\ d_1\ } \xrightarrow{\ d_1\ } \quad r^E \overset{?}{=} h_1(g^{d_1}(g^a)^{e_2})$$
$$d_2 = t_{A_2} - a e_3 \bmod q \qquad \xrightarrow{\ d_2\ } \xrightarrow{\ d_2\ } \quad r^E \overset{?}{=} h_1(g^{d_2}(g^a)^{e_3})$$
$$k_{AB_{(1)}} = h_0(g^b, g^{r_{A,1}}, (g^b)^{r_{A,1}}) \qquad\qquad\qquad k_{BA_{(1)}} = h_0(g^b, g^{r_E}, (g^{r_E})^b)$$
$$k_{AB_{(2)}} = h_0(g^b, g^{r_{A,2}}, (g^b)^{r_{A,2}}) \qquad\qquad\qquad k_{BA_{(2)}} = h_0(g^b, g^{r_E}, (g^{r_E})^b)$$

Attack 10.3: New attack 2 on Protocol 10.1

10.3 Analysing Another Two Protocols With Claimed Proofs of Security

Both Protocols 10.2 and 10.3 carry claimed proofs of security in the CK2001 model [14]. The notation used is as follows:

- A, B, and C denote the protocol participants exchanging a secret (session) key,
- $X_{\mathscr{E}_Y}$ denotes the encryption by X intended for Y,
- $MAC_{N_{XY}}(\cdot)$ denotes the generated MAC digest of some message using the one-time MAC key, N_{XY},
- N_{XY} denotes the randomly generated nonce by X intended for Y,
- a, b, and c denote the randomly generated ephermeral private keys of A, B, and C respectively.

The reader might notice that the session identifier, *sid*, in the specifications of Protocols 10.2 and 10.3 appear to be constructed differently from that discussed in Chapter 9.3. If we had follow the revised construction for session identifiers presented in

$$1.\ A \longrightarrow B : sid, [a]P, A_{\mathscr{E}_B}(N_{AB}), A_{\mathscr{E}_C}(N_{AC})$$
$$2.\ B \longrightarrow C : sid, [a]P, [b]P, B_{\mathscr{E}_C}(N_{BC}), B_{\mathscr{E}_A}(N_{BA}),$$
$$MAC_{N_{AB}}(sid, [b]P, A), A_{\mathscr{E}_C}(N_{AC})$$
$$3.\ C \longrightarrow A : sid, [b]P, [c]P, C_{\mathscr{E}_A}(N_{CA}), C_{\mathscr{E}_B}(N_{CB}),$$
$$MAC_{N_{AC}}(sid, [c]P, A),$$
$$MAC_{N_{BC}}(sid, [c]P, B),$$
$$B_{\mathscr{E}_A}(N_{BA}), MAC_{N_{AB}}(sid, [b]P, A)$$
$$4.\ A \longrightarrow B : sid, [c]P, MAC_{N_{BA}}(sid, [a]P, B),$$
$$MAC_{N_{CA}}(sid, [a]P, C), C_{\mathscr{E}_B}(N_{CB}),$$
$$MAC_{N_{BC}}(sid, [c]P, B)$$
$$5.\ B \longrightarrow C : sid, MAC_{N_{CB}}(sid, [b]P, C),$$
$$MAC_{N_{CA}}(sid, [a]P, C)$$
$$\text{Session key } SK = e(P,P)^{abc}$$

Protocol 10.2: Hitchcock–Boyd–González Nieto tripartite key exchange protocol 8

$$1.\ A \longrightarrow B : \quad sid, [a]P, A_{\mathscr{E}_B}(N_{AB}), A_{\mathscr{E}_C}(N_{AC})$$
$$2.\ B \longrightarrow C : \quad sid, [a]P, [b]P, B_{\mathscr{E}_A}(N_{BA}),$$
$$MAC_{N_{AB}}(sid, [b]P, A), A_{\mathscr{E}_C}(N_{AC})$$
$$3.\ C \longrightarrow A : \quad sid, [b]P, [c]P, C_{\mathscr{E}_A}(N_{CA}),$$
$$MAC_{N_{AC}}(sid, [c]P, A),$$
$$B_{\mathscr{E}_A}(N_{BA}), MAC_{N_{AB}}(sid, [b]P, A)$$
$$4.\ A \longrightarrow B : \quad sid, [c]P,$$
$$MAC_{N_{BA}}(sid, C, [a]P, [c]P, B),$$
$$MAC_{N_{CA}}(sid, [a]P, [b]P, C)$$
$$5.\ A/B \longrightarrow C : sid, MAC_{N_{CA}}(sid, [a]P, [c]P, C)$$
$$\text{Session key } SK = e(P,P)^{abc}$$

Protocol 10.3: Hitchcock–Boyd–González Nieto tripartite key exchange protocol 9

the earlier discussion, session identifiers should be

$$sid_A = \mathscr{H}(A||B||C||N_{AB}||N_{AC}||N_{BA}||N_{BC}||N_{CA}||N_{CB}) = sid_B = sid_C,$$

where sid_U denotes the session identifier of some protocol participant, U.

However, such a construct does not appear to be feasible for Protocols 10.2 and 10.3 since not all protocol participants have full view of the messages exchanged. For example, B does not know N_{AC} and C does not know N_{AB}.

10.3.1 Protocol Analysis

The attack sequences and the internal states can be examined by viewing the reachability graphs produced by SHVT. The analyses were run on a Pentium IV 2.4 GHz computer with 1024 Mb of RAM and the analysis statistics are shown in Figure 10.6.

Protocol Analysis	# Players	# Runs	Run-Time	New Flaws?
Protocol 10.2	3	2	Approximately 3 mins	Yes
Protocol 10.3			– ditto –	

Fig. 10.6 Analysis statistics

10.3.1.1 Analysis of Protocol 10.2

State space analysis in SHVT reveals that goal state 2 of Definition 10.1.1 is violated. The attack sequence is described in Attack 10.4.
At the end of Attack 10.4,

- Oracle Π_A^{sid} has accepted with $SK_A = e(P,P)^{abc}$.
- Both oracles, $\Pi_B^{sid_{\mathscr{A}}}$ and $\Pi_C^{sid_{\mathscr{A}}}$, think that a session (associated with session identifier, $sid_{\mathscr{A}}$) has been initiated by the adversary, $\mathscr{A}$. However, both $\Pi_B^{sid_{\mathscr{A}}}$ and $\Pi_C^{sid_{\mathscr{A}}}$ are asked Session-State Reveal queries prior to accepting any session keys.
- Since Π_A^{sid} and ($\Pi_B^{sid_{\mathscr{A}}}$ and $\Pi_C^{sid_{\mathscr{A}}}$) have different session identifiers, they are not partners (according to Definition 2.3.10). Therefore, the adversary, $\mathscr{A}$, is allowed to reveal both B and C without rendering session key of Π_A^{sid} unfresh (according to Definition 2.3.1).
- Internal states of $\Pi_B^{sid_{\mathscr{A}}}$ and $\Pi_C^{sid_{\mathscr{A}}}$ are revealed to the adversary, $\mathscr{A}$, with the Session-State Reveal queries, which includes (N_{AB}, b) and (N_{AC}, c) respectively. With knowledge of these internal states, $\mathscr{A}$ is able to "make" Π_A^{sid} accept the session key, $SK_A = e(P,P)^{abc}$.
- With knowledge of b and c from earlier Session-State Reveal queries, $\mathscr{A}$ is able to compute the session key accepted by A, $e(aP,P)^{bc} = SK_A$. Hence, $\text{Adv}^{\mathscr{A}}(k)$ is non-negligible, in violation of Definition 2.3.11.

10.3.1.2 Analysis of Protocol 10.3

State space analysis in SHVT reveals that goal state 2 of Definition 10.1.1 is violated. The attack sequence is described in Attack 10.5.
Similar to Attack 10.4, at the end of Attack 10.5,

- Oracle Π_A^{sid} has accepted with $SK_A = e(P,P)^{abc}$.
- Both oracles, $\Pi_B^{sid_{\mathscr{A}}}$ and $\Pi_C^{sid_{\mathscr{A}}}$, think that a session (associated with session identifier, $sid_{\mathscr{A}}$) has been initiated by the adversary, $\mathscr{A}$. However, both $\Pi_B^{sid_{\mathscr{A}}}$ and $\Pi_C^{sid_{\mathscr{A}}}$ are asked Session-State Reveal queries prior to accepting any session keys.
- Since Π_A^{sid} and ($\Pi_B^{sid_{\mathscr{A}}}$ and $\Pi_C^{sid_{\mathscr{A}}}$) have different session identifiers, they are not partners (according to Definition 2.3.10). Therefore, the adversary, $\mathscr{A}$, is allowed to reveal both B and C without rendering session key of Π_A^{sid} unfresh (according to Definition 2.3.1).

1. $A \longrightarrow B:$ $sid, [a]P, A_{\mathscr{E}_B}(N_{AB}), A_{\mathscr{E}_C}(N_{AC})$

The adversary, $\mathscr{A}$, intercepts and deletes message from network. $\mathscr{A}$ then sends intercepted message as her own to B, however, with a different session identifier, $sid_{\mathscr{A}}$.

Note that $\mathscr{A}$ is able to claim ownership of the intercepted message because the identity of the sender is not included in the encryption.

1. $\mathscr{A} \longrightarrow B:$ $sid_{\mathscr{A}}, [a]P, A_{\mathscr{E}_B}(N_{AB}), A_{\mathscr{E}_C}(N_{AC})$

B upon receiving this message will think that $\mathscr{A}$ wants to establish a session (associated with session identifier, $sid_{\mathscr{A}}$) and proceeds as per protocol specification.

2. $B \longrightarrow C:$ $sid_{\mathscr{A}}, [a]P, [b]P, B_{\mathscr{E}_C}(N_{BC}),$
       $B_{\mathscr{E}_{\mathscr{A}}}(N_{B\mathscr{A}}), A_{\mathscr{E}_C}(N_{AC}),$
       $MAC_{N_{AB}}(sid_{\mathscr{A}}, [b]P, \mathscr{A})$

3. $C \longrightarrow \mathscr{A}:$ $sid_{\mathscr{A}}, [b]P, [c]P, C_{\mathscr{E}_{\mathscr{A}}}(N_{C\mathscr{A}}),$
       $C_{\mathscr{E}_B}(N_{CB}), MAC_{N_{AC}}(sid, [c]P, \mathscr{A}),$
       $MAC_{N_{BC}}(sid, [c]P, B), B_{\mathscr{E}_{\mathscr{A}}}(N_{B\mathscr{A}}),$
       $MAC_{N_{AB}}(sid, [b]P, \mathscr{A})$

Note that both B and C think that the session (associated with $sid_{\mathscr{A}}$) is being established with the adversary, $\mathscr{A}$, because $SID_B = SID_C = sid_{\mathscr{A}} \neq SID_A = sid$. Therefore, A, B, and C are not partners (see Definition 2.3.10) and $\mathscr{A}$ is allowed to reveal both B and C without rendering session key of A unfresh (see Definition 2.3.1).

$\mathscr{A} \longrightarrow C:$ Session-State Reveal$(C, sid_{\mathscr{A}})$
$\mathscr{A} \longrightarrow B:$ Session-State Reveal$(B, sid_{\mathscr{A}})$

The internal states of $\Pi_B^{sid_{\mathscr{A}}}$ and $\Pi_C^{sid_{\mathscr{A}}}$ are revealed to the adversary, $\mathscr{A}$, after asking the Session-State Reveal queries, which includes (N_{AB}, b) and (N_{AC}, c) respectively. With knowledge of (N_{AB}, b, N_{AC}, c), $\mathscr{A}$ is able to construct respective ciphertexts and MAC digests, and send fabricated messages to A impersonating C.

3. $\mathscr{A}_C \longrightarrow \mathscr{A}:$ $sid, [b]P, [c]P, C_{\mathscr{E}_A}(N_{C\mathscr{A}}),$
       $C_{\mathscr{E}_B}(N_{CB}), MAC_{N_{AC}}(sid, [c]P, A),$
       $MAC_{N_{BC}}(sid_{\mathscr{A}}, [c]P, B),$
       $B_{\mathscr{E}_A}(N_{B\mathscr{A}}), MAC_{N_{AB}}(sid, [b]P, A)$

4. $A \longrightarrow B:$ Some message.

The adversary, $\mathscr{A}$, intercepts and deletes message from the network. Note that the session key accepted by A is $SK_A = e(P, P)^{abc}$.

Attack 10.4: Attack Sequence on Protocol 10.2

- Internal states of $\Pi_B^{sid_{\mathscr{A}}}$ and $\Pi_C^{sid_{\mathscr{A}}}$ are revealed to the adversary, $\mathscr{A}$, with the Session-State Reveal queries, which includes (N_{AB}, b) and (N_{AC}, c) respectively. With knowledge of these internal states, $\mathscr{A}$ is able to "make" Π_A^{sid} accept the session key, $SK_A = e(P, P)^{abc}$.

- With knowledge of b and c from earlier Session-State Reveal queries, $\mathscr{A}$ is able to compute the session key accepted by A, $e(aP, P)^{bc} = SK_A$. Hence, $Adv^{\mathscr{A}}(k)$ is non-negligible, in violation of Definition 2.3.11.

1. $A \longrightarrow B$: $sid, [a]P, A_{\mathscr{E}_B}(N_{AB}), A_{\mathscr{E}_C}(N_{AC})$

The adversary, $\mathscr{A}$, intercepts and deletes message from network. $\mathscr{A}$ then sends intercepted message as her own to B, however, with a different session identifier, $sid_{\mathscr{A}}$.

Note that $\mathscr{A}$ is able to claim ownership of the intercepted message because the identity of the sender is not included in the encryption.

1. $\mathscr{A} \longrightarrow B$: $sid_{\mathscr{A}}, [a]P, A_{\mathscr{E}_B}(N_{AB}), A_{\mathscr{E}_C}(N_{AC})$

B upon receiving this message will think that $\mathscr{A}$ wants to establish a session (associated with session identifier, $sid_{\mathscr{A}}$) and proceeds as per protocol specification.

2. $B \longrightarrow C$: $sid_{\mathscr{A}}, [a]P, [b]P, B_{\mathscr{E}_{\mathscr{A}}}(N_{B\mathscr{A}}),$
        $MAC_{N_{AB}}(sid_{\mathscr{A}}, [b]P, \mathscr{A}),$
        $A_{\mathscr{E}_C}(N_{AC})$

3. $C \longrightarrow \mathscr{A}$: $sid_{\mathscr{A}}, [b]P, [c]P, C_{\mathscr{E}_{\mathscr{A}}}(N_{C\mathscr{A}}),$
        $MAC_{N_{AC}}(sid_{\mathscr{A}}, [c]P, \mathscr{A}),$
        $B_{\mathscr{E}_{\mathscr{A}}}(N_{B\mathscr{A}}),$
        $MAC_{N_{AB}}(sid_{\mathscr{A}}, [b]P, \mathscr{A})$

Note that both B and C thinks that the session (associated with session identifier, $sid_{\mathscr{A}}$) is being established with the adversary, $\mathscr{A}$, because $SID_B = SID_C = sid_{\mathscr{A}} \neq SID_A = sid$. Therefore, A, B, and C are not partners (see Definition 2.3.10) and $\mathscr{A}$ is allowed to reveal both B and C without rendering session key of A unfresh (see Definition 2.3.1).

$\mathscr{A} \longrightarrow C$:   Session-State Reveal$(C, sid_{\mathscr{A}})$
$\mathscr{A} \longrightarrow B$:   Session-State Reveal$(B, sid_{\mathscr{A}})$

The internal states of $\Pi_B^{sid_{\mathscr{A}}}$ and $\Pi_C^{sid_{\mathscr{A}}}$ are revealed to the adversary, $\mathscr{A}$, after asking the Session-State Reveal queries, which includes (N_{AB}, b) and (N_{AC}, c) respectively. With knowledge of (N_{AB}, b, N_{AC}, c), $\mathscr{A}$ is able to construct respective ciphertexts and MAC digests, and send fabricated messages to A impersonating C.

3. $\mathscr{A}_C \longrightarrow \mathscr{A}$: $sid, [b]P, [c]P, C_{\mathscr{E}_A}(N_{C\mathscr{A}}),$
        $MAC_{N_{AC}}(sid, [c]P, A),$
        $B_{\mathscr{E}_A}(N_{B\mathscr{A}}),$
        $MAC_{N_{AB}}(sid, [b]P, A)$

4/5. $A \longrightarrow B/C$: Some message.

The adversary, $\mathscr{A}$, intercepts and deletes messages sent by A for both B and C from the network. Note that the session key accepted by A is $SK_A = e(P, P)^{abc}$.

Attack 10.5: Attack Sequence on Protocol 10.3

10.3.2 Flaws in Refuted Proofs

The general notion of the existing proofs is to assume that there exists an adversary, $\mathscr{A}$, who can gain a non-negligible advantage in distinguishing the test key, and use $\mathscr{A}$ to break the underlying DBDH problem. Such an adversary, $\mathscr{A}_{\mathscr{DBDH}}$, against the DBDH problem is built using $\mathscr{A}$. The objective of $\mathscr{A}_{\mathscr{DBDH}}$ is to distinguish between $\widehat{e}(P,P)^d \in \mathbb{G}_2$ and $\widehat{e}(P,P)^{abc} \in \mathbb{G}_2$ when given a bilinear map $\widehat{e}$, a generator of P of $\mathbb{G}_1$, an element $\widehat{e}(P,P)^d \in \mathbb{G}_2$, and a triple of elements $aP, bP, cP \in \mathbb{G}_1$ with $a, b, c, d \in \mathbb{Z}_q^*$, where q is the prime order of the distinct groups $\mathbb{G}_1$ and $\mathbb{G}_2$. Note that the triple of elements a, b, c is not known to $\mathscr{A}_{\mathscr{DBDH}}$.

In Attacks 10.4 and 10.5, the adversary, $\mathscr{A}$, is allowed to ask for the ephemeral secret keys (i.e., b and c) with a Session-State Reveal query (recall that sessions with non-matching session identifiers and non-agreeing partner identifiers are non-partners). Clearly, such a query is unable to be answered by $\mathscr{A}_{\mathscr{DBDH}}$ since $\mathscr{A}_{\mathscr{DBDH}}$ does not know b and c as $\mathscr{A}_{\mathscr{DBDH}}$ is using $\mathscr{A}$ to break the underlying DBDH problem. If $\mathscr{A}_{\mathscr{DBDH}}$ randomly selects two elements, $b' \in \mathbb{Z}_q^*$ and $c' \in \mathbb{Z}_q^*$, and returns this to $\mathscr{A}$, $\mathscr{A}$ is able to check that $b'P \neq bP$ and $c'P \neq cP$.

Hence, the proof simulation is aborted and $\mathscr{A}_{\mathscr{DBDH}}$ fails. Consequently, $\mathscr{A}_{\mathscr{DBDH}}$ does not have a non-negligible probability in breaking the underlying DBDH problem although $\mathscr{A}$ has a non-negligible advantage against the security of the underlying protocols. This is in violation of the underlying assumption in the proofs.

10.3.3 A Possible Fix

In both Protocols 10.2 and 10.3, the identity of the sender is not included within the encrypted messages. This effectively allows a malicious adversary, $\mathscr{A}$, to intercept the encrypted message and claims as its own. We observe that Hitchcock, Boyd, and González Nieto [14] suggest that specifying the sender in the encryption only clarify the purpose of each encryption in protocol descriptions, although in practice the sender does not necessarily need to be specified.

However, these observations contradict earlier findings of An, Dodis, and Rabi [3]. An et al. suggest that in a multi-user setting, the sender's identity must be included in every encryption and the recipient's identity must be included in every signature. Similar conclusion is also suggested by Choo, Boyd, and Hitchcock [13] in their recent findings on the conference key agreement protocol of Boyd and González Nieto [9].

However, including the identity of the sender in every encryption alone will not help in preventing Attacks 10.4 and 10.5 as the adversary, $\mathscr{A}$, is still able to hijack the first message. Then the adversary is able to send the hijacked message with a fabricated $sid_{\mathscr{A}}$. Consequently, $\mathscr{A}$ is still able to ask Session-State Reveal query to instances of B and C without rendering the session key of A unfresh (recall that sessions with non-matching session identifiers are non-partners).

Hence, as a possible fix, we propose to include the identity of the sender and the partnering mechanism, sid, in every encryption. Informally, Attacks 10.4 and 10.5 will no longer be valid since the adversary, $\mathscr{A}$, is unable to claim ownership of the intercepted messages or cause confusion among the protocol participants' sessions.

10.4 Analysing Protocols with Heuristic Security Arguments

In this section, we examine several previously unbroken key establishment protocols with only heuristic security arguments; namely the Jan–Chen two-party mutual authentication and key establishment protocol [16], two Yang–Shen–Shieh trusted three-party authenticated key establishment protocols [22], Kim–Huh–Hwang–Lee key agreement protocol [17], Lin–Sun–Hwang improved Diffie–Hellman based encrypted key exchange protocols MDHEKE I and II [18], and the Yeh–Sun authenticated key agreement protocol [23].

10.4.1 Case Studies

10.4.1.1 Jan–Chen Mutual Protocol

Protocol 10.4 describes the Jan–Chen mutual authentication and key establishment protocol (MAKEP) [16]. There are two entities in Protocol 10.4; namely a client of limited computing power, A, and a server, B. The security goals of Protocol 10.4 are mutual authentication and key establishment. In Protocol 10.4, the notation $x \in_R \mathbb{Z}_n^*$ denotes that x is randomly drawn from $\mathbb{Z}_n^*$. At the end of Protocol 10.4's execution, both A and B will share a secret session key SK_{AB} known only to the particular instances of A and B.

10.4.1.2 Yang–Shen–Shieh Protocols

Two trusted three-party authenticated key establishment protocols (with and without public key systems) due to Yang–Shen–Shieh [22] are shown in Protocols 10.5 and 10.6. There are three entities in Protocols 10.5 and 10.6; namely a trusted server S, an initiating client A, and a responder client B. The security goals of Protocols 10.5 and 10.6 are mutual authentication and key establishment. The notation used in Protocols 10.5 and 10.6 is as follows: N_U, R_U denotes some randomly cho-

Registration Phase

Client A Server B

$x \in_R \mathbb{Z}_n^*$

$v = g^{-x} \bmod N$

public/private key pair (y,x) $\xrightarrow{\quad v \quad}$ $y = (v - ID_A)^d \bmod N$

$\xleftarrow{\quad y \quad}$ public/private key pair (e,d)

Session Key Generation

$r_s \in_R \mathbb{Z}_n$ $\xrightarrow{\quad ID_A, y \quad}$ $w \in_R \mathbb{Z}_n$

$\xleftarrow{\quad r_s \quad}$

$u = g^w \bmod N$ $k \in_R \mathbb{Z}_n$

$g^s \cdot v^{\mathcal{H}(r_s\|\iota\|u)} \overset{?}{=} u \bmod N$ $\xrightarrow{\quad u, \iota, s \quad}$ $\iota = \{k\}_e, s = w + x \cdot \mathcal{H}(r_s\|\iota\|u)$

$\xleftarrow{\quad \mathcal{H}(k) \quad}$

$\sigma = k \oplus s$ $\mathcal{H}(k) \overset{?}{=} \mathcal{H}(k)'$

$SK_{AB} = \sigma = k \oplus s \bmod N = SK_{BA}$

Protocol 10.4: Jan–Chen MAKEP

sen nonces; K_S denotes the public key of S; and $K_{U,S} = (g^{X_u, Y_u} \bmod \beta)$ denotes the key for long term use between U and S, where g and β are two large primes.

1. $A \longrightarrow B: \{A, N_A, K_{AS}\}_{K_S}, R_A$
2. $B \longrightarrow S: \{A, N_A, K_{AS}\}_{K_S}, \{B, N_B, K_{BS}\}_{K_S}$
3. $S \longrightarrow B: \{A, B, K_{AB}\}_{N_A}, \{B, A, K\}_{N_B}$
4. $B \longrightarrow A: \{A, B, K_{AB}\}_{N_A}, \{R_A, R_B\}_{K_{AB}}$
5. $A \longrightarrow B: \{R_B\}_{K_{AB}}$

Protocol 10.5: Yang–Shen–Shieh protocol 1

At the end of both protocol runs, A and B will share a secret session key K_{AB} known only to the particular instances of A and B. The session identifiers (*SIDs*) for both A and B in Protocol 10.5 are $SID_A = SID_B = \{R_A, R_B\}$, and in Protocol 10.6 are $SID_A = SID_B = \{N_A, N_B\}$.

1. $A \longrightarrow B: A, \{g^{X_a} \bmod \beta\}_{K_{AS}}, N_A$
2. $B \longrightarrow S: A, B, \{g^{X_a} \bmod \beta\}_{K_{AS}}, \{g^{X_b} \bmod \beta\}_{K_{BS}}$
3. $S \longrightarrow B: \{g^{Y_a} \bmod \beta\}_{K_{AS}}, \{A, B, K_{AB}\}_{K_{A,S}},$
   $\{g^{Y_b} \bmod \beta\}_{K_{BS}}, \{B, A, K_{AB}\}_{K_{B,S}}$
4. $B \longrightarrow A: \{A, B, K_{AB}\}_{K_{A,S}}, \{N_A, N_B\}_{K_{AB}}$
5. $A \longrightarrow B: \{N_B\}_{K_{AB}}$

Protocol 10.6: Yang–Shen–Shieh protocol 2

10.4.1.3 Kim–Huh–Hwang–Lee Protocol

Protocol 10.7 describes the Kim–Huh–Hwang–Lee key agreement protocol [17]. Both the initiator A and responder B have a shared password, pwd_{AB}. Prior to running Protocol 10.7, A and B compute Q and Q^{-1} from pwd_{AB} respectively. At the end of the protocol run, both A and B share a secret session key SK_{AB} and SK_{BA} respectively, where $SK_{AB} = g^{ab} \bmod n = SK_{BA}$.

$$A\ (Q, pwd_{AB}) \qquad\qquad\qquad B\ (Q^{-1}, pwd_{AB})$$

$$a \in_R \{0,1\}^k, b \in_R \{0,1\}^k$$

A		B
$X_1 = g^{aQ} \bmod n$	$\xrightarrow{\quad X_1 \quad}$	$Y_1 = g^{bQ^{-1}} \bmod n$
$X \overset{?}{=} g^a \bmod n$	$\xleftarrow{\quad Y_1, X \quad}$	$X = (X_1)^{Q^{-1}} \bmod n$
$Y = (Y_1)^Q \bmod n$	$\xrightarrow{\quad Y \quad}$	$Y \overset{?}{=} g^b \bmod n$
$SK_{AB} = Y^a = g^{ab} \bmod n$		$SK_{BA} = X^b = g^{ab} \bmod n$

Protocol 10.7: Kim–Huh–Hwang–Lee key agreement protocol

We observe that Protocol 10.7 is susceptible to an offline dictionary attack, as explained in Attack 10.6. We note that in a later independent yet related work by Lu and Cao [19], the same attack described in Attack 10.6 was presented.

---

1. By observing the protocol execution shown in Figure 10.7, a passive adversary, $\mathscr{A}$, knows the values of $X_1 = g^{aQ} \bmod n$ and $X = (X_1)^{Q^{-1}} \bmod n$, where both Q and Q^{-1} are computed from pwd_{AB}.
2. From the password space of pwd_{AB}, $\mathscr{A}$ selects a password $\alpha_{\mathscr{A}}$ at random.
   a. $\mathscr{A}$ computes $Q_{\mathscr{A}}^{-1}$ from $\alpha_{\mathscr{A}}$.
   b. $\mathscr{A}$ computes $X' = X_1^{Q_{\mathscr{A}}^{-1}} \bmod n$.
   c. $\mathscr{A}$ compares if $X \overset{?}{=} X'$.
   d. If $X = X'$, then $\mathscr{A}$ terminates as $pwd_{AB} = \alpha_{\mathscr{A}}$, else exclude $\alpha_{\mathscr{A}}$ from the password space, and repeat Step 2.

Attack 10.6: Offline dictionary attack on Protocol 10.7

An offline dictionary attack presents a more subtle threat as the adversary, $\mathscr{A}$, can impersonate a legitimate party to initiate transactions. Our analysis model does not capture dictionary attacks. In the next section, we will show the attacks captured by our analysis model.

10.4.1.4 Lin–Sun–Hwang Key Protocols MDHEKE I and II

Protocols 10.8 and 10.9 describe the Lin–Sun–Hwang improved protocols MD-HEKE I and II [18]. Both the initiator, A, and the responder, B, share a secret password pwd_{AB}. At the end of both protocol runs, both A and B accept with the same session key $SK_{AB} = g^{ab} \bmod n = SK_{BA}$.

$A\ (pwd_{AB})$		$B\ (pwd_{AB})$
$x \in_R \{0,1\}^k, R_A = g^x \bmod n$	$\xrightarrow{\quad A,\{R_A\}_{pwd_{AB}}\quad}$	$y, C_B \in_R \{0,1\}^k$
$SK_{AB} = \mathscr{H}((R_B)^x \bmod n)$	$\xleftarrow{\quad R_B,\{f(R_B),C_B\}_{SK_{BA}}\quad}$	$R_B = g^y \bmod n$
Decrypt $\{f(R_B),C_B\}_{SK_{BA}}$		
Verify $f(R_B)$	$\xrightarrow{\quad C_B\quad}$	$SK_{BA} = \mathscr{H}((R_A)^y \bmod n)$

Protocol 10.8: Lin–Sun–Hwang Key improved protocol MDHEKE I

$A\ (pwd)$		$B\ (pwd)$
$x \in_R \{0,1\}^k, R_A = g^x \bmod n$	$\xrightarrow{\quad A,\{R_A\}_{pwd_{AB}}\quad}$	$y, C_B \in_R \{0,1\}^k$
$SK_{AB} = \mathscr{H}((R_B)^x \bmod n)$	$\xleftarrow{\quad R_B,\mathscr{H}(R_B,SK_{BA})\quad}$	$R_B = g^y \bmod n$
Verify $\mathscr{H}(R_B,SK_{BA})$	$\xrightarrow{\quad \mathscr{H}(SK_{AB})\quad}$	$SK_{BA} = \mathscr{H}((R_A)^y \bmod n)$

Protocol 10.9: Lin–Sun–Hwang Key improved protocol MDHEKE II

10.4.1.5 Yeh–Sun Key Protocol

Protocol 10.10 describes the Yeh–Sun key authenticated key agreement protocol [23]. A and B share a secret password pwd_{AB}. At the end of the protocol run, A and B accept session keys $SK_{AB} = \mathscr{H}(K_1) = \mathscr{H}(K_2) = SK_{BA}$.

10.4.2 Protocol Analyses

In this section, the protocols discussed in Chapter 10.4.1 are specified using APA and the automated state space analyses performed with SHVT reveal that the pro-

A (pwd)		B (pwd)

$$x \in_p \mathbb{Z}_p*, X = g^x \bmod p$$
$$\xrightarrow{X \oplus pwd_{AB}}$$
$$X = X \oplus pwd \oplus pwd$$
$$Y = Y \oplus pwd_{AB} \oplus pwd$$
$$\xleftarrow{Y \oplus pwd_{AB} || \mathcal{H}(K_2,X)}$$
$$y \in_p \mathbb{Z}_p*, Y = g^y \bmod n$$
$$K_1 = Y^x = g^{xy} \bmod p$$
$$K_2 = X^y \bmod p = g^{xy} \bmod p$$
$$\mathcal{H}(K_1,X) \stackrel{?}{=} \mathcal{H}(K_2,X)$$
$$\xrightarrow{\mathcal{H}(K_1,Y)}$$
$$\mathcal{H}(K_1,Y) \stackrel{?}{=} \mathcal{H}(K_2,Y)$$

Protocol 10.10: Yeh–Sun authenticated key agreement protocol

tocols violate the respective requirement(s) of Definition 10.1.1, as shown in Table 10.1.

Protocol	Requirement(s) No. Violated	Associated Security Goals Violated
10.4	1, 2, and 4	Key establishment, Entity authentication
10.5	3 and 4	Key establishment, Entity authentication
10.6	3 and 4	Key establishment, Entity authentication
10.7	1	Key establishment
10.8	1	Key establishment
10.9	1	Key establishment
10.10	1	Key establishment

Table 10.1 Violations of Definition 10.1.1 in protocol analyses

10.4.2.1 Protocol Analysis 1

Attack 10.7 describes an execution of Protocol 10.4 in the presence of a malicious adversary, $\mathcal{A}$.

At the end of Attack 10.7, A and B accept the respectively session keys, SK_{AB} and $SK_{B\mathcal{A}}$, where

$$SK_{AB} = \sigma_{AB} = k \oplus s \bmod N$$
$$SK_{B\mathcal{A}} = k \oplus s_{\mathcal{A}} \bmod N$$
$$\neq SK_{BA}.$$

B thinks that the key $SK_{B\mathcal{A}}$ is being shared with the adversary, $\mathcal{A}$. Such an attack is also referred to as an unknown key share attack.

State space analysis performed in the SHVT analysis reveals that both requirements 2 and 4 of Definition 10.1.1 are violated. As shown in Attack 10.8, the adversary, $\mathcal{A}$, sends a Reveal query to a non-partner oracle of A, B, as B believes $SK_{B\mathcal{A}}$ is

$$A\ (y,x) \qquad\qquad \mathscr{A}'(y_{\mathscr{A}}, x_{\mathscr{A}}) \qquad\qquad B\ (e,d)$$

$$\xrightarrow{\quad ID_A, y \quad} \qquad\qquad \xrightarrow{\quad ID_A, y \quad} \quad r_{sA} \in_R \mathbb{Z}_n$$

$$\xrightarrow{\quad ID_{\mathscr{A}}, y_{\mathscr{A}} \quad} \quad r_{s\mathscr{A}} \in_R \mathbb{Z}_n$$

$$\text{Intercept} \quad \xleftarrow{\quad r_s \quad}$$

$$w \in_R \mathbb{Z}_n \quad \xleftarrow{\quad r_{s\mathscr{A}} \quad} \quad w_{\mathscr{A}} \in_R \mathbb{Z}_n \quad \xleftarrow{\quad r_{s\mathscr{A}} \quad}$$

$$u = g^w \bmod N \qquad u_{\mathscr{A}} = g^{w_{\mathscr{A}}} \bmod N$$

$$k \in_R \mathbb{Z}_n \qquad\qquad k_{\mathscr{A}} \in_R \mathbb{Z}_n$$

$$\iota = \{k\}_e \qquad\qquad \iota_{\mathscr{A}} = \{k_{\mathscr{A}}\}_e$$

$$s = w + x \cdot \mathscr{H}(r_{s\mathscr{A}} \| \iota | u)$$

$$\xrightarrow{\quad u, \iota, s \quad} \qquad \text{Intercept}$$

$$s_{\mathscr{A}} = w_{\mathscr{A}} + x_{\mathscr{A}} \cdot \mathscr{H}(r_{s\mathscr{A}} \| \iota \| u_{\mathscr{A}})$$

$$\xrightarrow{\quad u_{\mathscr{A}}, \iota, s_{\mathscr{A}} \quad}$$

$$g^{s_{\mathscr{A}}} \cdot v^{\mathscr{H}(r_{s\mathscr{A}} \| \iota \| u_{\mathscr{A}})} \stackrel{?}{=} u_{\mathscr{A}} \bmod N$$

$$\mathscr{H}(k) \stackrel{?}{=} \mathscr{H}(k)' \quad \xleftarrow{\quad \mathscr{H}(k) \quad} \qquad\qquad \xleftarrow{\quad \mathscr{H}(k) \quad} \quad \sigma_{B\mathscr{A}} = k \oplus s_{\mathscr{A}}$$

Attack 10.7: Attack sequence on mutual authentication goal of Protocol 10.4

being shared with $\mathscr{A}$. $\mathscr{A}$, by asking for the session key of B (i.e., $SK_{B\mathscr{A}}$), will be able to compute the session key SK_{AB} accepted by A ($SK_{AB} = SK_{BA} \oplus s_{\mathscr{A}}$).

$$\text{Continue from Attack 10.7}$$

$$\mathscr{A}\ (y_{\mathscr{A}}, x_{\mathscr{A}}) \qquad\qquad B\ (e,d)$$

$$\xrightarrow{\quad \textit{Reveal} \quad}$$

$$\xleftarrow{\quad SK_{B\mathscr{A}} \quad}$$

$$SK_{\mathscr{A}} = K_{B\mathscr{A}} \oplus s_{\mathscr{A}} \oplus s = SK_{AB}$$

Attack 10.8: Attack sequence on key establishment goal of Protocol 10.4

Hence, Protocol 10.4 is not secure since both the key establishment and mutual authentication goals are violated. This is demonstrated in Attacks 10.7 and 10.8.

10.4.2.2 Protocol Analysis 2

Attack 10.9 describes an execution of the Protocol 10.5 with public key systems in the presence of a malicious adversary, $\mathscr{A}$. Let $\mathscr{A}_U$ denote $\mathscr{A}$ impersonating user U. At the end of Attack 10.9, neither A nor B are partnered since they do not have matching SIDs as show below.

$1(R1).\ A \longrightarrow B: \quad \{A, N_A, K_A\}_{K_S}, R_A$

$2(R1).\ B \longrightarrow S: \quad \{A, N_A, K_A\}_{K_S}, \{B, N_B, K_B\}_{K_S}$

$\qquad\qquad\qquad\qquad \mathscr{A}$ starts another protocol run - Protocol Run 2 (R2)

$1(R2).\ \mathscr{A}_B \longrightarrow A: \{B, N_B, K_B\}_{K_S}, R_A$

$2(R2).\ A \longrightarrow S: \quad \{B, N_B, K_B\}_{K_S}, \{A, N_{A(R2)}, K_A\}_{K_S}$

$3(R1).\ S \longrightarrow B: \quad \{A, B, K_{R1}\}_{N_A}, \{B, A, K_{R1}\}_{N_B}$

$\qquad\qquad\qquad\qquad \mathscr{A}$ intercepts message in protocol flow 3 (R1)

$3(R2).\ S \longrightarrow A: \quad \{B, A, K_{R2}\}_{N_B}, \{A, B, K_{R2}\}_{N_{A(R2)}}$

$\qquad\qquad\qquad\qquad \mathscr{A}$ reveals A to obtain K_{R2} and uses A as a decryption oracle.

$3(R1).\ \mathscr{A}_S \longrightarrow B: \{A, B, K_{R1}\}_{N_A}, \{B, A, K_{R2}\}_{N_B}$

$4(R1).\ B \longrightarrow A: \quad \{A, B, K_{R1}\}_{N_A}, \{R_A, R_B\}_{K_{R2}}$

$5(R1).\ \mathscr{A}_A \longrightarrow B: \{R_B\}_{K_{R2}}$

Attack 10.9: Attack sequence on Protocol 10.5

$$sid_A = \{g^{R_A}, g^{R_E}\}$$
$$sid_B = \{g^{R_E}, g^{R_B}\}$$
$$\neq sid_A.$$

However, A has not accepted a key, in violation of Definition 10.1.1. Also, both A and B have different SIDs; hence according to Definition 10.4.1, A and B cannot be partners. Although B has accepted the key K_{R2}, B believes that K_{R2} is being shared with A when, in fact, K_{R2} is being shared with the adversary $\mathscr{A}$. This violates requirement 3 of Definition 10.1.1.

10.4.2.3 Protocol Analysis 3

Attack 10.10 describes an execution of Protocol 10.6 in the presence of a malicious adversary, $\mathscr{A}$.

At the end of Attack 10.10, neither A nor B are partnered since they do not have matching SIDs (i.e., $sid_A = \{g^{R_A}, g^{R_E}\}$ and $sid_B = \{g^{R_E}, g^{R_B}\}$). A has not accepted a key, thus violating requirement 4 of Definition 10.1.1. Both A and B have different SIDs; hence, according to Definition 10.4.1, A and B cannot be partners. Although B has accepted the key K_{R2}, B believes that K_{R2} is being shared with A when, in fact, K_{R2} is being shared with the adversary $\mathscr{A}$ (i.e., unknown key share attack). Requirement 3 of Definition 10.1.1 is violated.

10.4.2.4 Protocol Analysis 4

Attack 10.11 describes the attack sequence on Protocol 10.7.

At the end of Attack 10.11, A and B have accepted session keys, SK_{AB} and SK_{BA}, where

$1(R1). \ A \longrightarrow B: \quad A, \{g^{X_a} \ mod \ \beta\}_{K_A}, N_A$

$2(R1). \ B \longrightarrow S: \quad A, B, \{g^{X_a} \ mod \ \beta\}_{K_A}, \{g^{X_b} \ mod \ \beta\}_{K_B}$

$\qquad\qquad\qquad \mathscr{A}$ starts another protocol run - Protocol Run 2 (R2)

$1(R2). \ \mathscr{A}_B \longrightarrow A: \quad B, \{g^{X_b} \ mod \ \beta\}_{K_B}, N_A$

$2(R2). \ A \longrightarrow S: \quad B, A, \{g^{X_b} \ mod \ \beta\}_{K_B}, \{g^{X_{a(R2)}} \ mod \ \beta\}_{K_A}$

$3(R1). \ S \longrightarrow B: \quad \{g^{Y_{a(R1)}} \ mod \ \beta\}_{K_A}, \{A, B, K_{R1}\}_{K_{A,S,(R1)}},$

$\qquad\qquad\qquad \{g^{Y_{b(R1)}} \ mod \ \beta\}_{K_B}, \{B, A, K_{R1}\}_{K_{B,S,(R1)}}$

$\qquad\qquad\qquad \mathscr{A}$ intercepts message in protocol flow 3 (R1)

$3(R2). \ S \longrightarrow A: \quad \{g^{Y_{b(R2)}} \ mod \ \beta\}_{K_B}, \{B, A, K_{R2}\}_{K_{B,S,(R2)}},$

$\qquad\qquad\qquad \{g^{Y_{a(R2)}} \ mod \ \beta\}_{K_A}, \{A, B, K_{R2}\}_{K_{A,S,(R2)}}$

$\qquad\qquad\qquad \mathscr{A}$ reveals A to obtain K_{R2} and uses A as a decryption oracle.

$3(R1). \ \mathscr{A}_S \longrightarrow B: \{g^{Y_{a(R1)}} \ mod \ \beta\}_{K_A}, \{A, B, K_{R1}\}_{K_{A,S,(R1)}},$

$\qquad\qquad\qquad \{g^{Y_{b(R2)}} \ mod \ \beta\}_{K_B}, \{B, A, K_{R2}\}_{K_{B,S,(R2)}}$

$4(R1). \ B \longrightarrow A: \quad \{g^{Y_{a(R1)}} \ mod \ \beta\}_{K_A}, \{A, B, K_{R1}\}_{K_{A,S,(R1)}}, \{N_A, N_{B(R2)}\}_{K_{R2}}$

$\qquad\qquad\qquad \mathscr{A}$ intercepts message in protocol flow 4(R1)

$5(R1). \ \mathscr{A}_A \longrightarrow B: \{N_{B(R2)}\}_{K_{R2}}$

Attack 10.10: Attack sequence on Protocol 10.6

A	$\mathscr{A}$	B
$X_1 = g^{aQ} \ mod \ n$ $\longrightarrow$	Intercept	$(X_1)^E = g^{aEQ} \ mod \ n$ $\longrightarrow$
$Y_1, (X_1^E)^{E^{-1}}$ $\longleftarrow$	Intercept	$Y_1, (X_1)^E$ $\longleftarrow$
$Y = g^b \ mod \ n$ $\longrightarrow$		$(Y)^E = g^{bE} \ mod \ n$ $\longrightarrow$
$SK_{AB} = Y^a = g^{ab} \ mod \ n$		Reveal $\longrightarrow$
		$SK_{BA} = g^{abE} \ mod \ n$ $\longleftarrow$
	Compute $SK_{BA}^{E^{-1}} = g^{ab} = SK_{AB}$	

Attack 10.11: Attack sequence on Protocol 10.7

$$SK_{AB} = g^{ab} \ mod \ n$$
$$SK_{BA} = g^{abE} \ mod \ n$$
$$= SK_{AB}.$$

Both A and B are not partners since they have accepted different session keys with different SIDs, as shown below.

$$sid_A = \{X_1, Y_1, X, Y\}$$
$$sid_B = \{X_1^E, Y_1, X^E, Y\}$$
$$\neq sid_A$$

By revealing B, the adversary $\mathscr{A}$ is able to obtain the session key $SK_{BA} = g^{abE}$ and is able to compute the session key of A by computing $SK_{BA}^{E^{-1}} = g^{ab} = SK_{AB}$. Protocol 10.7 is, therefore, insecure.

10.4.2.5 Protocol Analysis 5

Attack 10.12 describes the attack sequence of a reflection attack on Protocol 10.8. Let $\mathscr{A}_U$ denote $\mathscr{A}$ impersonating some user U.

A		$\mathscr{A}_B$
	$\xrightarrow{\quad A,\{R_A\}_{pwd} \quad}$	Intercept
	$\xleftarrow{\quad B,\{R_A\}_{pwd} \quad}$	Initiate concurrent session
	$\xrightarrow{\quad R_{A2},\{f(R_{A2}),C_A\}_{SK_{AB}^{S2}} \quad}$	Intercept
	$\xleftarrow{\quad R_{A2},\{f(R_{A2}),C_A\}_{SK_{AB}^{S2}} \quad}$	Reflect message back to A
$SK_{AB}^{S1} = \mathscr{H}(g^{xx_2})$	$\xrightarrow{\quad C_A \quad}$	Intercept
$SK_{AB}^{S2} = \mathscr{H}(g^{xx_2})$	$\xleftarrow{\quad C_A \quad}$	Reflect message back to A

Attack 10.12: Attack sequence on Protocol 10.8

At the end of Attack 10.12, A thinks that she has completed two concurrent sessions with B and has accepted session keys $SK_{AB}^{S1} = \mathscr{H}(g^{xx_2}) = SK_{AB}^{S2}$. B has no knowledge of these two sessions. This implies that A has no partner. By revealing session 2 at A to obtain SK_{AB}^{S2}, the adversary, $\mathscr{A}$, is then able to obtain a fresh session key SK_{AB}^{S1}.

Protocol 10.8 is, therefore, insecure since the adversary, $\mathscr{A}$, is able to obtain the session key of a fresh oracle of a non-partner oracle by revealing a non-partner oracle holding the same key (i.e., violating the key establishment goal).

10.4.2.6 Protocol Analysis 6

Attack 10.13 describes a reflection attack on Protocol 10.9.

At the end of Attack 10.13, A thinks that she has completed two concurrent sessions with B and has accepted session keys $SK_{AB}^{S1} = \mathscr{H}(g^{xx_2}) = SK_{AB}^{S2}$. B has no knowledge of these two sessions. This implies that A has no partner. By revealing session 2 of A to obtain SK_{AB}^{S2}, the adversary $\mathscr{A}$ is then able to obtain a fresh session key SK_{AB}^{S1}.

Protocol 10.9 is, therefore, insecure since the adversary, $\mathscr{A}$, is able to obtain the

A		$\mathscr{A}_B$
	$\xrightarrow{A,\{R_A\}_{pwd}}$	Intercept
	$\xleftarrow{B,\{R_A\}_{pwd}}$	Initiate concurrent session
	$\xrightarrow{R_{A2},\mathscr{H}(R_{A2},SK_{A,B,S2})}$	Intercept
	$\xleftarrow{R_{A2},\mathscr{H}(R_{A2},SK_{A,B,S2})}$	Reflect message back to A
$SK_{AB}^{S1}=\mathscr{H}(g^{xx_2})$	$\xrightarrow{\mathscr{H}(SK_{AB,S2})}$	Intercept
$SK_{AB}^{S2}=\mathscr{H}(g^{xx_2})$	$\xleftarrow{\mathscr{H}(SK_{AB,S2})}$	Reflect message back to A

Attack 10.13: Attack sequence on Protocol 10.9

session key of a fresh oracle of a non-partner oracle by revealing a non-partner oracle holding the same key (i.e., violating the key establishment goal).

10.4.2.7 Protocol Analysis 7

Attack 10.14 describes the attack sequence (i.e., reflection attack) on Protocol 10.10. At the end of Attack 10.14, A thinks that she has completed two concurrent sessions with B and has accepted session keys $SK_{AB}^{S1}=\mathscr{H}(K_2)=SK_{AB}^{S2}$. B has no knowledge of these two sessions. This implies that A has no partner. By revealing session 2 of A to obtain SK_{AB}^{S2}, the adversary $\mathscr{A}$ is then able to obtain a fresh session key SK_{AB}^{S1}.

A		$\mathscr{A}_B$
	$\xrightarrow{X \oplus pwd}$	Intercept
	$\xleftarrow{X \oplus pwd}$	Reflect message
	$\xrightarrow{X_2 \oplus pwd||\mathscr{H}(K_2,X)}$	Intercept
	$\xleftarrow{X_2 \oplus pwd||\mathscr{H}(K_2,X)}$	Reflect message
$SK_{AB}^{S1}=\mathscr{H}(K_2)$	$\xrightarrow{\mathscr{H}(K_1,X_2)}$	Intercept
$SK_{AB}^{S2}=\mathscr{H}(K_2)$	$\xleftarrow{\mathscr{H}(K_1,X_2)}$	Reflect message

Attack 10.14: Attack sequence on Protocol 10.10

Protocol 10.10 is, therefore, insecure since the adversary $\mathscr{A}$ is able to obtain the session key of a fresh oracle of a non-partner oracle by revealing a non-partner oracle holding the same key, in violation of the key establishment goal.

10.5 Summary

We have described a formal model which can complement computational complexity proofs in the Bellare–Rogaway model. In our model the adversary capabilities closely match those in the BPR2000 model. Through a detailed study of

- the unpublished pre-proceedings version of the Jakobsson-Pointcheval protocol [15],
- two Hitchcock–Boyd–Gonzalez-Nieto tripartite key exchange tripartite key exchange protocols [14],
- the Jan–Chen two-party mutual authentication and key establishment protocol [16],
- two Yang–Shen–Shieh trusted three-party authenticated key establishment protocols [22],
- Kim–Huh–Hwang–Lee key agreement protocol [17],
- Lin–Sun–Hwang improved Diffie–Hellman based encrypted key exchange protocols MDHEKE I and II [18], and
- the Yeh–Sun authenticated key agreement protocol [23],

we have demonstrated that this approach can capture structural flaws in protocols. We were able to find both existing and previously unknown flaws in the protocol using SHVT. Such a tool is useful in checking the hand-generated Bellare–Rogaway proofs. We speculate that if the protocol designers had access to such a tool when constructing their original proof of security or heuristic security arguments they could have spotted the flaw in the protocol.

References

1. Martín Abadi & Phillip Rogaway 2000. Reconciling Two Views of Cryptography (The Computational Soundness of Formal Encryption), in J van Leeuwen, O Watanabe, M Hagiya, P D Mosses & T Ito (eds), Proceedings of 1st IFIP International Conference on Theoretical Computer Science – IFIP TCS 2000. Lecture Notes in Computer Science 1872/2000: 3–22
2. Martín Abadi & Phillip Rogaway 20020. Reconciling Two Views of Cryptography (The Computational Soundness of Formal Encryption). *Journal of Cryptology* 15(2): 103–127
3. Jee Hea An, Yevgeniy Dodis & Tal Rabin 2002. On the Security of Joint Signature and Encryption, in Lars R Knudsen (ed), Proceedings of Advances in Cryptology - EUROCRYPT 2002. Lecture Notes in Computer Science 2332/2002: 83–107
4. Michael Backes 2004. A Cryptographically Sound Dolev-Yao Style Security Proof of the Needham–Schroeder–Lowe Public–Key Protocol. *IEEE Journal on Selected Areas in Communications* 22(10): 2075–2086
5. Michael Backes 2004. A Cryptographically Sound Dolev-Yao Style Security Proof of the Otway-Rees Protocol, in Samarati P & Gollmann D (eds), Proceedings of 9th European Symposium on Research in Computer Security - ESORICS 2004. Lecture Notes in Computer Science 3193/2004: 89–108
6. Michael Backes & Christian Jacobi 2003. Cryptographically Sound and Machine-Assisted Verification of Security Protocols, in Alt H & Habib M (eds), Proceedings of 20th International Symposium on Theoretical Aspects of Computer Science - STACS 2003. Lecture Notes in Computer Science 2607/2003: 310–329

7. Michael Backes, Christian Jacobi & Birgit Pfitzmann 2002. Deriving Cryptographically Sound Implementations Using Composition and Formally Verified Bisimulation, in Lars-Henrik Eriksson & Peter A Lindsay (eds), Proceedings of International Symposium of Formal Methods Europe – FME 2002. Lecture Notes in Computer Science 2391/2002: 310–329

8. Bruno Blanchet 2006. A Computationally Sound Mechanized Prover for Security Protocols. *Proceedings of IEEE Symposium on Research in Security and Privacy 2006.* IEEE Computer Society Press: 140–154. Extended version available from http://eprint.iacr.org/2005/401

9. Colin Boyd & Juan Manuel González Nieto 2003. Round-optimal Contributory Conference Key Agreement, in Yvo Desmedt (ed), Proceedings of Public Key Cryptography - PKC 2003. Lecture Notes in Computer Science 2567/2003: 161–174

10. Colin Boyd & Kapali Viswanathan 2002. Towards a Formal Specification of the Bellare-Rogaway Model for Protocol Analysis, in *Proceedings of Formal Aspects of Security - FASec 2002.* British Computer Society Press: 209–223

11. Ran Canetti 2000. Universally Composable Security: A New Paradigm for Cryptographic Protocols. *Cryptology ePrint Archive, Report 2000/067.* http://eprint.iacr.org/2000/067/

12. Ran Canetti & Marc Fischlin 2001. Universally Composable Commitments, in Joe Kilian (ed), Proceedings of Advances in Cryptology – CRYPTO 2001. Lecture Notes in Computer Science 2139/2001: 19–40

13. Kim-Kwang Raymond Choo, Colin Boyd & Yvonne Hitchcock 2005. Errors in Computational Complexity Proofs for Protocols, in Bimal Roy (ed), Proceedings of Advances in Cryptology - ASIACRYPT 2005. Lecture Notes in Computer Science 3788/2005: 624–643. Extended version available from http://eprint.iacr.org/2005/351

14. Yvonne Hitchcock, Colin Boyd & Juan Manuel González Nieto 2004. Tripartite Key Exchange in the Canetti-Krawczyk Proof Model, in Anne Canteaut & Kapaleeswaran Viswanathan (eds), Proceedings of 5th International Conference on Cryptology in India - INDOCRYPT 2004. Lecture Notes in Computer Science 3348/2004: 17–32

15. Markus Jakobsson & David Pointcheval 2001. Mutual Authentication and Key Exchange Protocol for Low Power Devices, in Paul F Syverson (ed), Proceedings of 5th International Conference on Financial Cryptography - FC 2001. Lecture Notes in Computer Science 2339/2002: 169–186

16. Jinn-Ke Jan & Yi-Hwa Chen 2004. A New Efficient MAKEP for Wireless Communications, in *Proceedings of 18th International Conference on Advanced Information Networking and Applications - AINA 2004.* IEEE Computer Society: 347–350

17. Young-Sin Kim, Eui-Nam Huh, Jun Hwang & Byung-Wook Lee 2004. An Efficient Key Agreement Protocol for Secure Authentication, in Antonio Laganà, Marina L Gavrilova, Vipin Kumar, Youngsong Mun, Chih Jeng Kenneth Tan & Osvaldo Gervasi (eds), Proceedings of International Conference On Computational Science And Its Applications - ICCSA 2004. Lecture Notes in Computer Science 3043/2004: 746–754

18. Chun-Li Lin, Hung-Min Sun & Tzonelih Hwang 2000. Three-Party Encrypted Key Exchange: Attacks and A Solution. *ACM SIGOPS Operating Systems Review* 34(4): 12–20

19. Rongxing Lu & Zhenfu Cao 2006. Off-line Password Guessing Attack on an Efficient Key Agreement Protocol for Secure Authentication. *International Journal of Network Security* 3(1): 35–38

20. Roland Rieke 2002. Implementing the APA Model for the Symmetric Needham-Schroeder Protocol in State Transition Pattern Notation in the SH Verification Tool. *Technical report:* Fraunhofer Institute for Secure Telecooperation SIT

21. Duncan S Wong & Agnes H Chan 2001. Efficient and Mutually Authenticated Key Exchange for Low Power Computing Devices, in Colin Boyd (ed), Proceedings of Advances in Cryptology - ASIACRYPT 2001. Lecture Notes in Computer Science 2248/2001: 172–289

22. Wen-Her Yang, Ji-Chiang Shen & Shiuh-Pyng Shieh 1999. Designing Authentication Protocols Against Guessing Attacks. *Technical report* 2(3): Institute of Information & Computing Machinery, Taiwan. http://www.iicm.org.tw/communication/c2_3/page07.doc

23. Her-Tyan Yeh & Hung-Min Sun 2002. Simple Authenticated Key Agreement Protocol Resistant To Password Guessing Attacks. *ACM SIGOPS Operating Systems Review* 36(4): 14–22

Chapter 11
An Integrative Framework to Protocol Analysis and Repair

In the previous chapter, we provided a formal specification and machine analysis of the adversary model from the BPR2000 model and demonstrated that this approach can capture structural flaws in protocols.

We are motivated by the observation that although there have been recent advances in the integrative approach, no researchers have propose an integrated framework to analys and (automatically) repair protocols that were found to be flawed (during the analysis). For example, in the approaches of Backes *et al.* [1, 2, 3], Blanchet *et al.* [7, 8], and Canetti *et al.* [9, 10], the focus is to prove the protocols secure using some automated tools whilst in the approach described in the earlier chapter, the focus is to analyse protocols proven secure in the Bellare–Rogaway model [5, 6].

In this chapter, we propose an integrative framework that allows us to analyse protocols using a modified version of the BR93 adversarial model[1] and, more importantly, to repair protocols that are found to be insecure against certain types of attacks[2]. Note that our approach differs from the approaches of Chen, Clark and Jacob [11, 12, 13]. In their approaches, the focus is on how to develop a particular protocol in some automatic way in terms of a set of property specifications about the application, and not to analyse and repair protocols.

We now present an overview of our framework.

1: The Adversarial Model.   We provide a formal specification and machine analysis of a *modified* version of the widely accepted indistinguishability-based model of Bellare and Rogaway [6], the BR93 model, from computational proofs in the setting of a planning problem.

---

[1] We remark that another distinctive feature of our framework as compared to other existing computer security approaches is that we are able to analyse protocols proven secure in the BR93 model (and also the CK2001 model with some minor modifications).

[2] To the best of our knowledge, this is the first work that utilises an automated tool to update "insecure" protocols specifications.

- The planning problem, an ongoing research area in artificial intelligence, is about composing a workable plan (a sequence of actions) that allows the agent to achieve its given goal(s) from the initial state [14, 23]. This is also known as goal-directed reasoning. In our context, the given goal is defined as a state of insecurity and if a workable plan exists, then we have found an attack on the protocol that we are analysing.

- Our choice of formalism for this work is Asynchronous Product Automata (APA), a universal state-based formal method. APA is supported by the Simple Homomorphism Verification Tool (SHVT) [20] for analysis and verification of cooperating systems and communicating automata. Once the possible state transitions of each automaton have been specified, SHVT (the planner) can be used to automatically search the state space of the model. SHVT provides a reachability graph of the explored states. In our APA specification, the abstract communication model captures the representation of the protocol, the message transmission, and the communication channels.

2: Protocol Specification. As a case study we specify and analyse the three-party identity-based secret public key (3P-ID-SPK) protocol of Lim and Paterson [15]. The protocol claims to provide explicit key authentication – implicit key authentication and key confirmation.

3: Protocol Analysis. Our planner, SHVT, reveals a workable plan that allows us to achieve our defined goals (states of insecurity) from the given initial state. In other words, previously unpublished flaw on the Lim–Paterson protocol is revealed by the automated state space analysis performed with SHVT.

4: Protocol Repair. In our framework, we have a set of generic patches to overcome certain attacks, such as the known session key attack, unknown key share attack, reflection attack, and the key-replicating attack, which we term the "repairable" attacks. Once some attack has been revealed using SHVT in the earlier analysis, we proceed to repair the protocol using a pre-defined checklist (described in Chapter 11.2.3). This checklist can be updated when new patches are discovered (in the same sense as an anti-virus signature file being updated when new virus signatures are discovered). The repaired protocol is then re-analysed and a message will be output as a result of the protocol re-analysis, indicating whether the protocol has been successfully repaired or not.

We regard the main contributions of this chapter to be two-fold:

1. confirmation of the feasibility of using formal specifications to identify problems in human-generated computational complexity proofs by revealing previously unpublished flaw in the case study protocol, and

2. an automated approach to repair protocols that were found to be insecure against certain types of attacks.

Material presented in this chapter has appeared in the following publication:

- Kim-Kwang Raymond Choo. An Integrative Framework to Protocol Analysis and Repair: Bellare-Rogaway Model + Planning + Model Checker. *Informatica*, 18(4):547–568, 2007.

11.1 Case Study Protocol

Protocol 11.1 involves three parties, a trusted server S and two principals, A and B, who wish to establish communication. The security goal of Protocol 11.1 is to distribute a session key between two communication principals (i.e., implicit key authentication), which is suitable for establishing a secure session. Key confirmation is also provided by Protocol 11.1, and hence, achieving explicit key authentication [16, Definition 12.8].

The notation used in Protocol 11.1 is as follows.

- $\{\cdot\}_K$ denotes the encryption of some message under some key K,
- r_U denotes some randomly chosen nonce, $||$ denote concatenation of messages,
- $MAC_{K^{MAC}(\cdot)}$ denotes the computation of a MAC digest under some MAC key K^{MAC},
- $Sig_{K^{Sign}}(\cdot)$ denotes the signature of some message under some signature key K^{Sign},
- $K_{U_1 U_2}$ denotes the session key shared between users U_1 and U_2,
- pwd_{US} denotes some secret password shared between some user U and the server S, and
- $\mathcal{H}$ denotes a secure cryptographic hash function.

$$1.\ A \longrightarrow B : A, r_A, \{A, ST_A\}_{PK_{A1}}$$
$$2.\ B \longrightarrow S : B, \{B, ST_B\}_{PK_{B1}}, A, r_A, \{A, ST_A\}_{PK_{A1}}$$
$$3.\ S \longrightarrow B : Sig_{SK_{B2}}(K_{AB}), Sig_{SK_{A2}}(K_{AB})$$
$$4.\ B \longrightarrow A : Sig_{SK_{A2}}(K_{AB}), MAC_{K_{AB}}(r_A), r_B$$
$$5.\ A \longrightarrow B : MAC_{K_{AB}}(r_B)$$

Protocol 11.1: Lim–Paterson three-party identity-based secret public key protocol

1. Protocol 11.1 begins by having A randomly select a random string, ST_A, and a nonce, r_A. A then computes the encryption key, $PK_{A1} = \mathcal{H}(A||S||pwd_{AS})$, and encrypts (A, ST_A) using PK_{A1}. The message, $A, r_A, \{A, ST_A\}_{PK_{A1}}$, is then sent to B with whom A desires to communicate.
2. Upon receiving the message from A, B also randomly selects a random string, ST_B, computes the encryption key, $PK_{B1} = \mathcal{H}(B||S||pwd_{BS})$, and encrypts (B, ST_B) using PK_{B1}. $B, \{B, ST_B\}_{PK_{B1}}, A, r_A, \{A, ST_A\}_{PK_{A1}}$, is then sent to the server, S.

3. S computes the corresponding private key pairs for PK_{A1} and PK_{B1}, SK_{A2} and SK_{B2} respectively. Using SK_{A2} and SK_{B2}, the respectively ciphertexts are decrypted and ST_A and ST_B obtained. S then runs the session key generator to obtain a session key K_{AB}, which has not been used before. K_{AB} is then signed under the respectively SK_{A2} and SK_{B2}, and sent to B.

4. B recovers K_{AB} from $Sig_{SK_{B2}}(K_{AB})$ using PK_{B1}, computes the MAC digest $MAC_{K_{AB}}(r_A)$, and randomly chooses a nonce, r_B. The following message is then sent: $Sig_{SK_{A2}}(K_{AB}), MAC_{K_{AB}}(r_A), r_B$.

5. A recovers K_{AB} from $Sig_{SK_{A2}}(K_{AB})$ using PK_{A1}. If the MAC digest received verifies true, then A will compute MAC digest $MAC_{K_{AB}}(r_B)$ and sends $MAC_{K_{AB}}(r_B)$ to B.

6. At the end of Protocol 11.1's execution, both A and B have accepted a session key of the same value, K_{AB}.

11.2 Proposed Integrative Framework

In this section, we present an overview of our APA formal specification framework. We follow the general adversarial formalism of the BR93 model described in Chapter 2.3, except that we now have a definition of insecurity rather than a definition of security. Consequently, we do not require the Test query that models the indistinguishability of the session key. We then specify Protocol 11.1 using APA and demonstrate that SHVT (or any model checker tool) can be used to find previously unknown flaws in the protocols. We conclude this section by showing a repaired Lim–Paterson protocol.

11.2.1 Protocols Specification

As mentioned earlier, the setting of our approach is based on the planning problem. Therefore, similarly to the formulation of the planning problem [23], we have three inputs in the formulation of our framework, as follows.

Description of Initial State.   We describe the internal states and knowledge of (e.g., keys that are known to) the agents. Agents in our formal framework comprise the protocol participants and a malicious adversary (adopted from the BR93 model described in Chapter 2.3.4).

Description of Goal State.   Before an agent can achieve its goal(s), we need to provide a formal description of the goal state that the agent has to achieve. In our framework, we define a desired goal as a state of insecurity. Hence, if an agent manages to achieve the defined goal, then the protocol is insecure.

Description of Possible Actions.   This input provides a formal description for the set of possible actions that can be performed by the agents.

For the rest of the paper, we use the terms agent and automata interchangeably. In our formal framework using APA specification, protocol principals are modelled as a family of elementary automata. The various state spaces of the principals are modelled as a family of state sets. The channel through which the elementary automaton communicates is modelled by the addition and removal of messages from the shared state component Network, which is initially empty. Each of the elementary automata only has access to the particular state components to which it is connected. In addition to the regular protocol principals, we specify an adversary, $\mathscr{A}$, which has access to the shared state component Network, but no access to the internal states of the principals.

This adversary, $\mathscr{A}$, is adopted from the BR93 model described in Chapter 2.3.4.1 whereby $\mathscr{A}$ is able to intercept messages in the Network, swap data components in the intercepted messages to form new messages, remove messages from the Network, or fabricate new messages. $\mathscr{A}$ is then able to send these messages to the oracles via the Network (corresponding to Send queries in the BR93 model). Also, once an oracle, Π_U^i, has accepted and holds a session key, the session identifier associated with that oracle becomes visible to the adversary, $\mathscr{A}$, via the shared state component Transcript. If $\mathscr{A}$ so chooses, $\mathscr{A}$ is able to obtain the session key of Π_U^i (stored in the state component Keys) via a Reveal query. The shared state component Transcript also contains a log of all sent messages.

11.2.1.1 Defining SIDs in Protocol 11.1

Bellare, Pointcheval, and Rogaway [5] suggested that SIDs can be constructed on-the-fly using fresh unique contributions from the communicating participants. Uniqueness of SIDs is necessary since otherwise two parties may share a key but not be partners (in the sense of Definition 2.3.6), and hence the protocol would not be considered secure. The importance of partnership is also higlighted in the recent work of Rogaway [21].

Within Protocol 11.1, the only values that A and B can be sure are unique are r_A, r_B, ST_A, and ST_B. However, only r_A and r_B are both known to A and B. Hence, a naive construct for SIDs in Protocol 11.1 is the concatenation of r_A and r_B where r_A and r_B are the unique nonces contributed by individual protocol participant.

Another possible SID construct is the concatenation of the protocol participants' identities and the unique nonces contributed by individual protocol participant. Including the identities of the participating parties is to provide a binding to the session identifier. This avoids scenarios where two or more sessions have identical keys but different session identities as protocol participants have different perceived partners. Such an approach is adopted by several other researchers [17, 18, 19] and is also recommended by NIST [4]. Therefore for Protocol 11.1, we define SIDs as the concatenation of the protocol participants' identities and unique nonces contributed by individual protocol participant.

11.2.1.2 Description of Goal State

In using automated tools, we find it more natural to define the goal state to be the **state of insecurity** – reachability of this state implies that the protocol being analysed is insecure – rather than the state of security due to the limitations of model checking tool (i.e., state explosion problem). Definition 10.1.1 depends on the notions of partnership in Definition 2.3.6 and freshness in Definition 2.3.1. Violation of the first requirement in Definition 10.1.1 also implies that the protocol is vulnerable to a *key replicating attack* first described by Krawczyk [18] – see Definition 2.3.12.

Since our formal framework is closely based on the BR93 model, protocols that were proven secure in the BR93 model but found to be violating any of the first two goal states (or any of the three goal states if the protocol provides key confirmation) described in Definition 10.1.1 will be insecure in the BR93 model. Consequently, the existing proof of the (insecure) protocol will also be invalid.

11.2.1.3 Description of Possible Actions

Possible actions refer to the message exchanges among the agents (i.e., protocol participants and the adversary). As Russell and Norvig [22] suggested, actions are represented by logical descriptions of pre-conditions and effects (which we term post-conditions). To model actions, we now need to specify the properties of all states of components associated with the particular elementary automaton, and the changes of the states caused by the state transition.

Step 1.   The name of the transition pattern has to be first defined, e.g., Protocol Step 1.

Step 2.   The variables to be used in this transition pattern, $(x_1, \ldots, x_n)$, is then defined. Note that the variables defined here are local to this transition pattern.

Step 3.   The required (pre-)conditions prior to performing a state transition is now defined. If any of the defined conditions is not satisfied, this transition pattern will proceed no further.

Step 4.   The changes of the states caused by this state transition is now specified, i.e., the post-conditions / effects.

State Transition.   A state transition can only occur when all the above steps are executed.

11.2.2 Protocols Analysis

Figure 11.1 presents an example reachability graph describing how searches are performed in the SHVT analysis, namely: forward from the initial state to the finish state when an agent has achieved its goal (i.e., achieving any of the goal states described in Definition 10.1.1).

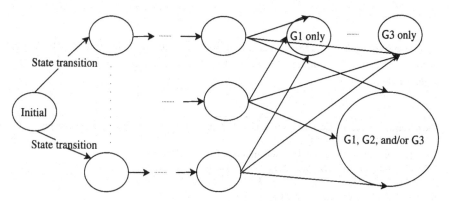

Fig. 11.1 A reachability graph: protocol analysis in SHVT

If a workable plan exists (i.e., the agent manages to reach any of the finish states, achieving G1, G2, and/or G3 of Definition 10.1.1), we can then trace the path that it takes and hence, find the attack sequence. This is also known as a solution – a plan that an agent can execute, which guarantees the achievement of the goal [22] – in the planning problem. Note that the nodes in the reachability graph described in Figure 11.1 represent the various states of the protocol execution and the arcs (arrows) represent the state transitions between two states.

The search approach in our SHVT analysis is also known as a progression planner in the planning problem. Consequently, the inherent limitations associated with a progression planner, i.e., the high branching factor and thus the huge size of the search space [22], are also present in our approach. For example, in several of our earlier experiments, we observe that certain interleavings of the protocol message exchanges and actions of the adversary that are "obviously" immaterial in achieving the goal are explored by SHVT. In other words, what is obvious to us, human, are not necessarily obvious to the progression planner or SHVT.

Hence, for run-time efficiency, and to avoid enormous branching factors in the search space, we restrict the actions of the adversary so that certain actions are possible for only some message types. The attack sequence and the internal states can be examined by viewing the reachability graphs produced by SHVT. The analyses were run on a Pentium IV 2.16 GHz computer with 1024 Mb of RAM and the analysis statistics are shown in Figure 11.2.

# Players	# Runs	Run-Time	Goal state(s) achieved
4	2	Approximately 2 mins	Yes (G2 and G3 of Definition 10.1.1)

Fig. 11.2 Analysis statistics of Protocol 11.1

State space analysis in SHVT reveals that both G2 and G3 of Definition 10.1.1 are violated. The attack sequence is described in Attack 11.1. Let C_B denotes C impersonating B.

The adversary, $\mathscr{A}$, asks a Corrupt query to C, a client participant – *static corruption*. $\mathscr{A}$ now runs as C.

1. $A \longrightarrow B$: $A, r_A, \{A, ST_A\}_{PK_{A1}}$

The adversary intercepts and deletes this message from the Network.

2(C). $C \longrightarrow S$: $C, \{C, ST_C\}_{PK_{C1}}, A, r_A, \{A, ST_A\}_{PK_{A1}}$

3. $S \longrightarrow C$: $Sig_{SK_{C2}}(K_{AC}), Sig_{SK_{A2}}(K_{AC})$

4(C). $C_B \longrightarrow A$: $Sig_{SK_{A2}}(K_{AC}), MAC_{K_{AC}}(r_A), r_C$

5. $A \longrightarrow B$: $MAC_{K_{AB}}(r_B)$

The adversary intercepts and deletes this message from the Network.

Attack 11.1: Attack Sequence on Protocol 11.1

In Attack 11.1,

Static Corruption.   The adversary, $\mathscr{A}$, asks a Corrupt query to C, a client participant, prior to the execution of Protocol 11.1 between A and B – *static corruption*. $\mathscr{A}$ now runs as C since the Corrupt query enables the adversary to learn the entire internal state of C including the password shared between C and S, pwd_{CS}.

Step 1 of Protocol 11.1. A randomly selects a random string, ST_A, and a nonce, r_A. A then computes the encryption key, $PK_{A1} = \mathscr{H}(A||S||pwd_{AS})$, and encrypts (A, ST_A) using PK_{A1}. The message is then sent to B as per protocol specification.

Message Interception.   The adversary intercepts and deletes this message sent by A from the Network.

Step 2 of Protocol 11.1 by C. C also randomly selects a random string, ST_C, computes the encryption key, $PK_{C1} = \mathscr{H}(C||S||pwd_{CS})$, and encrypts (C, ST_C) using PK_{C1}. The message, $C, \{C, ST_C\}_{PK_{C1}}, A, r_A, \{A, ST_A\}_{PK_{A1}}$, is then sent to the server, S.

Step 3 of Protocol 11.1. S computes the corresponding private key pairs for PK_{A1} and PK_{C1}, SK_{A2} and SK_{C2} respectively. Using SK_{A2} and SK_{C2}, the respectively ciphertexts are decrypted and ST_A and ST_C obtained. S then runs the session key generator to obtain a session key K_{AC}, which has not been used before. K_{AC} is then signed under the respectively SK_{A2} and SK_{C2}, and sent to C.

Step 4 of Protocol 11.1 by C. C recovers K_{AC} from $Sig_{SK_{C2}}(K_{AB})$ using PK_{C1}, computes the MAC digest $MAC_{K_{AC}}(r_A)$, and randomly chooses a nonce, r_C. The message, $Sig_{SK_{A2}}(K_{AC}), MAC_{K_{AC}}(r_A), r_C$, is then sent to A by C **impersonating** B.

Step 5 of Protocol 11.1. A recovers K_{AC} from $Sig_{SK_{A2}}(K_{AC})$ using PK_{A1}. The MAC digest received will certainly verified true since C already recovers K_{AC} from $Sig_{SK_{C2}}(K_{AB})$ using PK_{C1} in the earlier step. Hence, A will compute MAC digest $MAC_{K_{AC}}(r_C)$ and sends $MAC_{K_{AC}}(r_C)$ to B.

Message Interception.   The adversary intercepts and deletes this message sent by A from the Network.

Session Key.   If the MAC digest received verifies true, then C (the adversary) knows that A has accepted session key, K_{AC} and A believes is being shared with B. However, B is unaware of such a session with A since all messages sent by A to B have been intercepted and deleted from the Network by the adversary. Hence, A has accepted and terminated without a partner – G3 of Definition 10.1.1. Moreover, the adversary knows the session key accepted by A after receiving the message from S in step 3 of the protocol execution – G2 of Definition 10.1.1.

11.2.3 Protocol Repair

As mentioned earlier, we have a set of generic patches to overcome attacks, such as the unknown key share attack, which we term the "repairable" attacks. We can check manually (if we want) to determine if the revealed attack is in our pre-defined list of "repairable" attacks. Attack 11.1 can be considered an unknown key share attack since A believes the key is being shared with B when in fact, the key is being shared with C (the adversary). Hence, Attack 11.1 is in our pre-defined list of "repairable" attacks, which we know can be repaired.

Alternatively, we can proceed directly to repair the protocols. For readability, we present an informal overview of our repairing procedure (in plain english rather than in the unwieldy APA specifications). Note that we assume that the session identifier, sid, is the concatenation of the protocol participants' identities and other unique messages.

1: Session Key Derivation Function Checking.   Is sid part of the keying material?

If yes,   proceed to Step 2,

Otherwise   modify the key derivation function within the protocol specifications to a hash of the concatenation of the session identifier and existing keying materials using an independent hash function (i.e., in the case of Protocol 11.1, session key is now constructed as

$$\mathcal{H}_1(sid||K_{AB}) = \mathcal{H}_1(A||B||S||r_A||r_B||K_{AB})$$

where $\mathcal{H}$ and $\mathcal{H}_1$ are independent secure cryptographic hash functions).

2: Encryption Scheme Checking   Does the protocol use any encryption scheme?

> If yes,   check if the identities of the sender and the intended recipient / protocol participants are included within the message to be encrypted?
> If yes,   proceed to Step 3.
> Otherwise   modify the encryption function within the protocol specifications to include the identity of the sender and the intended recipient so that these identities are included within the message to be encrypted.

Otherwise   proceed to Step 3.

3: MAC Scheme Checking   Does the protocol use any MAC scheme?

> If yes,   check if the identities of the sender and the intended recipient / protocol participants are included within the MAC digest to be generated?
> If yes,   proceed to Step 4.
> Otherwise   modify the MAC function within the protocol specifications to include the identity of the sender and the intended recipient so that these identities are included within the MAC digest to be generated.

Otherwise   proceed to Step 4.

4: Signature Scheme Checking   Does the protocol use any signature scheme?

> If yes,   check if the identities of the sender and the intended recipient / protocol participants are included within the signature to be generated?
> If yes,   proceed to Step 5.
> Otherwise   modify the signature function within the protocol specifications to include the identity of the sender and the intended recipient so that these identities are included within the signature to be generated.

Otherwise   proceed to Step 5.

5: Protocol Analysis   Restart the protocol analysis described in Chapter 11.2.2 with the repaired protocol. Check to see if any of the goal states in Definition 10.1.1 are violated.

> If yes,   output error message "Protocol cannot be repaired!".
> Otherwise   output message "Protocol successfully repaired!" and then terminated.

Protocol 11.2 describes the resulting repaired Protocol 11.1.

---

1. $A \longrightarrow B : A, r_A, \{A, B, ST_A\}_{PK_{A1}}$
2. $B \longrightarrow S : B, \{B, A, ST_B\}_{PK_{B1}}, A, r_A, \{A, B, ST_A\}_{PK_{A1}}$
3. $S \longrightarrow B : Sig_{SK_{B2}}(S, A, B, K_{AB}), Sig_{SK_{A2}}(S, A, B, K_{AB})$
4. $B \longrightarrow A : Sig_{SK_{A2}}(S, A, B, K_{AB}), MAC_{K_{AB}}(B, A, S, r_A), r_B$
5. $A \longrightarrow B : MAC_{K_{AB}}(A, B, S, r_B)$

Session identifier, $sid_A = A||B||S||r_A||r_B = sid_B$
Session key, $\mathscr{SK}_A = \mathscr{H}_1(sid_A||K_{AB}) = \mathscr{H}_1(sid_B||K_{AB}) = \mathscr{SK}_B$

Protocol 11.2: A repaired Protocol 11.1

We remark that in our generic patches, we ensure that the identities of the protocol participants are explicitly exchanged in every encryption, MAC digest, and signature; and also include the session identifier in the key derivation function. In so doing, we provide a binding between the messages and the protocol participants, and between the session key and the session identifier. However, our approach has the drawback of making the protocol scheme non-symmetric as the participants will have to be ordered (see Chapter 9). We hope that by having access to such an automated tool will help to prevent future cases of old attacks making their way into new protocols (e.g., our case study protocol was only recently published in *Security Protocols Workshop 2006* [15]).

It is also important to note that Protocol 11.2 is not proven secure, as this is not the purpose of our work. Our work here is to show that we are able to reveal flaws, particularly previously unknown flaws, in protocols and repair the revealed flaws using an automated model checker tool. We now present an informal discussion to provide a better insight into the protocol failures and the basis for our repair procedures.

In Protocol 11.1, the identities of the protocol participants are not included within the encrypted messages, the signatures generated, and the MAC digests generated. This effectively allows a malicious adversary, $\mathscr{A}$, to intercept messages and cause confusion on who are the actual partipants of this protocol session. Hence, by including the identities of the protocol participants within the encrypted messages, the signatures generated, and the MAC digests generated, we should be able to thawrt Attack 11.1.

Moreover, as pointed out in Chapter 9, including the unique session identifiers (SIDs) comprising the identities of the participants and their roles within the session key deriviation function ensures that session keys will be fresh and effectively ensures some sense of direction. If the role of the participants or the identities of the (perceived) partner participants change, the session keys will also be different.

11.3 Summary

We extended the framework presented in Chapter 10 in the setting of the planning problem, and an artificial intelligence problem, to analyse protocols. As a case study, we specified and analysed the three-party identity-based secret public key (3P-ID-SPK) protocol of Lim and Paterson [15]. We then refuted its existing heuristic security arguments by revealing a previously unpublished flaw in the protocol with SHVT. More importantly, we described how our formal framework can be used to repair protocols that were found to be insecure against certain attacks. There are, however, limitations of our approach presented in this chapter.

1. Due to the nature of our tool, our approach is not fully automatic as there does not exist an automatic way to pass from (the hard to read) SHVT reachability graph outputs to the attack sequences, e.g., the "nicely" drawn attack sequence presented in Attack 11.1. Hence, for readability, the reachability graph output by SHVT have to be translated manually (computer-aided). Moreover, if a protocol with claimed security proof is found to be insecure in our approach, the reasoning behind the failures of the claimed security proof cannot be provided.

2. As mentioned earlier, protocols that are found to be insecure in our framework will also be insecure in the BR93 model. However, due to the deterministic nature of our tool, some attacks might be left out in our analysis. Hence, protocols that are not found to be insecure in our approach, do not automatically imply security in the BR93 model (i.e., not sound).

References

1. Michael Backes 2004. A Cryptographically Sound Dolev-Yao Style Security Proof of the Needham–Schroeder–Lowe Public–Key Protocol. *IEEE Journal on Selected Areas in Communications* 22(10): 2075–2086

2. Michael Backes 2004. A Cryptographically Sound Dolev-Yao Style Security Proof of the Otway-Rees Protocol, in Samarati P & Gollmann D (eds), Proceedings of 9th European Symposium on Research in Computer Security - ESORICS 2004. Lecture Notes in Computer Science 3193/2004: 89–108

3. Michael Backes & Christian Jacobi 2003. Cryptographically Sound and Machine-Assisted Verification of Security Protocols, in Alt H & Habib M (eds), Proceedings of 20th International Symposium on Theoretical Aspects of Computer Science - STACS 2003. Lecture Notes in Computer Science 2607/2003: 310–329

4. Elaine Barker, Don Johnson, & Miles Smid 2006. Recommendation for Pair-Wise Key Establishment Schemes Using Discrete Logarithm Cryptography. *Special Publication (SP 800-56A)*. National Institute of Standards and Technology

5. Mihir Bellare, David Pointcheval & Phillip Rogaway 2000. Authenticated Key Exchange Secure Against Dictionary Attacks, in Bart Preneel (ed), Proceedings of Advances in Cryptology - EUROCRYPT 2000. Lecture Notes in Computer Science 1807/2000: 139 – 155

6. Mihir Bellare & Phillip Rogaway 1993. Entity Authentication and Key Distribution, in Douglas R. Stinson (ed), Proceedings of Advances in Cryptology - CRYPTO 1993. Lecture Notes in Computer Science 773/1993: 110–125

7. Bruno Blanchet 2006. A Computationally Sound Mechanized Prover for Security Protocols. *Proceedings of IEEE Symposium on Research in Security and Privacy 2006*. IEEE Computer Society Press: 140–154. Extended version available from http://eprint.iacr.org/2005/401

8. Bruno Blanchet & David Pointcheval 2006. Automated Security Proofs with Sequences of Games, in Cynthia Dwork (ed), Proceedings of Advances in Cryptology – CRYPTO 2006. Lecture Notes in Computer Science 4117/2006: 537–554

9. Ran Canetti 2000. Universally Composable Security: A New Paradigm for Cryptographic Protocols. *Cryptology ePrint Archive, Report 2000/067*. http://eprint.iacr.org/2000/067/

10. Ran Canetti & Marc Fischlin 2001. Universally Composable Commitments, in Joe Kilian (ed), Proceedings of Advances in Cryptology – CRYPTO 2001. Lecture Notes in Computer Science 2139/2001: 19–40

11. Hao Chen, John A. Clark & Jeremy L. Jacob 2004. Synthesising Efficient and Effective Security Protocols, in Alessandro Armando and Luca Viganò (eds), Proceedings of 2nd International Joint Conference on Automated Reasoning – ARSPA 2004. Electronic Notes in Theoretical Computer Science 125(1): 25–41

12. John A. Clark & Jeremy L. Jacob 2000. Searching for a Solution: Engineering Tradeoffs and the Evolution of Provably Secure Protocols, in *Proceedings of IEEE Symposium on Security and Privacy 2000*. IEEE Computer Society Press: 82–95

13. John A. Clark & Jeremy L. Jacob 2001. Protocols are Programs too: The Meta-Heuristic Search for Security Protocols. *Information & Software Technology* 43(14): 891–904

14. Vladimir Lifschitz 1999. Answer Set Planning, in Michael Gelfond, Nicola Leone & Gerald Pfeifer (eds), Proceedings of 5th International Conference on Logic Programming and Nonmonotonic Reasoning – LPNMR 1999. Lecture Notes in Computer Science 1730/1999: 373–374

15. Hoon Wei Lim & Kenneth G Paterson 2006. Secret Public Key Protocols Revisited, in Proceedings of Security Protocols Workshop 2006. Lecture Notes in Computer Science. Available from http://www.isg.rhul.ac.uk/~hwlim/

16. Alfred J Menezes, Paul C van Oorschot & Scott A Vanstone 1997. *Handbook of Applied Cryptography*. CRC Press

17. Ik Rae Jeong, Jonathan Katz & Dong Hoon Lee 2004. One-Round Protocols for Two-Party Authenticated Key Exchange, in Markus Jakobsson, Moti Yung & Jianying Zhou (eds), Proceedings of Applied Cryptography and Network Security - ACNS 2004. Lecture Notes in Computer Science 3089/2004: 220–232

18. Hugo Krawczyk 2005. HMQV: A High-Performance Secure Diffie–Hellman Protocol, in Victor Shoup (ed), Proceedings of Advances in Cryptology - CRYPTO 2005. Lecture Notes in Computer Science 3621/2005: 546–566. Extended version available from http://eprint.iacr.org/2005/176/

19. Caroline Kudla & Kenneth G Paterson 2005. Modular Security Proofs for Key Agreement Protocols, in Bimal Roy (ed), Proceedings of Advances in Cryptology - ASIACRYPT 2005. Lecture Notes in Computer Science 3788/2005: 549–569

20. Peter Ochsenschläger, Jurgen Repp, Roland Rieke & U Nitsche 1998. The SH-Verification Tool - Abstraction-Based Verification of Co-operating Systems. *Journal of Formal Aspects of Computing* 10(4): 381–404

21. Phillip Rogaway 2004. MOn the Role Definitions in and Beyond Cryptography, in Michael J Maher (ed), Proceedings of 9th Asian Computing Science Conference - ASIAN 2004. Lecture Notes in Computer Science 3321/2004: 13–32

22. Stuart Russell & Peter Norvig 1995. *Artificial Intelligence: A Modern Approach*. Prentice Hall

23. Daniel S Weld 1999. Recent Advances in AI Planning. *AI Magazine* 20(2): 93–123

Chapter 12
Conclusion and Future Work

In this final chapter, a summary of the book and a discussion of open problems and possible research directions are presented.

12.1 Research Summary

In this book, we have achieved all the four research goals identified in Chapter 1.2.3 as explained below.

1: To examine the computational complexity models critically.

- In Chapter 3, we studied the BR95 model and revealed that its partnership function used in the 3PKD protocol [8] is flawed, which invalidates the proof for the 3PKD protocol.
- In Chapter 4, we studied the Bellare–Rogaway models and the CK2001 model and identified several variants of the key sharing requirement.
- In Chapter 5, we presented a comparison of the relative strengths of the notions of security between the variants of the Bellare–Rogaway models and the CK2001 model. We then demonstrated that protocol 3PAKE of Abdalla and Pointcheval [1], though proven secure in the BPR2000 model, is vulnerable to an unknown key share attack. This attack illustrated the drawback of the BPR2000 model.
- In Chapter 6, we extended the BR93 model to model the compromise of long-term keys, not currently captured in the existing model.

2: To analyse published protocols in the literature.

- In Chapters 3, 4, and 8, we revealed new flaws in several published protocols and a message authenticator of Bellare, Canetti, and Krawczyk [7]. We then pointed out the corresponding flaws in their proofs and proposed solutions to these protocols and their proofs. We also identified three areas where protocol proofs are likely to fail; namely an inappropriate proof model environment,

Send, Reveal and Corrupt queries not adequately considered in the proof simulations, and the omission of proof simulations in Chapter 8.

- In Chapters 10 and 11, we used our formal framework to reveal new flaws in several protocols.

3: To contribute towards the design principles.

- In Chapter 9, we proposed a way to construct session keys in protocols which can result in significant benefits for the security of the protocols. We propose keying materials, comprising the identities of the participants and roles, unique session identifiers (SIDs), and some other ephemeral shared secrets and/or long-term (static) shared secrets, to be included in the key derivation function.

  Note that our observation on the session key construction is cited in a special publication (SP 800-56A) – Recommendation for Pair-Wise Key Establishment Schemes Using Discrete Logarithm Cryptography by National Institute of Standards and Technology (NIST) [6].

- In Chapter 10, we provided a formal specification and machine analysis of the BPR2000 model that can be used to reveal structural flaws in protocols. Such an approach is complementary to the computational complexity approach. We then extend this framework to automatically repair protocols found to be insecure in Chapter 11.

4: To design new provably secure and efficient protocols.

- In Chapters 3 and 4, we presented improved provably-secure 3PKD protocols and an improved Protocol $\mathscr{TS}2$. The improved 3PKD protocol proposed in Chapter 4 is included in a submission to the IEEE 802.11, the working group setting the standards for wireless LANs [2].

- In Chapter 6, we proved a revised protocol of Boyd [11] secure in the BR93 model. We also proposed an alternative protocol that is efficient in both rounds and messages, and proved it secure in the BR93 extended model.

In our results, we demonstrated the importance of rigorous proofs of security against active attacks in a well-defined and robust model and that specifying correct proofs for protocols remains a hard problem. More importantly, we believe the techniques and methods outlined in this book represent a step toward a better understanding in the construction of provably-secure key establishment protocols.

12.2 Open Problems and Future Directions

Much work in this area remains to be done. We list several interesting dimensions on how this research can be extended.

Extending our work in Chapter 5.   While our studies in Chapter 5 focus only on the Bellare–Rogaway and Canetti–Krawczyk models, it would be interesting to extend our work to other computational complexity proof models (e.g., the proof model due to Shoup [18]) or other simulation-based proof models (e.g., the universal composability approach and the black-box simulatability approach due to Canetti *et al.* [12, 13, 14] and Backes *et al.* [3, 4, 5] respectively).

Extending our work in Chapter 6   While our work in Chapter 6 allows us to detect a known weakness of key agreement protocol of Boyd [11] that cannot be captured in the original BR93 model, it would be interesting to know what other symmetric-key protocols may also have this property. One example is a protocol with similar properties which was proven secure in the BR93 model by Shoup and Rubin [19]. Another possible extension is to investigate and propose a modular proof approach with a formal statement of security that allows server-based three-party key establishment protocols like those introduced in Tables 6.1 and 7.1 to renew session key(s) in subsequent sessions without the server's further involvement, even in the event that the long-term key or the earlier session key are compromised.

Extensions to existing computational complexity models. As mentioned in Chapter 6, we find existing models insufficiently rich to capture all reasonable actions of the adversary. A possible extension is to enhance the models to include attacks such as key compromise impersonation attacks, and denial of service attacks. We speculate that the models can also be extended to other types of protocols, such as fair exchange protocols as we observe that there does not exist any published provable-secure fair exchange protocols.

Extending our work in Chapter 10.   While our studies in Chapter 10 only examine the original version of the Jakobsson–Pointcheval protocol [17] and several other protocols with heuristic security arguments, it would be interesting to extend the work to other cryptographic protocols with proofs of security in order to gain better confidence in their correctness. We would also like to explore other computational complexity models, in particular Shoup's model [18], to gain a better understanding of the uses of a complementary model.

Computer-aided cryptographic proofs.   The many examples of new attacks on published protocols mentioned in this book clearly illustrate the pitfalls of publishing protocols without providing rigorous proofs of security against active attacks and the pitfalls in constructing proofs of security. A possible extension is to investigate a potential approach to making the process of writing and verifying cryptographic proofs routine and less prone to human errors. For example, the popular sequence of games technique employed in many cryptographic proofs [9] might be specified and verified using some automated tool or computer program verification [10, 15, 16].

References

1. Michel Abdalla & David Pointcheval 2005. Interactive Diffie–Hellman Assumptions with Applications to Password-based Authentication, in Andrew Patrick & Moti Yung (eds), Proceedings of 9th International Conference on Financial Cryptography - FC 2005. Lecture Notes in Computer Science 3570/2005: 341–356

2. Jonathan Agre, Wei-Peng Chen, Mohammed Refaei, Anuja Sonalker, Chenxi Zhu & Xun Yuan 2005. Secure NOmadic Wireless Mesh (SnowMesh). Submission to the IEEE 802.11, The Working Group Setting the Standards for Wireless LANs. http://www.flacp.fujitsulabs.com/publications.html

3. Michael Backes 2004. A Cryptographically Sound Dolev-Yao Style Security Proof of the Needham–Schroeder–Lowe Public–Key Protocol. *IEEE Journal on Selected Areas in Communications* 22(10): 2075–2086

4. Michael Backes 2004. A Cryptographically Sound Dolev-Yao Style Security Proof of the Otway-Rees Protocol, in Samarati P & Gollmann D (eds), Proceedings of 9th European Symposium on Research in Computer Security - ESORICS 2004. Lecture Notes in Computer Science 3193/2004: 89–108

5. Michael Backes & Christian Jacobi 2003. Cryptographically Sound and Machine-Assisted Verification of Security Protocols, in Alt H & Habib M (eds), Proceedings of 20th International Symposium on Theoretical Aspects of Computer Science - STACS 2003. Lecture Notes in Computer Science 2607/2003: 310–329

6. Elaine Barker, Don Johnson, & Miles Smid 2006. Recommendation for Pair-Wise Key Establishment Schemes Using Discrete Logarithm Cryptography. *Special Publication (SP 800-56A)*. National Institute of Standards and Technology

7. Mihir Bellare, Ran Canetti & Hugo Krawczyk 1998. A Modular Approach to The Design and Analysis of Authentication and Key Exchange Protocols, in Jeffrey Vitter (ed), Proceedings of 30th ACM Symposium on the Theory of Computing - ACM STOC 1998. ACM Press: 419–428

8. Mihir Bellare & Phillip Rogaway 1995. Provably Secure Session Key Distribution: The Three Party Case, in F. Tom Leighton & Allan Borodin (eds), Proceedings of 27th ACM Symposium on the Theory of Computing - ACM STOC 1995. ACM Press: 57–66

9. Mihir Bellare & Phillip Rogaway 2004. Code-Based Game-Playing Proofs and the Security of Triple Encryption. *Cryptology ePrint Archive, Report 2004/331*. http://eprint.iacr.org/2004/331/

10. Bruno Blanchet 2006. A Computationally Sound Mechanized Prover for Security Protocols. *Proceedings of IEEE Symposium on Research in Security and Privacy 2006*. IEEE Computer Society Press: 140–154. Extended version available from http://eprint.iacr.org/2005/401

11. Colin Boyd 1996. A Class of Flexible and Efficient Key Management Protocols, in *Proceedings of 9th IEEE Computer Security Foundations Workshop - CSFW 1996*. IEEE Computer Society Press: 2–8

12. Ran Canetti 2000. Universally Composable Security: A New Paradigm for Cryptographic Protocols. *Cryptology ePrint Archive, Report 2000/067*. http://eprint.iacr.org/2000/067/

13. Ran Canetti & Marc Fischlin 2001. Universally Composable Commitments, in Joe Kilian (ed), Proceedings of Advances in Cryptology – CRYPTO 2001. Lecture Notes in Computer Science 2139/2001: 19–40

14. Ran Canetti & Hugo Krawczyk 2002. Universally Composable Notions of Key Exchange and Secure Channels, in Lars R Knudsen (ed), Proceedings of Advances in Cryptology - EUROCRYPT 2002. Lecture Notes in Computer Science 2332/2002: 337–351. Extended version available from http://eprint.iacr.org/2002/059/

15. Ricardo Corin & Jerry den Hartog 2006. A Probabilistic Hoare-style logic for Game-based Cryptographic Proofs, in Ingo Wegener, Vladimiro Sassone & Bart Preneel (eds), Proceedings of 33rd International Colloquium on Automata, Languages and Programming - ICALP 2006.

Lecture Notes in Computer Science 4052/2006: 252–263. Extended version available from http://eprint.iacr.org/2005/467/

16. Shai Halevi 2005. A Plausible Approach to Computer-Aided Cryptographic Proofs. *Cryptology ePrint Archive, Report 2005/181.* http://eprint.iacr.org/2005/181

17. Markus Jakobsson & David Pointcheval 2001. Mutual Authentication and Key Exchange Protocol for Low Power Devices, in Paul F Syverson (ed), Proceedings of 5th International Conference on Financial Cryptography - FC 2001. Lecture Notes in Computer Science 2339/2002: 169–186

18. Victor Shoup 1999. On Formal Models for Secure Key Exchange (Version 4). *Technical report* no RZ 3120 (#93166). IBM Research, Zurich

19. Victor Shoup & Aviel D Rubin 1996. Session Key Distribution Using Smart Cards, in Ueli M Maurer (ed), Proceedings of Advances in Cryptology - EUROCRYPT 1996. Lecture Notes in Computer Science 1070/1996: 321–331

Index

Asymmetric encryption, 24
Authentication, 2
   Data origin authentication, 2
   Entity authentication, 2

Bellare–Rogaway model, 38, 42, 83
   BPR2000 model, 45
   BR93 model, 43
   BR95 model, 44
   Extension to the Bellare–Rogaway model,
     108

Canetti–Krawczyk model, 46, 83
Computational complexity approach, 5
Computer security approach, 4
Confidentiality, 2

Data integrity, 2
Diffie–Hellman-based protocols, 29
Digital signature, 26

Hash function, 27

Identity-based (ID-based) key agreement
    protocols, 29
Indistinguishability (IND) game, 24

Key compromise impersonation resistance, 36
Key establishment protocol, 3, 29
   Group-based protocol, 33
   Three-party (tripartite) protocol, 33
   Two-party protocol, 33

Message authentication code (MAC), 26

Polynomial time algorithm, 21

Random oracle, 28
RSA-based protocols, 29

Security attributes, 35
   (Joint) key control, 36
   Forward secrecy, 35
   Key integrity, 36
   Known (session) key security, 35
   Unknown key share security, 35
Semantic security, 24
Session identifiers (SIDs), 125
Session key construction, 157
Session key generation, 31
   Hybrid protocol, 32
   Key agreement protocol, 32
   Key transport protocol, 31
Symmetric encryption, 25

Types of attacks, 36
   Cryptanalysis attack, 37
   Eavesdropping, 36
   Information replay attack, 37
   Key replicating attack, 48, 59, 96, 131, 136
   Modification attack, 37
   Oracle attack, 38
   Parallel session attack, 38
   Passive attack, 36
   Protocol interaction attack, 38
   Reflection attack, 37, 159, 186, 187
   Typing attack, 37
   Unknown key share attack, 97, 131, 135,
    184, 199